New Turkey and the Far Right

New Turkey and the Far Right

How Reactionary Nationalism Remade a Country

Selim Koru

I.B. TAURIS
LONDON • NEW YORK • OXFORD • NEW DELHI • SYDNEY

I.B. TAURIS
Bloomsbury Publishing Plc
50 Bedford Square, London, WC1B 3DP, UK
1385 Broadway, New York, NY 10018, USA
29 Earlsfort Terrace, Dublin 2, Ireland

BLOOMSBURY, I.B. TAURIS and the I.B. Tauris logo are trademarks
of Bloomsbury Publishing Plc

First published in Great Britain 2025

Copyright © Selim Koru, 2025

Selim Koru has asserted his rights under the Copyright, Designs and Patents Act, 1988,
to be identified as Author of this work.

For legal purposes the Acknowledgements on p. viii constitute an extension
of this copyright page.

Cover design by Charlotte Daniels
Cover image © Leonid Andronov/Alamy Stock Photo

All rights reserved. No part of this publication may be reproduced or transmitted
in any form or by any means, electronic or mechanical, including photocopying,
recording, or any information storage or retrieval system, without prior permission in
writing from the publishers.

Bloomsbury Publishing Plc does not have any control over, or responsibility for, any
third-party websites referred to or in this book. All internet addresses given in this
book were correct at the time of going to press. The author and publisher regret
any inconvenience caused if addresses have changed or sites have ceased to exist,
but can accept no responsibility for any such changes.

A catalogue record for this book is available from the British Library.

A catalog record for this book is available from the Library of Congress.

ISBN: HB: 978-0-7556-5643-1
PB: 978-0-7556-5644-8
ePDF: 978-0-7556-5646-2
eBook: 978-0-7556-5647-9

Typeset by Deanta Global Publishing Services, Chennai, India
Printed and bound in Great Britain

To find out more about our authors and books visit www.bloomsbury.com
and sign up for our newsletters.

Contents

List of Figures vii
Acknowledgments viii

Introduction 1

1 Roots 15
   A Nation among Nations 15
   Resentment, Revaluation, and Romanticism in Europe 17
   Turkish Romanticism 21
   The Turkish Far Right during the Cold War 25
      Two Men of Ressentiment 28
   Conclusion: Revaluing the Republic 38

2 The Institutional Structure of "New Turkey" 41
   A Messy Solar System 41
   The Road to the Executive Presidency 45
   Ruling through the Oligarchic Networks 57
   Where Is the System Going? 68

3 Making Strategy in New Turkey 71
   Imagining a New Normal 71
   The Factory Settings: Liberalization 72
   Blood Touches the Wolf's Tooth: The Syrian Civil War and the Kurds 81
   Catharsis: The Coup Attempt 94
   The New Normal 100

4 Turkey's Relations with Russia and China 103
   A Career of Geopolitical Proportions 103
   Turkey–Russia: Hot Steel Quenched in Water 107
      Case Study: Turkey–Ukraine Relations during the War 118
   China–Turkey Relations: The Dog That Didn't Bark 129
      Case Study: The Uyghur Question 135

5	The Vision of Greater Turkey	141
	Territory	142
	Population	156
	Military Development and Alliance Structure	169
Conclusion		177
Notes		181
Index		241

Figures

1	The Republic of Turkey State Institution Guide	42
2	Government structure breakdown for the 2018 Turkish presidential system	44
3	A popular map depicting how Turkey would establish a "safe zone" along the southern border	90
4	Erdoğan's contacts with the leaders of Russia and the United States, as reported in Anadolu Agency and other Turkish state news agencies	117
5	The Turkish National Pact of 1920 and The Lausanne Treaty of 1923	150
6	A story on the website of the state news agency Anadolu Agency delineating Mîsâk-ı Millî borders on Turkey's southern border via Google Maps	151
7	Historian Nicholas Danforth's interpretation of the January 20, 1920 version: "Regions in red were an 'indivisible whole,' while regions in pink would have their status determined by referendum"	152
8	Population rate by age group, 1935–2080	161
9	Number of international students 2001–21	164

Acknowledgments

The idea for this book started to take shape after the 2016 coup attempt in Turkey. The country was changing rapidly, and I was broadening my reading to try and make sense of it. In 2019, I was a fellow at the Foreign Policy Research Foundation (FPRI), and Chris Miller, who was director of the Eurasia Program at the time, approached me about writing a series of reports on Turkey. We came up with a two-year project, and I was lucky enough to receive funding from the Smith Richardson Foundation, but only on the condition that the reports amount to a monograph. The pandemic stretched out the project's lifetime, and James Ryan, who was the head of research at FPRI, encouraged me to upgrade my work into a full book.

While writing, I was also doing a PhD at the University of Nottingham, studying Nietzsche's politics under the supervision of Hugo Drochon. While my book and thesis shared a theoretical foundation, they were otherwise very different, and researching and writing two very demanding texts at the same time has taken its toll. I am thankful to Hugo for his patience as well as his opinions on the first chapter of this book.

Sam Harshbarger was my research assistant on this project, and I thank him for his meticulous work and boundless enthusiasm. Nicholas Danforth read parts of the book and gave useful comments. Two anonymous readers gave very insightful comments and made the book much better.

Most of all, I thank my wife, Müjge Küçükkeleş, who has been my invaluable reader, editor, and guiding light.

Introduction

Rabbim isterse sular, *bük*l*üm* b*ük*l*üm* burulur
If my Lord wills it, the waters will part, bend by bend
          Necip Fazıl Kısakürek, Sakarya Türküsü

In the summer of 2013, a predominantly young crowd gathered to protest the demolition of a park adjacent to Istanbul's central square. The police met them with barricades, tear gas, and clubs. The protest turned into a popular uprising across Turkey's major cities in which crowds called for the resignation of the prime minister. To the government, this was embarrassingly similar to the Arab uprisings roiling the Middle East in previous years.

As clouds of tear gas rose from city centers, four leaders of the ruling Justice and Development (AK) Party gathered in a "sitting of friends" [dost meclisi] to discuss where the country was heading. Among them was Beşir Atalay, the former minister of interior and, at that point, the deputy prime minister. A short, bald man in his mid-sixties, Atalaty was from the inner Anatolian city of Kırıkkale. He was trained in law and sociology, and came to be known within the Islamist movement as a scholar-practitioner. He never smiled if he could help it, and wasn't one to waste words. He liked to think of himself as a radical but placed great value on institutions and deliberation. On this day, Atalay was concerned.

"We are missing the Obama opportunity," he told the others, including the then prime minister Recep Tayyip Erdoğan.[1]

———

Being Muslim has been politically complicated for a long time. For centuries, most of the Islamic world had been poor and divided, watching as Western countries rose in power and prestige. The recent history of Turkey's conservative intelligentsia, as with others in the Muslim world, was one of soul-searching and self-doubt. Why had the Muslim world fallen behind? How was it to catch up? Would this entail a conflict with the West? In the Arab world, things had already taken a violent turn. With the 2001 attack on the Twin Towers in New York, and the subsequent US-led invasions of Afghanistan and Iraq, tensions rose to new heights. The "Clash of Civilizations" was in the air.

After two terms of the Bush administration and the "war on terror," Barack Obama was elected in 2008 on a broadly progressive agenda. As "Barack Hussein Obama"—the middle name alone induced optimism—took the oath of office, he promised that he would seek a "new way forward" with the Muslim world, one "based on mutual interest and mutual respect."[2] To find that new way, Obama embarked on an international tour, and his first stop was Turkey.

Among the Muslim-majority countries at the time, Turkey was a rising star. Under the AK Party government, it was no longer curtailing its Muslim identity, nor did it reject globalization and modernity as they existed in the West. It aspired to be a Muslim version, sometimes of Christian Democrats in Europe, at others, third-way liberals in the Anglo-American world. Scholars and policy analysts from Ankara to Washington believed that the AK Party could reconcile "Muslim civilization," however loosely defined, with Western modernity. The "Clash of Civilizations" need not be inevitable. Just as the American civil rights movement had chosen the nonviolent path, and yielded as its fruit the Obama presidency, the Muslim world, too, could choose the path of integration and development. Globalization was now malleable enough to adapt to the newcomers, and these newcomers were mature enough to overcome past resentments and join the liberal international project. It could channel historical grievance into the international system and realize its claims of social justice and the equality of nations.

Muslims did not have to replicate the mistakes of the West—the military interventions, the discrimination of immigrants, extreme inequality. They could rise above the need to meet violence with violence, and work with progressives in the West to find a new way forward. As leaders, Obama and Erdoğan could each use the symbolic powers of African American and Islamic heritage to drive this movement and create momentum for others to follow. When Atalay spoke of missing the "Obama opportunity" in 2013, he was thinking about a political problem far greater than merely bilateral relations with the United States.[3]

He was right to be concerned. Despite Obama's promising 2009 visit to Turkey, the geopolitical mending wasn't materializing. Turkey's accession process to the European Union (EU) slowed down, and eventually stopped over the failure to resolve the conflict over Cyprus, as well as French opposition to Turkey's accession.[4] Turkey's relationship with Israel deteriorated in 2009–10, never to fully recover. Disagreements were also emerging with the United States over how to handle the bloody civil war in Syria.[5] All the while, the

Erdoğan government became more repressive at home, centralizing power and demonizing its opposition. The Gezi Park protests of 2013 indicated robust grassroots opposition to the government.

Overall, however, it seemed less and less likely that Turkey's citizens could ever reconcile their political differences. The country looked less unique in the Muslim world, and less able to achieve the progressive mission it sought with, and ultimately within, the West. Atalay thought that the AK Party government was pulling in a perilous direction and needed an urgent course correction to salvage Turkey's role on the global stage.

So what did Erdoğan think? Did he believe, as Atalay did, that Turkey needed to seize the "Obama opportunity," to distinguish the country's unique position in the Muslim world and reassert its strategic importance to the West?

"He did not adopt that idea [o düşünceyi benimsemedi]," Atalay told me.

The transition to what we now call "New Turkey" was underway.

———

This transition from liberalism to reactionary nationalism—one that is all too common today from the United States to India—is reflected in the term Turks have used to describe this new regime: New Turkey. It helps to think on that term, not least because this New Turkey is not the first New Turkey. In his exposition of the term, Tanıl Bora, a veteran scholar of political ideas in Turkey, points out that the Republic's founder, Mustafa Kemal Atatürk, often spoke in the 1920s of "the New Turkish state," "the state of New Turkey," "the New Turkey Republic," and simply "New Turkey." This marked the country's rupture from the Ottoman state, the "Old Turkey," brought down, in this view, by sloth and superstition.[6] Publications in French and English at the time also used the phrase to describe the Kemalist state. In 1947, Turkish-American author Selma Ekrem published a book entitled *Turkey, Old and New* in which she reflected on the interaction between Ottoman-era customs and modern reforms.[7] The adjective seems to have dropped off in the 1950s, when Turkey had aged a few decades and had its first democratic government.

Turkey became new again in the accounts the foreign press wrote about the AK Party era. As early as 2005, BBC journalist Chris Morris published a book entitled *The New Turkey: The Quiet Revolution on the Edge of Europe*. The cover showed the silhouette of a man in traditional garb, looking out from the dark arcade of a mosque onto the gleaming glass façade of the European Parliament. The book, like international news reports at the time, used "New Turkey" in reference to the liberal wave of reforms at the time.[8] In this usage, there was no

"Old Turkey," probably because the words "new" and "Turkey" already presented enough of a contrast, implying that Turkey connotes backwardness unless appropriately modified.

The AK Party adopted the term in its Turkish form. The earliest such instance appears to have been at a 2007 election rally, when the party used a song entitled "Yeni Türkiye" (New Turkey) by pop singer Işın Karaca, allegedly editing out a part that praised Mustafa Kemal Atatürk. Karaca wasn't pleased, but the conservative electorate liked the phrase, and the AK Party kept using it. The Foundation for Political, Economic and Social Research (Siyaset, Ekonomi ve Toplum Araştırmaları Vakfı, SETA), a think tank close to the AK Party, used the phrase in its reports during the late 2000s.[9] Unlike in the English version, however, "Old Turkey" (Eski Türkiye) also entered common use. It referred to the years before the AK Party's dominance, describing an autocratic country governed by a militarist elite.[10] "Yeni Türkiye," meanwhile, was liberal, European, and enthusiastically reconnecting with its Ottoman and Islamic heritage.

As the police were firing gas canisters at protesters in Gezi Park in the summer of 2013, "New Turkey" changed meaning yet again. The AK Party was shedding its liberal credentials and assumed a nationalistic tone, and it took the "New" adjective along with it. This "New Turkey" was about God and country, the home-grown arms industry and the sanctity of the family. It was a self-assertive place no longer beholden to what it considered to be the malign influence of Western power and culture. Its corollary, "Old Turkey" was no longer militarist and authoritarian; it was weak and treasonous, governed by a class that had capitulated to Western supremacy. The Old–New dichotomy now described two ways of positioning the country in relation to the West.

In this New Turkey, the promise of cultural progressivism and liberal democracy looks like little more than a stepping stone. The country is no longer governed through a parliamentary system, but by a super-presidency with ever-growing powers. Its political and economic structure has ossified into a wide pyramid where very few loyalists rule at the top, and everyone else gets pushed further to the bottom. On the world stage, Turkey is among a league of revisionist powers. Its relations with the United States and Europe are crisis-prone, while its relations with local and Eurasian powers are stable and growing. Turkey is also assuming a strategic culture that is more interventionist, engaging in several wars and armed conflicts in its region.

———

The "New Turkey" of this book's title is this last iteration. I will argue that this is a political regime based on a reactionary strand of far-right Turkish nationalism. This is informed by my reading of the political tradition that the Erdoğan generation grew up in and my observations of Turkish politics in the last two decades. My account is part of what has been called the "resentment paradigm," explaining political events, and especially right-wing politics, in terms of status anxiety and existential resentment.[11] This approach was prevalent in the late nineteenth and early twentieth centuries, but lost purchase toward the end of the Cold War. In recent years, however, some writers in the non-Western world have been observing convulsions of resentful nationalism in their countries. Western countries also tuned back into the analytical framework in the 2010s, especially with the 2016 election of Donald Trump, linking the event to resentment among the white working class.[12]

The English-language literature on Turkish history and politics is only recently starting to develop a clearer picture of Turkey's various right-wing movements. As a discipline, Turkey studies since the 1970s focused on the sins of the Kemalist establishment in the early decades of the Republic, seeing that period as the root of the country's problems with democracy.[13] Liberal scholars believed that it was the Kemalist establishment's exclusion of conservative-Islamist and Kurdish groups that prevented democracy from taking root. They argued that only by including these identity groups into its electoral and bureaucratic processes could Turkey find peace. It is becoming increasingly obvious, however, that what is now called "post-Kemalist" scholarship failed to consider that the conservative movements, and the Islamists in particular, might not conform to the liberal system they envisaged. They assumed that participation in the liberal world order would be so compelling that these groups would jettison their more eccentric beliefs. When the AK Party's leadership claimed to have "taken off the shirt" of Islamist politics, and started life in the 2000s as a liberal, center-right force, most professional Turkey analysts wanted to believe them.[14]

Some in the AK Party's leadership may indeed have been sincere in their liberal conversion, but the dominant strain embraced a different path. When it became clear that Islamist forces were not reliably democratic, they were merely labeled with negations: undemocratic and illiberal. Conspicuously absent from the literature on the Erdoğan regime, and the Islamist political tradition from which it emerged, is the term "far-right." In popular writing on Turkey, the "far-right" designation is almost exclusively used for pan-Turkic nationalists, which is represented by the Nationalist Action Party (MHP), as well as the "Idealist Hearths" (sometimes called "Grey Wolves"). As my first chapter will make clear,

I consider "far-right" to denote an identitarian, and at root, romantic opposition to the Kemalist Republic's founding ethos. In this sense, both the Islamist and the pan-Turkic traditions are on the far-right of Turkey's political spectrum.

It is the Islamists, however, that became politically successful and took the country through the metamorphoses it has undergone in the past decades. This book therefore takes seriously the worldview of Turkey's Islamists and seeks to understand them on their own terms, describing them for what they are, rather than what they aren't. I base my analysis on my reading of the writers and theorists that shaped the worldview of the Erdoğan generation of AK Party leaders. I also rely on the work of leftist scholars in Turkey, since many of them have long studied Turkey's far-right movements with far greater rigor than those in liberal and international circles.

———

My intellectual path has been shaped by my personal story. I grew up along the confluence of Islamist and liberal politics, and had a front-row seat to New Turkey's formation from its early days.

My father was a Turkish diplomat, and during my childhood, our family rotated between living between Ankara and locations abroad, first in Europe and then in the United States. This exposed me to various historical narratives. In American and German schools, our teachers taught us that history had been a complicated struggle, but that for the most part, good had prevailed over evil. Yes, these countries had committed the atrocious crimes of colonialism, slavery and genocide, but they had had seen the errors of their ways. The liberal model advanced in the United States had allowed for constitutional government and eventually, the civil rights movement, to yield a better society. Despotic regimes had been defeated in the Second World War, and eventually, in the Cold War as well. The "good guys" had won. The task of today's politics was to build on that victory by refining liberal institutions, making them more inclusive and efficient. The Martin Luther King quote Obama liked to use sums it up: "the Arc of the moral universe is long, but it bends towards justice."[15]

The narrative I was taught at school in Turkey was similarly optimistic. Our country was the main heir of the Ottoman Empire, a world power that couldn't keep up with the times. By the twentieth century, it was collapsing, and in the First World War, Turkey had been invaded by colonial powers. The imperialists intended to occupy and dissolve the Ottoman state permanently, but on the brink of catastrophe, a few Ottoman soldiers, led by Mustafa Kemal, defeated the invaders and carved out an independent nation-state. Mustafa Kemal, now taking on the name "Atatürk," founded a Republic and steered Turkey toward modernist ideals emanating from Europe. The "good guys" had won, and they looked a lot like the good guys in the American and European textbooks. Our task, again, was to be custodians of victory.

During summers I spent with my extended family; however, I was educated in a different history. This is because, unusual for Turkish diplomatic families of the time, my parents weren't from the secular, wealthy establishment. Growing up as the son of a shopkeeper in Izmir, my father went to an Imam Hatip School (originally vocational schools for the Muslim clergy, now simply a more conservative education track), but he made it into Ankara University's prestigious Faculty of Political Science. He was probably the first imam-hatip graduate to ever become a career diplomat, and certainly the first to make the rank of ambassador. My mother was from a family of conservative emigres from Kayseri to Izmir. She excelled in her studies and trained in the top medical schools in the country, but gave up her career as a doctor to raise my sister and me as we traveled around the world. My parents were always outsiders in the secular, Kemalist diplomatic service. My mother remembers how, upon finding out that my parents didn't drink alcohol, one of my father's bosses early in his career advised them to break the Islamic taboo. "You'll eventually have to anyway," he told them, "you might as well start now."

All this meant that as a kid, I led a double life of sorts. During the school year, I'd get an official education in Ankara, Mainz, or Chicago. Over the holidays, we'd go back to Izmir and spend long stretches of time with our extended family. We would mostly stay in my mother's old neighborhood, called Akevler (literally ak-evler, meaning "White Homes," foreshadowing the AK Party, founded decades later).[16] Akevler was founded by radical Islamists as an exclave in the famously secular city of Izmir.[17] The brains behind it, Süleyman Karagülle, was a chief advisor to Necmettin Erbakan, the most prominent Islamist politician of the time. Karagülle is known for "Adil Düzen" (Just Order), Erbakan's policy for a systematic redesign of the state and the economy according to Islamist principles. While this "Just Order" remained a utopian slogan, Akevler could be seen as its local experiment. Here, Karagülle and his followers wanted to build a financial model that would isolate this compound from the outside world. They tried to create their own currency pegged to the price of iron and cement ("demir-çimento," DÇ) that would separate them from the interest-based financial system of Turkey. They set up Quranic schools and prayer rooms in each apartment block, so that children could get a supplementary religious education and adults could teach and debate. Like most utopian projects, Akevler's model didn't stick, and by the time I was a kid, it was already fusing with the urban sprawl around it. Still, it remained a conservative, even quietly radical neighborhood.

At Akevler, I soaked in a story that turned the historical narratives I had received in school—abroad and at home—upside-down. Here, I was told that we had not been the winners of modernity, we had been its losers. My late grandfather, a deeply pious man from the inner Anatolian city of Kayseri, would tell my cousins and I how Muslims had been oppressed by European colonialists, and how the Ottoman Empire had been cheated out of its territories by sneaky English imperialists and their collaborators in our midst. The Quran had been proven to be scientifically accurate in study after study, but Western scientists were sitting on the evidence.[18] Atatürk had been a great leader and the nation was indebted to him for winning the war of independence, but his reforms abolishing the Ottoman alphabet, the dress code, and educational curricula were unforgivable. İsmet İnönü, the Republic's second president, pushed these even further, including the infamous Turkish-language call to prayer. Both men led secular lifestyles, drank alcohol, and spoke foreign languages. They severed the nation from its spiritual roots. The first democratically elected prime minister, Adnan Menderes, was gradually moving back into a conservative policy, but had been hanged after the country's first coup in 1960. As a consequence, Muslims in Turkey were made to apologize for their faith. Some of this history was accurate, some of it wasn't, but with family, one didn't want to split hairs. According to my grandfather, the reality we lived in was a silent catastrophe. The bad guys had won. Our inheritance was defeat.

The correct posture in the face of this, we were taught, was dignified resistance. My grandfather told us stories of his youth to inculcate us with this spirit. While in the military, his superior officer, upon finding out that he doesn't drink alcohol, orders him to sit and drink with the others. Grandfather refuses. Just as the officer raises his hand to hit him, grandfather reaches out to grab his wrist.

"Orders are for the line of duty," he says.

In another story, he's in an important meeting at the ministry for agriculture, where he was a cotton inspector. It's time for Friday prayers, and grandfather tells his superior that he is stepping out briefly because he has "an appointment." When the superior insists he move the date, grandfather says, "this is an appointment with the divine sir [bu ilahi bir randevü]. It cannot be moved." The lesson was always to "stand up to pharaoh," to refuse to yield to the predominant culture. I loved hearing those stories, and I thought of them often as a student abroad. I still do.

Still, our families were afraid that we, the children, might forget. It was the 1990s, globalization had hit its stride, and American culture was an unstoppable force rolling across the globe, including Turkey. The boom in post–Cold War optimism hit Turkey at least just as hard as it did Europe. Every time we came back from abroad, my cousins rifled through our bags to examine the new cultural artifacts we had brought. A defining song of the era was Rafet El Roman's "Macera Dolu Amerika" ("America, full of Adventure")—in the fast-paced song he was writing a letter about the wonders of New York City, to a boy named Mehmet in Rural Turkey. We stayed up all night and watched (badly) dubbed American blockbusters and looked forward to the once-in-the-summer trip to McDonalds one of my aunts would take us on. The idea among young people, as in most transition economies in the world at the time, was to emulate Western, and specifically American, behaviors: following one's dreams, dating, traveling, starting a business were all getting baked into Turkish culture. Our family thought that my sister and I were especially in danger because we spent large chunks of our childhood in Western countries. As is usually the case in these situations, they feared that we would be estranged from their world and slip away into the dominant culture, not to be heard of again.

The word of caution to us, who lived in the West, was always to "learn the techniques [teknik] of the West, not its morality [ahlak]." This was, and remains, a ubiquitous phrase in conservative circles. It sounds deceptively simple: we were to disaggregate Western modernity, extract the knowledge that allowed it to generate power, which primarily lay in science and organizational structure, and leave the cultural offerings on the table. It wasn't necessarily that that culture was poisonous—though there was that too—it was that it sidetracked us from the primary task. Our collective goal of reverting history to what it was supposed to be, to amass power and turn defeat into victory. Thus empowered by Western power and technology, our uniquely moral nation would produce benevolent outcomes. Things like the internet or armed drones, which acted as tools of cultural degeneration and destruction in the West, would become the tools of peace and prosperity in our hands.

Like any counterculture, this conferred on us a sense of dignity, which then became a sense of superiority. As the AK Party's star was rising in the 2000s, we thought we could see around the corner. Things were changing. While freshly minted civil servants of my parents' generation were encouraged to drink alcohol and flout their foreign language skills, they now made a show of fasting during Ramadan and highlighting their provincial origins. The Islamist "neighborhood," as it is often called, had held its ground, and the rest of the country was now shifting in its direction.

In my twenties, I was excited about this transformation but also felt uneasy about it. The advice we had received as children assumed that one can disaggregate "technique," meaning technology and institutional structure, from "morality," meaning culture. But can one separate, for example, the scientific method from the enlightenment principles that also underpin individualism and secularism? Can we reverse-engineer modernity to get the benefits of technology, but roll back what Islamists consider moral degeneration? Was Islam, the last of the great Abrahamic faiths, really so different in its moral infrastructure? Was the West uniquely evil, and we as Muslims innocent and wholesome? How serious were we about all this?

The best aspects of the Islamist tradition were serious about facing these questions. They wanted to distill from Islam principles that would govern modern life and thus generate a serious alternative to Western liberalism and Soviet Communism. Akevler was to be a laboratory to develop these ideas. The most successful Islamists, however, did not lose time with theory. They simply adopt the already present economic and political models of the twentieth century, adorned them with the symbols of the Ottoman past, and revise the country's history of defeat. This reactionary strain won out, and what emerged was *New Turkey*.

―

The book begins with historical and conceptual background, then analyzes Turkey's domestic transformation during the AK Party years, and finally moves outward, to the country's foreign relations and geopolitical vision.

Chapter 1 describes the idea at the core of New Turkey: an existential resentment of the West. This is an outgrowth of Turkish romanticism, which, in turn, can be traced to continental Europe, and particularly to Germany. In the nineteenth century, the newly unified Germany was inspired by romantic notions of civilizational destiny and greatness. Most importantly, these thinkers defined the German nation in contrast to the French and English nations. The late Ottoman and early Turkish romantics were also caught up in this dynamic, defining themselves in contrast to the broader West. This yielded two contending systems of valuation: Aspirational Occidentalism, which sought to imitate the West in order to be accepted by it, and Competitive Occidentalism, which sought to imitate the West in order to overcome its geopolitical dominance. The former tendency set the official state ideology, while the latter was relegated to the Islamist and Turkist far-right of the political spectrum during the Cold War.

This chapter also introduces two figures who shaped far-right thinking in the 1970s and 1980s. The first is Necip Fazıl Kısakürek, a charismatic Islamist who wrote some of the most compelling nationalist poetry of his time. The second figure is Kadir Mısıroğlu, a self-styled historian who engaged in virulent polemics against the Kemalist republic. The figures pushed for a shift in the values that animate the Turkish state apparatus, a process that culminated in the AK Party government. This revaluation, I argue, is the essence of the transition from "Old" to "New" Turkey.

Chapters 2, 3, and 4 examine different strands of development during the AK Party era of almost twenty-five years. They start with developments in Turkey, then turn outward into Turkey's approach to the wider world and its relationships abroad. Readers uninitiated to Turkey's recent history might do best to read them in order, but I hope that the chapters can also hold their own for a specialist audience.

Chapter 2 describes the institutional transformation Turkey has undergone during the AK Party years. It begins with a description of the political landscape in the 2000s, specifically how the AK Party at the time overcame constitutional obstacles to win election after election, gradually changing the system every time. By the mid-2010s, Erdoğan had sidelined his fellow AK Party founders and outside allies, consolidating the movement in his own hands. He sought to reform the constitution to establish a presidential system, but successive polls indicated that the idea was deeply unpopular. His movement appeared stuck. The failed coup attempt in 2016 revitalized Erdoğan's efforts, allowing him to purge his enemies, as well as centralize legislative, executive, and juridical power in a newly created executive office in 2017. While the hyper-centralized system was meant to streamline government, it came to rely heavily on networks of informal actors in the bureaucracy and private sector. These include *cemaat*, as well as ethnic and regional networks.

Chapter 3 evaluates the development of the AK Party's "intellectual defense complex," made up of a community of policy experts populating Ankara and Istanbul, and the strategic culture they created. It argues that Turkey has gone through two major strategic shifts in the past two years. The first was in 2002, the "factory settings" of the AK Party influenced heavily by third-way liberalism in the United States and the United Kingdom, as well as the need to overcome the military's political dominance within Turkey. The tone of Ankara's policy community during this period was internationalist and eagerly pro-EU. The second shift occurred in 2015, when, reacting to events in Syria and a hung parliament after the June elections that year, the Erdoğan government abandoned the nascent peace process with the PKK and embarked on a nationalist path. It embraced resentment-fueled politics and, in subsequent years, began to stage military operations in its near abroad. The policy community now took on a hard-nosed realist tone. Military and intelligence officers, as well as defense industry specialists were its most valued members. This chapter weaves in small professional biographies of specific characters in the Turkish policy scene. Some of these are civil servants— ambassadors, generals, and intelligence chiefs—who negotiate the transition from Old to New Turkey. Others are political advisors, academics, and journalists who surround the men in power and drive events behind the scenes.

Chapter 4 analyzes Turkey's relations with Russia and China, presenting a case study for each. Like these two Eurasian powers, Turkey under Erdoğan is a revisionist country, but is that enough to create lasting bonds? With Russia, this seems to be the case. Despite a history of conflict and various flash points in Syria, the Caucasus, and Ukraine, Ankara and Moscow enjoy a robust relationship. This goes back to the early twentieth century, when both countries sought to "catch up" with Western Europe, and the mid-to-late stages of the Cold War, when they built cordial relations across the Iron Curtain. After the Cold War, Erdoğan and Putin both felt snubbed by the West, and both built political brands on subverting Western dominance in international affairs. This allowed them to establish a remarkably stable working relationship. Though significant differences remain between the countries, and can at times result in proxy battles, the relationship at the top remains congenial, even cooperative. The case study on Russia is the Ukraine war, perhaps the biggest test of Turkey–Russia relations. For Turkey's new elite, Ukraine's pro-Western policy was regressive and misguided, but also contains opportunities for Turkey. Ankara has therefore chosen to chart a path that is "pro-Ukrainian without being anti-Russian." Interviews with serving Turkish officials, as well as a close reading of pro-government Turkish media, indicate that Ankara anticipates Kyiv to be disappointed with its Western allies. In that eventuality, Turkey seeks to engage Ukraine and cultivate in it a more Turkish form of sovereignty—one that is integrated neither into liberal Western institutions nor into the Russian civilizational sphere.

On China, the story is different. Turkey sought to establish strong relations with the emergent superpower but has continuously fallen short. It has not been able to deepen economic relations significantly, nor acquire a solid place in

China's Belt and Road Initiative. This is largely because, unlike countries like Germany, Turkey did not devote the diplomatic and institutional resources into understanding and penetrating the Chinese system. Part of the obstacle here is cultural: Turkey's business and cultural elite are highly focused on the West and reluctant to develop connections in Asia. The case study in this section is the Uyghur question: the long-suppressed Muslim-Turkic population in western China. Throughout his time in power, Erdoğan has struggled with the task of balancing its solidarity with the Uyghur and his eagerness to build up relations with China. At the beginning of this career, he seemed interested in the former but, in the 2010s, firmly emphasized the latter. China, meanwhile, has been demanding of Turkey in this respect, pressuring it to conform to its narratives and suppress public sentiment at home. The Uyghur question therefore still poses a challenge to the development of Turkey–China relations, albeit one that authorities on both sides are working to overcome.

Chapter 5 seeks to lay out the patterns of Turkey's grand strategy. There are three elements to this. The first element is geographic expansion. This can entail broadening connectivity in the liberal sense, increasing the network of commerce, tourism, and cultural engagement with the world at large, especially building vibrant South–South relations. It also has an irredentist aspect, in which Turkey's new elite keeps an eye toward broadening its military control over territory and, ultimately, expanding its borders. The second element entails the expansion of Turkey's population. In order to be a great power, Turkey's new leadership has sought to ensure that the country's population continues to expand and accepts their new values, but has only met limited success. At the same time, Turkey is also becoming a recipient of migrants across its southern and eastern borders. While this has created significant political backlash, it could make the country more cosmopolitan and imbue it with the young population its leaders want. The third element is Turkey's military-industrial buildup and alliance politics. Turkey has been a NATO member since 1952, and while this history has not been without significant friction, the country has always taken its alliance obligations seriously. Under its new elite, Turkey is pursuing a policy of self-reliance that is unique among NATO allies, save perhaps the United States. Considering the political tradition of its ruling elite, as well as the material push in the defense industry, I conclude that the country is preparing for a future in which it will be less dependent on its Western treaty allies and seek to develop an alliance of its own.

1

Roots

For he might have been a Roosian,
A French, or Turk, or Proosian,
Or perhaps Itali-an!
But in spite of all temptations
To belong to other nations,
He remains an Englishman!
He remains an Englishman!
H.M.S. Pinafore, by Gilbert & Sullivan

England is our model and our rival, our guiding light and our enemy.
Marquis de Luchet[1]

Oh my enemy, you are my expression and my endeavor
As day needs night, so do I need you![2]
Necip Fazıl Kısakürek

They say that I am angry. Anger too is an oratory art![3]
Recep Tayyip Erdoğan

A Nation among Nations

Reaction to Western modernity lies at the heart of Turkish politics today. Every election, every speech, every news item is marked by it. This is not an ideological commitment. Ideologies, like communism and liberalism, are theories about how to organize society that might be based on observations in human nature, historical patterns, or faith traditions. While some ideologies like Islamism, neoliberalism, and Turanism (pan-Turkic nationalism, or Turkism) play a prominent role in Turkey's transformation, they are not its animating force. Nor is it useful to talk about geopolitical leanings packed into an "-ism", such as "anti-Westernism," "anti-Americanism," or "Eurasianism." These terms may describe some outcomes of Turkey's policies, but they fail to go beyond that.

When explaining Turkish politics, too often we focus on the ways the country is distinct from its European neighbors: its Islamic and Ottoman heritage, its location straddling Europe and Asia, its history of military conflict with the West. It doesn't help that Turkey's new elite also likes to accentuate these factors, proudly holding them up as evidence of the country's special place in history. Ironically, such exceptionalism is the quintessential aspect of nation formation in Europe. I aim to de-exceptionalize Turkey and locate its current regime within a wave of reactionary nationalist movements raging across the world today, from Israel to China, and India to the United States.[4]

The literature on nationalism is vast, and tells it story from many different perspectives. Modernist theorists like Ernest Gellner and Benedict Anderson have argued that nationalism emerged in Europe, either through new modes of industrial production, which changed the nature of labor, or through the proliferation of mass communication, which allowed otherwise disparate societies to imagine themselves into a national collective.[5] Eventually this process spread beyond the West, transforming the globe into a patchwork of nations. In his study of nationalism in the Middle East and Africa, Elie Kedourie emphasized the role of elites, and how their sense of humiliation has shaped ideas of nationhood.[6] Liah Greenfeld, meanwhile, has based her theory of nationalism on reactionary feeling, particularly with her work on the Russian elite.[7]

In telling the story of New Turkey, I can't hope to offer a full discussion of Turkish nationalism, nor would this be useful. My purpose is to explain the recent shift between Old and New Turkey, which is not about Turkish nation formation as much as a competition between different facets of Turkish nationalism. To do this, I will rely on explanations based on status anxiety among cultural elites. I will enhance this with my reading of Nietzsche and his ideas concerning the relationship between values and politics.

The chapter will begin with an exploration of the spread of nationalism in Europe, and the ideas of exceptionalism and competition this entailed. It will then trace these ideas among the intelligentsia of the late Ottoman Empire, arguing that the Ottoman reading of the West, or its "occidentalism," at this time, split into two camps: one aspiring to European culture, the other seeking to compete with it. This dual reading of the West among the Turkish intelligentsia, I will argue, made up two strands of values that can be traced throughout the late Ottoman Empire, the long twentieth century, and into our present. The "Old Turkey" of the Kemalist elite sought to emulate the West with the intention of joining it, while the "New Turkey" of today seeks to emulate the West in order to compete with it. Its competitive drive is animated by existential resentment of the West, a high-order status anxiety that suffuses the Islamist tradition. I end the chapter with a brief examination of the two romantic writers who were most influential in this respect: Necip Fazıl Kısakürek and Kadir Mısıroğlu.

Resentment, Revaluation, and Romanticism in Europe

In medieval Europe, the term used to describe foreigners was "natio," Latin for "something born." In the thirteenth century, it described church councils in Paris, then came to refer to the political and cultural elite.[8] The sixteenth-century English users of "natio" then did something strange. They began to describe the lower classes, hitherto denigrated as "plebeians" or "rabble," as "the nation." This implied that it was a badge of honor to be among the multitude as long as one could claim to be among the *English multitude*. This linguistic inversion, Liah Greenfeld argues, signaled the creation of the first nation.

The spread of this concept has been a long and painful process. Other societies compared themselves to the already formed nations, wrestling with feelings of provincial inadequacy in the face of a dominant external model.[9] The first to undergo this process was France. The various subjects of the king of France were increasingly speaking the same language, concentrating around a few major cities, and comparing themselves to the English. The more "national" the French became, and the closer they came to catching up, the harsher their anti-English sentiment developed. By the late eighteenth century, the French saw the English as too capitalist, too greedy, and too arrogant.[10] It is with this emotional backdrop that the French supported the uprisings in the English colonies in the Americas and continued to see the English as their chief rivals in the Napoleonic era. Greenfeld labels this emotion as "ressentiment," an existential envy toward England that was becoming the norm among the French elite.[11]

Ressentiment was most famously used by Friedrich Nietzsche in his *Genealogy of Morals*.[12] The term is of French origin, and though it shares a root with its English cousin "resentment," it indicates a different, and deeper emotion. The French verb "ressentir" (re-sentir) means to "feel again," suggesting the continuous re-living of an offensive or humiliating sensation, be it personal or historical. While the English "resentment" can result from an offense suffered in a conjectural manner (example: being cheated), the Nietzschean "ressentiment" specifically describes a resentment that cannot be acted upon, an existential envy directed not only against a subject but against time itself (example: having been born into poverty). In *Thus Soke Zarathustra*, Nietzsche writes:

> "It was": thus is called the will's gnashing of teeth and loneliest misery. Impotent against that which has been—it is an angry spectator of everything past.
> The will cannot will backward; that it cannot break time and time's greed—that is the will's loneliest misery.[13]

The subject of *ressentiment* is rebelling against the circumstances that gave rise to his own being. He is haunted by the impossibility of achieving the counterfactual in which he has power and prestige and the subject of his envy is desperately trying to catch up. Nietzsche's "man of ressentiment" can be a socialist or nationalist—ideology here is secondary—what matters is that he is obsessed with a history of defeat that has made him lesser than others. His will seeks to bend backward and revise the chain of contingencies that has made him what he is. Unable to do this, he develops an obsession with the subject of his *ressentiment*, the bumbling nobleman sitting atop the victories of his vicious forefathers. In his book of the same name, German philosopher Max Scheler gave us one of the sharpest descriptions of this emotional state:

> It is as if it whispers continually: "I can forgive everything, but not that you are—that you are what you are—that I am not what you are—indeed that I am not you." This form of envy strips the opponent of his very existence, for this existence as such is felt to be a "pressure," a "reproach," and an unbearable humiliation."[14]

Ressentiment is a relatively modern phenomenon because it assumes that the subject and object of envy are fundamentally comparable and equal in principle, but, in reality, are separated by irreconcilable differences. Premodern feudal societies were divided between nobles and peasants, but these were not comparable groups. A peasant didn't resent a nobleman, for example, because it didn't occur to him that they should be equals. As subjects gradually became citizens, they were equal under law, but separated by the vastly unequal distribution of wealth and opportunity. This was a *ressentiment*-prone structure.[15] A disenfranchised citizen could resent the powerful citizen because there was now a presumption of equality. Similarly, the emerging international environment was in principle predicated on the equality of sovereign nations, but in reality it was defined by the vast differences between them. The forces of modernity—capitalism, state formation, the change brought about by technology—accelerated the creation of inherently unstable, ressentiment-prone situations within and between societies.

This kind of ressentiment has been an essential aspect of nationalism's diffusion across the world. French ressentiment toward the English pushed them into military, economic, and cultural competition, culminating in the conflicts of the Napoleonic era. The Germans and Russians humiliated during that time nourished ressentiment toward the French and English and engaged in similarly competitive behavior in the late nineteenth and twentieth centuries. Each wave expressed itself in convulsions of romantic nationalism, in which artists of the "backwards" nation implored an ancient Volk to "wake up" and take its rightfully glorious place in the global hierarchy that was taking shape.

The German romantic tradition, in particular, was paradigmatic. Johann Gottfried Herder, the eighteenth-century philosopher, writer, and theologian, sought the acceptance of French cultural circles, but also thought the country decadent, mechanized, and ugly.[16] His method of consoling himself will sound familiar to us: the French and English may be more powerful and advanced, he thought, but they would never match the authentic spirit, or *Volksgeist*, of the German nation. Here, the romantics took the traits that were considered to be "backward" and re-valued them to be the mysterious source of German power. The playwright Heinrich von Kleist, for example, was passionately anti-Napoleonic, decrying French power as a lifeless, mechanical force, an "Allworld-Consul," or, citing Shakespeare, the "Universal Wolf."[17] What Germany lacked in technical advancement, it made up for in a deep well of spiritual strength that would allow it to ultimately defeat this monster. Von Kleist's 1809 play, *Die Herrrmannsschlacht*, depicted Germanic tribes heroically resisting the soulless onslaught of Roman legions.

Once Germany was unified and could match French military might, its nationalists saw their newfound military achievements as proof of inherent superiority. In his 1873 essay entitled *David Strauss: The Confessor and the Writer*, Nietzsche lamented how the supposed intelligentsia saw the German military victory over France in the Franco-Prussian war (1870–1) as testament to their cultural superiority and distinctiveness. He believed the opposite was true: Germany had achieved military victory because it managed to copy French industrial and cultural accomplishments. This is why the newly emerging Germany harbored a "grotesque juxtaposition and confusion of different styles," rather than an authentic and productive culture:

> Only if we had imposed upon the French an original German culture could there be any question of a victory of German culture. In the meantime, we should not forget that we are still dependent on Paris in all matters of form, just as before and that we have to go on being dependent, for up to now there has been no original German culture.[18]

The new German elite Nietzsche wrote of may have seemed "anti-French" to use the current expression, but they were only continuing a pattern set by the French. Their nationalism was petty, subjugating culture to politics, domestic well-being to geopolitical glory. Yet the newly unified German Empire would continue to grow in this vein. In the late nineteenth and early twentieth centuries, Germany's educational attainment, industrial output, and military power were growing at breakneck speed.

Perhaps the most important area where Germany had to "catch up" was in the acquisition of colonies, the mark of a truly great nation. In 1897 Bernhard von Bülow, who would go on to serve as chancellor of the German Empire from 1900 to 1909, gave a speech on the subject of German presence in China. German missionaries had been killed in China, and Germany had seized on this as pretext to send warships to ensure its continued trade and cultural expansion in the East. The "place in the sun" speech, as it is remembered, is worth quoting at length:

> We definitely do not feel the need to have a finger in every pie. But we believe it is inadvisable, from the outset, to exclude Germany from competition with other nations in lands with a rich and promising future. The days when Germans granted one neighbor the earth, the other the sea, and reserved for themselves the sky, where pure doctrine reigns – those days are over. We see it as our foremost task to foster and cultivate the interests of our shipping, our trade, and our industry, particularly in the East.[19]

Here Bülow seeks to establish a contrast between what we might call a weak "Old Germany," which was overly deferential to the French and British, and a powerful "New Germany," which would compete with them. He wants his country to travel up in the hierarchy of nations, and for its elevated status to be acknowledged by everyone he deems above and below it:

> We must demand that German missionaries, merchants, goods, as well as the German flag and German vessels be treated with the same respect in China that other powers enjoy. We are happy to respect the interests of other powers in China, secure in the knowledge that our own interests will also receive the recognition they deserve.

> In short, we do not want to put anyone in our shadow, but we also demand our place in the sun. True to the tradition of German policy, we will make every effort to protect our rights and interests in East Asia and West India—without unnecessary harshness, but without weakness either.

The phrase "place in the sun" captured the spirit of the times, and Kaiser Wilhelm II adopted it to express the driving force of German policy. Any real change in geopolitical hierarchy, the Germans recognized, was bound to involve violence, and Germany prepared its military for the impending clash with France, Russia, and Britain. This could be presented as a defensive investment for the protection of growing trade links, but the undercurrent of power politics flowed decisively in a revisionist direction.[20]

This is not to make a historical comparison between Wilhelmian Germany and Turkey under Erdoğan, and what that would mean for global politics. Such comparisons have been made in relation to China's rise today, which, considering its geopolitical scale, may be more appropriate.[21] For our purposes, the comparison serves to highlight the internal mechanisms of these rising powers, and their ressentiment-infused national cultures. To observe this dynamic in Turkey, we must extend the history of European romanticism to the late Ottoman period.

Turkish Romanticism

At the peak of their power in the sixteenth century, the Ottomans ruled over a vast empire spread across three continents. As Europe modernized, however, the Ottomans struggled to keep up. The small European countries that once felt provincial in Istanbul's eyes were growing in power and prestige. By the late nineteenth century, every bit of territory the empire lost further unbalanced the sensitive European power dynamic, a phenomenon that became known as the "Eastern Question."[22] The Ottomans were grappling with modernizing reforms, but seemed unable to catch up.[23] There was clearly something to the European experience that was far better at generating military and economic power, but it was extremely difficult to identify and replicate, and the Ottoman intelligentsia was haunted by this problem. Boarding trains and steam ships to Europe, the empire's intellectuals learned Europe's languages, read its literature, and marveled at its technological accomplishments. When they came back home, they were brimming with ideas.

The most influential of these figures was Nâmık Kemal (1840–88), a poet, playwright, and journalist. He criticized the Ottoman government in his pamphlets and newspapers, arguing forcefully for a parliamentary monarchy. Forced into exile in Paris and London, where he published the *Muhbir* and *Hürriyet* newspapers. Nâmık Kemal's plays and theoretical essays infused the Turkish sphere with the ideas of *Volksgeist* from European thinkers like Rousseau and Herder.[24] He took concepts like "fatherland" and "parliament" in their European contexts and pegged them to Ottoman concepts of vaguely similar meaning, seeking an authentic transition to modernity.[25]

What made the Ottoman modernization process different from that of European societies is that it seemed to involve far greater material and cultural differences. The Germans, despite their perceived "backwardness," were still able to compare their military, economic, and cultural accomplishments to those of the French and British at this time. Ottoman intellectuals had to acknowledge that their empire did not merit such comparison. The yawning gap between Ottoman and Western examples of modernity—especially in technological, economic, and institutional matters—became an obsession for Ottoman intellectuals. The scholar of Turkish intellectual history Hasan Aksakal writes:

> Turkey did not experience a Napoleonic occupation, a people's revolution, or an industrialization ordeal. Rather than any other thing, Turkish romanticism is related to the encounter of the representatives of Turkish political culture in the 19th Century with European modernity, and their realization that their own society had remained far more backwards than they thought. Open evidence for this is the effort behind every product of Turkish romanticism to explain the discrepancy between modern peers and their local representatives, the desire to "prove oneself to Europe" and the "expectation of acceptance/the Occidentalist anger at not being accepted."[26]

Aksakal here identifies two ways Turkish romantics dealt with the problem, amounting to two aspects of Turkish Occidentalism.[27] These are distinct systems of valuation, and they have been reverberating across Turkey's recent history. The first is what I will call "Aspirational Occidentalism." This is the belief that Western superiority is a natural outgrowth of its scientific and cultural accomplishments, while Turkey is held back by some of its non-European features, chief of which is its Islamic heritage. Aspirational Occidentalism sees the West as a model and seeks to replicate it as closely as possible, with the aspiration of transforming

Turkey into a Western country. It considers "Westernness" to be good, even beautiful, and sees "Easternness" as backward and ugly. The second value system is what I will call "Competitive Occidentalism." This is based on the belief that Western supremacy is the result of uniquely immoral and predatory conduct.[28] Like ressentiment movements in Europe, Competitive Occidentalism seeks to replicate Western methods while maintaining its cultural distinctiveness, which, in this case, are symbols of Islamic, Turkic, and Eastern heritage. In this value system, Westernness is evil, and Easternness is good. In order to defend the good, however, one must learn to replicate the methods of evildoers. The West is therefore not a model here, but an anti-model. Most political movements in Turkey's modern history have born aspects of both forms of valuation, but emphasize one over the other.

In the late Ottoman Empire, as in many European countries at the time, secret student societies began to form around nationalistic and enlightenment ideals. These "Young Turks" argued for a constitutional monarchy. They had a largely admiring attitude toward the West, learned its languages, and kept up with its trends. Many adhered to a simplified version of *Vulgärmaterialismus*, a creed that advocated the radical implication of scientific methods to overcome social problems.[29] This view tended to treat religion as the root of modernity's problems and experimented with either reforming it or rooting it out. On the other side of the political spectrum stood Sultan Abdülhamid II, who emphasized the empire's Islamic characteristics and sought to stamp out constitutionalist ideas. He also sought to modernize, but did so in large part to maintain the Ottomans' ability to compete with European powers and defend its Islamic distinctiveness.[30] After a very brief constitutional period in 1876–8, Abdülhamid II ruled with an iron fist. In 1908, however, the Young Turks, through the Committee of Union and Progress (CUP), succeeded in restoring parliamentary government and took control. It would be simplistic to say that these two political fronts embodied the two sides of Turkish Occidentalism, but they harbored early manifestations of those tendencies.

Following the First World War, European powers moved to finally occupy all of the Ottoman Empire and break it up. Mustafa Kemal, a military officer who broadly shared the CUP's ideas but was marginalized due to his opposition to some of its policies, now forged a movement of national liberation.[31] His army defeated the Western-backed Greek occupying forces, forces, managing to carve out Anatolia and a slice of the Balkan territory for the foundation of the Republic of Turkey, proclaimed in 1923. This Republic held up Western modernity as a cultural and economic model, and enacted strict reforms, most notably by abolishing the

Caliphate, transitioning to the Latin alphabet, instituting women's rights, the civil code, and a program of secular education. Its leading lights, chief among them Ziya Gökalp, fashioned Turkishness into a national identity somewhere between ethnic and civic nationalism in Europe. There was little ideological content to this—the Kemalists flirted with socialism, liberalism, and fascism—but at the height of its influence, Kemalism was a moral commitment, prescribing good and bad behavior, beautiful and ugly, as being roughly Western and non-Western.

Ironically, it had taken a war against the West to break into what has since become the paradigmatic case of Aspirational Occidentalism. After all, if Turkey had been permanently occupied by Western powers and adopted their ways by force, it would have meant capitulating to a superior civilization. Since Turkey defeated Western forces in the field of battle, however, Mustafa Kemal could argue that Westernization was a sign of the Turkish nation's advancement in the hierarchy of nations. This made Kemalism a model for Muslim-majority countries such as Egypt and Iran.[32] It also freed its hand to embrace Westernization without reserve.

An anecdote by Hasan Rıza Soyak, one of Mustafa Kemal's closest associates, illustrates the values of the new regime. One day, "when the great victory was still fresh," writes Soyak, the Mustafa Kemal was sent a painting.[33] As it was unpacked in front of him, it became apparent that it depicted an Ottoman soldier bayoneting a Greek soldier lying on the ground. "Suddenly his [Mustafa Kemal's] face wrinkled, he leaped up and shouted: 'cover it up, take it away . . . what a revolting scene . . . I marvel at the wretched mind.'"[34] Soyak writes that he later learned that the piece had been painted in 1897, during the Greco-Turkish war, and presented to Sultan Abdülhamid II. "The person sending it must have thought it appropriate for the mood at the time, and thought that the victorious commander would take pleasure in this," he writes.

Many at the time would have seen the Turkish war of independence as revenge against the West, which oversaw the dissolution of the Ottoman Empire, and the Greeks who occupied parts of Anatolia. The person sending it was likely reflecting notions of Competitive Occidentalism, seeing the West as evil, and therefore a valid object of revenge. Perhaps Mustafa Kemal had already satisfied that desire; perhaps he had risen above it. Revenge implies a past defeat and victimhood. The Kemalist project was about burying victimhood, draping itself in victory, and moving forward.

But the legacy of defeat wouldn't be forgotten. As Soyak also writes, "the painting was put back into the box and stored in the attic. When I left the mansion [köşk] years hence, the painting was still there."[35] In the following years, the Kemalist regime prosecuted its opponents mercilessly, but a systemic opposition always remained, biding its time.

The Turkish Far Right during the Cold War

For much of the Kemalist Republic, centrist politics was firmly occupied by the values of Aspirational Occidentalism. Turkey followed the modernization reforms set by its founder and sought to be a member of the European family of nations. It was only the politics on the fringes that challenged these values, most successfully among far-right movements of the Cold War.

There is some contention concerning what constitutes a far-right movement in Turkey. In much of the English-language scholarship and journalism on the country, the term "far right" is generally used for the "Türkçü" meaning "Turkists" (sometimes also called pan-Turkic nationalists or "Ultranationalists").[36] This classification has less to do with Turkey and more with European history, where revanchism manifested itself in fascist movements, most prominently in Nazi Germany. The Turkist nationalists followed some of these forms. They glorified the nation-state through mythical symbols of a manufactured Turkic lore, such as that of the "grey wolf." They organized in rigidly hierarchical student groups and after the 1990s, even had their own version of the Roman salute, in the form of an outstretched arm with the hand making a wolf sign. Some among them assumed an explicitly racist ideology. All this makes it seem compelling to designate this group as the "far right" in Turkey, and placing all other movements, including the Islamists, in a centrist category. This, however, places an excessive focus on form and misses the underlying dynamic of far-right nationalism.

For a better approach, consider a framework put forward by scholars İlker Aytürk and Tanıl Bora. They see right-wing politics broadly as a tendency to accept the inequalities that have historically manifested in the social structure and then take the resulting hierarchy as an organizational principle.[37] In this sense, a Sunni Muslim is superior to an Alevi or a non-Muslim (e.g., Armenian, Greek, Assyrian), a Turk is inherently superior to a Kurd, a boss is superior to his workers, and men are superior to women. This order need not be explicitly stated and can be (and often is) denied by right-wing movements. Their policies, organizational structure, and, most importantly, institutional culture, however, will rely on this order and reinforce it. While left-wing politics seeks to flatten these social hierarchies, right-wing politics seeks to conserve them.[38]

In Turkey's recent history, center-right leaders accepted the traditional social hierarchy, but felt it inappropriate to carry the issue of identity to the core of their politics. For them, economic development projects, such as building dams and bridges, were the core mission of governance. Turkey's two most influential center-right leaders, Süleyman Demirel and Turgut Özal, were both engineers, trained at the prestigious Istanbul Technical University (İTÜ). Both were reserved about their conservatism, preferring to talk about economic policy while quietly signaling that they were protective of the cultural hierarchies that were in place.[39] Their politics rested on an unarticulated, yet firm, notion that the matter of identity could lead to questioning the Kemalist foundations of the republic, destabilizing the country and delaying its economic progress.

Turkey's far right saw it the other way around, placing identity ahead of economic development. These movements believed that the nation's core strength, its *Volksgeist*, was eclipsed by the Kemalist regime. Although the country appeared to have maintained its sovereignty through Mustafa Kemal's leadership in the war of independence, it had succumbed to a form of metaphysical enslavement to the West. The center-right's emphasis on policy over identity, therefore, was addressing the symptoms of the disease, rather than its cause. Without a metaphysical revival, Turkey could not generate intellectual, economic, and military power on a geopolitically competitive scale. Only if and when the country was led by an authentically "national" leader who would restore its true identity would all questions of policy—from healthcare to the defense industry—fall into place.[40] Turkey would then generate power in the same way that it had at the peak of the Ottoman Empire and experience a geopolitical rise, or in the vernacular experience a "diriliş," meaning something between "resurrection" and "reawakening." Only a revival of core Turko-Islamic identity and a fresh confrontation with the West could restore the nation's natural place in the world.

Within the far right, there were two main ideological traditions: the Turkists and the Islamists. Many Turkists in the Republican era actually saw themselves within the Kemalist framework, but there was an anti-Kemalist Turkists strain as well. This was embodied most strongly by the writer Nihal Atsız, who harbored pan-Turkic, often racist, and irredentist views that went against Kemalist foundations, especially toward the end of the Second World War, when Turkey sided with the Allies against Nazi Germany.[41] The Islamists, meanwhile, emphasize Turkey's Islamic character over its Turkic one. This is not necessarily a modern ideology based on a methodical reading of the Quran and Sunnah (the deeds of the prophet Muhammad), as is the case with thinkers like Hasan al-Banna or Abul A'la Maududi. In Turkey's daily parlance, "Islamist" is often used interchangeably with "Anatolianist" or "Mukaddesatçı" and refers to a form of romantic nationalism with Islamic overtones.[42] I will stick to this convention for the sake of simplicity.

The Turkists and Islamists were not always on good terms. There was often friction between their youth wings and polemical magazines.[43] The Turkists tended to be more active on the streets, had armed wings, and joined the apparatus of state, especially the police and military.[44] The Islamists were a more bookish movement, and once their young men graduated from their student groups, they mostly avoided state employment, remaining in the private sector. Some Turkists saw the Islamists as being backward and effeminate, and many Islamists saw the Turkists as thuggish and racist idol-worshippers.[45] While there was some overlap and some ideologues switched back and forth between them, for the most part, the Turkists and Islamists remained separate spheres.

One thing Turkists and Islamists of all stripes could agree on, however, was their opposition to the left. Like right-wing movements in the West, they saw Marxist materialism as the ultimate antithesis to their country's metaphysical core. Kemalist Westernization was a fact of life, but further degeneration into the complete destruction of metaphysical values could still be avoided. The Kemalist regime maintained cordial relations with the Soviet Union but, starting in the 1950s, came to be deeply integrated into the institutional structure of the capitalist West, including membership in NATO.[46] In the eyes of the Islamists and non-Kemalist Turkists, this made it at once a problem but also a bulwark against further catastrophe.

During the Cold War, the pool of intellectuals, poets, writers, and philanthropists that far-right movements drew upon is wide and deep. The essayist and translator Cemil Meriç and the academic and poet Nurettin Topçu are some of the most scholarly and respectable across the political spectrum. Nihal Atsız was the foremost intellectual of the non-Kemalist Turkists, most famously writing the serialized novels *The Death of the Grey Wolves* and *The Revival of the Grey Wolves*, which would today place somewhere between the genres of fantasy and historical fiction. The Kurdish polymath and mysticist Said Nursi founded the Islamist "Nurcu" movement, the most successful branch of which was that of the mystic preacher and cult leader Fetullah Gülen, known in the 1970s and 1980s for his wildly popular sermons, and later for his sprawling secret networks. Islamists in the cities, meanwhile, hewed closer to the tradition of Mehmet Âkif Ersoy, a late Ottoman Islamist most famous for composing the Turkish national anthem at the dawn of the Republic.

Among these figures, two men stand out: Necip Fazıl Kısakürek and Kadir Mısıroğlu. This is not necessarily because they are the best scholars or most reputable. Far from it—others in this tradition, such as Meriç, Safa, and Topçu, far surpass them in those respects. Yet Kısakürek and Mısıroğlu have channeled the spirit of *ressentiment* far more effectively and forcefully than any of their contemporaries.[47] More than any other figures, they had a clear sense of the values of their enemy, the Aspirational Occidentalists, and sought to turn them upside down, achieving a revaluation into Competitive Occidentalism. The West wasn't beautiful and just; it was ugly and evil. Ottoman and Islamic history wasn't decadent and weak; it was harmonious and powerful. Like the romantic nationalists in Europe, Kısakürek and Mısıroğlu didn't shift values through meticulous research and tight argumentation, but through poetry, polemics, and their unique aesthetics. Erdoğan once said that "anger too, is an oratory art," and these are the masters he learned it from.

Two Men of Ressentiment

Necip Fazıl Kısakürek (1904–83) was a poet of unusual power and charisma. He edited and published the popular *Büyük Doğu* (Great East) magazine, and his poetry was the most popular reading in Islamist student groups. But Necip Fazıl, as he is known, did not cut the ascetic figure one might expect from a political Islamist. His life was a curious mix of vice and piety, privilege and revolt.

Necip Fazıl was born in 1904 as the sole child of a well-to-do family. He grew up in Istanbul, graduated from the Naval Academy in 1924, one year after the Republic was founded, and was selected by the nascent administration as one of a handful of young scholars to study in Europe. In a personal letter sent to the members of this group, Atatürk famously wrote: "I am sending you as sparks, you must return as flames."[48] This was a group handpicked to be the vanguard of the Kemalist Westernization project. Necip Fazıl was sent to Paris, but did not focus on his studies. When asked about his time there, he liked to say that he drank and gambled so much that he never saw Paris in daylight.[49] His scholarship was canceled after a year, and upon his return to Turkey, Necip Fazıl began to work as an administrator in banks and gave lectures on language and literature at universities in Ankara and Istanbul. He became a published poet, writing some of his most popular verses, such as *Kaldırımlar* (Sidewalks), and rubbed shoulders with some of the leading artists of the time.[50]

The 1930s saw Necip Fazıl's transformation from bohemian poet to virulent polemicist, a sworn enemy of the left and the Kemalist order. He met Abdülhakîm Arvâsî, a leader of the Nakşibendi order, a powerful group of Sufi origin, but which by this time had assumed a more traditionalist line.[51] Much has been made of Arvâsî's influence on Necip Fazıl, not least based on his autobiographical book on the subject entitled *Him and I*.[52] The book is dripping with romantic descriptions, culminating with Necip Fazıl's meeting with the great sheik, but is characteristically thin on the actual beliefs the relationship is said to have engendered. Indeed, for all his Islamist bluster, Necip Fazıl was seldom seen at prayer or displayed little in the way of religious sensibilities, even after coming under Arvâsî's influence.[53] Still, the prevailing narrative has been that Necip Fazıl may have led a life of sin up until this moment in 1934, but that after meeting Arvâsî, he devoted himself to the wholesome cause of Islamic revival. The association helped him assume an air of spirituality and sharpened his contrast with the left and the Kemalist intelligentsia.

A lesser known, but actually formative, influence on Necip Fazıl during this time was his fellow right-wing polemicist Cevat Rıfat Atilhan. Twelve years Necip Fazıl's senior, Atilhan had been an Ottoman major who fought on the empire's various fronts in the 1910s, as well as in the war of independence.[54] Atilhan's formative experience was as a spy hunter, pursuing Jewish agents whom he believed to be betraying the Ottomans to Western powers. In civilian life, he became the most committed and influential Turkish anti-Semite of his time. He imported Western anti-Semitic tropes into Turkish, publishing dozens of books on Jewish and Masonic conspiracies, translating texts such as the *Protocols of the Elders of Zion*, and maintaining close relations with the Nazi regime. He served jail time for having incited attacks against Jews in Eastern Thrace (Trakya) in 1934, and staged a coup in 1942, for which he was mysteriously pardoned.[55] In 1943, Necip Fazıl founded his famous magazine *Büyük Doğu (Great Asia)*, where Atilhan became a contributor. He was also a founding member of the *Büyük Doğu Cemiyeti* (Great Asia Society), an order aiming to advance the cause of political Islamism.[56] Since the Nazis lost the Second World War, Atilhan had dropped scientific racism and become more Islamist, but the enemy he pursued remained the same: Western "globalist" forces and the Kemalist regime as their representative in Turkey. Under Atilhan's influence, Necip Fazıl's work evolved from romantic musings to sharp, and often vicious polemics. Anti-Semitic tropes, venomous attacks on Eastern Communism and Western capitalism, and dreams of an Islamo-

Turkic revival became his favorite themes. In later years, Necip Fazıl would fall out with Atilhan, but the man had an indelible impact on him.[57]

By the 1940s, Necip Fazıl was one of the foremost enemies of the Kemalist order, attacking it as being a soulless imitation of the decadent West. He stood out for the level of craft in his invectives, his relatively intimate knowledge of Western writers and the Kemalist elite, and, above all, the sheer confidence with which he called for a post-Kemalist revival of authoritarian Islamist politics.[58] Necip Fazıl's followers came to call him "üstat" meaning "master," and he reveled in the attention especially young people showered on him. He was known to speak at exhausting length at student events, stringing together biological analogies and combative aphorisms. His enemies were "living corpses," they were sick, the "microbes" in the body politic, to be extirpated by vigorous action.[59] This was the language of rancor, and it was especially appealing to young men. In 1952 Necip Fazıl and Atilhan were found guilty of having incited a student to attempt the murder of Ahmet Emin Yalman, a liberal, anti-fascist journalist and professor.[60] Necip Fazıl justified his conduct saying he was duty bound to "shape the souls and minds" of the nation's youth.[61]

Unlike Islamist or communist ideologues of his time, Necip Fazıl was not concerned with setting up coherent systems of thought. He published more than a hundred books, but these were patchy collections of aphorisms and contained little in the way of solid, considered prose. He certainly wrote no "big book" of his entire political philosophy. He was a fundamentally reactive writer, preferring verse, plays, short articles, and speeches that tore into the Westernizing powers that be. One short piece entitled "This Is Me" (ben buyum) helpfully lays out his politics for posterity:

> Hazy [muallakta] thought, hazy art, hazy community, are not substances I understand. It is for this reason that I shall inform my readers of what I am, rather than to wait for them to put together, as if solving a puzzle, clippings of my writings. These acts of informing, like headings to books containing whole causes, are titles of thought brought down to their last summations.
> Asianist (opposed to copied Europeanism).
> Extreme nationalist
> —Anatolianist (opposed to thought systems outside of the nation).
> Identitarian
> —Essentialist [Şahsiyetçi - Keyfiyetçi] (opposed to adrift individual rights, to standard measurements).
> In property, in favor of limitations (opposed to personal capitalism on the large scale).

In art, thought and science, isolationist-minimalist (opposed to rootless and rough systems of diagnosis).
With respect to the perfection of thought and spirit, in favor of class structure (anti-democratic).
Interventionist around a single perspective (anti-liberal).
In summary regarding today's world regimes: from a personal vantage point anti-communist, anti-fascist, anti-liberal. There you have my outline![62]

In true reactionary fashion, Necip Fazıl sets his principles against their opposing poles, mostly being ideas he associates with the Kemalist structure of his time. Some of these are contradictory, but most significantly, his "copied Europeanism," heading the list, corresponds to what I have called Aspirational Occidentalism. By calling himself "anti-fascist," Necip Fazıl likely rejects scientific racism most prominently seen with the Nazis, rather than the reactionary nationalism that animates it, or the rigidly hierarchical structure that it brought about.[63] Indeed, despite his many disagreements with the Kemalist project, Necip Fazıl was partial to its top-down nature, seeking to retain this structure, but to reverse the charge of its occidentalism. He put forward a vision of politics that is simple, yet robust: an extremely nationalist country where the state (or presumably an oligarchic caste) controls the means of material and cultural production. He wanted society stratified into strict classes and governed by a collectivist ethos: a Sparta in Anatolia. This country was to be "Asianist" in that it rejected Western modernity and cherished its own distinct mode of modernity, thereby turning the values of the Kemalist order upside-down.

The greatest symbol of this kind of reversal, Necip Fazıl believed, would be the restoration of Hagia Sophia into a mosque. The ancient Byzantine cathedral had been converted into a mosque when the Ottomans conquered Istanbul in 1453 and became the holiest site of Ottoman civilization. In the early republic, Atatürk had the building converted into a museum, which, to the Islamist and Turkist far-right, was an unforgivable act of desecration. On December 29, 1965, Necip Fazıl gave a speech in which he prophesied that the Kemalist period would end, that Turkic-Islamic civilization would rise once again, and that Hagia Sophia—restored into a mosque—would be the centerpiece of this epic reawakening.[64]

Today, President Recep Tayyip Erdoğan speaks warmly of meeting Necip Fazıl as a young man. As a member of the Islamist youth groups organized under the Millî Türk Talebe Birliği (National Turkish Student Union, MTTB), Erdoğan read his poems in front of audiences and, to this day, recites his poetry in his speeches. Since 2014, Erdoğan also gives out the annual Necip Fazıl

Kısakürek awards to poets, writers, and researchers who follow in the footsteps of "the master." Arguably the only poet who might rival Necip Fazıl's standing in the eyes of the state today would be Mehmet Âkif Ersoy, the poet of Turkey's national anthem, and another devoted Islamist romantic. Yet even he would not come close to the political influence of the failed exchange student-turned-polemicist. Necip Fazıl is the driving force behind Erdoğan's most symbolic moves, including the 2020 re-conversion of Hagia Sophia into a mosque.[65] In his speech celebrating the occasion, the president said:

> We opened Hagia Sophia as if opening the heart of the conservative [mukadessatçı] Turkish youth, exactly as the master expressed it. I praise my Lord a thousand times for giving me the opportunity to fulfill master Fazıl's will.[66]

Necip Fazıl had opposed the Kemalist state at the peak of its power, and at the darkest time for Islamists. Erdoğan could look back on his hero the way one might, in peacetime, look back on a wartime general. At an event in 2022 commemorating the poet's life, Erdoğan said that Necip Fazıl

> took on the arduous task of restoring a history that had been erased, forgotten, distorted and even turned inside-out. He fearlessly spoke the truth about the Ottoman Empire and Republican Turkey, the single party era, society and politics. Although he had the opportunity to live his life as he wished, he chose hardship, adversity and suffering.[67]

The emphasis on choice is crucial here. What made Necip Fazıl so powerful a figure was that he joined the cause despite having other alternatives. He could have been a banker or a bohemian poet, but he chose the life of the subversive polemicist. He moved through the world with the confidence of an aristocrat and the self-righteousness of a zealot. For all the glaring contradictions in his writing and in his life, not once did he show an inkling of self-doubt or remorse.

That is why, like most romantics, Necip Fazıl is remembered for the feelings induced by his poetry. The pieces in which he aspired to be more doctrinaire and prescriptive have largely been forgotten. He believed, for example, that a "Başyüce" (a strange composite of the Turkic words *baş* meaning "head" and *yüce* meaning "holy" or supreme") in the mold of Abdühamid II, would one day, after Kemalism embarrassing enthrallment to the West, rule Turkey once again. He penned a series of "Başyücelik Emirleri" (the orders of the Başyücelik) in which he stipulated Islamist rules on anything from financial to sartorial regulations. While a single authoritarian leader of this description has emerged in our time, his policies were a far cry from those set out in Necip Fazıl's conception. The more specific, theoretical, and ideological figures like Necip Fazıl became, the less interesting their writing generally was to posterity. The pieces that are most popular today are the ones focusing on big symbols or historical turning points: the Hagia Sophia speech, the war of independence in *Sakarya Türküsü*, or the figure of Abdühamid II in the hagiographic *Ulu Hakan* (The Great Khan).[68] It is these symbols that fueled the *ressentiment* of the generation that went on to found the AK Party and consolidate around the Erdoğan presidency.

The second figure of the revaluation is Kadir Mısıroğlu (1933–2019), the self-styled historian who attacked the foundational agreements of the Kemalist Republic. Like Necip Fazıl, Mısıroğlu was a relentlessly combative polemicist and civilizational revivalist. Unlike the poet, however, Mısıroğlu was more orthodox in his proclivities and lived long enough to see the Islamist movement in power.

Mısıroğlu was born in 1933 in the Black Sea town of Akçaabat, close to the city of Trabzon. He studied law in Istanbul, where he devoured Islamist magazines and quickly met their foremost editors. In a 2010 interview, Mısıroğlu described himself as "a man who woke up early into the Islamic cause" and "matured early" from an ideological perspective.[69] He wrote perhaps his most influential tract in these early years and spent the rest of his long life defending it, seeing its ideas move from the farthest corners of exile, to the highest levels of the state. His book, *Lausanne, Victory or Defeat?*, came out in 1965 and sought to revise the official history of Kemalist Turkey.

That history claimed to have rescued the country from great disaster. Western powers and their surrogates had defeated the Ottoman Empire during the First World War. In 1920, the government of the Ottoman sultan signed the Treaty of Sèvres, which was going to divide his territory between the victors, restricting Turkey to a small territory in central Anatolia.[70] Mustafa Kemal rebelled against the sultan's decision and led the war of independence, pushing back the occupying Western powers. This much was undeniably true. Mısıroğlu's objections lay with what happened next: Mustafa Kemal's second-in-command, İsmet İnönü, went to Lausanne, Switzerland in 1922–3 and negotiated the territorial and legal arrangements of what became the Republic of Turkey we know today. The official Kemalist line was that Lausanne was the best possible deal Turkey could get, and that it represented Turkey's ultimate victory in the nation's quest for survival. This, Mısıroğlu said, was a lie. Lausanne was not a victory snatched from the jaws of defeat; it *was* defeat. The Turkish delegation in Lausanne, he argued, made monstrous blunders by ceding territory on Turkey's southern border, as well as the islands on the Aegean.[71] They ceded far more territory than they had to, and did so because they were gripped by an inferiority complex and did not dare speak out in the presence of European diplomats.[72] If the Turkish delegation had conducted themselves honorably and built on the military victory of the war of independence, Mısıroğlu said, Turkey could have been a much larger power.

Mısıroğlu based his assertions mostly on the memoirs of Rıza Nur, one of the statesmen who were present during the negotiations and served as Republican Turkey's first minister of health. In subsequent years, Rıza Nur had a falling out with Atatürk and went into exile, where he wrote his memoirs in opposition to the Kemalist project in Ankara. Mısıroğlu had no patience for anyone critical of his selection of sources. He claimed well into his later years that he considered Rıza Nur's account to be perfectly accurate, and that if anything, Nur was holding back in his criticism.[73]

As Chapter 5 will develop in detail, Mısıroğlu's book on Lausanne now forms the basis of Turkey's very own "stab-in-the-back" myth. Turkey is deemed to have won the war but lost its empire at the negotiating table. As discussed earlier, the foundational claim of Kemalism was that it had beaten the West in battle, and that its Westernization effort therefore wasn't a capitulation, but a natural progression. Mısıroğlu attacked this foundational narrative by arguing that there was no victory at its beginning. The Kemalist Republic and its Westernizing policies amounted to nothing more than civilizational capitulation. The continuation of the historical argument, and one he made for the remainder of his years, was that the Kemalists and the Young Turk movement it sprang from were nefarious figures in the pay of an international Masonic-Jewish conspiracy, and that the abolishing of the sultanate and the caliphate was an inexcusable offense. Ottoman power hadn't declined due to its internal flaws; it was brought down by a global conspiracy directed by the Western powers.

Mısıroğlu led a turbulent and highly productive life after his famous book. Unlike Necip Fazıl, he assumed a fairly disciplined lifestyle and was meticulous about Islamic practice.[74] Like him, however, he ran into trouble with the Kemalist state. In 1977, Mısıroğlu ran for parliament for the Islamist National Salvation Party, but lost. After the 1980 coup, he fled to Germany and the UK and was stripped of his citizenship in absentia.[75] Mısıroğlu was a popular speaker in the diaspora, and continued writing. He returned to Turkey in 1991, re-acquired his citizenship, and saw the AK Party's rise to power. Mısıroğlu had been running his own publishing house, *Sebil Yayınevi*, through which he published books and pamphlets, as well as *Sebil*, his weekly magazine. Sebil Publishing still sells books such as *Pages from the CHP's Gallery of Sins, The Black Muslim Movement in America*, and *Three Persons of the Caliphate*, these being among Mısıroğlu's dozens of works.⁷⁶ *Lausanne, Victory or Defeat?* however, remained his most popular work.

As with Necip Fazıl, Mısıroğlu crafted a unique and compelling aesthetic. Kemalism's Aspirational Occidentalism, as he understood it, was a symbolic affair, and, among other reforms, demanded the erasure of Ottoman sartorial traditions: men were to wear suits and hats, women to unveil themselves and don modern dresses. Most Islamists opposed these reforms by refusing to wear hats and insisting on female headscarves. Mısıroğlu went further and wore Ottoman-era headgear, a kalpak at first and, in later years, a fez. The point, he explained, was not to dress in a premodern fashion. He wore suits after all, and the fez itself had been an Ottoman-era reform away from the turban. Rather, Mısıroğlu believed that one needed to maintain some form of sartorial distinction from the world of infidels ("gavur") even if it was a simple piece of headgear. In later years, the fez was accompanied by a cane, which together made him appear similar to Abdulhamit II, the Islamist favorite among late sultans. Mısıroğlu said that he used the cane due to leg injuries he sustained in jail and during an attempt on his life.

Above all, Mısıroğlu was a powerful speaker. He made a point of using Ottoman and Islamic vocabulary, believing that they conveyed the mindset of a ruling culture. He could captivate his audiences of young men for hours, stringing together historical narrative, theory, anecdotes, and admonition in an authoritative, masculine style. He would often raise his voice and bang the table, so that especially emphatic points would be punctuated by the sound of clinking tea glasses. In a session in 2015, for example, when finishing up a response, he was fantasizing about the day the Kemalist regime would fall. "We will—you will" the old man corrected himself "walk to Topkapı Palace with the prophet's banner, and loudly chant in unison, the ayat [Quranic verse] 've ku ca-el hakku ve zehekal batil, innel batil ekane zehuha!'"⁷⁷ He banged his fist on the podium, then twisted it, as if holding a knife. Gritting his teeth, he translated the Arabic verse "falsehood [batıl] is not written, and thus cannot survive" and hammering the podium again, shouted "falsehood is bound to be destroyed!"⁷⁸ In his later years, these question-and-answer sessions were put on YouTube, where they became wildly popular among a new generation.

For all his antics, Mısıroğlu had a deep understanding of the transition from Old to New Turkey. He was systemically opposed to the regime, but didn't believe in an Iranian-style revolution. The struggle of Islamism, he believed, was about shifting political norms gradually. He explained this in another 2015 lecture, in which he likened recent Ottoman-Turkish weakness to a solar eclipse in history:[79]

> When there is a solar eclipse, it stays dark for five minutes, then the sun begins to come out again. Consider 1939-1950 as the time of full eclipse. In 50, the opening begins.
> The first hero of this opening is Menderes. Its second hero is Demirel. Its third hero is Özal. Its fourth hero is Tayyip bey.
> Of these, every hero is more solid than the one before. Every hero makes fewer mistakes than the one before.
> We saw Demirel in a mosque despite him being a Freemason. We did not see Menderes in a mosque. I have met Menderes many times, and I never once saw him in a mosque, neither at Friday [prayers], at bayram, nor at a funeral. But Demirel had his Mercedes parked in front of Hacıbayram [mosque] and prayed the Friday prayer.
> Özal, in the seat of the president, had Mawlid prayers recited and had the taraweeh prayer recited with khatm. He assembled the hafız [these are non-mandatory forms of Islamic prayer, usually performed by especially pious people. A hafız is a person who can recite the Quran from memory].
> These things had been made into a big deal when Erbakan did them.[80]
> Tayyip bey has done more than the three combined.
> What does this show us? It shows us a retreat in the enemy ranks, and an improvement and abundance among those representing Islam. It is the stage of lessening mistakes. This shows us fate, fate!

In Mısıroğlu's thinking, the identitarian notions of the far-right had slowly gained currency with center-right leaders, blossoming in the Erdoğan era. Given his ideological commitments, Mısıroğlu thinks of it as being one from secular conduct to Islamic observance, but we can just as easily think of it as an inversion of values, from Aspirational to Competitive Occidentalism. Mısıroğlu continues and, in true romantic fashion, draws up a cosmic picture in which the audience can feel unique and significant. He is mixing metaphors here, but it is worth hanging on:

> It's akin to how now, as we are approaching summer, it is getting warmer. If it had been fall, this progression would have been towards the cold.
> When there is a cold day in between, we aren't worried because it is against the essence of the season.
> Seasons of transition contain contrasts.
> Turkey is in the season of transition from kufr [disbelief, or denial of faith] to iman [faith]. You will see the time when this progression has reached its perfect

state. [Smacks the podium] But to earn the thawab [merit] you get from one step in this time, you will have to take a thousand steps at that time. [Smacks the podium, is now shouting] Don't forget! A few good deeds in times of deprivation are more important than a lot of good deeds in times of plenty. A small feat on the path of Islam's victory today is more important than a large feat at the time of Islam's victory! These days will pass! Have something written in your ledger.

The idea that "transition contains contrasts" is critical for the gradual revolutionary. As later chapters will detail, Erdoğan was able to engage in conduct that his far-right core of supporters did not approve of. During the liberal posture in the 2000s, he could support gay rights and maintain strong military relations with NATO allies, because his supporters understood that he was gradually moving the country into a future where this would change. Unlike many liberal or centrist voters, who want to see candidates enact the policies they campaigned on, Islamist voters had long horizons. They voted for what they thought of as a grand civilizational transformation, rather than immediate policy outcomes. In politics, Mısıroğlu said, one had to remain ambiguous. "You don't say white and you don't say black. You say grey. He who wants white will say 'he has said something approaching white,' he who wants black will say 'he has said something approaching black,'" Mısıroğlu said, amounting perhaps to the most concise summary of the AK Party's electoral tactics.[81]

Mısıroğlu understood that his role was different from that of the politician or the crowd. Islamist politicians had to compromise on their core beliefs, meet the public where they were, then pull them in the right direction. Mısıroğlu was already in the future, and he had already assumed the values of Competitive Occidentalism as perfectly as possible. His task was to show the way, to supervise the revaluation as it unfolded and to make sure that it did not stagnate midway through. "I am a man of liberty" he said in a 2015 lecture, "like an unsheathed sword, I want to speak the way I want to! Conditional sentences, tentative sentences don't satisfy me. I want my sentences to crash down on the brains of the Kuffar, as if crushing the heads of snakes," Mısıroğlu was banging his fist on the podium, "like atom bombs!" the audience was clapping, "this cannot be done in politics! This cannot be done in politics!" he shouted. Mısıroğlu wanted "to assume a role in building the future. I am not out to save the day." He cared deeply about the ideas among Islamist youth and wanted to keep them as "pure" as possible. This is why his most vicious polemics were against fellow Islamists who bent to the times. He was one of the first major Islamist figures to speak strongly against the Gülenist movement, a powerful group of Islamists who emphasized "intercultural dialogue" and were known to infiltrate state institutions. Mısıroğlu even spoke in derisive fashion about Islamist luminaries like Mehmet Âkif Ersoy, who eventually softened to the Kemalist order. Again and again, he insisted that there could be no compromise with the forces of Westernization.

When Mısıroğlu died in 2019, thousands of his followers, including senior AK Party cadres, attended his funeral. It was public knowledge that Mısıroğlu's will had been that "nobody who feels even the slightest bit of affection for Mustafa Kemal" could attend his funeral.[82] Erdoğan had visited Mısıroğlu in hospital the year before. Attending the funeral would declare his enmity to Kemalism—and the Aspirational Occidentalism is espoused—too openly. He tweeted his condolences, while his younger son, Bilal Erdoğan, attended the funeral in person.

Conclusion: Revaluing the Republic

In mainstream discussions, the most basic way of distinguishing between Turkey's two political halves has been Islamist vs. secular, Ottoman vs. Europan, East vs. West. My approach is substantially different. I argue that the civilizational distinction between Turkey and Europe is superficial, and that Turkish nationalism follows European patterns. Since the Cold War, a romantic and reactionary strand of Turkish nationalism has moved to the center of politics, shifting the country's core from what I have called Aspirational Occidentalism to Competitive Occidentalism. This is not an ideological shift but a shift in the value propositions undergirding the country's politics.

The new regime does not scrap Kemalist symbols and traditions but revalues them. For example, Turkey's presidents and prime ministers visit Mustafa Kemal Atatürk's mausoleum every year, commemorate him, and sign what is called the Book of Honor. It is customary that in this ceremony, they quote a phrase from Atatürk's tenth-year speech:

> We shall raise our country to the level of the most prosperous and civilized countries in the world. We shall lend our nation the most extensive welfare and resources. We shall raise our national culture above the level of contemporary civilization.

The visiting leader is to state what they have done to bring the nation closer to reaching "contemporary civilization," by which—it is universally understood—Atatürk meant the West. This phrase therefore expresses the highest order strategic goal of the Republic. In "Old Turkey," the phrase was often shortened to "reach the level of contemporary civilization," implying that the goal was parity with the West. Atatürk was also usually referred to by his last name, a European convention adopted as part of his Westernization reforms. He was mostly depicted wearing a frock coat and top hat, or in front of a black board instructing students in the Latin alphabet. Most importantly, school curricula would emphasize his role as the man who ended the caliphate and sultanate, and founded the Republic.

Erdoğan hasn't stopped visiting Atatürk's mausoleum, nor has he jettisoned his famous phrase. Instead, he has been quoting it slightly differently, usually speaking of the goal of "rising *above* the level of contemporary civilization."[83] The preposition is back. Turkey is no longer content to reach parity with the West; it now wants to surpass its level of modernity. After more than two decades of his rule, Atatürk has also changed in the public consciousness. Successive education reforms have shifted the emphasis away from his Westernization reforms, and toward his long career as a general, fighting Western armies in Libya, Gallipoli, and Anatolia. He is often depicted in military uniform, and the country's new elite shies away from using the name "Atatürk," speaking rather of "Mustafa Kemal" or "Gazi Paşa," a title in reference to his status as a veteran general.

The change illustrates the ways in which the two political cultures change the past for their own purposes and, thus, the value propositions that the country operates on. In the new value system, there are many thoroughly secular Kemalists who support the Erdoğan government. There are also many who are in the opposition but still ascribe to the Competitive Occidentalist mindset of the West being Turkey's main antagonist.

The following chapters will explore how the Islamist movement imprinted this value system onto Turkey's institutional structure, its strategic culture, and foreign relations.

2

The Institutional Structure of "New Turkey"

A Messy Solar System

The Turkey and Middle East Public Governance Institute, an official body training high-level bureaucrats, used to publish a reference book entitled The Republic of Turkey State Institution Guide.[1] It was printed as a high-quality hardcover booklet and aimed to present a comprehensive inventory of state institutions, beginning with the highest institutions in the legislature, executive, and judiciary, then moved down to the presidency, parliament, high courts, prime ministry, and high councils. It contained impartial or independent institutions, such as the supreme election council and the central bank; local administrative structures, such as city and municipal governorates; oversight institutions; government-owned for-profit businesses; and "professional organizations qualified as government institutions." There were page-long summaries for each of these, with an institution logo and official title, along with their mandates, budgets, current leaders, and international associations.

Akin to the United States Government Manual, this book was meant to be a compact picture of Turkey's government.[2] If you were working in the municipality of the city of Adana and someone from the "Presidency of the Turkey Water Institute" asked for an appointment, you might have checked this book to learn about that institution. If you ever wonder when the "High Council for Privatization" was founded, page 33 would tell you it was on November 27, 1994, under law "4046/3 md."

Figure 1 was found at the end of the book. It is headed by a box entitled "Constitution," from which three lines branch out into boxes labeled "Judiciary," "Executive," and "Legislature." Underneath each box are additional boxes marking the institutions for the respective branch of government, and these are divided by dotted lines separating them into three different spheres.

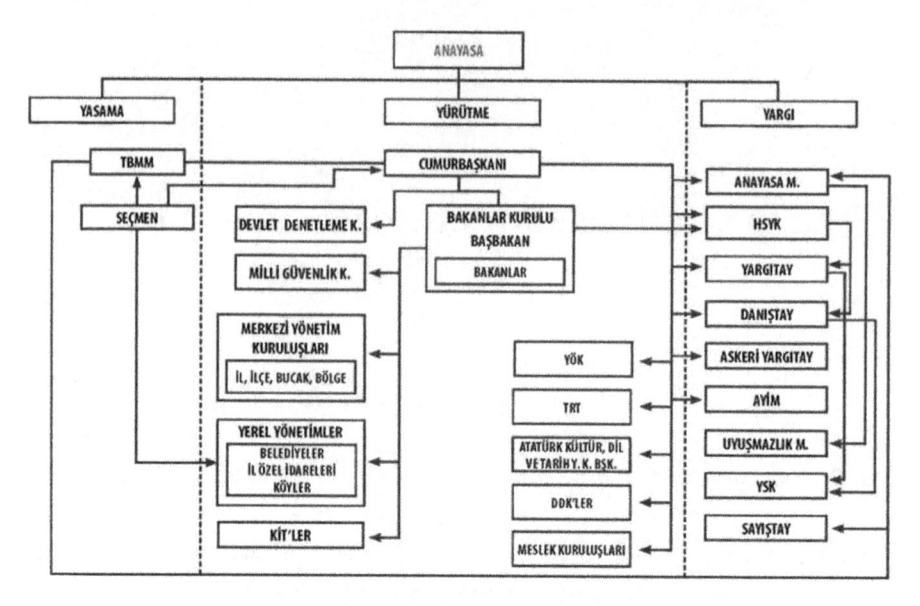

Figure 1 The Republic of Turkey State Institution Guide, page 254.

The diagram, of course, should be taken with a hefty grain of salt. Turkey experienced a military coup almost every decade or so since its first free elections in 1950 (the current constitution was drafted, with later amendments, after the 1980 coup), and even in the 2000s, when Turkey was in European Union (EU) accession negotiations, the military loomed large over the political sphere. Still, the constitutional democracy laid out in this chart expressed the aspiration of more than 150 years of parliamentary politics, stretching back to the Ottoman Empire. "Normalization," in Turkish political discourse, meant that the country would eventually resemble Western European democracies. It would reduce the influence of the military, rationalize governance, and make room for individual liberty.

A few months after its last update in 2017, the Republic of Turkey State Institution Guide was all but useless. The Turkey and Middle East Public Governance Institute was shut down in 2018, and the work of keeping track of the state's institutions was transferred to the "Presidency Digital Transformation Office."[3] There are now different institutions, such as the main e-government portal, or the Information and Communication Technology Authority (BTK), that maintain lists of institutions, but these are not as comprehensive, and either way, the breakneck pace of institutional change in the past years would make it extremely frivolous to aim for that goal.[4] In the meantime, Turkey's system of governance has radically changed. The closest thing to a visual of the system of government today is Figure 2, an English-language version of the graphic depicting the "Presidential Executive System."

This figure is only a chart for the institution of the presidency, rather than all of government. The rest of the government of Turkey at that time officially remains the same, with the separation of powers remaining enshrined in the constitution. In practice, however, the system has changed. This new chart is the only one anyone in Turkey is likely to recognize, and it is the one that best illustrates the country's system of government. The presidency is the center of gravity, the sun around which all institutions of state revolve. The ministries, councils, and offices of the executive form the inner orbits, with the judiciary and legislature merely forming outer ones. The constitution is now a mere organizing schematic, rather than the source of legitimacy.

In the previous chapter, I discussed how far-right romantic writers thought about the transition from "Old" to "New" Turkey, from Aspirational Occidentalism to Competitive Occidentalism. But how did the process take place? Specifically, how did the Islamists take over the apparatus of the state and use it to enact this revaluation? In this chapter, I will trace the process with a focus on Turkey's institutional structure, and especially its system of government. There is a debate on the nature of sovereignty that is helpful in illuminating this process. Here, the liberal tradition claims that the law arises from moral principles and thereby constitutes its own sphere—meaning that in a liberal republic such as the United States, even Congress and the White House are ultimately constrained by the constitution. Another is the realist tradition, most prominently represented by twentieth-century German theorist Carl Schmitt, that argues that politics—or a sovereign decision-maker—precedes the law. "The sovereign is he who decides on the exception," wrote Schmitt, meaning that the mark of the sovereign is that he may suspend the law when political necessity demands it.[5] In this conception, constitutional frames or even rule-bound legislative bodies cannot be the origins of sovereignty: sovereignty precedes them and rests ultimately within the political sphere. It is embodied in a person who, as a matter of historical circumstance, can act outside the law. The difference between the liberal and realist traditions is in the first and second charts: the first is a maze of rules and regulations, while the second is a central point, surrounded by a series of deceptively simple concentric circles.

The first section of this chapter will narrate the change in the character of the presidency, specifically how it acquired a new political charge. According to Schmitt, the spheres of economics, aesthetics, ethics, and others are separate, and defined by dichotomies (profitable-unprofitable, beautiful-ugly, good-evil).

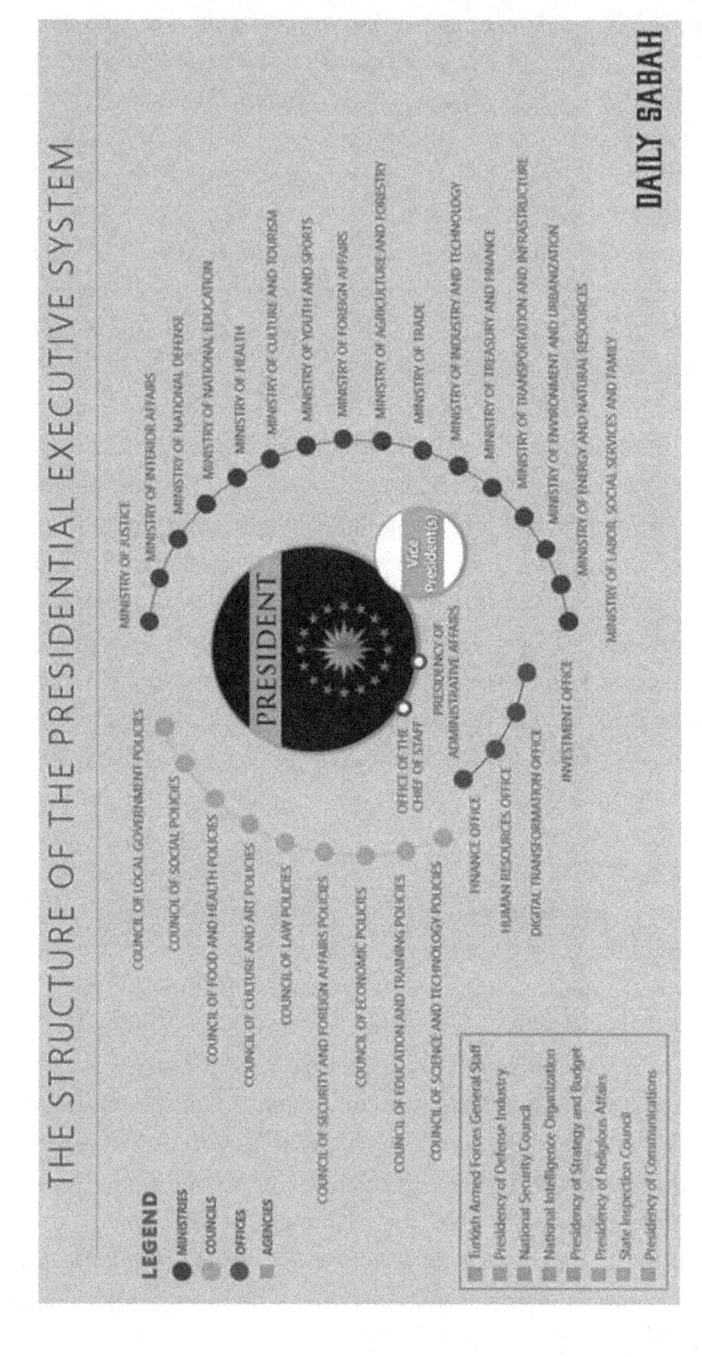

Figure 2 Government structure breakdown for the 2018 Turkish presidential system. Source: "Major changes in store after Sunday's election," *Daily Sabah*, June 22, 2018.

The political sphere is constituted and defined by the friend–enemy distinction, an association that extends to the willingness to go into existential struggle, meaning war.[6] The choice that Turkish president Recep Tayyip Erdoğan has made, again and again throughout his political career, has been to privilege the political sphere over all others. More than ever before, life has become about the friends and enemies of the nation, inside and outside of the country. In the language of the state, the word "terrorist" no longer just describes armed groups, but student protesters, journalists, or opposition politicians. Without constitutional safeguards, this implies a rule of the majority and, in its advanced stages, a regime of Sunni-Turkish supremacy. The way in which this dynamic has manifested itself is in a need to "normalize" the country away from its recent past, what Turkish nationalists believe to be a state of tutelage under Western imperialism, to become a geopolitical power in its own right. This perceived indignity is the "emergency" that Turkey lives under and the engine of its immense institutional transformation. Though it is ongoing, the emergency became most acute with the 2016 coup attempt, which the Erdoğan government, along with the majority of Turks, believes to be an intervention by the United States. This event has allowed the government to enact the presidential system, which was initially a deeply unpopular idea. It also continues the wellspring of its legitimacy with the public today.

"New Turkey," however, also significantly departs from Schmitt's pattern. As expanded upon in the chapter's second section, the institutional planets orbiting the sun of the president do not do so in an orderly fashion. "New Turkey's" solar system of institutions is a treacherous and unpredictable place. Ministries, police forces, regulatory authorities, construction firms, financial institutions, and universities grow or shrink rapidly, orbit in strange formations or crash into each other. These are often loosely linked through *cemaat*, political factions, organized crime networks, or regional "hometown" [memleket] networks, none of which are officially supposed to be part of government. In the absence of a credible constitutional framework, governance occurs through these networks and is anchored to the political authority of the president, rather than his legal right.

The Road to the Executive Presidency

The present system—like any other—grew out of the circumstances of its predecessor. That is why we need to look at the last years of the parliamentary system in Turkey and the chain of events that led to the creation of the Erdoğan-sized presidency.

While "Old Turkey's" presidency was not a ceremonial office, it was not an executive one either. It was designed in the post-coup constitution of 1980 to be occupied by a figure who represented the priorities of the military-led Kemalist elite. Presidents appointed the top judges, generals, and other important bureaucrats, such as university rectors, and had a soft veto on legislation (parliament could override it with a two-thirds majority), but they did not preside over the cabinet; the prime minister did. Prime ministers were often middle-aged figures with the energy to immerse themselves in the day-to-day tasks of governance. Presidents were usually older and concerned themselves with appointments and broad legislative issues that set the tone for the state in the medium-to-long term. Presidents also crucially took an oath of office that bound them to be nonpartisan in their conduct.

For the most part, Ahmet Necdet Sezer was such a president. The son of a school teacher, he studied law and rose up the ranks to become chief justice of the Constitutional Court and, in 2000, president of the Republic. Though most of his tenure coincided with the first AK Party government, it went by without major incidents. In 2007, Sezer's presidency was due to end, and according to the 102nd clause of the constitution at the time, candidates to the office needed to receive a two-thirds majority (367 votes) in the first two rounds of parliamentary voting, or a simple majority (251 votes) in another two rounds. The Justice and Development Party (AK Party), having a majority of 354 in the 550-seat parliament (the Republican People's Party had all remaining seats), was in a strong position to get its candidate elected. It put forward Abdullah Gül, who was one of the three senior founding leaders of the AK Party (the other two being Bülent Arınç and Recep Tayyip Erdoğan) and foreign minister at the time. For the first time in Republican history, someone with an Islamist background was positioned to occupy the highest office of the land.[7]

That summer, the opposition, judiciary, and military acted together to block Gül's election.[8] After initial voting in parliament, the opposition took the matter to the Supreme Court, which ruled that a quorum of 367 was needed to hold the vote in the first place. Much of the public, going well beyond the AK Party's voter base, saw this as an overtly political and deeply unjust decision. The opposition tried to control the optics by organizing massive rallies across major cities, calling for the protection of the country's secular character.[9]

Most alarming perhaps was a message that the military put on its website, threatening to intervene in politics to protect what it perceived to be a threat to the secular Kemalist order. The act is still remembered as the "e-coup." The establishment was tolerating an Islamist government, but it had decided that the presidency was off limits.

These events put government into deadlock, forcing the country into early elections. In the ensuing campaign, the AK Party argued that they represented inevitable change, and that the establishment was bending the rules to cling to power. It was a resounding success. The AK Party strengthened its share of the popular vote from 34.3 percent to 46.6 percent.[10] The Nationalist Movement Party (MHP), the main Turkist outfit, also entered parliament and announced that they would participate in subsequent parliamentary sessions. This meant that a quorum would be established in presidential voting—allowing the AK Party to elect Abdullah Gül to the presidency. Using its new majority, the AK Party government also put to a referendum a constitutional amendment for all subsequent presidents to be elected by popular vote.[11] It passed with 67 percent. Put together, 2007 marked the growth of the AK Party from a strong plurality into the voice of the majority.

It may not have been immediately apparent at the time, but the office of the president had been changed forever. The generals had designed the presidency as a "captain's bridge," and they would always own the captain. The most popular center-right politicians, Turgut Özal and Süleyman Demirel, had served in the position before, but never despite the military's wishes. The AK Party was not only denying them the office, it was also making sure that they could never attain it again. Abdullah Gül would be the last president elected by a parliamentary vote. The presidency now belonged to the majority vote, and that was the AK Party's territory.

Still, the next vote was scheduled for 2014. Gül had been elected in parliament, and he took his oath of impartiality seriously. His remaining link to party politics was his relationship to Erdoğan. One of the most memorable moments of that year was Erdoğan's much-anticipated announcement of the candidate. "Our candidate for president," he had said, "is my brother Abdullah Gül."[12] It expressed the complicated relationship between the men. It seemed as though Erdoğan was picking his own superior. He was clearly the more popular of the two, but privately, the men conversed as equals and talked through important decisions before announcing their united positions. While Erdoğan had unparalleled political instincts and charisma, Gül brought strategy and long-term policy planning. It was his picks for ministerial posts (e.g., Ali Babacan, Beşir Atalay, Ahmet Davutoğlu) that made the first terms of the AK Party relatively successful.

By the early 2010s, however, tension was building between the two leaders. Erdoğan no longer consulted Gül on matters relating to the party and, most importantly, lists of MP candidates before elections. In public events where both leaders were due to attend, there was often a waiting game of sorts. Erdoğan was often late for events, while Gül liked to be punctual. The problem was that the president could not be seen to be waiting for the prime minister, so Gül's staff would have to time his departure according to the tardiness of Erdoğan. This was vexing to the president since it made people think that he was holding up events.

The tension gradually spilled over into public view as well. In 2013, the government sought to demolish Gezi Park in Istanbul's Taksim square to rebuild an Ottoman-era barracks in its place. This triggered a nationwide civil resistance movement against it. For well over two months, thousands of people occupied Taksim square, as well as many of the central squares of Turkey's major cities. Erdoğan was enraged at attacks against his person and ordered a police crackdown. President Gül remained quiet, however, and is best remembered for tweeting out the phrase "one truly wonders sometimes," which seemed like a comically obtuse objection to the government's conduct.[13] Another incident occured on May 10, 2014, when Erdoğan and Gül were sitting next to each other at the Council of State, listening to a speech by the president of the Turkish Bars Association Metin Feyzioğlu. When Feyzioğlu leveled criticism against the government, Erdoğan lost his temper and began shouting from his seat. Gül motioned him to calm down, but Erdoğan kept shouting.[14] It was incidents like these that illustrated how Erdoğan did not consider himself bound by the hierarchy enshrined in the constitution. He believed that he represented the will of the people in a unique way and deserved a unique office.

There was always something about Erdoğan that didn't fit into the constitutional structure. His mentor Necmettin Erbakan had been called "hoca," meaning "teacher" in reference to his background as an engineer. Erdoğan's close circle called him "reis," meaning "head" or "chief." In Turkey, the term is used mostly in Turkist circles and has a slightly thuggish connotation. Erdoğan was the only Islamist leader to use the title, but it fit his masculine style of leadership. His official titles, in comparison, Erdoğan wore like ill-fitting suits. Prime ministers presided over the cabinet and, effectively, the legislature, but were always in a precarious position. Like any parliamentary system, Turkey's was designed to prevent the emergence of any one person as the undisputed ruler of the state. Presidents had the power to shape the state in the long term, especially the judiciary and military, but did not have executive powers. The system was designed for government through messy negotiations and compromise. There was no room for a "reis." Starting in the early 2010s, however, Erdoğan floated the idea of a "reinforced presidential system."[15] Though Erdoğan was as popular as ever, the idea polled terribly. The term "presidential system" (*Başkanlık Sistemi*) sounded like an alien concept, carrying a whiff of the American federal system.[16] People also associated it with "one man" dictatorship, which suggests a reversion to the founding years of the Republic. Polls in 2011 and 2013 indicated that at most, only 17 percent of the population favored a presidential system.[17] Even within his party, Erdoğan had trouble keeping the idea on the agenda.

By August 2014, when President Gül's term would expire, Erdoğan had been prime minister for almost twelve years and was making no secret of his desire to become the next president, reinforced or not. He declared that since he would be the first elected president in Republican history, he would, in effect, ignore his oath of impartiality and continue to weigh in on politics. In a parliamentary speech in July of that year, Erdoğan said, "Were İsmet İnönü, Evren, Demirel, Sezer impartial? They all had their political opinions." He argued that these centrist figures didn't ruffle any feathers because "their politics overlapped with that of the state, not with that of the people." In this view, impartiality was not only undesirable, it also was a fiction designed to cover up the establishment's subversion of the democratic will. "If I get elected, I will not be impartial. I will be a president on the side of the people. That is what Turkey needs."[18] Erdoğan was arguing that political impartiality was a fiction designed to conceal a Westernization project going back to the roots of the Republic. If he was elected by popular will, he would take that as a mandate to reverse that project.

Erdoğan won the 2014 presidential election with 52 percent of the popular vote, resigned his position as chair of the AK Party, and ascended to what was—formally at least—a position above politics.[19] Then–foreign minister Ahmet Davutoğlu succeeded Erdoğan as chairman of the AK Party and prime minister. Davutoğlu was a highly recognized figure, but lacked his own base of support within the party and among the electorate.[20] Erdoğan clearly meant for the professor to be his extension, not his replacement.

In the following months, Erdoğan ruled exactly the way he said he would, using his informal, but decisive, influence over his former party to continue controlling the executive and legislative branches of government. This meant that during this period, Turkey was governed through a heavy constitutional infringement at the highest echelons of the state. In retrospect, this was the moment when the defining characteristic of "New Turkey"—the supremacy of the political sphere over the legal one—first came to life. The transition, however, was anything but smooth. The opposition criticized this heavily and repeatedly, and the Erdoğan government was clearly uneasy about the situation.[21] It urgently needed to merge the offices of the president and prime minister, but the idea of a "reinforced presidency" continued to be unpopular. Metropoll, a reputable polling agency, said in late 2015 that it had polled the presidential system "at least ten times in the past two years" and that the idea never received more than 32 percent approval, which was roughly the pre-2007 voting base of the AK Party.[22] So widely acknowledged was this problem that when Minister of Justice Bekir Bozdağ was pressed early that year on this issue, he lamented, "they do not want the citizen to learn about the presidential system. They are afraid that if he does learn about the presidential system, he could change his mind," in effect acknowledging that the government wasn't able to shift public opinion in their favor.[23] The public had given Erdoğan the presidency, and it was fairly tolerant of his daily violations of his oath of office, but it wasn't ready to go further. The idea of one all-powerful office remained politically untenable.

As the country approached the June 2015 national elections, the AK Party struggled with what was widely referred to as "two headedness."[24] Davutoğlu spoke in front of traditional campaign stops with huge crowds, while Erdoğan held political speeches in glitzy halls of a more presidential nature. He was not being impartial, but the expectation of impartiality still prevented him from rolling up his sleeves. Meanwhile, the opposition was gaining momentum. In particular, the Peoples' Democratic Party (HDP), which was the most recent incarnation of the Kurdish movement, was changing the political landscape. Born out of the 2013 Gezi Protests, a nationwide movement against the AK Party, the HDP was shaping up to be something akin to the European Greens. It was reaching out to a young, well-educated, liberal urban base in the big cities, merging that vote with its traditionally Kurdish base in the southeast. The right considered the Kurdish movement to be the political wing of the Kurdistan Workers' Party (PKK), a trojan horse sent to Ankara to undermine Turkey's territorial unity. The HDP's charismatic leadership worked hard to overcome this image, arguing that it was *Türkiyeli*, or "of Turkey" rather than "Turkish."[25] Its new co-chairperson, Selahattin Demirtaş, was arguably the most talented politician after Erdoğan, cutting through the mainstream Turkish media's resistance with razor-sharp wit. Given that the peace process between the government and PKK was underway, some floated the idea that the Erdoğan government might enter into a tacit alliance with the HDP. The price of such an arrangement would certainly be the presidential system on the government's side and the continuation of the peace agreement on the HDP's side.

Demirtaş's campaign focused relentlessly on the government's weakest point: the daily constitutional infringement at the highest level of government. He called Davutoğlu, who was officially leading the AK Party ticket, the "intern Prime Minister" and chose to address President Erdoğan directly as the real force behind the AK Party.[26] This was key to Demirtaş's appeal. Throughout the campaign, Demirtaş, a leftist and a leader from an ethnic and linguistic minority, spoke to Erdoğan, the leader of the religious and cultural majority, as an equal. Demirtaş boasted that he didn't answer the president's phone calls and addressed him in the colloquial "sen" rather than the formal "siz" in his speeches.[27] This appeared to be intended to break the spell that Erdoğan was the providential leader of the country and thus entitled to a super-presidency. Battling the president on that basis gave him tremendous symbolic power. His most memorable speech from that time was at a party group meeting in parliament on March 17, 2015, in which he said:

> Mr. Recep Tayyip Erdoğan, as long as the HDP exists, as long as the members of the HDP breath on this soil, you will not be president. Mr. Recep Tayyip Erdoğan, we will not make you president, we will not make you president, we will not make you president.[28]

It may sound like a straightforward statement, but this was an electrifying moment. Its circumstances were unprecedented. Demirtaş was saying that the Sunni-Turkic majority Erdoğan represented was not sacrosanct, and that its supremacy could be opposed at the parliamentary podium, the very heart of the Republic. Legitimacy did not come from an inherent ownership of the state; it came from being represented in those chambers.

The statement also bore a linguistic twist that needs to be unpacked to make sense in English. Erdoğan at this point already was the "president" but not quite the kind Demirtaş was referring to here. In Turkish, the President of Turkey is a "Cumhurbaşkanı," a combination of the words "cumhur," roughly meaning "the people," and "başkan," dervied from the Turkic word for "head," being the common translation for president. While the presidents of some other countries (Azerbaijan, France, Portugal, Ukraine) are also called "Cumhurbaşkanı," most others have no cumhur- prefix and are only "başkan." The most prominent such "başkan" is the president of the United States, and due to the weight of that particular office, the plain title of "başkan" for a head of state has a powerful ring to it. In the executive system that Erdoğan was proposing at the time, he would have ceased to be a "Cumhurbaşkanı" and become a "Başkan," just like the president of the United States. This would separate him from previous Turkish presidents and elevate him to a higher level.[29]

By choosing to pound his rhetorical hammer on this particular word, Demirtaş was isolating Erdoğan, turning his nationalistic rhetoric against him. Turkey's conventions were not good enough for the president. He sought a foreign title, one which indicated that he was at least as power-hungry and imperialistic as the Westerners he railed against. The statement fed into the image of Erdoğan that had been growing among the opposition for some time: a man consumed by vanity, resentment, and the quest for power.[30] This was all the more daring since Demirtaş was the representative of the left-Kurdish movement with whom Erdoğan was still officially in peace talks. Demirtaş might still have been angling for a deal with the government, but he wanted to maximize his party's performance at the ballot box and negotiate from a position of strength.

In the June 2015 national elections, the AK Party lost its governing majority in parliament for the first time since 2002. A hung parliament ensued, and opposition leaders began to eye each other for a possible governing coalition. Had they succeeded, it might have trapped Erdoğan in an "Old Turkey" presidency without executive powers, sidelined his party, and possibly crippled his political movement. Demirtaş's promise might have become reality. Coalition negotiations never began, however, since the Turkist MHP would not sit down with the left-Kurdish HDP, which they saw as an extension of the PKK. Speaking about the post-election climate five years later, Osman Baydemir, a leading HDP MP at the time, said in a later interview that the HDP sent an emissary to Erdoğan, giving him three options: form a coalition with the CHP and receive HDP support; form a minority government and receive HDP support; or form a coalition directly with the HDP, without giving up any ministries. All the HDP asked for in return was for the peace process to continue. According to Baydemir, Erdoğan merely dismissed the emissary, saying, "you will see."[31]

That summer, the foundation of Turkish politics shifted. As talks in parliament failed to take place, a second election was set for November 1. Erdoğan now campaigned with full force on behalf of the party that he had officially left behind. As the next chapter will explore in detail, it was during this period that the peace process broke down, and the war between the state and the PKK-led Kurdish movement resumed with a vengeance. The state eventually deployed heavy military units to extract PKK forces from the South-East.[32] Erdoğan now assumed a hawkish stance, moving him closer to the MHP. In the November election, the AK Party received its parliamentary majority again with 49.5

percent, its highest share of the vote up to that point.[33] Constitutional or not, it had become clear that Erdoğan needed to violate his oath and campaign actively for "New Turkey" to survive.

In the early months of 2016, pressure was mounting on Prime Minister Davutoğlu. Many in the party thought that he had failed in the June 2015 elections, and most dangerous of all, there were constant rumors that he was trying to take the reins from Erdoğan.[34] The "two-headedness" of the government was causing it to expend a great deal of energy on squashing these rumors. Davutoğlu also appeared to be doing well in his negotiations with the EU, attaining the holy grail of visa-free travel into the Schengen zone in exchange for a migration deal, pending conditions.[35] It was increasingly looking like he wanted to step out of Erdoğan's shadow and actually govern himself. His lieutenants were trying to convince key figures in the party, as well as Erdoğan himself, to abandon plans for the deeply unpopular executive presidency. A backlash was inevitable. In April 2016, an anonymous blogger wrote an entry called "The Pelican files," a dramatic insider's account of the bureaucratic infighting between Erdoğan and Davutoğlu.[36] Among the many accusations it made against Davutoğlu was that he was trying to introduce transparency laws that would expose and limit AK Party corruption, creating his own media sphere, being dovish on the PKK, and deferential to Western leaders. In summary, Davutoğlu was trying to imprison Erdoğan within the presidency while assuming the full powers of the executive. Much of this was true, and the accusations undercut Davutoğlu's position. Erdoğan's charisma was the wellspring of AK Party rule and could not be challenged openly. In May, Davutoğlu resigned, and Erdoğan installed the ever-loyal Binali Yıldırım.[37] There would no longer be friction between the president and prime minister, but the constitutional infringement continued.

Erdoğan was trapped in this informal arrangement until the night of July 15, 2016, when a group within the military tried to stage a coup. As the next chapter will discuss in detail, this was a spectacular failure. There was little doubt among the public that the Gülenists, an organization that had infiltrated state institutions for decades, were behind it and that they had been supported by the United States. Erdoğan declared a state of emergency and made the case that the nation had entered a new stage in its existential struggle against Western powers. All discussion on the presidential system faded into the background as the nation's focus shifted to almost daily waves of the purges against the Gülen network. The post-coup environment gave Erdoğan unprecedented political power. A referendum on the presidential system no longer looked unwinnable.

The pan-Turkic nationalists in parliament were more vulnerable than ever in this period. In the 2015 elections, the MHP's seats in parliament had dipped below those of the HDP. This situation was humiliating and sparked an internal challenge against party leader Devlet Bahçeli.[38] The MHP rebels sought to hold extraordinary party congresses to vote for a new leader, but Bahçeli fought their demands in court. He also began to make regular trips to the presidential palace.[39] The Islamist and Turkist traditions were ideologically separate, but they were both far-right nationalists, united in Turkey's culture of ressentiment. Now the short-term interests of their leaders also converged. Erdoğan could make sure that the challenge against Bahçeli would fail, and in return, Bahçeli would support him behind opposition lines. In November 2016, Bahçeli spoke on the idea of an executive presidency. The speech set the groundwork for a formal alliance between the Islamist and Turkist factions:

> In these days, when the Republic of Turkey is in an existential struggle, it is exceedingly dangerous and objectionable for our future, that the president, who is at the head of the government and the state, should be on the wrong side of the law. For this danger to be eliminated, there are two alternative paths before us. The first of these and the one which is the most correct, most wholesome to us, is for the honorable President to give up on enforcing the de facto presidency, and to retreat to his legal and constitutional boundaries. If this isn't going to occur, the second path is for there to be a rapid inquiry for a way to legalize the de facto situation. It shall not be seen, nor talked about, in any civilized and democratic country in the world, that a government and power structure commit a crime every day.

Though ostensibly objecting to the president's violation of the constitution, Bahçeli was suggesting that the offense could be rectified through a post-facto legalization. He then went on to lay out a roadmap to how this could be done:

> Faced with this situation, if the Justice and Development Party is to continue its stubbornness with regards to the presidential system, there are again two options before us.
>
> First, if the AKP has a constitution already prepared or in preparation, it can bring it to the GNA [Grand National Assembly, Turkey's parliament], granted that it contains previously agreed upon articles. Members of parliament can vote according to their principles and beliefs, and listening to the voice of their conscience, will surely arrive at a decision.
>
> Second, this proposal for constitutional amendment will either become law in the GNA's General Assembly by surpassing the 367 threshold, or it will

remain above the 330 threshold and be presented to the people's decision in a referendum.

The Nationalist Movement Party is respectful and bound to every decision the Turkish nation will make. Our preference, as always, is for the continuation, strengthening, and reform, of the parliamentary system. If our nation should say the opposite, however, we will naturally have nothing to say to the contrary.[40]

These "options" were stages of a process likely discussed in great detail during Bahçeli's meetings with Erdoğan. It was telling that Bahçeli neglected to mention, for example, the possibility of the motion falling below 330 votes in parliament and being rejected without ever going to a referendum. He insisted that he was opposed to the presidential system but also hinted that he would be open to change his mind about it. Bahçeli was becoming the example Erdoğan needed: an opposition figure who, seemingly guided by patriotic duty, edged closer and closer to his side. The more public this transition was, the more "patriots" in the opposition camp were likely to follow him.

Bahçeli's speech was therefore an attempt to rescue the presidential system from being Erdoğan's vanity project. It may have fallen flat at an earlier time, but since the coup, the threat perceptions of the West, and particularly the United States, had gone up. The night of the coup saw the most ideologically charged Islamist and Turkist elements take to the streets.[41] Now, the broader social segments of these groups, represented by Erdoğan and Bahçeli, were fusing into a "patriotic" front against foreign intervention. The coup had been an attack on Erdoğan, and it seemed appropriate in these circles that the point of enemy attack should be fortified with more power. The AK Party's design for what was now called "Turkish Type Presidential System" was put before parliament in January, where it received a three-fifths majority, and was scheduled for a referendum in April 2017.[42]

In early 2017, the AK Party's own polling still indicated that public support for the system was in the low 30s. A highly effective campaign, as well as support from the MHP leadership raised the number into the 40s. What pushed the "yes" vote into a thin majority was a very public fight with the Netherlands. Turkey has a sizable and politically charged diaspora in Western Europe, including the Netherlands, but the government there was not allowing AK Party politicians to campaign there.[43] AK Party supporters, egged on by politicians from Ankara, faced riot police in Rotterdam, and the incident escalated into a full-blown crisis.[44] Nationalist voters rallied around the flag, staging protests across Turkey in which they symbolically stabbed oranges and held up signs saying "faşit Hollanda." On April 17, 2017, less than a year after the coup attempt, a referendum on the presidential system passed with 51.4 percent.[45] Erdoğan had finally legalized his total control of the state rule by expanding into a new, broader nationalistic base. The first elections under the new system were scheduled for the following year.

The new electoral system was designed to reinforce majoritarian rule. The presidential and parliamentary elections are held simultaneously every five years. If no presidential candidate manages to get a majority of votes, then a second round is held.[46] There is an assumption in the new system that whoever is elected president is also the leader of the most successful political party, or party coalition, as Erdoğan was. There are also no midterm elections. This makes it highly likely that a single party is in charge of the executive and legislative branches of parliament. The president and his parliamentary group can act without the need to compromise with the opposition for a period of five years.[47] Technically, it would be possible for someone to be elected without his political party gaining a parliamentary majority, or being elected while not affiliated with a political party. Muharrem İnce, Erdoğan's main opponent in the 2018 presidential election, had been an MP with the CHP, but was not its leader. Had he been elected, he would either have had to replace the party chairman to combine positions, or go through the chairman to enact parts of his legislative agenda. He was not. Erdoğan won the 2018 presidential election in the first round, with 52.59 percent of the popular vote.[48]

The presidency officially remains one of the three branches of government, subject to checks and balances. In practice, it is unimpeachable and in control of the legislative and judiciary branches of government. Technically, Article 105 of the revised constitution allows a three-fifths majority of the now 600-seat parliament to vote that the president be tried for crimes, or a two-thirds majority for him to be put to the Supreme Court.[49] According to Turkey's long-standing Political Parties Law, however, party bosses decide on regional candidates before elections. This translates into nearly perfect party discipline, even when the party boss in question does not happen to be in total control of the levers of state. There is also a culture of conformity in Turkish politics that makes political dissent extremely difficult. In the 2017 voting for the executive presidency in parliament, there were many AK Party MPs who wanted to vote against the motion. They held meetings and discussed their ideas, but decided that it was not worth the risk. "Everything bad that happened after this would have been blamed on us," said one of these MPs.[50] Up until 2022, the only MP to resign from the AK Party was Mustafa Yeneroğlu, who was raised and educated in

Germany, and therefore a cultural outlier. The legal architecture it is embedded in, combined with the culture of Turkish politics, therefore makes Article 105 a very light check on the president.[51] It certainly hasn't been in question under President Erdoğan's term under the new system. As he often says, he has never "recognized a will above the national will."[52] The "national will" is under the new system expressed by the razor slim majority.

The institutional structure of the country is evolving accordingly. An article on the presidential system published by legal scholar Kemal Gözler more than a year after it went into effect enumerated its severe procedural failings and laid out in painstaking detail the system's contradictions.[53] There are many institutions, such as the Sovereign Wealth Fund, he wrote, which are in effect both run and supervised by the president. The presidency engages in what Gözler calls "the problem of parthenogenesis," meaning that the various "cells" of the system are replicating themselves without outside interference. "One of the most fundamental principles of our administrative law is the legality of administration [*idarenin kanuniliği*]. This principle means that the power to establish administrative institutions does not rest with the administration [*idare*] but with the legislature," he writes. An example of such parthenogenesis, according to Gözler, is Presidential Decree 4, clause 186, in which the president decreed that he could establish development institutions by presidential decree. Gözler points to this as a bug of the presidential system, but it makes more sense to think of it as a feature. In the absence of a real constitutional order, every action of the state, no matter how small, must be traced to a decision made by President Erdoğan. This creates a monumental task of governance, one that has to be assisted by informal means.

Ruling through the Oligarchic Networks

Formally impartial institutions often have well-known political leanings. The *BBC* and National Health Service (NHS) in Britain, for example, are known for being staffed largely by people who are progressive, while members of the British Armed Forces are mostly conservative.[54] In the United States, Evangelical Christians are overrepresented in the armed forces, and Jewish people are overrepresented in fields requiring a high degree of education, such as medicine, law, and academia.[55] While this is subject to conspiracy theories, it is not surprising, nor should it be alarming. Different groups of people may be inclined toward different areas of life, and given the history of the twentieth century, paying too much attention to this is rightly considered distasteful. As long as individuals adhere to the law, institutions work as intended.

In Turkey, there are similar dynamics. Broadly defined, there are networks that display political, regional, or religious affiliations, which are then used to build support within government or semi-governmental institutions. The Presidency of Religious Affairs, the government institution that centrally assigns imams to mosques, tends to be conservative and inner Anatolian. The mainstream left used to be well represented in the legal profession and in academia, and continues to have influence in semi-governmental institutions, such as the Chamber of Mechanical Engineers (TMMOB) or the Turkish Medical Association (TTB). The Turkists and the "Idealist Hearths" (*Ülkü Ocakları*), their nationwide network of student organizations, are feeders for institutions like the police and armed forces, in which they maintain group coherence.[56] There are also micro-groupings: A department head from the province of Konya might be inclined to hire his fellow Konyans, for example. By themselves, these things are not problems and may be considered natural expressions of the country's diversity.

What happens, however, when these groups of people no longer share a set of rules that govern their interactions? What happens when the interplay between them becomes a competition, rather than cooperation of the diverse parts of the nation? In recent decades, this kind of thinking has made some groupings in Turkey far more powerful and dynamic than what one might see in most other countries. Specific groups can take over whole areas of public policy or orchestrate complex political operations. In this environment, institutions become strongholds to be defended, besieged, infiltrated, taken over, purged, and re-taken, sometimes over the course of only a few years.

The Erdoğan government springs from a far-right Islamist movement with relatively little access to or influence on institutional networks. Like all outsiders, it attributed great importance to what was happening in the institutions of state. The Islamists imagined shadowy networks of Freemasons, Jews, and others, generally seeing them as sinister forces obstructing the "the will of the people." Once they entered politics, members of the early AK Party moved away from such talk, but they did think of themselves as fighting "tutelage" (*vesayet*), which generally refers to the military elites who set the boundaries of acceptable politics and have intervened through military coups when politicians overstepped those boundaries.[57] The paradigmatic case in recent memory was the "367 affair" of 2007—when the high courts, military, and CHP came together to block the AK Party's candidate for president. In the 2010s, when Erdoğan was thinking about systemic reform, he began using another term for the evil he saw lurking within the state: "the bureaucratic oligarchy" (*bürokratik oligarşi*).[58] This may be Erdoğan's own innovation, and though some of these terms are overlapping in meaning, this one implies a more diffuse structure. Erdoğan used "bureaucratic oligarchy" to refer to any interest groups within government bureaucracy that were not subservient to him and, therefore, "the will of the people." Having become the establishment, politics was now about finding and replacing the remaining pockets of resistance.

From this point of view, it is easy to conflate democratic checks and balances with subversive forces within the state. Speaking to the Konya Chamber of Commerce on December 18, 2012, for example, then–prime minister Erdoğan addressed problems he was having with "City Hospitals," a policy for shutting down smaller hospitals in big cities and centralizing medical care in newly built massive medical complexes. Erdoğan said:

> We have not been able to bring to life the City Hospitals project for 6 years because of the bureaucratic oligarchy. We no longer want to see patients being carried outside in stretchers on the campuses of hospitals. But we have not been able to overcome this. Why not? Because of the bureaucratic oligarchy and the judiciary. But those looking in from the outside think "you have 326 MPs, 326 MPs and you are still making excuses?" But that thing that is called the separation of powers ... it comes and plants itself in front of you as an obstruction. And you have a playing field.
>
> The legislative, executive and judiciary in this country need to first think of the benefit of the people and then of the benefit of the state. If we are to become strong, we can only be so in this way, but if the investment I'm going to make is going to get delayed by a mere word for 3 months, 6 months, then one year, two years are gone, then you will never be able to answer for this country, these people, not to history, nor to those lying under this soil.[59]

Erdoğan begins his reasoning from the premise that he is the undiluted expression of "the will of the people." This makes him, and the people following him, unlike any of the other interest groups within the country's institutions. He therefore has no choice but to see parts of the state that are not directly subservient to him—of which, according to the constitution, there are many—as forces that are against the popular will. These are not merely sources of inefficiency and obstructions to progress, but enemies that prevent Turkey from becoming more powerful in relation to other countries. While the enemy on the party-political level has been defeated, as Erdoğan's reference to "his" MPs indicates, their presence within the country's institutions remains and forms the most significant obstacle for the country's "reawakening."

In this environment, Erdoğan moves according to the popular adage, "Politics does not accept vacuums" (*siyaset boşluk kabul etmez*).[60] Right-wing political leaders sometimes use this as a catch-all phrase, but behind it is a particular zero-sum approach to governance. Erdoğan by no means invented the phrase, but he has often invoked it and has been more disciplined than others in implementing it.[61] The idea is that institutions are vessels to be filled by a political force. Thinking that they can somehow remain politically neutral is dangerously naïve—institutions always have a political content, and if it isn't yours, it is that of your enemy. This attitude is disguised under a thick coating of liberal language. When it was first running for office in 2002, for example, the AK Party argued that the Council of Higher Education (YÖK), a regulatory body, exercised undue power over universities. In its electoral platform, the party promised universities "managerial and academic independence."[62] During successive AK Party governments, however, party loyalists took over YÖK and tightened their grip on universities. They did this first to ostensibly de-politicize them, and, later, to re-politicize them in their favor.[63] More recently, the Erdoğan government's surrogates tried to gain control of the Turkish Bars Association, a body where all lawyers must register. When lawyers resisted the interference, the government passed a law that opened the way for the establishment of alternative bars, which has allowed them to dilute the system, empower their own institutions, and disempower those who resist them.

Suffusing the country's institutions in this way, however, has not been easy. In its early days, when the AK Party was besieged on all sides by the coup-prone "oligarchs" of the Kemalist order, it could not have survived on its own. European and Turkish liberals supported the Islamists in public. More significantly, a silent ally among the bureaucratic oligarchs themselves aided the young government: the Gülenists. This alliance is the original sin of the AK Party, one which opened the country's institutions to the corrosive effects of *cemaat*, political ideologies, and criminal networks.

The Gülenists were originally one of many religious groups known as *cemaat*, which roughly translates into "religious community" or "lodge," and are typically organized around a charismatic leader.[64] Starting out in the 1970s, Fetullah Gülen was a preacher with a particularly strong appeal. Cassette tapes of his sermons circulated widely among conservative circles and allowed him to build a cult following. Over time, the group developed a unique hierarchy, built up common funds, extended into the worlds of business, charity, media, and, most importantly, education. The Gülenists became known in political circles but did not take a firm political stance. In 1999, Gülen moved to the United States, where he set up residence in a 26-acre property in Saylorsburg, Pennsylvania.[65]

Unlike most other networks, many in the bureaucracy who paid fealty to Gülen kept their association hidden, especially in critical institutions like the military and judiciary. According to an infamous video recording of Gülen, their strategy was to "move within the arteries of the system" until his covert adherents were in key positions, and only reveal themselves when they were ready to take over the state.[66] Gülenists would have their own hierarchies within institutions and answer to a chain of command that went up to Saylorsburg, PA, rather than the constitution of the Republic of Turkey. When the AK Party was founded in 2001, it became the first political party that the Gülenists openly supported. Gülen's business and educational empires threw their weight behind the government, and its media championed Erdoğan's policies. When the AK Party battled the traditional nodes of power within the bureaucracy, covert Gülenists in Ankara's central institutions supported them. The most infamous of such cases are the Sledgehammer and Ergenekon trials, in which scores of Kemalist and nationalist officers—the Kemalist "oligarchs" and bureaucratic rivals of the AK Party and the Gülenists—were jailed.[67]

In 2010, the AK Party government proposed a major constitutional amendment package aimed at reforming the judiciary. It argued that this was essential to overcome the oligarchic hold of "Old Turkey's" Kemalist elites, and to drive the point home, they scheduled the plebiscite on the thirtieth anniversary of the July 12, 1980, coup d'état. On the campaign trail, Erdoğan also repeatedly implied that the country's Alevi minority had undue influence on the judiciary. "The time for making appointments with orders from the dede [Alevi spiritual leaders] is ending," he said at a campaign stop in Sincan.[68] This was an old, but notoriously vague claim that circulated in Islamist circles, where the Alevi were often seen as quasi-Shia heretics.

The Gülenists were also vigorously campaigning for the "yes" vote. Fetullah Gülen himself said on television that "even those in their graves must be awakened to use their 'yes' vote in that referendum," a characteristically bizarre phrase.[69] Gülenist newspapers also argued that there was an Alevi hold on the judiciary that needed to be broken. The claims were baseless. The judiciary was predominantly Kemalist in outlook, and the Alevi may have been overrepresented, but there was no reason to think of this as institutional capture or even favoritism. Ironically, however, the Islamists who made these accusations did want to capture the institution.

The referendum passed with 57.9 percent of the vote.[70] In his victory speech, Erdoğan said he thanked "his brothers" who supported the campaign "from across the ocean," a euphemism for the Pennsylvania-based Gülen. The remark received especially strong applause, and Erdoğan, smiling, added that since the opposition liked to criticize his "transatlantic" allies, it was up to him to defend them.[71] Gülenist power within the state was a secret between him and his base, a mysterious force that worked its way through the bowels of the state on their collective behalf. In the end, the 2010 referendum restructured the Supreme Court and the Supreme Board of Judges and Prosecutors, among other reforms, and gave the Gülenists a commanding view of the bureaucratic landscape.

In the following years, the Gülenist network reached the peak of its power. "They walked the halls swinging their arms around, like they owned the place," a bureaucrat active during those years told me, and it is common to hear the same from people across private and public institutions. "They had bright people with fancy degrees applying for key public institutions," said another, "it was government policy to hire them. It came straight from the minister."[72] The Gülenists had won at the game of "bureaucratic oligarchy."[73] Their huge informal network meant that they could make or break careers, funnel money through lucrative backroom deals, and have worldwide reach without any oversight. Particularly concerning was the Gülenist presence within the police since it was widely believed that they were using its mandate for intelligence gathering to listen in on the nation's phone conversations.[74] The idea of privacy was disappearing. The investigative journalist Ahmet Şık wrote about their wiretapping activities in a book entitled *The Imam's Army*. The police confiscated its copies before publication and promptly arrested Şık on March 3, 2011. As he was being tucked into a police car, Şık famously exclaimed, "whoever touches [them] burns!"[75]

Even AK Party circles were gradually afraid of the burn, and rightly so. The Gülenists were becoming too powerful for the Erdoğan government to control. There are rumors that the first cracks appeared over MP seats. As part of their understanding, the AK Party had been allocating Gülen a handful of seats before every election. Before the 2011 elections, the Gülenists are said to have asked for dozens of seats. Some later put this number over 100.[76] This was a radical increase that would effectively have given Gülen veto power over legislation. Erdoğan apparently rejected the request outright, which amplified the already festering ill-feeling between the camps. The Gülenists were also critical of the government's policy to make peace with the PKK, a process that was headed by the National Intelligence Organization (MIT). In February 2012, prosecutors summoned Hakan Fidan, the head of MIT, to testify in a case that involved the government's talks with the PKK. The case was heading in a direction that could implicate Fidan with charges of conspiring with the PKK against the state, and therefore deeply concerning to the government. This would later be remembered as the first shot across the bow. AK Party leaders eventually saved Fidan from getting sucked into the case, presumably through backroom negotiations with the Gülenists.[77] Though both sides denied it, the alliance was now in question. In December 2013, embarrassing and incriminating phone conversations of top government officials and the Erdoğan family leaked on YouTube. What followed was a painful and very public unraveling of the alliance. Erdoğan declared the Gülenists network a terrorist group and a "parallel state" and began to purge them across public and private institutions.[78]

Millions of people were in some way affiliated with the Gülen movement. Their network of schools, banks, shops, prayer groups, and other institutions was so vast that especially for conservatives, it would have taken a conscious effort to avoid them all together. As the purge went on in 2014 and 2015, hundreds of thousands in public and private employment lost their jobs, the government seized more than a thousand companies, and many went to jail on bogus charges. In theory, the Erdoğan government aimed to punish those who were involved in what the Gülenists called "confidential service" (*mahrem hizmet*), meaning people who infiltrated institutions and formed a secretive parallel hierarchy. In reality, the purge went far wider, spilling over into the public sphere, turning into a regime of collective punishment of the organization, including the vast majority of Gülenists who were not involved in illegal activity. There were too many ordinary people who had long resented Gülenist power. The media was now full of credible stories about how the Gülenists systematically cheated on government and university exams and engaged in workplace mobbing that, in some cases, led to suicide.[79] Gülenists who lost their jobs and businesses couldn't be hired anywhere. Their civil rights were routinely violated with impunity, and the government was all too happy to feed the fire. When a senior government figure in one instance spoke on the need for mercy, Erdoğan quickly called to reprimand him.[80] The public instinct for revenge was to flow freely.

The purge picked up speed in summer 2016, and many believe that the coup attempt occurred prematurely on July 15 because the Gülenists network in the military received intelligence that it was about to be purged. There is consensus across Turkish politics that the Gülenists were behind the coup attempt. While there are some valid questions as to whether Gülenist officers were alone in planning and executing the coup, given recent history, as well as the bits of hard evidence publicly available, there is little reason to doubt the network's involvement at a very high level.[81] After that night, whatever reservations the public still had about the collective punishment of the Gülenists disappeared. The government's crackdown, as well as public persecution of the group, intensified. The public no longer referred to the Gülenists as a "parallel state" but adopted the government designation of "Fetullahist Terrorist Organization" (FETÖ). This put the group on an enemy status on par with the PKK. For years afterward, rarely a week went by that a group of bureaucrats, especially in the armed forces or police, weren't arrested on charges of being covert members of "FETÖ." Politicians regularly accuse each other of collaborating or having collaborated with the group at various points in the past.[82]

In terms of governance, the Gülenist saga is the single most defining event of the AK Party era. The Erdoğan government thought of itself as being superior to the "bureaucratic oligarchs" but was not above using the Gülenists as a weapon against others. After a destructive civil war, the AK Party's elite thought that the presidential system would finally grant them a blank slate to bring about the rule of "the majority" that they always envisaged. They seemed to think of the presidency as the center of a cosmic order, finally suffusing the country's institutions with the "will of the people." Instead, the pattern they set together with the Gülenists, of systematically subverting the law, setting up parallel hierarchies, and stacking institutions in their favor, has ingrained itself in the way the country's institutions—private and public—conduct business.

As the Gülenists were being purged from Turkey's schools, ministries, newspapers, and firms, gaping power vacuums opened up. It quickly became apparent that these could not be filled by generic Erdoğan supporters alone. So vast was the need for personnel that the government had to rely on other networks. The first people to rush into the breach were the Turkists, Kemalist Eurasianists, and similar nationalistic groups. Especially in the "armed bureaucracy" of police, gendarmerie and military forces, the Gülenists had relegated these groups to field work in far-off provinces or dead-end enforcement jobs. These groups played key roles in purging the Gülenists and defending the government in the coup attempt, and the government now gave them some of the most plum and influential jobs in Ankara. The Turkist especially are known to have connections to organized crime networks, and it once again became common to see politicians appearing in photos with figures from the underworld.[83] The country saw an unmistakable rise in the crime rate, while corruption probes in municipalities dropped to an all-time low.[84]

In areas where Islamists are more influential, such as education and the construction sector, there have been a mix of groups. TÜGVA (The Service for Youth and Education Foundation of Turkey) and TÜRGEV (The Youth and Education Service Foundation of Turkey), the charitable foundations managed by the elite around president Erdoğan, including Esra Albayrak and Bilal Erdoğan, his daughter and son, tried to fill the gap left by the vast educational network of the Gülenists (often literally, by appropriating their buildings).[85] A number of other cemaat also quickly moved into the vacuums left by the Gülenists. There are hundreds of cemaat in Turkey, and most are insignificant religious groups. The biggest grouping of them, however, is the Nakşibendi order, made up of four large cemaat: Menzil, İskenderpaşa, İsmail Ağa, and Erenköy. (Another grouping with many small branches are the Nurcu, the former home of the Gülenists)[86]) Previously relegated to their provincial origins, these religious groups have been developing bureaucratic, business, nongovernmental organizations, and international aid arms, much as the Gülenists had. None of them are nearly as institutionally coherent, well organized, and ambitious as the Gülenists, but they quickly filled the Gülen-shaped power vacuum across state, society, and industry.

In "Old Turkey," institutions were systemically unjust, but they had set rules, and it was difficult to bend them. In the 2000s, the country's institutions began to fray, and connections became more important. Entering the Gülenist network could carry a young person into a good school, secure job, or steady business contracts. In "New Turkey" of the late 2010s and early 2020s, the Gülenists were replaced by other groups fulfilling some of their old functions. A teacher looking to be transferred or promoted may text a family WhatsApp group to ask whether they have any contacts within Turkist circles and the MHP. A developer who wants to get a hospital tender might need contacts with the Menzil *cemaat*, which has significant pull in the Ministry of Health.[87] An ambitious judge—many of whom are now in their twenties and early thirties because older ones have been purged—will try to get into the more refined İskenderpaşa *cemaat's* afternoon discussion groups to meet important people.[88]

The various *cemaat*, as well as political identities such as Turkist nationalism or Eurasianist-Kemalist nationalism, all swerve around a central pillar of the Islamist political tradition, of which Erdoğan himself is the quintessential example. Those considering higher offices are well advised to build their resume accordingly. They should graduate from *Imam Hatip* high schools, where religious education is a priority, as well as involve themselves in AK Party politics at a young age.

Those from conservative parts of the country—especially the Black Sea region, where Erdoğan is also from—emphasize their origins. Those who aren't might try to marry into such families. Speaking at a public event, the former AK Party mayor of Balıkesir province made a distinction between a conservative caste of civil servants, "a human presence that represents the state within the military, in the civil service and so on," and a political caste, saying, "politics is represented by those from Trabzon, by those from the Black Sea." Laughing a little while adjusting his seat, he added, "if you want to attain [government] office, you have to be an *Imam Hatip* graduate and be from Trabzon. That is the way it is in our [the AK Party's] era."[89] For the higher rungs of power, in other words, *cemaat* or Turkist groups weren't enough.

There is also a set of small, but systemically important, institutions such as the Ministry of Finance, Foreign Ministry, and Central Bank, as well as regulatory bodies, such as the Banking Regulation and Supervision Agency (BDDK) or the Energy Market Regulatory Authority (EPDK) that are relatively free of peripheral identities and are politicizing in the more plain nationalism of the Erdoğan era. This may have several reasons. First, groups such as the Menzil cemaat or the Turkists like big pieces of institutional real estate, such as the Ministries of Health and Interior, which have the power to reach into the village level in the provinces, employ tens of thousands people, and hold extremely lucrative public tenders.[90] An institution like the Foreign Ministry employs only a few thousand people and puts out meager public tenders.[91] Its properties are scattered across the world, only serve narrow purposes, and are subject to the laws of different countries. Its entrance exams for career professionals also remain fairly competitive, which means that it cannot easily be stacked with the adherents of any specific group. Second, *cemaat* networks specifically are aware that they are regarded with suspicion since the Gülenists affair, and may want to give cause for concern by entering strategically critical institutions.

Many small, systemically important institutions have therefore been purged since the Erdoğan–Gülen civil war, but their "vaccums" have not been filled. The Foreign Ministry, for instance, purged a full third of its staff and did not replace them. The Central Bank purged a quarter of its staff and replaced a few top managers, mostly from government-friendly banks.[92] Those who remain understand what is expected of them. "New Turkey's" regulators, central bankers, diplomats and intelligence officers fold directly under the presidency, reflecting its cult of personality and nationalistic worldview. Those who do not have the stomach for such politicization either leave or refrain from applying in the first place.

The emerging challenge for the government is to maintain some degree of institutional capacity, and the place where this has been felt most acutely is the economy. Despite having a dynamic private sector, strong banks, and a resilient class of capable civil servants, Turkey's economy was in disarray throughout the late 2010s and early 2020s. It was first managed by Minister of the Treasury and Finance Berat Albayrak, Erdoğan's son-in-law. The Albayraks are a Trabzon-based Islamist family who own key assets in the country's media, construction, and energy sectors. Berat Albayrak also maintained a wide horizontal network across state institutions and, according to a source familiar with Ankara bureaucracy, "owned at least one floor in every [government] institution in Ankara." None of it translated into sound policy.[93] Having done away with Central Bank independence, Albayrak's approach was to cut interest rates, pump money into the private sector, and boost economic growth. As a consequence, the lira halved in value between 2017 and 2020, inflation shot up, and foreign investors pulled out billions of dollars from the country.[94] With the economic shock of the Covid-19 pandemic, Erdoğan went over Albayrak's head to appoint Naci Ağbal as governor of the Central Bank in November 2020. Albayrak resigned in protest, creating a minor bureaucratic vacuum in which the traditional bureaucracy could be called to fix the situation.[95] Ağbal raised interest rates and put Turkey back on an orthodox policy framework. The Albayraks, however, maintained pressure behind the scenes, and in March 2021, Ağbal was replaced with Şahap Kavcıoğlu, who was close to them. Kavcıoğlu dropped interest rates again and introduced hare-brained schemes to prop up the lira. Inflation rose to triple digits, wreaking havoc on wage earners. After the 2023 elections, Erdoğan appointed an orthodox economic team led by Mehmet Şimşek, a minister from the AK Party's liberal days. Şimşek's team raised interest rates again and introduced an austerity program. This was aimed at winning trust in international markets but has been devastating for the most vulnerable segments of society. The presidential system had promised a firm hand, but it turned economic policy into a carousel ride.

The structure of governance in Turkey's new system has some immediate political implications as well. For one, it means that, in Erdoğan's words, "the fate of the AK Party and the fate of our country have merged."[96] The bureaucracy's allegiance is to Erdoğan's leadership and his vision, and his adherents consider any peaceful transition of power as tantamount to coup plotting. The Erdoğan government could also not reshuffle its political deck, such as abandoning its coalition with the MHP and aligning with an opposition party. The MHP is a node connecting chunks of the police, armed forces, construction industry, and organized crime, all of which are vital for the government's operations. Putting pressure on those relationships, or attempting to rewire them, might not be beyond the Erdoğan government's powers, but it would be needlessly taxing. As MHP Chair Devlet Bahçeli likes to remind people, "The People's Alliance [the AK Party-MHP] was not built through negotiation. The People's Alliance was not formed through a process of give-and-take."[97] The MHP never asked for a ministry or other top political positions. Similarly, the various *cemaat*, regional, professional, and other groups may at different times have disputes between each other and the government, but these will be resolved through backroom deals, rather than negotiations in the public space.

While there is some room for negotiation, groups within the state cannot risk "walking out" and backing opposition political parties, nor even waiver in their support for the Erdoğan government. The political links between the presidency and the bureaucracy mean that any political group outside of that web of relations, such as leftist parties of the CHP or the HDP, are by definition foreign to the state. They can be tolerated to various degrees for the sake of public order, but they can never belong to government. Since the constitution has long been weakened, opposition membership in parliament, the legal positions they have gained through local elections, or the rights granted to them by their mere citizenship are greatly diminished. In recent elections, the government has argued to the electorate that they were engaged in an election of "beka," or "survival." Considering that an opposition victory would mean a fundamental uprooting of the country's power structure, this characterization is accurate in its own way.

Where Is the System Going?

In the lead-up to the 2023 elections, there was a discussion among Turkey's opposition about whether it would be appropriate to propose a return to the parliamentary system. Some cautioned against this approach, pointing out that a drive for the restoration of "Old Turkey" betrays a lack of understanding of its fundamental problems, and would not be able to establish a firm institutional and legal structure.[98] This did not stop Turkey's major opposition parties from coming together to chart the path to a "reinforced parliamentary system."[99] The proposal, however, was more a denunciation of the new Erdoğan-led regime than a clearly defined alternative.

Still, these calls have elicited a response from the government, which was remarkable in itself. The Erdoğan palace is the prime mover of Turkish politics and is extremely reluctant to seriously engage with criticism. In this case, however, Mehmet Uçum, a senior consultant to the president and vice president to the Presidency's Council of Law Policies, penned a relatively lengthy response entitled, "What does the reinforced parliamentary system signify?"[100] Here, Uçum argued that a return to the parliamentary system would choke the popular vote within a "bureaucratic-institutional tutelage" (*Bürokratik-kurumsal vesayet*) and, true to form, wrote that this would open up the country to foreign interference. The political opposition therefore sought to integrate Turkey into a "cast system relying on the steps of hierarchy and 'social evolution,' in other words, a global cast fascism," which was controlled by "imperialist globalists." Uçum's article confirmed the notion that there was very little nuance to the presidential system. It was a thin majority electing a single super-executive who is to govern the country through an ever-shifting combination of formal and informal rules.

Turkey's new approach to sovereignty should not sound particularly innovative. The regime that Erdoğan and his followers built follows a pattern of thinking that was theorized before in the nation states of Europe and is becoming popular again across the world. India under Narendra Modi, Hungary under Viktor Orbán, and other major countries are undergoing similar transformations.[101] In Israel, Benjamin Netenyahu faced accusations of graft and, in 2020, complained that he was being persecuted by a "deep state," saying "there is no democracy here, but a government of bureaucrats and jurists."[102] Once back in power at the head of a far-right coalition, he passed a law that would remove the Israeli Supreme Court's power to check executive and legislative power. The Trump administration in the United States also showed a tendency for this kind of "realist" thinking. Where Erdoğan's adherents seek to battle the "bureaucratic-institutional tutelage," Donald Trump's former chief strategist Steven Bannon sought to "deconstruct the administrative state."[103] Where AK Party surrogates try to rationalize the abolition of checks and balances, former attorney general William Barr made Schmittean arguments to lift checks and balances on the American presidency.[104] Most of these political movements build a narrative of great civilizational revival, promising their adherents that their country will be "great again."

Turkey stands out among these countries as a place where the ideas of far-right nationalists have been implemented at an advanced level. The state is firmly in the hands of the Islamist movement, and it is gradually transforming the country's institutions in its own image. Politically, the process is fairly robust. President Erdoğan's approval ratings have been relatively strong throughout times of high inflation, the Covid-19 pandemic, and a devastating earthquake in the country's south.[105] Legally, as Uçum has pointed out, getting out of the current system would be extremely difficult. The opposition would need to unify around a single leader, win the presidency and a parliamentary majority of 360 (out of 600 seats), then disperse the power they've accumulated, breaking up the office of the president and re-distributing its powers across different institutions, giving the opposition (now including the AK Party) power to place checks on them. Any return to the parliamentary system would likely itself require extra-legal action and in the regime's language constitutes a "counter revolution."[106]

Erdoğan's adherents, however, have other things to worry about. Even if they are able to manage the half of the country that does not support them, they will have to resolve at least two problems within the system they have built. First, the presidential system assumes that after Erdoğan's lifetime, there will be other leaders embodying Competitive Occidentalist values who will consistently be able to obtain the vote of the majority. This is possible but not guaranteed. The presidential system, after all, only became law on the back of slim majorities. Erdoğan himself has expressed doubts about what is called the "fifty plus one" rule.[107] There are popular opposition figures such as İstanbul mayor Ekrem İmamoğlu, who are not Competitive Occidentalists. If such a figure ever ascended to the presidency, the regime could come under threat.

The second and more pressing issue is "the problem of merit" (*liyakat sorunu*) as it is often referred to in government circles. Relentless politicization has hollowed out the country's most important institutions, making it less likely that competence meets responsibility. This is the subject of anxious discussion in Ankara and Istanbul. The fear is that this problem will prevent the country from generating the economic and military power needed to climb the rungs of international competition. It is difficult to say whether the Erdoğan government will be successful in tackling these problems, but its future depends on it.

3

Making Strategy in New Turkey

Imagining a New Normal

In the early 2000s, if you were to ask academics and think tankers close to the AK Party about Turkey's most pressing problems, you were sure to encounter the word "securitization," or "securitized policies" (güvenlikçi politikalar). Securitization theory comes from what is called the Copenhagen School of International Relations and became popular in the 1990s. It refers to a process in which state actors take a "normal" policy issue, which should be the subject of the domestic political process, and rephrase it in the language of an existential threat, putting it into the purview of the military, police, or intelligence. Coming out of the Cold War, this was a concern among liberal states. A culture of excessive securitization could be obstructing the work of parliamentary democracy. Many scholars argued that the Turkish state was doing just this with respect to Islamist and Kurdish politics. Its Kemalist character made the state intolerant to those groups, which meant that the political elite would always talk about them as a security threat to be contained. The AK Party, on the other hand, was an agent of "de-securitization" and "normalization." It was bringing Islam and the Kurdish issue in from the fringes, to be processed by the parliamentary system. Once that was done, Turkey would be unstuck, EU integration would commence, and even relations with neighbors like Syria and Iran would flourish.[1]

That is not what happened. Almost a quarter century on, it is also no longer the way the AK Party's experts think about politics. The vastly expanded pool of academics, consultants, and think tankers who make up the country's new foreign policy elite are no longer worried about securitization, but have themselves become the securitizers, seeing existential threats behind every problem: the opposition is treasonous and in the pocket of Western powers, making every election campaign a "beka sorunu," meaning a "problem of survival." There is no longer such a thing as a "Kurdish problem," only a "terrorism problem." The primary objective of foreign policy is no longer convergence with the European Union, but establishing Turkey's own sphere of influence. In their telling, politics is no longer about managing competing interests, it is about attaining mastery in a Hobbesian world. Violence is no longer a thing to be minimized, it is to be controlled, cultivated, and ultimately directed against enemies within and abroad. The Turkish military is therefore heavily involved in conflicts in neighboring countries, including Syria, Iraq, Azerbaijan, Armenia, and across the sea, Libya. Intelligence services grab and bag the regime's political enemies across the world. Indigenously built killer drones and warships get glowing coverage on the news; state-sponsored TV shows glorify the military prowess of Ottoman and Seleukid ancestors.

This transformation in strategic culture is an expression of the country's shift from Aspirational into Competitive Occidentalism at the state level. In this chapter, I will trace this process from the perspective of Turkey's "military intellectual complex," made up of defense analysts, think tanks, and state institutions.

The Factory Settings: Liberalization

Turkey has long been deeply attuned to the foreign policy establishment of the United States. Its elites have been educated in the country, and its private sector, academia, and media have assumed the trends they see in Washington. Since the end of the Cold War, many in Ankara dreamed of taking this one step further, gradually replacing American power in the region.[2] Among the old elite, this idea came from a feeling of being the extension of the Western alliance and, over time, taking on more responsibility within its structure.[3] Among the Islamists, it meant rolling back an imperial presence and returning to a natural order in which Turkey had its own sphere of influence. These two circles did not disagree on the competency of the United States—both believed that was the most advanced political structure in the world, and that it deserved to be emulated. Only the left, which had been waning since the 1980 coup, believed that the US-led order was not only immoral but also unsustainable.

To the Turkish political class, the most interesting part of the United States was its ability to create grand strategy. In this sense, people in Ankara in the 1990s found Washington D.C. to be a fascinating place. American academics, bureaucrats, and politicians came together to create long-term strategy in a way that the Europeans could not or would not do. The National Security Council,

State Department, the "marketplace of ideas" with its academics, journalists, and think tanks, seemed dynamic and powerful. Turkey, by contrast, had a National Security Council that was chaired by the ruling military cadre, and set a rigid national security policy.[4] Creative input here was not welcome. The country had some fairly innovative policy planning capabilities in the field of economic development (especially in its State Planning Organization), but this did not extend to larger strategic issues. When it came to geopolitics, Turkey was a strategy taker, not a maker. During the Cold War, the center right had been content with that arrangement. By the 1990s, there were stirrings of something new. True to the free market ethos of the time, this was not to happen through capacity within the government, but outside of it. A marketplace of ideas had to be built to develop the country's political creativity.

The state did become a little more open to outsiders during this time. Most of Turkey's bureaucrats, especially in the sphere of law and diplomacy, have traditionally come from Ankara University, or what is called "Mülkiye" after its Ottoman-era name, and worked their way up. Toward the end of the Özal era in the early 1990s, however, advisers of various stripes started to parachute into the top echelons of government, some becoming very influential. The renowned journalist Cengiz Çandar became a special advisor to Özal in the early 1990s and established contact with Kurdish groups in northern Iraq. The writer Mümtazer Türköne became a "spin doctor" for various center-right leaders. This world of high-flying advisers bled into daily newspapers, where "penslinger" columnists battled each with the juiciest political gossip of the day.[5] Politicians and diplomats kept a close eye on these columns, looking for hints on where the wind was blowing. The bureaucracy was still tightly knit, but it was gradually becoming a little more penetrable, something that could increasingly be influenced by outsiders.[6] "Think tanks" began to set up shop in Ankara and Istanbul, seeking to emulate American institutions like the geopolitical advisory firm Stratfor or the Brookings Institution.

Politically, this was a time when liberalism was on the ascendant. In the West, youthful "third way" liberals like Bill Clinton and Tony Blair were seemingly blurring the lines between the right and left, combining free market principles with progressive politics. In Turkey, young liberals in Istanbul and Ankara were rebelling against their parents' Kemalism. The "Second Republicanists," as they called themselves, focused on minority rights, the freedom of speech and religion, and they looked for allies, not among the country's traditional elite, but among a cadre of charismatic young Islamists.[7]

The Virtue Party (FP) was the latest incarnation of the Islamist "Milli Görüş" (National Vision) party, but it was being split between the "Traditionalists" (gelenekçi), who advocated for radical Islamist policies, and the "Innovationists" (yenilikçi), who wanted to explore a more gradualist approach. In 1998, the innovationist set up a think tank called ANAR under the leadership of Beşir Atalay, a reserved man with a background in sociology. Bureaucrats, academics, and businesspeople began to meet at ANAR and churn out policy reports. In the fateful FP party congress of 2000, the Innovationists, led by Abdullah Gül, challenged the Traditionalist leader Recai Kutan, but lost. Eager to break into politics, the Innovationists established the Justice and Development (Adalet ve Kalkınma) Party in August 2001. The abbreviation "AK" was the Turkic word for "white." The name had a rustic texture, yet signaled a tabula rasa.[8]

The AK Party built its first party platform based on ANAR reports. Its authors would later occupy important positions in government, with Atalay himself taking on several critical roles, including that of interior minister. ANAR operated on a shoestring budget, and, on economic policy, relied heavily on ideas and data coming in from the State Planning Organization (Devlet Planlama Teşkiları, DPT), which, in turn, relied heavily on the World Bank and International Monetary Fund (IMF).[9] Still, by repackaging this information creatively, ANAR probably remains the most successful think tank in Turkey's history. It did what most in this line of work can only dream of: it drafted a policy program, created a political strategy to defend it, and carried a young political party into government. A journalist who interviewed Erdoğan for a foreign newspaper at the time recalls how, with every question he asked, a group of advisors around the man frantically leafed through the party program before answering with the appropriate policy. The party was, as they say in the English-speaking world, "on message," partly because there was a black-and-white, ring-bound message to be on.

Going into its first election in November 2002, the AK Party was in a strategically unique position: it had some core supporters that it brought over from the Virtue Party years, as well as a firm base in Istanbul and Ankara from the mayoralties there in 1994. Having moved to the political center, it could also now appeal to liberal voters. The aging Kemalist elite was out of tune with the prevailing form of liberalism in Western countries, which emphasized minority rights, "authentic" religious identities, decentralization, and free markets.[10] The liberalism of the time, combined with the residue of Islamism, seemed to transcend the right–left divide, making politics about the old vs. the new, dysfunction vs. efficiency, corruption vs. transparency. The Innovationists could now claim that they were more Western than Kemalist Westernizers. They were efficient, hardworking, in tune with the times. In later years, commentators would refer to this mix of liberalism and conservative symbols as the "factory settings" of the AK Party.

The early AK Party strategy relied heavily on approval from the West. Its voter base live in the slums of Istanbul and Ankara, but it needed another kind of legitimacy as well. The staunchly Kemalist military had to be kept from smothering the AK Party government in its infancy, and strong support from the West was the only way to do so. When his party won the November 3 general election with 34 percent of the vote, Erdoğan was still officially banned from politics. On November 18, as Abdullah Gül was being sworn in as prime minister, Erdoğan was in Athens, meeting with a group of European MPs, then flew to Spain to meet with prime minister José María Aznar. In the following days, he would travel to Berlin, London, and Brussels to meet leaders there, and, on December 10, would be received by President George W. Bush at the White House.[11] Turkey had become a candidate for EU membership in 1999, and the young AK Party government now plowed its energy into the liberal and legal reforms required to reach the next stage. Support from Western states, however, was not enough. The AK Party also needed English-speaking policy professionals to convey its message to Western universities, think tanks, and newspapers.

The Islamist intelligentsia was already preparing to supply such people, and they built them on an American model. During the Cold War, Islamist writers and academics had been fairly secluded, keeping to polemical magazines and poetry readings. Here, they developed a cartoonish conception of Western hegemony: men in suits, sitting around a dimly lit map of the world, toppling governments, siphoning off foreign oil reserves, plotting coups, and erecting puppet regimes. The emerging generation of Islamists liked to talk of the "Üst Akıl," literally "the Mastermind." This entity was personified by suave academics-cum-strategists like Henry Kissinger and Zbigniew Brzezinski.[12] In the 1990s and the subsequent "war on terror" in the 2000s, another "Mastermind" figure was the historian Bernard Lewis, who had been a booster of Kemalism, and whose argument about "the roots of Muslim rage" had great influence on senior diplomats and politicians in the United States after the September 11 attacks. These figures had long been the objects of Islamist *ressentiment,* and their example would gradually be replicated at home.

The Science and Art Foundation (Bilim ve Sanat Vakfı, BİSAV) in Istanbul, supported by a handful of conservative businessmen, was to be a place where Islamist policy intellectuals could come together. Ahmet Davutoğlu, a scholar from Konya, was especially prominent in its design. He recruited undergraduates, mostly from his alma mater, the prestigious Boğaziçi University, and put them through a parallel curriculum at his weekend gatherings. There, the group read history, political science, literature, and philosophy. When Davutoğlu took a post at the Islamic University of Malaysia in the 1990s, he took some of those students with him. One of them was İbrahim Kalın, a lanky, thinly mustached history graduate. Unlike most recruits, Kalın had graduated from the relatively unimpressive Istanbul University, but proved himself to be exceptionally bright. He earned a master's in Malaysia and a PhD in Islamic theology from George Washington University.

Returning to Turkey in the early years of the AK Party, Kalın was put in charge of a new initiative: a think tank in Ankara. Founded sometime between 2005 and 2006, it was based in a house in the traditionally secular district of Çankaya, where the presidential compound and foreign embassies were still located at the time. It had three departments: politics, economics, and society, which in Turkish abbreviated to the "SET Foundation."[13] This sounded choppy, so after a while, someone thought of adding "research" ("Araştırmaları") to the title, making it "SETA."[14] BİSAV had been too high up in the ivory tower, and ANAR was too obscure and introverted, but SETA was to be more in the style of a Washington think tank. It sought to create narratives, inject them into the discussion, and shape the climate of high politics. Its director was to mingle with the Ankara crowd, attending embassy events, cultivating links to journalists, hosting visitors, and holding backchannel discussions. Kalın proved himself up to the task, growing the foundation's pool of experts, appearing on TV, attending events, and liaising with prestigious visitors.[15]

At this time, most International Relations departments and think tanks in Turkey were focused on EU studies. SETA took a different approach, focusing its work on the Middle East. This was in line with Davutoğlu's "bow and arrow" theory: the deeper Turkey drew its arrow Eastward, the farther it would shoot Westwards, meaning that the stronger Turkey's relationships were in the Middle East, Asia, and Africa were, the more important and desirable an ally it would be to Europe and the United States.[16] Not only was the AK Party leading the forces of civil society against the authoritarian establishment (and thus "normalizing"), it would extend liberal norms into places the West couldn't.[17] SETA scholars, like Bülent Aras, Hatem Ete, and Taha Özhan, argued that the AK Party was "de-securitizing" Turkish politics, rolling back irrational and undemocratic forces. SETA publications also made ample use of the term "soft power," put forward by the International Relations theorist Joseph Nye.[18] "New Turkey" was going to change the Middle East, and unlike the United States, it would do so by the power of its example, rather than miliary force.

SETA had an organic relationship with the AK Party, but it still set its own agenda. Davutoğlu remained behind the scenes, and while the more internationalist wing of the AK Party were tuned in to the institution, they did not take an active role in it. One thing that SETA was crucially missing, however, was a connection to Erdoğan's inner circles. The prime minister's core team had come together during his time as mayor of Istanbul and evolved from that basis onward. They were extremely effective political operators, but they didn't have academic expertise, didn't speak foreign languages, and hadn't traveled much. They were also not very approachable. One SETA employee at the time said that the institution even had trouble getting an appointment with Ankara mayor Melih Gökçek in those early years, and certainly couldn't get in the door with Erdoğan.[19] One day in the late 2000s, İbrahim Kalın and his team were attending a dinner at a famous Istanbul restaurant, where Erdoğan and his group were cordoned off at the top floor. Kalın was trying to go upstairs to briefly talk to the prime minister, but security wouldn't let him through. He ended up waiting in front of the stairs.[20]

At this time, Erdoğan began to develop an international voice more distinct and forceful than that of his party. One event, more than any other, would highlight this. On January 29, 2009, Erdoğan took part in a Davos panel on Middle East peace alongside Israeli president Shimon Peres. Most of the discussion was amicable, but at one point toward the end, Peres slightly raised his voice when speaking about Palestinian attacks, tilting his body toward Erdoğan. The moderator sought to wrap up the panel, but Erdoğan was offended. He repeatedly asked him for "one minute" to respond, raising his voice in response to Peres, saying that Israel knew "how to kill," and that its forces "hit the children on the beaches." When the moderator tried to cut him off, Erdoğan said that Peres had spoken twice as long as he had, said that he wouldn't come to Davos again. He got up and walked out. What came to be known as the "one-minute" incident was an expression of Erdoğan's undiluted anger, not only at Israel but at the world order as a whole. The AK Party's voter base loved it. Many party's grandees, however, while agreeing with Erdoğan's sentiment, found his actions undiplomatic and reactive.[21] Erdoğan was diverging from the AK Party's liberal playbook, and doing so unilaterally. He was no longer "on message"; he was the message.

This was a sensitive point in Erdoğan's political trajectory. As he was diverging from the party and letting more of his personality come through, some people were quietly backing away from him, while others rallied around him. For ambitious foreign policy types, it was the perfect time to look for new opportunities. In his weekly English-language column in *Today's Zaman*—eagerly read by foreign diplomats and Turkey watchers abroad—Kalın provided a spirited defense of the "one-minute" event. He argued that the Israel–Palestine issue was running on an artificial agenda, and that Erdoğan's natural reaction would once again ground it and thereby help resolve the conflict:

> From a purely diplomatic point of view, Erdoğan's reaction is more likely to cause concern than it is to bring comfort. But Erdoğan is not a diplomat. He is a political leader. His frustration does not simply show the limits of one man's patience, but underscores the boundaries of how much progress one can make with puppet diplomacy.[22]

This kind of post hoc defense was to become much more common in the new period. As his foreign policy was gradually reverting to the Islamist tradition's reactionary style, Erdoğan needed an analytical class to run interference in the liberal Western world. In May of that year, Ahmet Davutoğlu became foreign minister, and Kalın left SETA to become chief advisor to the prime minister.

SETA would henceforth be working more closely with the government, taking on more important tasks, and the most important agenda item in the late 2000s was the peace process with the Kurdistan Workers' Party (Partiya Karkerên Kurdistanê, or PKK), a Marxist-Leninist guerrilla group founded in the late 1970s. The Kurds are famously the largest nation without a state, spread across Syria, Iraq, Iran, and, most of all, Turkey. The PKK not only wanted to set up Kurdish self-rule, they wanted to end what they considered a feudal order and set up a redistributive, democratic, feminist, and atheist society in its place. The PKK had taken a hit after the Cold War, especially with the 1999 arrest of its leader Abdullah Öcalan, but it continued its insurgency against the Turkish state.[23] The Islamists had long argued that the Kurds were naturally conservative Muslims and, therefore, integral to the country's makeup. Kemalist secularism had distorted the natural, Ottoman-era bond between Turks and Kurds, resulting in the progressive aberration that was the PKK. Since the AK Party was now in power, and Kemalism was gradually receding, the PKK was effectively redundant. The challenge was to devise a policy platform that could gradually ease the country into this new normal.

SETA published on the issue extensively, conducting opinion polls and holding private meetings, often with senior AK Party officials. In 2008, it released a report by Taha Özhan and Hatem Ete entitled "The Kurdish Issue: Problems and Recommendations for Its Resolution" that packaged the Islamist position in academic language, specifically in that of the "securitization" literature.[24] This made the argument easier for liberals to digest, and even champion:

> The strategies implemented to solve the Kurdish problem so far have addressed the problem within the boundaries of the security perspective, which did not contribute to the solution and led to the problem becoming more layered. When ethno-secular language was added to these faulty resolution strategies, for the first time in Republican Turkey, Muslim subjects became two separate "ethnic elements" and were placed in "minority-majority antagonism" in a secular world of meaning.[25]

Westernization had shrunk Turkey's horizons, and its small-mindedness made it intolerant and violent toward non-Turkish groups, now turned into "minorities." In a footnote, Özhan and Ete argued that "any discussion that ignores the historical-cultural depth that makes these lands a homeland will only fuel alienation and accelerate disintegration."[26] This was a way of saying that leftist secularism, being a Western idea and thus ignorant of the deep religious ties between Turks and Kurds, was standing in the way of reconciliation. The peace process would only succeed in as far as it convinced the PKK to join the AK Party in its brand of romantic Islamism. Further work hashed out a plan to turn these ideas into reality. A comprehensive 2011 report by Hüseyin Yayman, entitled "Turkey's Memory of the Kurdish Question" was widely read at the time, also defending Islamist ideas while overtly setting up a dichotomy between security and "civil" forces.[27]

After years of furious conferencing, report-launching, and international consensus-building, much of which was conducted at SETA (and its newly established office in Washington D.C.), the peace process kicked off with Nevroz celebrations in March 2013. HDP politicians Pervin Buldan and Sırrı Süeyya Önder read out the imprisoned PKK leader Abdullah Öcalan's letter in Kurdish and Turkish, in front of a huge crowd in Turkey's Kurdish capital of Diyarbakır. In his letter, Öcalan proclaimed the dawn of a new age. The Middle East would be created anew, he wrote, its people would live side by side, free of outside interference. It was clear that the letter had been tightly negotiated with Turkish authorities. The phrase that stuck most in the minds of the Islamists was the promise that the Kurds and Turks would live "under the banner of Islam" and struggle together against Western imperialism's designs on the region. The PKK maintained many of its themes of class struggle, but it downplayed its progressive edge, saying exactly what the Islamists had long wanted them to say: that the problem between Turks and Kurds wasn't Turkish nationalism, imperialism, or even global capitalism, but

Western influence. The problem was that Western ideology an imperial outreach had gotten between two peoples who were bound by the ties of Islam. Removing this membrane of Westernness would be the first step toward rebuilding the relationship. While Islamist elites and Kurdish notables took note of this passage, liberals in Turkey, Europe, and the United States largely ignored it, reveling in the thought that a large ethnic minority was being recognized in the eyes of the state, and was no longer seen as a security threat.[28]

Part of the peace process was a government-picked group of sixty-three "Wise Persons," made up of businesspeople, artists, journalists, and scholars. The "Wise Persons" were split into groups covering Turkey's seven regions. The South-East group, which was to tour the Kurdish regions, was headed by Yılmaz Ensaroğlu, who was also the head of SETA's Law and Human Rights department at the time. The South-Western group included SETA's Hüseyin Yayman. The group toured the country, sat with local leaders, and sought to socialize the peace process.[29]

Other think tanks were also growing around this time and also acted as stepping stones for roles in government. The Center for Middle Eastern Studies (ORSAM), established in 2009, specialized on the close-up study of Iraq and Syria. It leaned more Turkist than Islamist and seemed closer to the security state. The Istanbul-based Center for Economics and Foreign Policy Studies (EDAM) was the more liberal, flashy, and atlanticist outfit. As a low-level researcher at the Ankara-based Economic Policy Research Foundation of Turkey (TEPAV) in the early 2010s, I was musing about my career prospects. Some of my colleagues were quitting to join the Foreign Ministry, paying their dues and moving up the ranks. Some people around me were advising me to do the same. An older colleague laughed when I told him of this, saying that I should simply get a PhD and write newspaper columns instead. "It's not as hard as it looks," he said. Over time, I would meet the right people and eventually become a bureaucrat. The goal in this wasn't to be just any kind of bureaucrat, but a "siyasi bürokrat," someone with fancy degrees and political connections who was parachuted into key institutions and told the straight-laced career professionals what to do.

In the meantime, Turkey's geopolitical needs were shifting. Germany's Angela Merkel and France's Nicolas Sarkozy did not want Turkey in the EU. The accession process had provided cover from military coups, but as the AK Party government solidified its place in power, it was also becoming comfortable with sovereignty, and appeared less willing to hand any of it over to Brussels.[30] New conflicts were also taking shape to Turkey's south. In the coming years, Turkey's geopolitical strategy would no longer be about engineering Turkey's accession to the liberal order; it would be about finding a way in Middle Eastern conflicts.

Blood Touches the Wolf's Tooth: The Syrian Civil War and the Kurds

The first decade of the AK Party's rule took place firmly within the traditional areas of Turkish foreign policy: the EU accession process and participation in NATO. The country's primary defense issue had traditionally been the fight against the PKK, and that was mostly on hold. In its second decade, the defining issue of Turkish foreign policy would be the Syrian Civil War, which took the country out of its multilateral framework. Ankara was at first confident that it could meet the challenge but quickly recognized that it was out of its depth. Its institutions weren't equipped to manage a proxy war, and the deeper Erdoğan waded into it, the more he lost control.

In 2011, popular protests in Tunisia, Egypt, and other Arab countries, often referred to as the "Arab Spring," dominated headlines. In March, protesters in Dara'a, southern Syria, also took to the streets. The Egyptian strongman Hosni Mubarak had been toppled in February of that year, and the Muslim Brotherhood was well positioned to replace him. It seemed possible that the same could happen to Syrian dictator Bashar al-Assad. As part of Ankara's "normalization" drive, its historically tense relations with Damascus had quickly been improving. Bashar al-Assad and Erdoğan visited each other in 2004, inked trade agreements, and resolved issues over water rights. Cross-border trade and investment was booming between the countries.[31] Turkey had a lot to lose by supporting the protests, but if the protests were to succeed, and free elections were held, it was likely that Damascus would be governed by Islamists friendly to the AK Party. Turkish Islamists often read Turkey's recent history into other Muslim-majority countries, and the popular overthrow of a fairly secular dictator in favor of an Islamist movement sounded like a very natural progression for their neighbor. During his visit to Cairo in September 2012, Erdoğan said, "the Syrian people at this time don't believe in Assad. I don't either, we don't either."[32]

In a similar vein, transatlantic policy circles began to talk of the "Turkish Model," implying that the protests sought to embark on a path of democratic elections, individual rights and market-based development.[33] This was close enough to the AK Party's vision for them to appear the same. It also meant that Turkey could garner strong international support when it called on Assad to step down. History had aligned behind the AK Party in Tunisia and Egypt, and it seemed only a matter of time until this wave of normative power would sweep over Syria as well.

Turkey's governing elite now sought to establish ties with its Islamist cousins south of the border. Ankara's budding policy experts were crisscrossing the region as de facto ambassadors of the AK Party. In a 2012 op-ed entitled "How Does One Become a Middle East Expert?" SETA analyst Ufuk Ulutaş bemoaned the inflation in armchair analysts. Political dynamics in the Middle East, he wrote, could not be understood by just anyone. The job required "a broad interdisciplinary study ranging from anthropology to theology, sociology to political science, geography to linguistics." Aspiring analysts had to speak several regional languages and be physically and spiritually grounded in the region. "Your feet must step on the soil you speak of," he wrote.[34] Yet Ulutaş fell short of his own standards in ways that were typical of his colleagues as well. He had very few academic publications, and those he had were razor thin on substance. He claimed to know some Arabic and Hebrew, but hadn't been heard to speak either. He did, however, step on the soil—or airport lounges—he spoke of. During a brief visit to Egypt in the winter of 2012, I found one group of young university students had named themselves the "Ufuk Group" after Ulutaş, who had been a frequent visitor. This was fairly typical of Turkey's "political bureaucrats" at the time. What they lacked in expertise, they made up for in enthusiasm and frequent flier miles.

Unlike Egypt's Hosni Mubarak, however, Assad wouldn't bend to popular pressure. Damascus sent its military to squash protesters in 2011, dragging the country into a bloody civil war. At this point, Ankara had a choice: either walk away or help the opposition fight back. It chose the latter, which meant that it had to support the newly forming insurgency across the border. Such work is usually done by intelligence services, which was not Turkey's strong suit. The country's main intelligence agency, the National Intelligence Organization (Milli İstihbarat Teşkilatı, MİT), was predominantly active in domestic intelligence.[35] Its operations abroad primarily entailed tight cooperation with the United States and the United Kingdom during the Cold War, as well as the protection of diplomatic personnel, which became an issue after the attacks of the Armenian Secret Army for the Liberation of Armenia (ASALA) on Turkish diplomats in the 1970s and 1980s.[36] Managing a proxy war in a large neighboring country was beyond MİT's capabilities.

The AK Party government had appointed Hakan Fidan to run MİT. This was an unorthodox choice for an institution that usually promoted its own, or very senior soldiers and diplomats, to the top job. Fidan's rise to this position is likely the result of long-term planning among the AK Party. He had been a noncommissioned officer in the Turkish military between 1986 and 2001. He was probably involved in intelligence at that time, considering that he wrote an MA thesis at Ankara's Bilkent University in 1999 entitled "Intelligence and Foreign Policy: A Comparison of British, American and Turkish Intelligence System."[37] Fidan then floated around policy circles during the early years of the AK Party, working as a consultant at the Australian embassy in Ankara and earning a second MA at the University of Maryland Global Campus, where students are mid-career civil servants, especially veterans and military-affiliated students.

In 2003, the AK Party government appointed Fidan as head of Turkish Development and Cooperation Agency (TİKA), Turkey's overseas development agency, which at the time was a relatively small institution.[38] This put Fidan on international trips with Foreign Minister Davutoğlu and Prime Minister Erdoğan, and allowed him to maintain a close relationship with President Abdullah Gül. In 2007, he left TİKA to became a deputy undersecretary to then-Prime Minister Erdoğan, and in 2010, when the position opened up, Fidan was finally appointed head of MİT. The meteoric rise suggests that this was planned. There were some young Islamists in the 1980s and 1990s who downplayed their conservative origins, joined the bureaucracy and the armed forces, but quietly maintained their ties to the Islamist movement. It seems plausible that Fidan could have had such ties to the AK Party's founding group, resigned when it was rising to power, burnished his international credentials, then joined the government as a well-credentialled senior bureaucrat. This would mean that Fidan didn't have to endure cut-throat competition to reach the top. In a region where spymasters have reputations for ruthlessness, he stood out for being mild-mannered, well-read, and reasonable. His most important task in those years was the peace process with the PKK, for which he frequently took part in meetings at SETA. It later emerged that in 2009, before becoming head of MİT, he was already involved in the organization's peace negotiations with the PKK, which took place in Oslo.[39]

In 2011, when the country waded into a proxy war across the border, Fidan had been the head of MİT for about a year. This was a task much different to the ones he and his institution had been preparing for. One of the first publicly available stories about MİT's involvement in Syria is about three agents in Hatay who unlawfully cooperated with the Assad regime. Hussein Harmoush, one of the founders of the Free Syrian Army, reportedly had a $100,000 bounty on his head in Syria and fled across the border into Turkey with his family. There were media reports that in August of 2011, three MİT agents abducted him and delivered him to the Assad regime, presumably to collect the bounty.[40] Fidan flew down to meet with the governor of Hatay and initiated prosecution against the MİT employees involved. This is only one incident, but it strengthens the prevalent idea in the policy community that MİT was not equipped for managing a war in Syria. MİT officers seemed neither competent nor aligned with the Erdoğan government's political stance.[41] In the following years, however, MİT managed to establish a relationship with Syrian rebel groups and began to arm and train them. The umbrella group was called the Free Syrian Army (FSO) and its base was first in Turkey's border region, and moved into rebel-held territories in Syria in 2012.[42] The United States would later express concern that these groups had extremist Islamist tendencies.[43]

Turkey's involvement in Syria was deeply entangled with the country's main domestic agenda item, which, in early 2012, was the Erdoğan–Gülen civil war. The Gülenists fired the first shot on February 7, 2012, when prosecutors presumably loyal to Gülen called for Fidan to be questioned and possibly detained over his role in MİT's talks with the PKK in Oslo. Erdoğan was able to block the summons, and the AK Party immediately passed a law that effectively cast a protective shield over MİT.[44] The judiciary could no longer touch the agency without going through the executive branch first. This sparked some debate at the time, and the AK Party's response, as with so much else, was that the prime minister was elected by the people and, therefore, did not need serious checks.[45] The Gülenist network, however, kept their aim on MİT and its involvement in Syria. As covered in the previous chapter, in December 2013, Gülenists elements leaked a trove of audio files of high-level conversations.[46]

One of these was the recording of a conversation between Fidan, Foreign Minister Ahmet Davutoğlu, Undersecretary of the Ministry of Foreign Affairs Feridun Sinirlioğlu, and Deputy Chief of the General Staff General Yaşar Güler. The leak was scandalous, mainly due to a part in the conversation where Fidan suggested that if it was necessary, he could easily stage a false flag attack on Turkish territory and thereby generate a *casus belli* for Turkish military incursion.[47] There is, however, far more to this glimpse of the inner workings of Syria policy at the time. The officials talk about the state of fighting on the ground, the limiting factors they face, and the public's view of events. This is a candid situation analysis between a group of senior foreign policymakers who feel that their room for maneuver is disappearing. Listening to the conversation, it quickly becomes apparent that at this point, Turkey was less a diabolic manipulator of the civil war (which the leakers probably sought to imply) and more a desperate bundle of loosely coordinated institutions, lacking a process for defining goals and devising the means to achieve them.[48] Here, for example, Davutoğlu and Yaşar Güler are talking about coordinating the provision of ammunition to the Syrian rebel groups:

Güler: Our prime minister should summon the chief of staff and the minister at the same time. He should speak in his presence.

Davutoğlu: Feridun bey and I have almost begged the prime minister to do just that, saying that we should all gather, that this business is going badly.

Güler: Also, my minister, it shouldn't be crowded. It should be your excellency, the minister of defense, the minister of interior and the chief of staff. The four of you should sit down. All these other people are not necessary. Because the need over there [in Syria], my minister, is weapons and ammunition. Not even weapons—just ammunition. We just talked about it sir. Let's say we are building an army of 1,000 people there. If we put these men into combat there without stockpiling 6 months of ammunition they need, my minister, these men will come back to us in two months.[49]

Much of this conversation is what one would expect in a country conducting a proxy war. Problems in intra-governmental coordination and competition for the ear of the executive are certainly common in these kinds of situations. Other aspects of it, however, are revealing of Turkey's strategic shift at the time. Despite his high military rank, Yaşar Güler's role among these civilians is clearly that of a subordinate. This is a major change for a country where the military has traditionally dominated the political class. That is no longer the case because by 2013, the Gülenist allies of the AK Party had whittled away the politically assertive military officers through the Ergenekon and Sledgehammer trials, which accused them of coup-plotting based on faulty evidence. Many of the remaining officers were either Gülenists or lacked the anti-Islamist zeal of their elders. A few, like Fidan before he left, or Hulusi Akar, who later became Chief of the General Staff, had long-standing relationships with the AK Party. Güler had served as an aide to Akar, and appears to have been part of this group. In the leaked conversation, General Güler's high-pitched, obsequious voice complains about the lack of ammunition and the general dearth of resources. He also seems uncomfortable with MİT dominating the Syria file, but remains too reserved to express it outright, saying at one point, "this is an issue that has been left on Hakan bey's back! I mean, we don't understand. Why?"

Paradoxically, as the power of the military was dwindling, the importance of military force in Turkish foreign policy was becoming more apparent. Here is another telling exchange in the conversation:

Güler: My minister, we just talked about that as your excellency was in the other room. Openly. The armed forces are a tool that is going to be necessary to you at any time.

Davutoğlu: Of course. Everywhere, when we talk to the Prime Minister [Erdoğan] in your absence, I tell him in the academic manner, that without hard power, one cannot remain on this soil. Without hard power, there cannot be soft power.[50]

This seems like a strange comment for a foreign minister to make. Statesmen usually don't feel the need to justify the existence of as fundamental a capability as that of military force. At this point, however, Davutoğlu had spent the previous decades arguing that the Kemalist status quo was a coercive, "securitizing" force, and counterposed the Islamist movement as a normative corrective. When arguing for the deployment of more military force in Syria, he justifies it—somewhat circuitously—by claiming that such interventions form the bedrock of "soft power." Davutoğlu also seems to suggest that he has been couching his advice to Erdoğan in academic language in order to magnify its impact.

It is worth noting here that Davutoğlu was not alone in trying to convince Erdoğan. In March of that year, Erdoğan and his foreign policy team visited the White House, where Obama pushed him to send the Turkish Armed Forces into Syria. Erdoğan pushed back, saying that he would only commit forces as part of a larger NATO intervention on the ground. Obama, who was trying to extricate his country from the Afghanistan and Iraq wars, and might already have been regretting the NATO intervention in Libya in 2011, had no appetite for any involvement but kept pushing for Turkey to take the initiative.[51] Years later, based on in-depth interviews with Obama for a profile in *The Atlantic*, the journalist Jeffrey Goldberg would write that the president considered Erdoğan to be "a failure and an authoritarian, one who refuses to use his enormous army to bring stability to Syria." Given the mood at the time, as well as later reporting from Washington, it seems very likely that Davutoğlu was aligned with the Americans on this issue.[52] Obama and Davutoğlu, two famously professorial statesmen, were trying to convince the notoriously unlettered Erdoğan to engage in military action in Syria, but failed. In his comments to Güler, Davutoğlu implied that Erdoğan was reluctant due to his belief in "soft power" and his commitment to the liberal paradigm of the 2000s.

That seems fanciful. There is no reason to think that Erdoğan had normative reservations about the use of military force. It is much more likely that he was suspicious of his own military. He probably thought that sending the Turkish military into Syria on its own would have opened him up for political attack at home and abroad. As the first major Islamist leader in the country's history, he must have been aware that he would be judged by different standards than Bülent

Ecevit, the leftist prime minister who ordered the intervention in Cyprus in 1974. If Erdoğan invaded a neighboring country with only dubious international backing, Western governments, as well as liberals at home, could have made him out to be a warmonger. They could also have argued that Erdoğan was waging a personal vendetta against Bashar al-Assad, who was part of the Alawite minority in Syria. Erdoğan also knew that the Gülenist network had been planting their recruits into the military academy for a generation, and that in the event of a major Turkish operation, many of the officers on the ground would not only answer to Ankara but also to a potentially hostile cult leader in Pennsylvania. The fact that the Gülenist later leaked the tapes of this conversation attests to their proclivity to portray Erdoğan as an aggressor at this stage of the conflict. As events would amply demonstrate, Erdoğan did not have compunctions about the use of force itself. It is far more likely that he resisted sending the military into Syria because he saw it as a trap.

Another key figure in the leaked tapes was Undersecretary of Foreign Affairs Feridun Sinirlioğlu, who says at one point that "our national security has become the exceedingly shabby material of domestic politics." Sinirligolu was highly influential in this period, but unlike Davutoğlu, the famously laconic diplomat received little international attention. He was born in a small town in the Black Sea province of Giresun and earned a PhD in international relations from the prestigious Boğaziçi University. After he joined the service, Sinirlioğlu served in critical posts like Tel Aviv and Beirut, as well as in official appointments as advisor to prime ministers and presidents in the 1990s. His tall, wide frame meant that he towered over his colleagues, a quiet giant who was unusually analytical for the protocol-oriented Foreign Ministry. He was as secular as anyone in the old guard, but his no-nonsense demeanor and instinct for power appealed to Erdoğan early on. One time at a social event, he overheard a group of his fellow ambassadors complaining that the prime minister never listened to them. Sinirlioğlu chuckled and said, "he always listens to me." He would serve as undersecretary for an unusually long period of seven years, before being assigned as permanent representative at the UN in New York.[53]

In retrospect, Sinirlioğlu and Fidan were crucial figures in Turkey's transformation. They came up in the Atlanticist framework of the Cold War, but were intellectually and temperamentally open to Erdoğan's revaluation of the Republic. They weren't as rigidly internationalist or Kemalist, as others of their generation, nor were they as overtly political as most others around Erdoğan in the 2010s. Western diplomats came to see them as capable professionals who could relay their messages to the otherwise unreachable class of Competitive

Occidentalists at the top echelons of government. This worked because, unlike Davutoğlu, Sinirlioğlu and Findan did not aspire to cultivate a political base of their own, and their loyalty never seems to have been in question. Their power came from the necessity of continuing Turkey's high-level relationship with the West at a time when the political basis of the relationship was gradually disappearing.

A unified Turkish-American strategy on Syria, however, continued to elude even the most adept bureaucrats. In 2014–15, the countries launched a joint "Train and Equip" program that would pick Syrian rebels, train them on Turkish territory, then send them into the conflict. The program never worked as intended. Rebel groups could not be vetted properly, and those who received training proved to be poor fighters.[54] Gradually, Turkey and the United States gravitated toward different sides of the war. Ankara's priority in those years was to topple the Assad regime, and it continued to unilaterally arm groups that the United States considered Islamist extremists, eventually forming them under the banner of the "Free Syrian Army" (FSA). Washington's priority was to "degrade and destroy" the newly emerging Islamic State of Iraq and the Levant (ISIS), and it came to believe that the best ally for it in that endeavor was the Democratic Union Party (PYD), the Syrian offshoot of the PKK. Starting in 2013, the PYD effectively set up and governed the Autonomous Administration of North and East Syria (AANES), also known by the Kurdish name "Rojava" (meaning "the West" in Kurdish, referring to Western Kurdistan).[55] The Syrian Civil War now had multiple fronts: Assad's forces, backed by Iranian militias and the Russian air force; Islamist rebels, backed by Turkey as well as some Gulf states; the armed wing of the SDF, backed by the United States; and ISIS.

The growth and complexity of the war started to put pressure on Turkey's domestic political alignments, most importantly concerning the Kurdish issue. The Erdoğan government was still in talks with the PKK at this time, but the group's success in Syria was changing the architecture of the arrangement. The PKK had a presence in Syria, Iraq, and Iran, but it was an organization born of Turkey and always sought Kurdish self-rule in that country. That had given Ankara leverage, which was the basis of the peace process, but the war in Syria was changing that equation. The PKK was no longer dependent on "winning" in Turkey and now saw a future across the border in Rojava. Ankara was in danger of losing its leverage on the group. Salih Muslim, the chairman of the PYD at the time, visited Turkey several times and met with Sinirlioğlu and Turkish ambassador to Syria, Ömer Önhon. He claimed that they tried to convince him to work with the Islamist rebels, but since they did not recognize Kurdish rights, talks never went further. Meanwhile, the SDF was not only successful in the battlefield but was also earning a place in Western public opinion. ISIS was across the news on a daily basis in the West, and in this narrative, the SDF fashioned itself as the anti-ISIS: a radically progressive, secular, feminist group, and the biggest ethnic minority in the world without a state. This publicity reached a high with the 2014 siege of Kobanê, when ISIS sought to take over a town on the Syria–Turkey border.[56] The Western press was enamored with the Kurds, which only deepened Ankara's concerns.[57]

"The PKK chose its war," a retired military officer, who had spent his professional life fighting the PKK, told me at the time, "and it is winning." The PKK was pivoting away from Turkey, focusing on the prospect of a more permanent territorial presence in Syria. Its challenge was now to alleviate Ankara's concerns. The founder and leading theorist of the PKK, Abdullah Öcalan, was in prison since 1999, where he was said to read widely, including the theories of the anarchist Murray Bookchin. From his prison cell, he denounced the top-down, Marxist-Leninist ideas of his youth, arguing that states were inherently repressive, and that the future for Kurds lay in a confederal structure. The PKK's declared aim was no longer independent statehood, but self-government, be it within other states or on its own.[58] Being the left-Kurdish movement's political arm, the HDP duly campaigned for local government within Turkey's constitution. The Rojava cantons in Syria were based on a system of "democratic confederalism." They were open to talks with Damascus as long as Kurdish rights were guaranteed, presumably through the continuation of its governance structure.

To Turkey's security establishment, the PKK's anarchism, confederalism, feminism, and peace talks with Damascus all looked like window dressing intended for a gullible Western public. National struggle and statehood were the only ways to unify and consolidate political power. Ankara's decision-makers had no doubt that the PKK thought along similar lines and was trying to dress up its plans in progressive language to woo Westerners and calm regional powers. Its aim was nothing less than an expansionist Kurdish state, and the Syrian Civil War had opened up a power vacuum for just such an arrangement. Bureaucrats and academics in Ankara believed that Rojava aimed to grow into an unbroken land bridge from northern Iraq, across northern Syria, to the Mediterranean. This would mean that the PKK was able to extract oil from fields in northern Iraq and Syria, transport it to the port of Latakia, and ship it to global markets. Later dubbed the "terror corridor," this was feared to literally put a perennially stateless and landlocked people onto the map (Figure 3). Turkey would be "encircled" by a "terror state," a hostile, Western-backed entity akin to Israel.[59]

Leveraging political sympathy in the West, this left-Kurdish state could even, in time, make claims on Kurdish-majority territories in Turkey.

The growing geopolitical anxiety vindicated fears among the opponents of the peace process in Ankara, primarily made up of officers of Kemalist or pan-Turkic nationalistic backgrounds who had been sidelined by the Gülenists and the AK Party government. They thought that the Islamist government had at best been naive. It had cooked up its "peace process" in its think tanks and was trying to score points with Western capitals, and all while the enemy was gaining ground. For the past few years, soldiers who served in the South-Eastern regions were troubled to see the PKK collecting taxes and running parallel institutions within reach, while they were told to stand down. In one such account I heard at the time, a car had been stolen in Diyarbakır, and its GPS signal tracked to a known PKK location. The owners of the vehicle asked law enforcement to intervene, but were told that there was nothing to be done. Such stories circulated freely among the security bureaucracy, ramping up anxiety.

As the state apparatus was returning to a war footing, SETA was also undergoing serious changes. The institution was growing by leaps and bounds, having set up offices in Washington D.C., Istanbul, Cairo, and Brussels. The old guard at SETA Ankara, however, was no longer as influential as it once was. Most of them were Kurdish Islamists who built their careers on the liberal wave of the 2000s and the peace process that followed. They now looked too understanding of the PKK, and far too reluctant about the use of Turkish military power. As the peace process was coming to an end, a more hawkish group moved in to steer

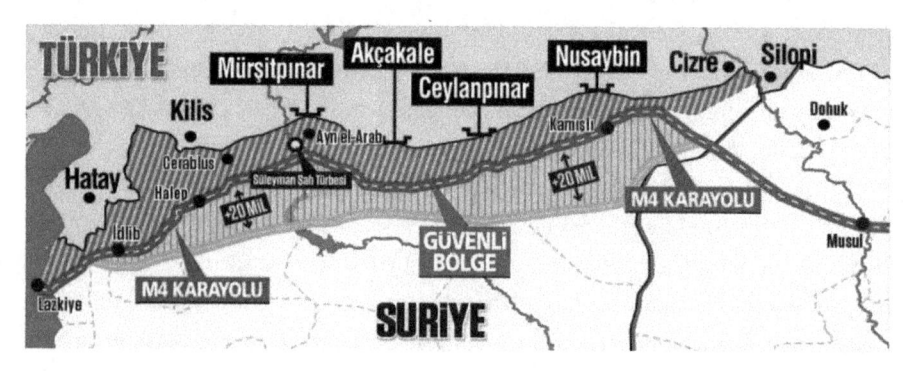

Figure 3 A popular map depicting how Turkey would establish a "safe zone" along the southern border, preventing a "Qandil-to-Mediterranean terror corridor" from emerging. It was shared by former AK Party parliamentarian Metin Külünk on Twitter. Metin Külünk, "Kandil Akdeniz terör koridoru ne demek? [What does the Qandil Mediterranean terror corridor mean?]," October 19, 2019, https://twitter.com/mkulunk/status/1181960104628965376.

SETA in a new direction. Burhanettin Duran, member of a powerful Islamist family from the Western Black Sea province of Sakarya, led the charge. He had written a PhD dissertation on the political thought of Necip Fazıl Kısakürek at Bilkent University in 2001, after which he took a job at Sakarya University. In 2009, he moved on to Şehir University in Istanbul, and in 2013, became head of SETA's Istanbul office. Duran and his associates were referred to as the "Sakarya clique" (Sakarya Ekibi) and were known for advocating a hard-nosed Turkish-Islamist view where liberal ideas like minority rights took a back seat. A longtime SETA staffer describes how in a meeting between Ankara and Istanbul staff at this time, she joked that the Ankara directors were almost all Kurdish. Afterward, one of her superiors in the Ankara office approached her in private and asked her to refrain from making such jokes. "These guys are sensitive to that issue. This is serious business," he said.[60] In 2014, Duran was appointed head of SETA, cementing the organization's shift into its post-liberal stance.

In his public writing and speaking, Duran always cut straight through the PKK's leftist rhetoric. He argued that the group, as well as the HDP, which the state saw as the civilian party representing it in parliament, wasn't holding up its end of the bargain in the peace process. Rather than approaching the Erdoğan government with civilizational language, they were painting it as a pernicious Islamist force supporting extremist militants in Syria. In his column in the daily newspaper *Sabah* on November 4, 2014, Duran wrote:

> The HDP line abandons the discourse of civilization that can make trust and coexistence possible, and chooses the language of ideological conflict. In the chaotic environment of the region, marginalizing ISIS and identifying it with Islamists provides it with useful material, both domestically and abroad. This is where we encounter the perception of secular Kurds as the new allies of the West and the nationalist secularists, against the AK Party. In this way, they want to bring together those who support the Gezi protests and Kobane demonstrations. ... The aim is to create a new power bloc.[61]

By "discourse of civilization," Duran was referring to Öcalan's 2013 letter that promised to stand with Ankara "under the banner of Islam" and engage in the "anti-imperialist" struggle against the West. As the Islamists understood the peace process, the PKK was to lay down arms, and instruct its civilian movement to support the AK Party in parliament. In exchange, they would earn purchase in a new, Turkish-led, Ottoman-inspired regional order. Instead, the HDP was ramping up its anti-Islamist rhetoric, most notably by lumping the AK Party together with the Islamic State. It wasn't opposing Western power in the Middle

East; it was allying itself with the United States in Syria. It was ramping up Kurdish nationalism rather than assimilating into a softer Turkish identity. Its aim was to create "a new governing block," presumably with the opposition, against the AK Party.

It was in this environment, that in the summer of 2015, Turkey was heading for elections. Erdoğan was now president and had installed Davutoğlu as the chairman of the AK Party and prime minister. Davutoğlu was therefore leading the AK Party ticket, but the star of the campaigning season was Selahattin Demirtaş, the leader of the left-Kurdish People's Democratic Party (HDP). His style resonated not only with the left-Kurdish base of the HDP but with many progressive Turks in the big cities as well. On June 6, the AK Party lost its parliamentary majority, and the HDP won an unprecedented 13 percent of the vote and became the third-biggest party in parliament, surpassing the pan-Turkic MHP.[62] The only reason the opposition couldn't form a government was because the Turkist nationalists of the MHP refused to sit down to negotiate with the HDP.

The fog of war hangs heavy over the period between June 2015 and November 2015, but that is when the peace process broke down, and Turkey changed its strategic direction. Leftist and Kurdish groups were the victims of some of the most deadly bombings in Turkey's history. A group providing aid to the PYD-held town of Kobane was bombed on July 20, suffering the death of thirty-three people.[63] The HDP blamed the government, arguing that it was in league with Islamist militias, including ISIS, across the border. On July 22, two police officers in the border town of Ceylanpınar were killed in their homes, seemingly in retaliation. Turkish media first claimed that the PKK took responsibility, and the government announced the beginning of hostilities against the PKK. The PKK claimed that they did not order the attack, and that the peace process should remain in place.[64] It's difficult to say for certain who ended the peace process, but the PKK's side appears to have been benefiting from it far more from it than the state was.[65] Regardless of what actually happened, the process was now over, and pent-up violence exploded onto the scene.

Turkish military forces now laid siege to a few cities in the southeast. The PKK had trained a force under the name of Patriotic Revolutionary Youth Movement (Yurtsever Devrimci Gençlik Hareketi, or YDG-H) in urban combat. The YDG-H was deeply entrenched in several cities, in what seemed like a preparation for the possible breakdown of the peace process. Their young fighters put up stiff resistance, using a network of tunnels, trenches, and explosive devices to inflict maximum damage on military forces. What became known as the "trench operations" went on throughout early 2016 and involved heavy urban fighting. Increasingly frustrated at the pace of progress, special forces began to flatten entire neighborhoods, yielding high casualties on all sides, including civilians.[66] Within a year, more than 1,700 people were killed in the fighting.[67]

The "trench operations" also marked a cultural shift. The daily news was no longer about "wise men" councils and diplomatic talks, it was about military operations against a dangerous enemy. The Kurdish issue was no longer a political problem; it was a security problem. Social media was awash with footage of masked soldiers in the ruins of Kurdish cities, making the gesture of the gray wolf, a Turkist symbol. They also scrawled slogans on the walls of the cities they occupied. "Be afraid, blood has touched the wolf's tooth" was a popular one.[68] "If you are a Turk, be proud. If you aren't, obey" was another.[69] An especially notorious bit of graffiti read "love is experienced in *Bodrum*," this being the Turkish word for basement, where some families were found to have burned alive by heavy weaponry, as well as a coastal city known for its tourist resorts. The graffitis were often signed PÖH (Police Special Operations) or JÖH (Gendarmerie Special Operations), both of which were linked to the Ministry of Interior, rather than the General Staff. In a way, the "armed bureaucracy" was reclaiming its place in the public consciousness after years of taking a back seat during the peace process.

On TV, a new kind of journalism emerged around the conflict. Reporters were donning flack jackets and taking viewers into carefully curated accounts of soldiers on the front lines. Perhaps the best known of these was Mete Yarar. Himself a graduate of the Turkish Military Academy, Yarar had served as an officer for sixteen years, then went into business as a consultant, most notably for Turkish contractors in Iraq.[70] Yarar now made a documentary series through the state broadcaster TRT called "Witness" (Şahit Olun), in which he was embedded with special forces carrying out the trench operations in the southeast.[71] He prayed with soldiers ahead of battles, cruised with them in armored vehicles, and took cover under enemy fire. Most importantly, however, Yarar conducted intimate interviews with officers in the field, who invariably expressed patriotism, a deep sense of responsibility for their comrades, and an unshakable belief in the justice of their cause. Many explicitly claimed that the PKK had been feeding liberals and international audiences a false narrative of human rights violations, and saw Yarar's program as a place where they could set the record straight. The program reassured viewers that their military forces were spiritually attuned to the country's values and deeply sensitive to the moral responsibility they carried.

Any evidence to the contrary simply had to be fabricated, part of the enemy's disinformation campaign.

Catharsis: The Coup Attempt

The Arab Spring, the Syrian Civil War, and the resumption of hostilities against the PKK were changing Turkey's strategic outlook. The liberal notion of leading by example or "de-securitizing" long-festering conflicts no longer seemed relevant. The Turkish state was once again resorting to military solutions to its problems. But it still wasn't quite confident enough to take that approach beyond its borders. That would change with an intimately domestic event.

Given Turkey's recent history, people generally know when and how military coups happen. They know to expect them on a Friday, deep into the night. That's when the military generally mobilizes to capture politicians, ministries, and media organs. Most people only become aware of the coup Saturday morning, by which time the generals are already in firm control. The military then uses the weekend to reassure markets and NATO allies that Turkey will honor its obligations. Business starts on Monday, under a state of emergency, when opposition can be squashed and a new order established. Most of the time, the threat of overwhelming force is enough, and no serious violence takes place, at least not outside prison compounds.

That is not what happened with the most recent coup attempt. On Friday afternoon around 16:00, July 15, 2016, MİT director Hakan Fidan was alerted that there might be a serious problem with the military's chain of command. He convened with the General Staff to take preventive measures, including the grounding of military flights.[72] It appears that the measures moved the putschists to spring into action earlier than they had planned. At around 20:30 that night, when the nation was still having dinner and watching TV, military forces mobilized to take over airports, news channels, government buildings, and—to many people's puzzlement—the bridges spanning the Bosporus straits.[73] It was difficult to believe that this was indeed a coup attempt until government representatives called into TV channels to denounce the events and call on citizens to resist. The near-universal assumption in the country was that the remaining Gülenist officers in the military had initiated the coup.

F-16s were flying at low altitude at high speeds, casting window-rattling sonic booms over Ankara and Istanbul. This was terrifying, since, to our civilian ears, every boom sounded like a bomb. President Erdoğan was on holiday in

Marmaris and made a brief press statement at midnight, calling for calm, but stiff public resistance against what he called an "uprising" in the military ranks. Turkey is not a country to be ruled from Pennsylvania," he said, referring to Fetullah Gülen's place of residence, and said that "the Mastermind," a term that typically refers to Western conspiratorial action, would also pay a heavy price for incentivizing this action.[74] Erdoğan was then moved to the airport, right before a military squad reached his place of residence. From his plane, he conducted a video call with a CNN Türk reporter 00:28, in which he called on citizens to resist the coup attempt.[75] Mosque speakers began to recite prayers on loop, intending to call on the citizenry to resist the putschists. Some of the most documented scenes unfolded on the Bosporus bridge, where Istanbul's sizable population of government supporters faced down armed soldiers. Tactically, however, the fate of the bridge was relatively inconsequential. Most of the critical fighting took place around key government buildings in Ankara, where police and special forces fought putschists from the military. The most famous shootout occurred in front of the Special Forces Command in Ankara, where one of the coup's key organizers, Brigadier General Semih Terzi, was to take command and amass military special forces from the South-Eastern and Western regions in Ankara that night. CCTV footage shows that as Terzi approached the building, a noncommissioned officer named Ömer Halisdemir walked up to him and shot Terzi in the head, and was himself immediately shot by Terzi's men. Analysts say that his act denied the putschists the ability to concentrate their firepower where it mattered most, averting more bloodshed in Ankara and likely shortening the coup attempt significantly.[76]

It is difficult to imagine the coup's success, simply because mere minutes into the event, it was clear that the coup plotters had no political basis. Unlike previous coups, the public did not think of the coup attempt as a struggle between domestic forces, but as a foreign attempt at capturing Turkish sovereignty. Across the country, supporters of the government went out on the streets, and many faced down the soldiers who were desperately trying to enforce a curfew. I didn't join the people on the street, but I couldn't sit at home either. I lived in the affluent Ankara neighborhood of Çankaya. Perched uphill from the rest of the city, Çankaya is home to the old presidential complex, foreign embassies, and upscale shopping districts. Stepping outside, I found the streets to be dead quiet. I could hear shouting and see flashes of gunfire a few kilometers downhill, near parliament. I wanted to get a closer look. I walked down narrow side alleys, thinking that military vehicles wouldn't fit through them. Only once did I stop by a main boulevard, and that's when I saw tanks roll up the hill in the direction of the old presidential compound. At Güven Hospital, close to parliament, I saw the lobby full of trauma victims, most of whom were probably civilians who resisted the soldiers and were shot. Approaching the walls of parliament, I heard an explosion nearby and instinctively dived for cover. I would later find out that F-16s were bombing parliament, and this felt and sounded very different from sonic booms. Watching armored personnel carriers with soldiers in them from afar, it occurred to me that I could be killed with impunity, so I made my way back home.

I was able to sleep for a few hours, and in the early morning I saw on my social media feed that the coup had been averted. A combination of special forces loyal to the government and public resistance had prevailed. I went back to parliament, and found myself in a crowd of men who had confronted putschist soldiers. They were decked out in Turkish flags, chanting slogans that praised Erdoğan and cursed Fetullah Gülen in equally creative and forceful language. I was used to election rallies and sports events, but this was unlike anything I had ever experienced before. These were the men who had faced down the putschists' bullets and tanks, and they were ecstatic at having come out on top. They didn't look like average Erdoğan voters and rally goers; they looked like a mob at the sharp end of right-wing politics. Around me was a forest of hand signs, either of the gray wolf (extending the index and little fingers, joining the thumb with the middle and ring fingers) indicating Turkist nationalism, or the sign of the shahada (extended index finger), indicating radical Islamist commitments. I saw calloused hands, old clothes, and a few people wearing the thawb, a robe traditionally worn by men in the Arabian peninsula. I overheard a man saying to the other, "the *reis* told us to stay at home during Gezi [the 2013 opposition protests] and we did. Now he told us to come out and look at what we have done!" They were exhilarated to discover a long-lost agency finally returned to them.

As the sun rose higher, we saw group after group of special forces walk into the building of the Ministry of Interior, right across the street. Chants of "may the hands seeking to harm the police be broken!" rose up as well as plenty of takbir ("Allahu Ekber" meaning "God is great"). In front of the Interior Ministry, a man standing in front of the crowd held up a framed photo of President Erdoğan. He shouted slogans and the crowd followed. This was a cathartic moment. The Islamist movement of my youth had a sheepish character to it. A common reference point was that in the 1960 coup, when the military tried and hanged Prime Minister Adnan Menderes the Islamists could only observe. In the heady days of the 1970s too, it wasn't the Islamists who clashed with the leftists on the streets; it was the Turkists. The Islamists were preoccupied with commerce and religion; they weren't cut out for street fights. No longer. Under Erdoğan, the "reis," the Islamist movement had changed character. It subsumed the Trukists and formed a new, united far-right front.

Driving around Ankara for the next few weeks was a reminder of how violent the coup attempt had been. The national police headquarters was shot up with helicopter turrets. The think tank I work for is located across the street from the presidential palace, and the sidewalks and walls around our building were shot up, and several parked cars had been destroyed. The media was awash with footage from the Bosporus bridge, where civilians had put up stern resistance. In total, 253 people resisting the coup and 104 people perpetrating it were killed, and thousands were injured.[77] For weeks afterward, government supporters took to the main squares across the country on "democracy watch," but these were more about celebrating the victory rather than averting another coup attempt. Many people at these gatherings called for the return of the death penalty and hung Fetullah Gülen in effigy. Main squares, roads, bridges, and barracks were renamed with references to July 15 or the "national will."

In retrospect, the coup attempt had a far-reaching impact on Turkey's strategic culture and subsequent foreign policy stance. There are two reasons for this.

The first is a matter of perception. Although the coup attempt on July 15 was, almost by definition, a domestic struggle, it was widely seen as a confrontation between Turkey and the West. Given the context of the past few years, it made sense to suspect that the attempt had been led by covert Gülenists, a suspicion that was soon backed by emerging evidence.[78] Fetullah Gülen himself lived in Pennsylvania, and it was widely assumed that he worked with US intelligence. Considering also the United States' long history of supporting military coups, its ongoing support for the PKK's offshoots in Syria, and tensions between Ankara and Washington, it was not difficult to point the finger at Washington. President Erdoğan did not endorse that idea explicitly, but hinted at it very strongly. His surrogates across the media, including government-sponsored channels, further entrenched the belief that the coup attempt had been an American plot. This enflamed the country's already broiling Competitive Occidentalism. The West was no longer curtailing Turkish sovereignty by smearing its democracy and supporting its separatists; it was now sending assassins after the president and trying to take it by force. This called for a higher level of combat readiness, not just among state institutions, but across society as a whole.

A new tactical culture began to develop among Turkey's Islamist elite. Since the "trench operations," some people were more interested in the tools that the armed forces used in these operations, including rifles, thermal cameras, personnel carriers, and drones. With the coup attempt, the idea of gun battles traveled from the southeastern regions to Turkey's major cities, and young right-wingers with the means began to own and carry guns. While accurate numbers are hard to come by, gun ownership increased by about 27 percent in 2017 alone, and incidents involving guns increased by 61 percent.[79] Gun laws were significantly relaxed in following years, and between 2018 and 2023, the state-issued carrying licenses increased by more than 100 percent. Shooting ranges, once a rare sight, now mushroomed, especially in neighborhoods with a heavy Islamist and nationalist presence. YouTube videos of fitness influencers going through military training, or tactical trainers offering practical advice, became very popular in these circles.[80] In the relatively liberal days of the 2000s, Turkey's public sphere had a European aversion to violence. After the coup attempt, the country switched to an American culture, where politics and deadly violence are much closer intertwined.[81] Young people in right-wing circles began to fantasize about future coup attempts and foreign invasions, and armed themselves in anticipation of such events.[82]

The second factor was institutional. As argued earlier, it was likely that Erdoğan hadn't launched a military operation in Syria because he believed that there were senior officers in the Turkish military who were undercover agents of the Gülen movement. With the coup attempt, those officers had exposed themselves, and the government embarked on a sweeping purge of the remaining ranks. This meant that the Turkish armed forces were thin on skills, but the government could now be sure that the military would always remain within the chain of command.[83] Going forward, the overwhelming public anger at the putschists would mean that military officers would not only remain loyal to the government, they would hesitate to express any dissent whatsoever.

On August 24, a month after the coup attempt, Turkey launched operation "Euphrates Shield," in which Turkish armed forces, aided by Syrian rebels, drove a wedge between the PYD cantons of Afrin and Manbij. For the first time in decades, Turkey was using its military to take and hold foreign territory. The "terror corridor" that the PKK's offshoots were forming along the border was broken up. In nearly every speech he gave, sometimes several times a day, President Erdoğan asserted a new forward-defense doctrine: Ankara would henceforth play the game of geopolitics aggressively, break out of its shell of self-doubt, and prove its mettle to the world. At the opening ceremony of the Keçiören metro station in Ankara, in January 2017, the president said:

We must destroy the threats to our country at their source. Turkey's security does not begin in Gaziantep, but Aleppo, not in Hatay, but in Idlib, not in Mersin, but in Cyprus, not in Kars, but in Nahçıvan. This we must know.[84]

In the following years, Turkey staged several more military operations in northern Syria, taking and holding chunks of territory at a time. The cities were linked up to Turkey's domestic system through the governorate of Gaziantep. Anything from electricity to healthcare, clean water to construction, was provided through Turkey's system. Turkey also broadened its military presence in northern Iraq, played a decisive role in the civil war in Libya, as well as in the war between Azerbaijan and Armenia. With these foreign adventures, the power and prestige of the "armed bureaucracy"—including MİT, the TSK, and police forces—increased.

The military reviewed its conscription-based model, downgrading the importance of mandatory military service and boosting the ranks of its professional service significantly. Turkey had long been cited to maintain the second-largest military force in NATO, but the measure was largely an expression of its outsized population of conscripts. The military was a fairly flat pyramid, containing a relatively small number of professional soldiers at the top and a vast number of conscripts at the bottom. It now undertook reforms to drastically reduce the length and service for mandatory conscripts (narrowing down the bottom of the pyramid) and increased the number of professional staff (boosting the middle and top).[85] It also made it easier to transition from mandatory service to professional ranks, thus, like in the United States, the United Kingdom, and other frequently war-fighting countries, presenting military service as a place for unemployed young men to acquire professional skills, or a step in one's "personal development plan".[86] In 2022, for the first time, the number of professional soldiers surpassed those under conscription.[87] The purges conducted in the aftermath of the coup attempt, followed by reforms that increased the circulation of personnel, meant that the political makeup of the military would quickly change. While the ranks were traditionally filled with young people from Kemalists and Turkist nationalist families (as well as Gülenists who pretended to be from them), the state now tried to make them more attractive to men and women from Islamist backgrounds..[88] The transformed military leadership was to be housed in a massive new headquarters built on 12,620 square km. The building complex was designed in a polygonal shape and dubbed "Turkey's Pentagon," a rather overt nod at the American model.[89]

For understandable reasons, MİT was not nearly as transparent about its recruitment, but judging by its open announcements, it also made an effort to attract people with a wider range of skills, including foreign language expertise and engineering graduates. The agency was conducting daring grab-and-bag operations of Gülenists in Central Asia, Africa, the Balkans, and the Middle East.[90] It upgraded its technological capabilities, conducting CIA-style kinetic operations involving assault teams and drone strikes. Speaking at the opening ceremony of the massive new MIT headquarters dubbed "the castle," Erdoğan seemed pleased with the progress the institution was making. He looked back at a long history of Turkish patriotic intelligence agents, from the time of Sultan Abdulhamid II, until the "Special Organization" (Teşkilat-ı Mahsusa) of the Young Turks, active across and beyond the Empire's continental scale. The Republican era, however, only received an indirect mention. "Although our intelligence agency was deliberately kept weak for a long time," Erdoğan said, "circumstances and needs required us to strengthen this institution again." Those circumstances originated south of the border:

> Especially since the first day of the Syria crisis, our organization took an active role and contributed greatly to the success of our cross-border operations. Likewise, it is now fulfilling its duties in Libya. I wholeheartedly believe that you [MİT's staff] will continue to defend the interests of our state and nation in every geography, regardless of borders, distances or obstacles.[91]

Turkey's defense capabilities had radically transformed since the start of the Syrian Civil War, almost a decade in the past. The country was emerging out of an era of historical weakness, and its ability to gather intelligence and project power was at the core of that transformation. In the cabinet reshuffle of 2023, Hakan Fidan, who had overseen MİT's revival, became foreign minister, while İbrahim Kalın became the country's spy chief. In January 2024, MİT's newly founded "Intelligence Academy" released a report on far-right political movements in Europe, signaling that the agency would not constrain itself to the conflicts of the Middle East, but take a role in the civilizational conflict taking shape far beyond Turkey's borders.[92]

The New Normal

Turkey's strategic culture has fundamentally changed since the 2000s. The country is now a strategy maker, not a taker. It has a political class with a revisionist world view, and increasingly, the ability to project power to realize some of its goals. The goals of Turkish foreign policy, however, aren't up for discussion. Strategy is now generated at the high echelons of the state, and are seldom discussed in the open. Think tanks have acquired a more technical bend, churning out "who's who" lists, maps, and dry summaries. The buildings are bigger, the websites are more professional, the events are higher in profile, but the work seems less important. It would also no longer occur to anyone in this sector to write a report about the "securitization" of the Turkish state and its deleterious effects on the country's democratic makeup. Securitization is now the point. The task of the "policy expert" is to defend or promote positions passed down from above. Opposition politicians at times express discomfort at Turkey's alliance politics, or widening military footprint, but this doesn't rise to the level of serious discussion. The governing elite can safely deride it as "Old" Turkey thinking and move on.

The new foreign policy elite can hardly be said to have substantial intellectual differences, such as a division between idealists and realists, commercial interests, and humanitarian advocates. There are disagreements within the establishment, but these are less about substance than they are about allegiance. By 2021, for example, SETA was once again divided into two groups: one being Duran's "Sakarya Group," the other being loyal to senior Erdoğan advisor Fahrettin Altun, referred to as the "Istanbul group." In June 2021, the Sakarya group was able to purge the Altun group, firing more than twenty people in a day and seizing control of the institution on their own.[93] One might expect bureaucratic infighting at these institutions to involve some policy preferences, but this was remarkably light on that front. The best one might say about the two groups was that they had slightly different styles and priorities.

High above such infighting, at the center of the presidential palace, or newly built American-style headquarters, are a few defense intellectuals who have gone through the turbulent 2010s to secure the top jobs. It wasn't always obvious who among them would succeed. In the early years of the AK Party, many thought that Davutoğlu was Turkey's strategic genius. After all, he had made his name arguing against the likes of Samuel Huntington, Francis Fukuyama, and Bernard Lewis. He was a politically influential academic, accumulating disciplines and drawing huge crowds. He was hailed as "Turkey's Kissinger" but Davutoğlu was too much of a romantic, and even in the middle of his career, far too eager a man of the people to merit the comparison.[94] The role of the American defense intellectual fully formed in the aftermath of the Second World War, and its purpose was to bypass the democratic system, not participate in it. Realists of

European descent with a tragic view of world history, like Robert Strausz-Hupé and the RAND Corporation's Hans Speier, believed that the American public and its representatives were too fickle to be consulted on international affairs.[95] Their purpose was to develop a direct relationship with the political class, bypassing the public and stabilizing foreign policy decision-making.

Davutoğlu didn't understand that he faced a trade-off: he could either be effective or he could be popular. Trying to be the everyman strategist, he failed at both. His protege, İbrahim Kalın, on the other hand, accepted a position within Erdoğan's political project. From his relatively obscure origins, Kalın beat a path through academia, think tanks, and embassy dinners, to the top of Turkey's defense establishment. Fidan too, endured years of work in the bowels of the state, dealing with proxy wars, purges and scloretic institutions. If there ever was such a thing, the "marketplace of ideas" never materialized in Turkey, but a strategy-making oligarchy of sorts did emerge from this period. Kalın and Fidan came to run it because they never aspired to political leadership themselves. They submitted to Erdoğan, whose vision of Competitive Occidentalism now suffused Turkish foreign policy.

4

Turkey's Relations with Russia and China

A Career of Geopolitical Proportions

In the summer of 1999, Turkey was governed by a coalition led by the septuagenarian social democrat Bülent Ecevit. The AK Party had not yet been founded. İbrahim Karagül, a thirty-year-old journalist from the Black Sea city of Trabzon, had recently become a columnist for Yeni Şafak, an Islamist newspaper with a sharp take on geopolitics. Like some young Islamists of the time, Karagül had spent some time in Malaysia, and thought about the Muslim world beyond Turkey. He was alarmed by how the Western world associated Islam with political violence. Muslims were already a defeated civilization, and if they didn't unite, Karagül feared that their defeat would only deepen.

Karagül's threat perceptions were still colored by the Cold War at this time. He believed that a great geopolitical struggle between the West and non-Western world would take place in the twenty-first century, and that the Islamic world had to tread carefully.[1] Like many Islamists who grew up during the Cold War, he saw the Russian and Chinese states as communist giants bent on snuffing out organic Islamic life. He worried that Kemalist Turkey represented a similar mechanism of state oppression, as well as a materialist agenda that would try to scrub religion from the country. In a column entitled "Turkey's new adventure" on March 8, 2000, Karagül observed that "on the one side, Ankara is solidifying its relations with America and Europe, and on the other, approaching powers such as Russia and China, which are trying to counterbalance the West." This, he thought, was very dangerous. Dark forces were pushing Turkey toward Asia "despite Turkey's fundamental values, despite the Muslim peoples' struggle for freedom. Just like Chechnya and East Turkistan [Xinjiang] we will soon see that other Muslim societies will be sacrificed. For example Kashmir."[2] In his column on April 15, he wrote of a "Chinese-Russian front against Islam." He was worried that Turkey was cutting secret arms deals with the Chinese and found it appalling that Ankara did not react to the massacre of Uyghur Muslims "even as much as the USA or the Germans."[3] Karagül was probably thinking of Foreign Minister İsmail Cem's (1997–2002), and how he was exploring closer relations with China:

> Security-focused relations between Ankara and Beijing are seriously strengthening. Ankara is quickly approaching a choice between the West and Russia-China. If pressure from the U.S. and E.U. increase, Turkey could find itself in a state in which it is exposed to the mercy of Russia and China. Then we will live in a Turkey in which nobody will have the courage to voice the rights of democracy, human rights, and freedoms, nor religious and political rights.[4]

This kind of opinion would have been very common among Islamists at the time. In 1997, they had experienced what was called the "post-modern coup" or the "February 28 Process," in which the military threatened a coup, and thereby ousted the Islamist prime minister Necmettin Erbakan, initiating a process in which many citizens of overtly Islamist identity, such as people wearing headscarves or going to prayers during daytime, were forced out of public jobs and institutional affiliations.[5] European countries condemned the military for its undemocratic conduct, and Islamists largely protested on liberal, constitutional grounds. The experience reinforced among Islamist elite a perception of Europe as a protective force between them and state oppression. If Turkey's secular rulers grew tired of Western finger-wagging, Karagül feared, then Russia and China could pose as attractive alternatives.

As much as Karagül was alarmed by Russia and China, however, he also had an intuitive understanding of their nationalistic worldviews. In a column published three days after Putin's election on March 26, 2000, he wrote that "Putin has two goals in foreign policy: to develop a stance against U.S. world hegemony and to divide the U.S. and Europe" and "as Putin faces off with the U.S., he plans on getting closer with Europe in general, and Germany in particular. He measures the opposition to U.S. hegemony in Europe very well."[6] Mainstream publications in the West had similar ideas, but hedged their predictions and were prepared to give Putin a chance to play his part as a liberal reformer and partner of the West.[7] Karagül didn't have to doubt Putin's intentions in competing with the West—he probably recognized *ressentiment* in his neighboring nationalists.

He did seem worried that Turkey was falling behind as revisionist powers surged on. Putin was making strategic moves to safeguard Russia's dominion over Muslims in the Caucasus and Central Asia, which barely seemed to register with the geopolitically illiterate Ecevit government. Ankara's negligence,

Karagül feared, would even weaken American support for the Baku-Tbilisi-Ceyhan pipeline, and Washington would look for other partners to work with. All this was in no small part due to the activities of an unnamed "Russian lobby in Ankara," by which Karagül would have been referring to leftists.[8] This instinctive, yet loose, attachment to the transatlantic alliance was typical of Cold War Islamism.

As much as it was important for Turkey to have strong ties to Western liberals, Karagül also thought that they were also far more dangerous than they let on. The Western club of nations, with UN resolutions on one hand, and American military might on the other, had opened an era of military interventions. From Kosovo to East Timor, no national border was going to stop them as they expanded "the system."[9] This was part of the engine of globalization, which was twisting Muslim minds out of shape. In a piece entitled "Globalization Is Going to Destroy Us" Karagül wrote that "just as it did with the industrial revolution, so the Islamic world has entered the globalization and information revolution in defeat." He relayed how at the ministerial meeting of the Organization of Islamic Cooperation (OIC) in Kuala Lumpur, Malaysian prime minister Mahatir Muhammed made crucial points with "lessons for us all." He quoted Mahatir saying, "Muslims aren't the enemies of the West, but the West is being an enemy to Islam. It is destroying the values of Muslims. If we don't unite, globalization is going to turn us into banana republics" and "if they [the West] wanted to, they could wipe all of the Muslims from the surface of the Earth." Karagül agreed. The Islamic world was "not prepared to face the information age"[10] and defend itself against globalization. Muslims had to "question the repressive governments" ruling over them and form their own geopolitical unit. Only then could they intervene in the "global war" that sought to divide the spoils of their soil.[11] Karagül was fixated on Asia, rather than the Middle East or Africa, as the theater for this great struggle.

Fast-forward to 2018. The AK Party had been in power for nearly two decades, starting on a liberal and fairly pro-Western tone, and heading into a more centralized model of strongman rule. Geopolitically, it was adopting a tougher posture, with its military and economic footprint widening across the globe. Karagül's career had flourished in these years. He was now editor-in-chief of *Yeni Şafak* and a frequent flier on the presidential jet, posting selfies from different world capitals every other week. His writing, however, hadn't benefited from the success. He had become repetitive and was derided for his bombastic geopolitical statements. His shrill invectives against the opposition as "fifth columnists" of Turkey's enemies in the West were becoming a little more ridiculous than they were ominous.[12]

Karagül's threat perceptions had changed significantly from East to West in the intervening years. In a column on July 30, 2018, he sought to take stock of his career as a geopolitical analyst.[13] The defining event of the past decades, he wrote, was "fascism that has been rising on both sides of the Atlantic," by which he meant the United States and Europe. These powers, he wrote, sought to suppress Turkey's revival as a great power:

> Today, all of the threats to our country are from the West. The security threats, economic threats, technology embargoes, the covert attacks via terrorist groups, overt attacks like the July 15 coup attempt, come from the West, where they see our country's power accumulation as a threat to themselves.

Saying this, Karagül argued, did not mean that he was "anti-American," which he thought was an intentionally shallow accusation. His was no "blind ideological obsession." He never made things personal, and he never wrote out of resentment (kibir). He was simply making objective assessments, and time had proven him right. To be fair, young Karagül's concerns about the destructive consequences of liberal interventionism have been shared by reams of highly reputable literature, especially as it relates to the US-led invasions of Iraq and Afghanistan in the aftermath of September 11, 2001.

In Turkey, however, Western influence had long been something that came between the state and society. The EU always wagged its finger on issues relating to human rights and press freedom. Young Karagül had welcomed this when the Islamists were part of civil society, but when they ascended to become the governing class, he came to see this pressure as an intervention in Turkey's sovereignty. It was true, of course, that by the late 2010s, Western countries supported entities Turkey considered to be terrorists, put formal and informal embargoes on the Turkish defense sector, and funded opposition-leaning journalism in Turkey. From Karagül's perspective, these things were not manifestations of Western liberal commitments, nor a relationship unraveling at both ends, but unprovoked attempts at preventing Turkey's return to greatness.

Karagül's views of the Asian powers had changed even more radically. He no longer saw Russia and China as soul-crushing, materialist behemoths, but wholesome nations aligned against a mechanistic and hegemonic Western block. Their oppression of Muslims and Turkic peoples was now either a lie or something that had to be tolerated for the time being. Whenever, in recent years, the national discussion veered to the mass-incarceration of Uyghur

Muslims (which, by any objective measure, was worse than twenty years ago) or Russia's invasion of its neighbors (including Crimea, home to the Turkic Crimean Tatar people), Karagül simply wrote columns insisting that these issues were distractions. The West wasn't just the main threat, but "all of the threat" to Turkey.[14] The mission of a New Turkey required geopolitical focus, even when it was painful.

It was telling that the title of his self-reflective column was "Full Partnership with Shanghai and BRICS: Why Are All the Threats from the West? Turkey Is Not a Country, It Is Geography" (his titles became more verbose over the decades). Karagül now believed that Turkey had to "join the accumulation of power in the remaining [non-Western] part of the world," and that to this end, "Turkey must become a full partner to Shanghai [Cooperation Council] and BRICS." Anyone who opposed this was "using the sentences of the West, wanting to contain Turkey in their name, and generally follow secret agendas." The BRICS and Shanghai respected Turkey; they understood that "Turkey is not limited to Turkey, it is a geography," by which Karagül roughly meant that Turkey speaks on behalf of Muslims, Turkic peoples, and, in a broader sense, the downtrodden across the world. Turkey was not a mere country; it was an idea.[15] The West sought to deny Turkey that grand ambition, but the Eurasian powers, which were now civilization-states themselves, understood the need for an expansive Turkey.

Why, one may ask, should observers take Karagül's views seriously? Surely he exaggerates, or, more fitting perhaps, is himself an exaggeration. But that is the point. Just as a painting can be more faithful to reality than a photo, Karagül is a more faithful representation of Turkey's new geopolitical outlook than a thousand official statements could be. He doesn't bother with the facts and the mundane limitations that policymakers have to deal with, but he is synced into an emotional wavelength that drives relations in the long term. Turkey's new regime does indeed seek to connect to Eurasian powers through a shared revisionism. Taking a closer look at Turkey's relations with Russia and China, we will see that this can be the basis for a robust bilateral relationship but isn't quite enough to create deeper ties.

Turkey–Russia: Hot Steel Quenched in Water

Conventional geopolitical thinking in the West has a very specific model for relations between Turkey and Russia. It claims that Turkey has historically been vulnerable to Russian encroachment and hence needs Western support. That is why, during their long decline, the Ottomans looked for allies in Europe. The most memorable example of this was the 1853–6 Crimean War, when France and Britain propped up the Ottomans against the Russian Empire. In the Cold War, Republican Turkey feared Russian designs on its territories and sought the protection of the United States, joining NATO and hosting American military bases. Looked at it this way, the fear of Russian expansionism appears to be the basis for Turkey's Western orientation. That is why, no matter how "difficult" Turkish leaders get, Washington and Brussels can take comfort in knowing that they have nowhere else to go. Turco-Russian enmity is baked into the very fabric of Eurasia and can be relied upon as firmly as the law of gravity.

Events in the last twenty years have tested this line of thinking. In 2008, Russia invaded Georgia, and in 2014, started to edge its way into Ukraine, and in 2015, got involved in the Syrian Civil War. The government of Vladimir Putin has made no secret of its goal of re-establishing a Russian sphere of influence. As one might expect, Turkey did not appear pleased, most notably opposing Russia's annexation of Crimea, the home of the Tatar people, a Turkic minority. Yet Ankara's relations with Moscow also improved rapidly in this time frame. Trade and investment were increasing, and the emerging elite in the two countries—figures like Karagül—were singing each other's praises. The two countries continued to have significant disagreements, but unlike their crisis-prone relations with Western capitals, their relations with each other were remarkably robust. Turkey and Russia could be on opposite sides of a proxy war, yet come together and negotiate their differences.

The mainstream view in the transatlantic sphere was that this was an anomaly. As Russia continued to be more assertive, "adults in the room" would take over in Ankara, and Turkey's Western alignment (and rivalry with Russia) would snap back into place. There were hints of this kind of thinking across Western discourse on Turkey, including the very top. During a long interview with *The New York Times* ahead of the 2020 elections, for example, then-aspiring Democratic nominee Joe Biden was arguing that as president, he would get tougher on Erdoğan. "Because at the end of the day," he said, "Turkey doesn't want to have to rely on Russia. They've had a bite out of that apple a long time ago."[16] Upon Biden's election as president, some commentators argued that geopolitical forces were aligned to cause a new "recalibration" in Turkish foreign policy.[17] Now that the United States and Europe were tightening up the Western alliance, Turkey would rely more heavily on Western institutions. The "bromance" between Presidents Erdoğan and Putin would give way to the "frenemy" status between the countries.[18] The Russia–Turkey relationship, after all, was not shaped by "ideological convictions" but by economic necessity. Once Russian revisionism became more pronounced, Turkey would once again assume a more Atlanticist position.[19] This failed to materialize in the first years of the Biden presidency, but when Russia invaded Ukraine in February 2022, defenders of the prodigal son argument doubled down. Surely Turkey would be horrified by blatant Russian aggression and become a more ardent NATO ally. Footage of Turkish-made Bayraktar TB2 drones pounding Russian armor seemed self-explanatory.[20]

I call this the *prodigal son fallacy*.[21] It is predicated on the belief that "soft" considerations such as worldview don't play a significant role in determining Turkey's geopolitical orientation. Eventually, it posits, Turkey will be deterred by Russian expansionism and return—hat in hand—to the NATO fold.

There are two problems with this approach. First, it is based on a faulty reading of Turkey's Cold War history. Second, it gives so much weight to geographical and economic factors that it discounts values and strategic culture. Once we examine these factors more closely, an alternative view of Turkish-Russian relations will arise.

Let us look at the history first. Ottoman decline was indeed marked by a number of catastrophic defeats against the Russians in the late eighteenth and nineteenth centuries. The prodigal son narrative claims that this dynamic continued in the twentieth century, with Republican Turkey's accession to NATO. In recent years, however, a small group of Cold War historians reading Turkish, Soviet, and American archives have been making a different argument. In a landmark 2020 paper on the subject, historians Samuel J. Hirst and Onur İşçi have argued that the norm in Turkey–Russ relations from the 1920s on has not been hostility, but cooperation.[22] The elites in both countries were in a struggle to "catch up" with the European powers, and this common feeling improved their relationship considerably, despite the inherent tensions of the Cold War.

Turkish–Soviet cooperation goes back to the founding months of the Republic of Turkey. As Mustafa Kemal's forces were fighting Western occupiers in Anatolia, they signed a treaty with the Bolsheviks declaring "solidarity in the struggle against imperialism." The Soviets sent much-needed aid to Anatolia and maintained strong relations with Ankara in the early years of the Republic.[23] In the 1930s, Turkish statesmen found that the Europeans offered trade terms that would turn the country into an "agricultural colony," while the Soviets offered an arrangement that would allow for Turkey's industrial development.[24] Only in the period between 1939 and 1957 did Turkey's relations with the Soviets turn antagonistic. It started with the Nazi–Soviet pact in 1939, which alarmed Ankara, as it signaled renewed Russian territorial expansion, especially regarding the Straits. After the Second World War, the Soviets not only continued putting pressure on Turkey's rights over the Straits, but also claimed much of eastern Anatolia. It was during this time that Turkish diplomats steered the country westward in postwar summits; Turkey sent troops to the Korean War, and joined NATO in 1952. Turkey also hosted US bases and received development aid under the Marshall Plan.[25]

Already in the late 1950s, however, relations with the United States began to sour. The Americans were frustrated with Ankara's statism and cooled relations with the populist government of Adnan Menderes. At the same time, Nikita Khrushchev replaced Joseph Stalin as leader of the Soviet Union and adopted a softer approach to Turkey. In the following decades, Turkey remained within the Western block but never quite felt at home in it. Successive governments on the left and right were fixated on the country's underdevelopment vis-à-vis the West, and found that the Soviets, who harbored similar feelings, were willing partners in the game of catch-up. Moscow supported the development of Turkey's state-led heavy industry, helping to build some of the country's key factories, such as a glass factory in Çayırova and an aluminum factory in Seydişehir.[26] When Turkey launched its 1974 military intervention in Cyprus, the US Congress favored the Greek position, imposing an arms embargo on Turkey. The Soviets struck a more balanced tone, but stopped short of weighing in on what could have been an intra-NATO conflict. Turkey's rulers were more pro-American in the aftermath of the 1960 and 1980 coups, but usually flirted with the Soviets when popular politicians were at the helm. In short, Turkey was not as solidly anti-Russian and pro-American as transatlantic circles today tend to think. Turkey joined NATO in the 1939–57 time window, when it was most pro-Western, but for the remainder of the Cold War, Ankara maintained fairly productive relations with the Soviets.

This brings us to the second failing of the *prodigal son fallacy*, namely, the claim that Turkey's geopolitical orientation between Russia and the West is dominated by economic and regional security considerations, rather than the worldview of its political elite. This claim is inherently more difficult to dispute. We can hardly interview president Erdoğan on the factors behind his decisions. What we can do, however, is to observe the relations between the two countries over the past few years and try to think critically about the factors that direct them.

The political trajectories of Turkey and Russia during this quarter-century present significant parallels, especially in their relations with the West. In the early 2000s, Putin and Erdoğan had been newly elected as leaders of their countries. They had both inherited economies in the process of liberalization, and continued on that path.[27] They also styled themselves as center-right democrats, promising to bring stability to a turbulent political climate, which bought them favor in Western capitals. A few years into their tenures, however, both started having significant problems with the West. Turkey's EU accession process—the subject of great excitement in the early 2000s—ran aground in the later parts of the decade. Erdoğan now made bitter remarks, and disagreements about Cyprus soon clogged up the entire process. Russia, meanwhile, was dismayed at NATO enlargement. Since Poland and the Czech Republic's accession in 1999, the group of Central and Eastern European countries, including Bulgaria, Estonia, Latvia, Lithuania, Romania, Slovakia, and Slovenia, also joined shortly before the 2004 Istanbul summit. The alliance was now deep into what Russia considered its traditional sphere of influence. At the Munich Security Conference in 2007, Putin accused the United States of creating a world in which "there is one master, one sovereign."[28] In the following years, Russia began to invade its neighbors and expand its military footprint in the Middle East and Africa.

The debates on Western policy on both cases provide eerie similarities. On Turkey's EU accession, some observers emphasize Turkey's failure to meet the criteria of the acquis communautaire, the legal chapters countries need to fulfill in order to accede. Others argue that European prejudice was to blame, saying that the major center-right European leaders who took office at the time— especially Angela Merkel and Nicolas Sarkozy—were inherently opposed to its accession and sabotaged the process.[29] On Russia, hawks in Washington argued that NATO is an inherently defensive alliance, and that Russia was wrong to react to its enlargement in the way it did. Others argue that Western leaders should have taken Russia's objections more seriously and shown more restraint.

The EU, it seems, was too exclusive, while NATO was too expansionist. In both cases, the argument hinges not on the technical procedures involved but on perceptions. Turkey may or may not have had trouble with adhering to EU law, but what triggered its reaction was that its leadership *felt* that the Europeans were unwilling to deal with it because of its inherent characteristics. Beyond the legalistic arguments, Turks felt that Europeans thought of them as "too big, too poor, and too Muslim," as a European official once put it.[30] Similarly in Russia's disputes with the West, the issue wasn't whether NATO actually posed a threat to Moscow's interests, but whether the Russian leadership *felt* that it posed a threat to it. To liberal observers, the EU's selectiveness and NATO's expansion were signs that the thicket of rules and regulations were working as they should. If Turkey and Russia were upset by the results, that too was also part of the system's inevitable march toward progress. As these countries interacted with the institutions provided (the EU Council or the NATO-Russia Council), they would learn to moderate their feelings and reform their actions to the standard set by the West.[31] Leaders in Turkey and Russia, of course, saw it differently. Behind the institutional mechanisms, they felt the presence of a political will that sought to keep them down.

It would be wrong to suggest that Turkey and Russia turned to regimes of Competitive Occidentalism because they were snubbed by the West. These processes are the results of long historical patterns in both countries. It does, however, seem that the experiences activated reservoirs of *ressentiment* reaching deep into the political cultures of both countries, which manifested itself in revisionist politics. Going through the experience around the same time also improved the chemistry between presidents Putin and Erdoğan, elevating a historically cordial relationship to friendly levels.[32] Similar to the Cold War, the relationship between Turkey and Russia in the 2010s is one of economic cooperation, punctuated by political differences. Different from the Cold War, however, Turkey and Russia explicitly frame their relationship in terms of their opposition to the Western-led order.

What is remarkable about the Russia–Turkey relationship during this time wasn't that there were no problems, but that the two regimes could overcome their numerous problems very quickly. Like so much else in Turkey's recent foreign policy, this dynamic started with the Syrian Civil War. In the lead-up to the war, Russia was expanding into territories that Turkey had historical connections with. It invaded Georgia in 2008, eastern Ukraine (the Crimea and Donbas) in 2014, and began propping up the Assad regime in the same year. Turkey was fairly silent on the first, mildly censorious on the second, and almost confrontational on the third. In the early years of the Syrian Civil War, Turkey's intent was to support the Islamist rebels and topple the Assad regime. Russia rescued the Syrian regime in late 2015, embarking on a highly destructive bombing campaign of rebel positions. Islamist political circles were outraged that the rebels they supported, as well as women and children, were getting bombarded mercilessly by a faraway power.[33] Speaking to a TV station late that year, Erdoğan channeled some of this feeling, while trying to reach out to Moscow:

I would like to remind him [Putin] of my sadness concerning this matter. As two friendly countries, I will ask him to reconsider the step they took. Because we are the ones who suffer, who have problems in the region. Russia does not have a border with Syria. Why is Russia so involved in this business?[34]

As Russian targets were close to the Turkish border, their jets were frequently violating Turkish airspace. According to then–prime minister Davutoğlu, Turkey warned the Russian side several times, then changed its rules of engagement, authorizing its patrolling jets to shoot down aircraft that violated the border. Turkey then communicated this to the Russians on multiple levels, thinking that it would deter further violations. On November 24, 2015, a Russian Su-24 plane on a bombing run violated Turkish airspace for 17 seconds and was shot down by a Turkish F-16 on patrol.[35] This was the first time a NATO jet had shot down a Russian plane since the early months of the Korean War in 1952.[36] Putin called this a "stab in the back," presumably implying that Erdoğan had violated a revisionist understanding between the presidents. Russia placed sanctions targeting Turkish exports and tourism – two important foreign currency channels for the country – but not the more vital energy sector.[37] Turkey insisted that it was within its rights, while NATO and the UN called for de-escalation.[38]

For a few months, commentators in Washington breathed a sigh of relief, as it seemed that Turkey was finally distancing itself from Russia.[39] During an event with Balkan military chiefs in May 2016, Erdoğan said, "I told the NATO Secretary General 'you aren't in the Black Sea, that's why the Black Sea has turned into a Russian lake.'"[40] This sounded like Erdoğan wanted a bigger NATO presence in the Black Sea, which was well received in Atlanticist circles. But it did not last. Merely a month after those remarks, on June 27, Erdoğan sent Putin a letter expressing regret over the Su-24 shoot down, and relations began to thaw.[41] Two weeks later, Erdoğan and his government survived the July 15 coup attempt, for which both leaders held the United States responsible. It now seemed that Erdoğan's letter to Putin hadn't gone out a moment too soon. According to Turkish state news agencies, Putin called Erdoğan a day after the coup attempt and was the first world leader to express his support.[42]

While this may have been true, Russia was actually very late to make a public statement supporting the Erdoğan government on the night of the coup. The United States, major European nations, and the European Council made such statements between midnight and roughly 3:00 am, when much of the critical fighting was still taking place, President Erdoğan's plane was still airborne, and it was unclear what the outcome of the coup attempt would be. Russia merely expressed "deep concern" at the events until it made a more definitive statement after 9:20 am that morning, when the coup had been averted.[43] Putin then called Erdoğan on the next day, on July 17, while Obama called on July 19. Yet the Erdoğan palace built a narrative in which the Western world had waited for the coup to succeed, while the non-Western world, like Iran, Qatar, China, but most of all Russia, had expressed support for Turkey in its hour of need.[44] Erdoğan's first post-coup trip was to Moscow on August 9, when he said, "FETÖ and the forces behind it," by which he meant the United States, "are conspiring against Turkey-Russia relations."[45]

The two countries would now pick up where they left off, deepening trade and integrating their two economies. In Turkey's wider post-coup political environment, a stridently pro-Russian perspective began to take hold among the country's governing elite. American and European observers largely expressed doubt that the Gülenists were behind the coup, which in Turkish thinking, only served to highlight the complicity of their countries. The Russians, meanwhile, enjoyed an "I told you so" moment. State news broadcasters in Turkey and Russia ran stories of how Russia had banned Gülenist schools as far back as the early 2000s, citing their "totalitarian ideology" and links to the US government.[46] There were glowing news reports claiming that "the Russians also didn't sleep that night" and that a crisis desk at the Kremlin was ready to come to Ankara's aid should it fall to the will of American-backed putschists.[47]

The coup attempt supercharged the Turkish policy elite's deep-seated fears of the West. They believed that Washington would never truly respect Turkish sovereignty, while Moscow was a long-estranged friend and a good neighbor. There was also a hint of shame in Turkey regarding the Su-24 shoot down. Rumors resurfaced on national media that the pilot who had shot the Su-24 was a covert Gülenist.[48] It looked like Turkey had been ungrateful, even insolent, thinking that it could use its NATO membership as a club against Moscow when it was convenient. During his many meetings with Putin in these months, Erdoğan was unusually eager to express his thanks.[49] In November, Russian geopolitical strategist Alexander Dugin visited Turkey's parliament, attending the AK Party's weekly group meeting. When asked how he felt about Turkey's NATO membership, Dugin said, "that is your decision. You are an independent nation-state. You know who was among the people who bombed the Grand National Assembly. It definitely wasn't Russia."[50] For a while, Turkey actually slipped into the role of the prodigal son, but the father of the parable wasn't the United States, it was Russia.

Still, Turkey remained locked into Western structures. Short of an economy-destroying shift of geopolitical axis, Ankara couldn't act on the feelings unleashed by the coup attempt. Accusations against the United States remained on the level of angry insinuations, while the newfound partnership with Russia felt warm, but lacked policy substance. Ankara and Moscow needed something to solidify their bond. Turkey had been in need of a high-end air-defense system for at least a decade at this point and was in talks with several countries, including the United States, Russia, China, and a French–Italian joint venture. These failed, Turkish sources said, due to foreign refusals to meet Turkey's persistent demands for co-production and technology transfers.[51] In 2017, Turkey reconsidered Russia's S-400 air-defense system, and Ankara eventually loosened its expectations on technology transfers and signed a contract with the Russians.[52] The United States had warned Turkey against this on technical grounds: Turkey was part of the consortium to produce the F-35, the American-led fifth-generation stealth fighter jet since 1999.[53] The S-400 was designed to shoot down the F-35. American officials argued that the F-35 could not be "co-located" with the S-400, since this would allow the Russian system to collect information about the NATO plane.[54] If Turkey persisted in the purchase of the S-400, it would risk its place in the F-35 program. Turkish officials insisted that the two systems would not be in contact, and that American objections were unwarranted.

On July 12, 2019, three days before the second anniversary of the coup attempt, the first shipment of the S-400 system arrived in Turkey. The Russian plane carrying the equipment landed on Murted (formerly Akıncı) Airfield, which happens to have been the base where putschist planes took off on the night of the coup.[55] The delivery triggered the Countering America's Adversaries Through Sanctions Act (CAATSA), kicking Turkey out of the F-35 program and placing restrictions on its ability to purchase American weapons.[56] There was a flurry of speculation about the future of Turkey–US ties. To clear the air, Erdoğan invited a group of journalists on July 14, one day before the third anniversary of the coup attempt. He received them at the Vahdettin Pavilion, a Bosporus mansion named after the last Ottoman Sultan. At the event, Erdoğan said that Turkey was making momentous changes to its foreign policy and called the S-400 purchase "the most important agreement in our country's history."[57] He expected these journalists to support a narrative he was trying to build with the public across political lines:

> Despite the political and military pacts we have with the Western alliance, the fact is that we face the greatest threats from them. It is political, it is economic, it

is cultural, it is in all respects . . . we have been the forward garrison against the Soviet Union during the Cold War period, but it hasn't been enough to protect us from these threats.[58]

Note the causal assumptions beneath the argument. In the liberal transatlantic narrative, Russia posed a threat to Turkey, which is why Turkey sought alliances with the West. In the narrative of the Turkish far right, which was now in control, the West posed the main threat to Turkey, and Turkey neutralized that threat by turning itself into a Western "forward garrison" against Russia.[59] Erdoğan was saying that this model was now breaking down. Turkey was deeply integrated into Western markets and, through NATO, the West's security infrastructure. Yet these very ties forced the country into compromising its sovereignty in ways that were unacceptable. Erdoğan's historic task was to extricate Turkey from its dependencies on the West while also maintaining economic growth and security. The S-400 purchase was critical to Turkey's liberation, not because it deepened Turkey's partnership with Russia, but because it was a step toward gradually extricating the country from its enthrallment to the West. Russia was not a replacement to the United States, but a model in its actions against American hegemony.

The chain of events that began with Turkey's downing of the Su-24 in 2015 and ended with the delivery of the S-400 in 2019 set the mood of Turkey–Russia relations in the following years. Future historians might conclude that this period comparable to the 1939–57, only in reverse. Just as in the early stages of the Cold War, Turkey felt an acute geopolitical threat from Russia, it now felt it from the United States. Yet the Turkey–Russia relationship in this new period did not aspire to replicate Western alliance and economic systems. These were still two large countries that define themselves through insatiable geopolitical ambition. Rivalry, even bitter clashes, were built into the understanding between them. The bonds forged in the 2015–19 period, however, meant that the relationship could overcome these with remarkable speed. As Erdoğan said during Putin's visit in 2018, "like hot steel quenched in water, our bilateral relationship has hardened and strengthened with every failed provocation."[60]

The term "provocation" came up often when Erdoğan spoke to Putin. It referred to third parties that got in between the otherwise harmonious relations between the countries. On December 19, 2016, for example, an off-duty Turkish police officer fatally shot Russian ambassador to Ankara, Andrey Karlov. This might have been grounds for a crisis at any other time, but it only brought the countries closer. Both sides blamed the Gülen network and, by extension,

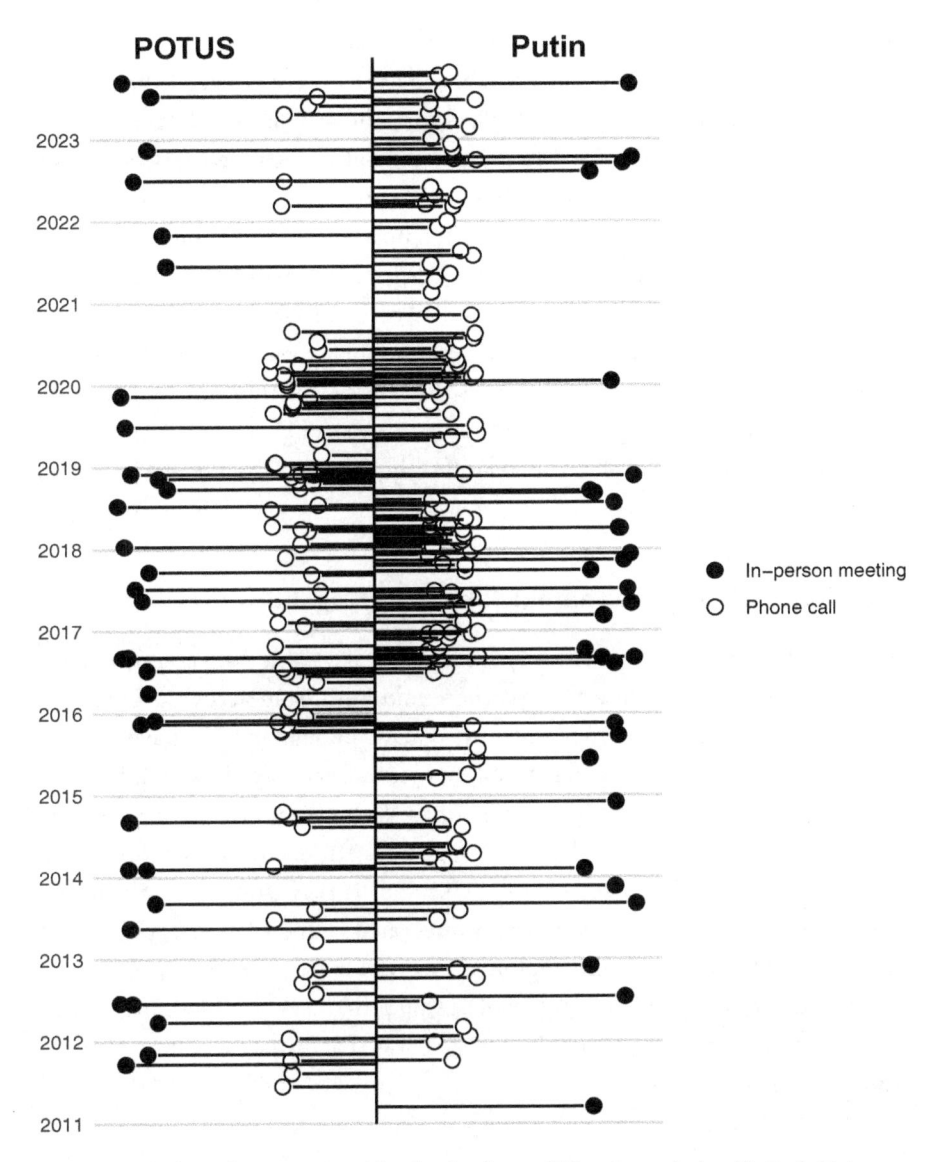

Figure 4 Erdoğan's contacts with the leaders of Russia and the United States, as reported in Anadolu Agency and other Turkish state news agencies.

the United States. In the Syrian Civil War, Erdoğan railed against American support for the YPG, the PKK's Syrian offshoot, but seldom spoke about the Russian support for Assad, or their relations with the PKK and its affiliates. On February 27, 2020, a Russian warplane bombed Turkish soldiers in Syria, killing at least thirty-four and wounding dozens more. Turkish authorities blamed the Assad regime, rather than Moscow. Turkey then embarked on a retaliatory bombing campaign.[61] The two countries also faced off in a bloody proxy war in Libya, with Russian mercenaries supporting the Libyan National Army (LNA), and Turkish-backed and internationally recognized Government of National Accord (GNA). In 2020, when the Russian-backed LNA was putting pressure on Tripoli, Turkey's armed drones destroyed Russian-made air-defense systems, putting the LNA on the back foot.[62] In the Caucasus, Turkey had long supported Azerbaijan's territorial claims over the Armenian-occupied and inhabited territories, while Russia maintained the status quo. This too changed in two Turkish-backed Azeri military operations, first in 2020, then in 2023, when Azeri forces reclaimed Nagorno-Karabakh. Despite their significant differences across these theaters of action, the relationship between presidents Erdoğan and Putin remained strong.

The biggest conflict to test this relationship, however, has been the war in Ukraine.

Case Study: Turkey–Ukraine Relations during the War

Turkey and Ukraine are in many ways compatible partners. Both countries have an interest in checking Russian expansion, and both want access to European markets and institutions. They are also distant enough not to have serious disagreements, yet close enough to enjoy cultural synergy. This could be the basis of a thriving partnership, but Ukraine's Westernization policy, as well as Russia's full-scale invasion of the country, has put Turkey in a difficult position. As Russia and the West faced off over Ukraine, Turkey sympathized with the former's revisionism, but was still deeply integrated with the latter. It couldn't fall neatly into either camp. As one diplomat involved in the relationship explained it to me, Turkey has pursued a policy of "being pro-Ukraine without being anti-Russia." Another way of saying this, perhaps, was that Turkey was "pro-Ukraine without being pro-Western."

In the following section, I will unpack this notion.

The Two Maidans

In 2013, Turkish and Ukrainian politics went through a similar, yet ultimately diverging, experiences. It just so happens that both took place in the countries' main squares, or as they are referred to in Ukrainian and Turkish, "maidans."

In May of 2013, protesters in Istanbul took to Taksim Square (Taksim Meydanı) to oppose the government's plans to demolish the adjacent Gezi Park and rebuild an Ottoman-era structure in its place. The issue turned into a lightning rod, especially for young people who were alarmed by Erdoğan's growing stature but also frustrated by the fecklessness of opposition politicians. In the weeks that followed, the protests grew into a nationwide movement of mostly progressive, left-leaning, and pro-European citizens. The Erdoğan government saw the Gezi movement as a Western-backed attempt to topple it and suppressed it with overwhelming force. It also imprisoned major civil society organizers, falsely accusing them of being behind some of the protests. The Erdoğan regime has since been unrepentant about its conduct in Gezi, making the events a major departure point between Turkey and European institutions, including the EU, the European Court of Human rights, and the Council of Europe.

A few months after Gezi, in November of 2013, two sides of Ukrainian politics also clashed on the country's main square. President Viktor Yanukovych was due to sign the European Union-Ukraine Association Agreement, which was designed to tighten Ukraine's political and economic relations with the block, but reversed the decision. Instead, Yanukovych announced that he would consider Ukraine's accession to the Eurasian Economic Union, an economic block dominated by Russia. A small group of young people gathered on Kyiv's "Independence Square" (Maidan Nezalezhnosti) to protest the decision. As in Turkey, the movement rapidly grew and broadened the scope of its demands, and just as in Turkey, the state responded with a heavy crackdown. The police began to use deadly force against the protesters, but they persisted and, by late February, succeeded in toppling the Yanukovych government. This set the basis of what is called the "Revolution of Dignity," resulting in the election of pro-Western politicians, the commencement of European reforms, and, eventually, the Russian invasion of Ukraine, and the country's deepening military cooperation with NATO allies.[63]

The outcomes of the two protests put Turkey and Ukraine on diverging paths. Turkey's new regime is built on the values of Competitive Occidentalism, while the present Ukrainian government has an aspirational attitude toward the West. Ukraine seeks to adopt Western political norms, join its multilateral institutions, and even accepts many of its values and lifestyles. Ukrainians seem to accept the idea that they are reliant on the West, and primarily the United States, in their war effort. They also do not seem averse to the idea of pooling sovereignty in Brussels. In a sense, Ukraine's geopolitical aims are more modest and, by post–Cold War standards, conventional than those of Turkey. This dissonance in values has a subtle, but definitive impact on the relations between the two countries.

A Note on Trade and Governance

On the surface, the Ukraine–Turkey relationship is light and full of possibilities. Traveling to Ukraine as a Turkish citizen before Russia's full-scale invasion was a thrilling experience. Most European countries put Turkish citizens through laborious and expensive visa processes, but entering Ukraine requires nothing more than a photo ID and a relatively cheap plane ticket. Once in the country, restaurants and hotels were affordable—also a rare luxury for those earning their living in the volatile Turkish lira. There were several Turkish websites tracking Ukrainian news and giving travel advice, as well as a thriving ecosystem of Ukrainian-Turkish social media influencers.[64] The relationship between the two countries remains unencumbered by a history of imperial rivalry or an overbearing colonial past. If anything, Turks are likely to bond with locals over Tatar food and their fate as peoples on the peripheries of Europe. This is as neighborly a relationship as Turkish citizens are able to find.

Economically, the two countries are often said to complement each other. Turkey has a relatively strong industrial base and a high appetite for risk. Ukraine has a strong agricultural base and highly skilled engineers. Ukrainians have long complained of shoddy road construction, a subject that the Erdoğan government has mastered since its early days. Construction giants like Enka, Limak, and Çalık Holding have therefore undertaken significant projects in Ukraine. An especially notable project was the Zaporizhzhia Bridge, a project that had been stalled since 2004 and was seen as a paradigmatic case of Ukrainian corruption. In 2020, the Zelenskyy government handed the project over to Turkey's Onur Group under what an anti-corruption NGO argued was a faulty process—but the results came in quick, and President Volodymyr Zelenskyy unveiled the bridge in January 2022.[65] Onur has taken on other high-profile projects in the country, including the repairs of Khreschatyk street in central Kyiv and the Kyiv–Borispol airport road project.[66] These substantiated the reputation Turkish firms have built for delivering big construction projects on time and at competitive costs.

Trade between the countries is growing but remains far below potential. Turkey exports machines and textiles, vehicle parts and chemicals, while importing mostly metals and agricultural products. In 2020, trade was fairly balanced and approaching the $5 billion mark. Turkish diplomats lament that Turkey has tried to negotiate an FTA with Ukraine for fifteen years and was only able to sign one just three weeks before Russia's full-scale invasion in February 2022, when President Erdoğan visited Kyiv.[67] Still, trade is unlikely to deepen soon. Ukraine joined Europe's Deep and Comprehensive Free Trade Area (DCFTA) in 2016, bringing it closer to the EU's single market, while Turkey's dysfunctional relationship with the EU has meant that it is stuck in the antiquated Customs Union agreement it signed with the EU in 1995.

Turkey tends to emphasize bilateral economic relations, and Turkish officials are frustrated at the slow pace at which these have developed. When asked about the problems they face, diplomats and businesspeople cite corruption on the Ukrainian side as a major impediment for progress. A 2018 report of the Foreign Economic Relations Board of Turkey (DEİK) also describes Ukraine as "one of the most difficult former USSR countries to do business in," which, it says, is due to the "political instability and the weakness of the legal infrastructure of economic activities."[68] It then goes on to list the various problems Turkish traders face in the country, like the inability to get tax refunds, obtaining payment from firms, problems obtaining work and residence visas, and security problems emanating from the conflict with Russia. Turkish officials and businessmen confirm the government's frustration with corruption, and more current reports continue to cite it as a problem.

This is odd. Western countries often highlight corruption as a problem in their partners, but Turkey is generally not too concerned with it. It prides itself on being a high-functioning trading nation with the ability to make inroads into some of the toughest markets in the world. The country's business community boasts of its growing presence in Africa, the Middle East, Central Asia, all of which are regions where corruption is fairly widespread. This is also why it is highly unusual for DEİK reports to even mention corruption, much less to detail its presence at length..[69] This may be due to the particular ways in which Ukraine is corrupt: it is decentralized in its corruption. Turkey is a highly centralized country, and its relations in emerging markets are usually built top-down. President Erdoğan usually travels to target countries with a large group of businessmen in tow, holds a leaders' summit, and signs a few big deals. Other business then flows down from the relationships he and his entourage build during those visits. Turkey therefore relies heavily on tight hierarchies to spread its influence across the map.

Ukraine, however, has been embracing a decentralized structure since the mid-2010s. Unlike in Turkey, the Ukrainian economy is fairly spread out, and Ukrainian presidents have limited say over who receives large contracts. After the Euromaidan protests in 2013–14, the government also launched administrative reforms that were meant to institutionalize the country's de facto decentralized structure.[70] Municipal governments in Ukraine have strong influence over their areas and are not easily penetrable to actors in Kyiv.[71] The Ukrainian military also has a decentralized mission command, giving a relatively high degree of autonomy to local decision-makers. Military experts have argued that this has been a strength against the highly centralized command of the Russian military.[72]

For Turkey, Ukraine's decentralized structure means that cooperation cannot flow down seamlessly from the presidential level to the level of local business. There are too many intermediaries and gatekeepers to contend with, and when they can't be resolved through phone calls from Kyiv, Turkish officials are frustrated. Turkey's concern with corruption in Ukraine may therefore not necessarily refer to unlawful or unregulated activity (though that is almost certainly also the case) but to the absence or inefficiency of hierarchical relations.[73]

Is Ukraine Lost to Freedom?

From the perspective of Turkey's new elite, the Ukrainian quest for membership in Western clubs like the EU and NATO is a regressive policy and is bound to collapse for two reasons. First, Turkey's new elite believes that the political basis for Ukraine's Westernization is shallow. They tend to believe that Euromaidan was engineered by Western capitals, that the ensuing Westernization drive does not represent the country's true spirit, and is therefore bound to falter when put under sufficient stress. Second, it believes that Western political will to support Ukraine in its war with Russia is also shallow, and will eventually disappoint Ukrainians, leaving their country mired in an irreconcilable territorial dispute with Russia. Turkey's Ukraine policy is predicated on the possibility of this outcome, and the potential it would yield in building a closer Turkey–Ukraine bond.

On the first point, Turkish mistrust of Ukraine's Westward tilt was already evident in the Turkish coverage of the Euromaidan protests. Though the protests didn't get much attention in Turkey, the coverage that did exist found it virtually impossible not to compare it to the Gezi protesters. Pro-government channels such as *A Haber* framed aspects of the protests, such as the formation of first-aid stations in a church, as "scenarios" similar to those seen in Gezi, implying that these were staged. In his September 19, 2014, column in *Yeni Şafak*, İbrahim Karagül implied that the CIA was behind both protests, and that they somehow used the same script for both countries. As evidence, he pointed to some of the similarities between emblematic images from the protests, like the presence of pianos and young women wearing red clothing:

> The scarlet woman, the man on the piano, masked people, spoiled girls, and the project of toppling governments over [the preservation of] trees, was all a Ukrainian scenario forced on Turkey.

A basic tenet of the Islamist tradition is that Westernizing elements in society are by their nature aligned against the "true" volk. Even if they aren't explicitly pro-Western, leftist or liberal popular sentiment that isn't explicitly against Westernization can —by definition—never reflect the feelings of even a segment of the nation. They are "scenarios," the production of foreign powers. Karagül applied this idea to Ukraine as well and took some of the similarities between the two Maidan protests as proof. By this measure, he concluded that Turkey was able to suppress what he saw as the Western-imposed politics of Gezi, while Ukraine succumbed to Euromaidan, derailing its politics from its "natural" nationalistic path and resulting in its territorial division. In this thinking, Russia's occupation of Ukrainian territory was a matter of course, a natural event almost beyond Russian agency. Agency lay only in Western meddling and national resistance:

> They [the West] have seen what chaotic fate Ukraine, which has lost Crimea, has been dragged into, and the fact that they unashamedly insist on this path is truly evil.
> Turkey, which is gaining ground quickly, was tripped up [çelme takılmış], but the country didn't stumble.[74]

As Ukraine succumbed to the false promise of the liberal empire, Karagül suggested, Turkey's strong leadership managed to keep it on the path of sovereignty. In this sense, Turkey's new elites considered Ukraine to be a cautionary tale. If Turkey had given way to the liberal-progressive wave that Gezi represented, they thought, it too would have seen its territorial integrity compromised. Hilal Kaplan, a powerful commentator close to Erdoğan, echoed this sentiment shortly after Russia's full-scale invasion in 2022, writing that "asking the question 'who is wrong?' is pointless, we must take this as a lesson [ibret almalıyız]." In the following months, she frequently derided Zelensky as a mere comedian and publicly cautioned her social media followers against presenting him as a hero.[75]

This interpretation of events among Turkey's ruling circles dovetailed nicely with a strand of pro-Putin right-wing sentiment in the English-speaking world. Oliver Stone, a filmmaker who was reviled among Turkish nationalists for his crude depiction of Turks in his 1978 film *Midnight Express*, was now feted in the same circles for his stance on Russia. Stone's 2016 film *Ukraine on Fire*, as well as his interviews with Putin, channeled the Russian perspective of the war with a Hollywood aesthetic, which pro-government commentators found immensely appealing. With Russia's full-scale invasion of Ukraine in 2022, many Turkish commentators were also drawn to a wave of critique among realist American scholars, chief among them the political scientist John Mearsheimer, who argued that the United States was ultimately to blame for the war. Much of this was well-intentioned criticism, but it was inevitably distorted in the Turkish media sphere. The fact that high-profile Americans were critical of their country's policies seemed more than analysis in such circles—it looked like an admittance of wrongdoing, a behind-the-curtain peek at how the world was *really* run.

These views not only dominated mainstream media, they were also endorsed at the highest levels of the state. In several interviews before and after Russia's full-scale invasion of Ukraine in 2022, İbrahim Kalın, who was at the time the Presidency Spokesperson and Deputy Chairman of its Council of Security and Foreign Policy, argued that the war in Ukraine was fundamentally caused by Western intransigence. The West expected the Russians to honor agreements they signed in the 1990s, right after the Cold War, when Russia was governed by Boris Yeltsin, at the nadir of its power. Russia under Putin believed that it had outgrown these agreements and wanted to renegotiate them, but Western leaders continually rejected these efforts. In an interview on October 11, 2022, Kalın said:

> Especially the Bucharest memorandum that was signed in 1997 [he probably meant the 1994 Budapest Memorandum on Security Assurances] no longer aligns with the realities of today. There is a new world today. The Russia that signed that understanding in the 1990s has remained in the past . . . Russia is saying "Come let us make a new treaty that will take into account these new balances." They have said this in different places and continue to say it.[76]

Kalın's tenor was closer to Mearsheimer than to Karagül, but the argument again hinged on the idea that Ukraine's agency was not to be taken too seriously. It only made sense if the Euromaidan protests, and Ukraine's overall Westward tilt, were not as much the expression of Ukraine's national sovereignty as that of Atlanticist meddling. Like Karagül, Kalın was also reflecting Turkish experiences on to his perception of the war in Ukraine. The second half of this particular interview was about Turkey's claims in the Eastern Mediterranean, where Kalın made a very similar argument: the partitioning of the Aegean islands and the maritime delimitations surrounding them had occurred after the First World War, a time when Turkey was historically weak, and the Western-backed Greeks were relatively strong. That had now changed. Turkey, Kalın said, far outweighed Greece in economic and military heft, and it was only right that the maritime maps between the countries be redrawn. This revision could either be done peacefully or it could be done through conflict.

Kalın did not state it openly, but it would not be a stretch to say that Turkey's policy elite saw in Russia's revisionist claims a pathway for their own. Like Russia, Turkey was more than a country—it was a civilization, and it was being boxed in by the liberal world order. And again like Russia, Turkey no longer wanted to "Westernize" but sought to present a civilizational alternative to the Western world. Movements such as Euromaidan, and the Ukrainian government born of it, supported the status quo. Ankara therefore dealt with the Zelenskyy government, not for what it was, but for the post-liberal potential it bore. A Turkish official told me months before the full-scale invasion that "a union of fate [kader birliği] is possible outside of the EU" for Turkey and Ukraine, "but Ukraine still has [EU] hopes." For Turkey–Ukraine relations to blossom, Ukraine's hopes of Westernization would first have to be dashed.

This brings us to the second belief that Turkey's new elite holds on Ukraine: that the West's political will to support Ukraine was also shallow and would ultimately disappoint Kyiv. Again, this was rooted in Turkey's own experiences with the West. Erdoğan had long accused the EU of blocking Turkey's accession process in large part out of anti-Muslim prejudice. To Turkish eyes, Ukraine's predominantly Orthodox makeup, historical connections with the Ottoman and Russian empires, and, most importantly, its status as a cultural outsider to Europe, put it in a similar situation. Ukraine's level of institutional and economic development placed it below EU member states like Hungary and Poland. Turkey's tendency was to see Ukraine's decentralization as corruption, which also made it less attractive as a member in these clubs. All this created a strong sense in Ankara that Ukraine would be rejected by the mechanistic West, and eventually join the "free" world of sovereign nations.

The weakest point in Ukraine's Westernization policy seemed to be its reliance on long-term Western military support. Ankara saw the United States as a serial betrayer of its allies, and supporters of the Erdoğan regime often derided progressive opposition parties, as well as the PKK, for "going down the well with America's rope," a version of a popular idiom implying that Washington is inherently unreliable and would drop its friends in their hour of need. This was not without basis: as a naval power influencing events far away from its shores, the United States has a history of working with actors in distant parts of the world, then leaving them to their own devices as its interests shift elsewhere. It has broken its promises to several Kurdish movements in the past, and in more recent years, withdrew from Afghanistan to leave its allies face to face with the Taliban and was even questioning its commitments to NATO.[77]

On February 24, 2022, when Russia launched its full-scale invasion of Ukraine, many in Ankara thought that hostilities could be over within a matter of days. The EU and the United States had stoked hopes of Westernization in Ukraine; they had encouraged reforms and promised the country's liberal elite that they would support them. Now that the Russians saw their bluff, however, the West would do the easy thing: it would condemn the invasion, perhaps sanction Russia, but ultimately watch as its friends in Ukraine were being rounded up by Russian soldiers. As a convoy of Russian military vehicles was making its way to Kyiv, Erdoğan cut short a multi-country trip in Africa and returned to participate in an extraordinary virtual NATO summit. It is rare for Erdoğan to make unscripted remarks, but he did so following Friday prayers on February 25:[78]

> At present, the European Union and with it, all Westernist [Batıcı] mentalities have unfortunately failed to display a serious, determined stance. They all give Ukraine plenty of advice [nasihat]. Of course it isn't possible to get anywhere on advice alone. I mean, what have you done? What are you doing? What are you going to do? Are you taking any steps? When we look at this, there are no steps taken.
>
> In today's [extraordinary virtual] NATO summit, we are going to discuss what kinds of steps you are taking, we are taking. Otherwise just giving lots of advice, condemnation–I mean one shouldn't run business as a hacivat-karagöz play [these being characters in a traditional shadow puppet show]. And the West, which merely gives plenty of advice on this issue, continues its advice. It is my wish that in today's NATO summit, we display a strong stance.
>
> In Zelenskyy's words, "they only give us advice, they don't give us any support," and this is unbefitting of friendship and solidarity.

The statement was remarkable for several reasons. First, Erdoğan was about to take part in a NATO summit, yet also levied attacks on it almost as an outsider. He started a sentence referring to NATO as "you," but then corrected himself to "we," reflecting the tension between his politics of Competitive Occidentalism and his formal position as head of a NATO country. Second, Erdoğan was calling for unified action in support of Ukraine, but his tone was very pessimistic. He used the term "advice" six times in about ninety seconds, suggesting that the West would merely watch as Ukraine was invaded. Erdoğan would presumably push for "taking steps" in the upcoming summit but seemed to think that his efforts were doomed to fail. NATO's inability to act in such moments was not merely a policy problem, it was a deeply ingrained attitude of "Westernist mentalities."

The wish was father to the thought here: Erdoğan wanted to see a preachy, yet limp, Western position, so he was eager to see it behind every turn. The sooner the Western world failed, the sooner non-Western powers could pick up the pieces and create their own order. Erdoğan's paraphrasing of Zelenskyy here also hinted at his aspiration for a post-liberal bond between the two countries. Ankara hoped that once it was abandoned by the West, Ukraine's hopes would be dashed, and they would assume a more Turkish form of sovereignty. Realistic talks with Russia could then take place. Since well before the full-scale invasion, Erdoğan also continually sought to reframe the conflict as a bilateral issue between "our Black Sea neighbors," rather than one between Russia and the wider West.[79] Turkey's numerous attempts at peace talks during the early months of the war were predicated on this trilateral framing. Removing the West from the room and holding talks only between natural leaders of "free" nations could resolve the problem. Putin could be reasoned with. Erdoğan's dealings with him in several antagonistic theaters proved as much.

We can't know what a deal in such an environment would have looked like, but Ankara's hopes are clear. Ukraine would have had to go through serious changes. European policies like the decentralization reforms would have stopped, and politics, business, and the media would have been consolidated in the hands of interests who were friendly to Russia. This would have made Ukraine resistant to liberal influence, but highly responsive to top-down deals made between presidents. Kyiv would have been neither Western in its orientation, nor Russian, instead deepening relations with Ankara. This "union of fate" would have meant that these midsized countries would build a healthy relationship while maintaining respectful boundaries.

Yet the full-scale invasion of Ukraine played out differently than Ankara thought it would. The Russian military was less capable, and Ukrainian political will was more robust than many assumed. Contrary to Ankara's assumptions, the collective West proved itself willing to support Ukraine's war effort with weapons, money, and refugee schemes. In Ankara's language, the West went from being fickle allies who would abandon Ukraine at the first sight of trouble, to warmongers who sought to prolong the war for their own geopolitical gains.

Turkey's own position was complex. Ankara refrained from participating in Western sanctions against Russia. It refused to close off its air space to Russian planes, and on March 1, it invoked the Montreaux Convention of 1936 and closed the straits between the Mediterranean and the Black Sea to all warship transits.

The Turkish arms industry, meanwhile, swung behind Ukraine, equipping it with armed drones, laser-guided missiles, and armored vehicles. In 2022, Turkey supplied Ukraine $275 million in arms, making it the country's sixth-largest supplier that year.[80] The most popular system by far was the Bayraktar's TB2 drone, which was useful during the early phases of the war but were later countered by stronger Russian air defenses.[81] Baykar is run by Haluk and Selçuk Bayraktar, the latter of whom is Erdoğan's son-in-law. The brothers seemed designated as the pro-NATO face of Turkey's regime, building strong relations with Ukrainian officials and investing into a $100 million drone complex in Ukraine. In 2024, Turkish companies also bolstered the US production of heavy ammunition, a critical bottleneck in Ukraine's war effort.[82] On the diplomatic front, Turkey gave vocal support to Ukraine's NATO and EU bids, which was consistent with Turkey's longtime commitment to the enlargement of both organisations.

Fulfilling its formal commitments to NATO while throwing its moral weight behind Russia, Turkey set itself up to become the interlockutor between the belligerent sides. In an interview, İbrahim Kalın, who was instrumental to these efforts, divided the Turkish diplomatic efforts into two phases: in the early months of the war, Turkey sought to negotiate bilateral peace treaties to end the war, but failed to get the two sides to agree.[83] In the second phase, Turkey began to negotiate several smaller, more practical deals. The most important of these was the Black Sea Grain Initiative, a UN-backed mechanism that was designed to transport grain and foodstuffs from Ukraine and Russia, two of the world's major suppliers, to global markets. Turkey also helped end a standoff over the Zaporizhzhia nuclear power plant and subsequent hostage negotiations. These were cases wherein Turkey was able to leverage its unique geopolitical position to alleviate some of the suffering inflicted by the war.

It is unclear to what extent Turkey's special role in the war has been coordinated with the broader Western strategy. At times it seemed as though Turkey was a geopolitical double agent, a go-between whose allegiance felt dubious, and was therefore courted on both sides. The West didn't seem to expect Turkey to be tough on Russia, nor did Russia expect Turkey to stop supporting Ukraine. One imagines that senior Turkish officials reassured both sides that they were really on their side. In a TV interview during the early days of the full-scale invasion, Kalın said that Turkey was speaking to both sides, and that "our Western friends are actually happy about this. Perhaps they don't openly say it or they won't say it, but at least to us, they say it openly."[84] Ukraine, which insisted on strong support among European allies, also seemed to place Turkey in a special category. The

Zelenskyy government took every opportunity to applaud Turkey's involvement and downplayed its links to Russia. Only occasionally have the Ukrainians let slip words of frustration. Speaking to the Greek public broadcaster ERT, president Zelenskyy said regarding Turkey, "a choice must be made–are you in favor of the truth or not?"[85] The Ukrainian ambassador to Ankara, who had himself made similar remarks, had to walk back these statements, expressing only undiluted thanks for Turkey's role.[86]

As the war in Ukraine drags on, Erdoğan's dismal predictions at its beginning could still turn out to be prescient. A Ukrainian counteroffensive in late 2023 was bogged down, and Ukraine's armed forces are suffering significant shortfalls, especially in heavy ammunition. Western politicians are souring on the idea of backing Ukraine, with far-right elements seeking to seize military support and end the war on Russia's terms. This means that there is a very real possibility that Ukraine could lose the war because it relied on Western support.

In such a scenario, Ukraine's hopes of Westernization would surely be dashed, and a "union of fate" between Turkey and Ukraine would be possible.

China–Turkey Relations: The Dog That Didn't Bark

The Communist Party of China has achieved for its country what Erdoğan envisions for Turkey: a highly competent civilization-state with a growing sphere of influence. China has a huge and sophisticated economy, a powerful military, as well as an informational and cultural ecosystem independent from that of the West. China's "wolf warrior" diplomats induce a degree of respect and trepidation in their erstwhile colonizers that even Russia can only watch with admiration. Erdoğan's New Turkey admires these qualities immensely. Official visits, strategy documents, Erdoğan's speeches, and the mood among political and business elite in Ankara and Istanbul all suggest that Turkey also wants stronger relations with China.

During his visit to Beijing in 2019, Erdoğan published an op-ed in the English-language *Global Times*, entitled "Turkey, China, Share a Vision for Future," stating:

> As late modernizers, Turkey and China are among countries seeking to bridge their development gap with Western nations in the 21st century. In other words, the 'Chinese dream' is to see China where it deserves to be on the world stage,

just as the 'Turkish dream' is to witness our nation secure the place it deserves in the international arena...

The world seeks a new, multipolar balance today. The need for a new international order, which will serve the interests of all humanity, is crystal clear. Turkey and China, the world's most ancient civilizations, have a responsibility to contribute to building this new system.[87]

Erdoğan clearly sought to draw a parallel between the Chinese and Turkish political projects. His piece went on to argue that the two states should increase their trade volume and cooperate in areas such as education and defense technology. Usually, when Erdoğan puts this much attention and force behind a policy, he sees some results. But that has not happened here. For decades, Erdoğan has not been able to close the gap between his ambitious rhetoric and reality. Turkey's relationship with China has improved, but remains far below the target Erdoğan has set. What accounts for the large gap? It seems that with regard to China, Turkey's new regime has come up against a conceptual limitation. It lacked an awareness of the scale of the task and the capabilities required for it. Unlike Russia, China had no special interest in establishing robust relations with Turkey. In this relationship, it was up to Turkey to develop its ties with the larger country. This meant that institutions in Ankara had to grow beyond their Occidentalist mindset, study the political and economic structure of the Chinese system, and find a way to make inroads. They have hitherto failed to do so. This section is therefore a short history of what hasn't happened.

What would an improvement in relations have looked like? There are two areas that the Erdoğan government saw as being areas that needed to be expanded in its relationship with China.

First, and perhaps the most pressing issue, was to develop a more balanced economic relationship with China. The Chinese economy was taking off in the 2000s, during the time of the first AK Party governments. The two countries competed in fulfilling a similar segment of the demand for manufactured goods in world markets, with China being a much larger and more efficient producer than Turkey. The challenge for Turkish firms was to build relationships in China and, like firms in developed economies, find a way to benefit from its rise. Otherwise Turkey's trade deficit with China would grow, and its exporters would lose out to their Chinese competitiors. This was one of the rare areas of policy in which Turkey's major business groups, the Foreign Ministry, as well as other policy arms, could agree with the young Islamists who had risen to power.

Erdoğan first visited China in January 2003, after the AK Party won the elections, but before he officially became prime minister. During this visit, he talked about Chinese capital investing in Turkey as a "little China" and the two countries conquering the European market together. He was also eager to think of China as a market for Turkish exports. Being from the Black Sea, one of the world's top hazelnut-producing regions, Erdoğan mused, "if only we could have every Chinese person eat just one handful of hazelnuts."[88] Since then, relations with China are always predicted to have "great potential" and to be on the verge of breaking through to new ground, but government bodies never followed through. Business groups such as TÜSİAD and MÜSİAD struggled to find a foothold in the Chinese market.[89] Turkey's trade deficit with China blew up and, in the late 2010s and early 2020s, fluctuated around a ten-to-one ratio.[90]

When asked, members of the business and bureaucratic class with experience in China argue that Turkish firms might have offshored the production to China and exported intermediate goods to those facilities. This might have been possible for Turkish firms with relatively high levels of know-how. Brands such as Arçelik, a subsidiary of Koç Holding, and one of the world's largest home appliance makers, set up some manufacturing in China, but not nearly on the level that could balance out Turkey's imports. It too, eventually sold its plant in 2020.[91]

Turkish business executives also point out that Turkey simply hasn't devoted enough resources to understanding China.[92] Germany, for example, decided to build deep economic relations with China in the 1980s, and the German government employs hundreds of staff across the country to maintain these relations. The political divergence between China and the West has now called this model into question, but that is not a problem Turkey would have if it had a similar relationship. Turkey claims that it seeks "strategic cooperation" with China but doesn't seem to have made a comparable investment in human resources. Its missions to China are fairly understaffed in comparison to those of European countries and employ only a handful trade attachés.[93] Chinese studies is an afterthought in Turkey's top universities, and there are very few China and East Asia specialists in the country.[94] The handful of Turkish business people who do think seriously about working in China are very limited in the Turkish resources and expertise they can find.

Emin Önen, Turkey's ambassador to China in 2017–23, reflected on his country's lack of focus in an extended interview with *Habertürk* in 2019, published upon President Erdoğan's visit to Beijing.[95] Unusual for such an important post at the time, Ambassador Önen was a political appointee. He had previously been a businessman, with a rare MA in East Asian Studies at Fatih University, and served two terms as an AK Party MP (2007–15), during which time he was involved with East Asian affairs. Unlike some other such appointees, however, he was well respected in the Foreign Ministry.

In the interview with *Habertürk*, Önen, like the handful of Turkish elites genuinely interested in China, expressed frustration with his countrymen's approach to the rising superpower. He lamented that Turkish businessmen neglect China, arguing that people in Turkey had grave misconceptions about the country as "'cheap labor,' 'people who work for $100 a month' or 'poor people wearing straw hats and working in rice paddies.'"[96] Not only was this vastly inaccurate, but it also prevented stronger relations between the countries. "I think we are settling into what is easy [biraz kolaya kaçtığımızı düşünüyorum], but this place requires patience" he said, and argued that China richly rewards those who learn its language, study its culture, and socialize into its business environment. "One must come and meet the people, eat the food, invite people to Turkey," Önen argued.[97] It isn't unusual for an ambassador to invite more attention to the country he serves in, but it was remarkable that China should require such invitation, especially in a country like Turkey, where the elite shares Beijing's revisionist outlook on world affairs. Being connected to the AK Party's thinking on China, Önen's comments also serve to illustrate the gap between the party's vision and the reality of China–Turkey relations. The underlying problem seemed to be that Turkey's new regime, like its old one, was deeply occidentalist. Despite the leadership's self-proclaimed interest in China, its strategic culture remained focused on the West, and its institutions were not equipped to understand China's history, institutions, and customs.

Unable to shape its relations with China, Turkey has continuously looked for global shifts as opportunities to get unstuck. In early 2020, when Covid-19 was new and quickly spreading across the globe, speculation was rife about what the pandemic would mean for the Chinese economy and the world at large. In March, President Erdoğan—rather unusually for him—disappeared from view for nearly a week. Once back, he had good news for the nation. Having evaluated the situation, Erdoğan and his strategists saw a new pathway for Turkey to become richer and more powerful than ever before. "The pandemic period in China has forced the world, and chiefly Europe, to look for alternatives for production," he said, "when producer alternatives are in question, one of the first places one thinks of is Turkey."[98] It was not uncommon at the time to think that the pandemic would reduce China's global status. Erdoğan developed a highly optimistic view of this situation, seeing behind it and opportunity for

Turkey. China produced low-value added goods on a scale and efficiency that Turkey simply couldn't match. If the Turkish economy was to continue growing, it had to move up the global value chains to produce higher value-added goods, which the country found difficult to do. If the pandemic knocked China out of the competition, he seemed to think, Turkey might be able to move in and take a much bigger slice of the European market. It would mean a difficult readjustment, Erdoğan said, but it would be worth it in the end. In June, he spoke of dropping oil prices (a major Turkish import), and how, thanks to its investment in the health sector, Turkey seemed to be doing comparably well in fighting the pandemic. "All leading indicators suggest that we are at the verge of a very serious leap forward" Erdoğan said.[99]

It's doubtful that Erdoğan and his team intended to draw parallels to Mao's "Great Leap Forward," but there was a very distant comparison in there—the state meant to undertake a radical readjustment of its economic model to "reshore" much of Chinese production to Turkey. The pandemic was a fast lane for Turkey, but only if it put its entire energy into it. "We must mobilize the entirety of our country's potential," the president said, which meant that heavy industry would be working through the pandemic and banks would finance the expansion.[100] Yet the Turkish Great Leap Forward (or what might have been "near shoring" from the Western perspective) did not materialize. Erdoğan and his team had overestimated the impact of the pandemic on China's standing in the world economy. Still, their ambitions illustrate Turkey's ambitions to become a "little China" and move beyond its trade deficit with the country.

Turkey's second policy objective in relations to China was to leverage its geographic location to become a crucial link in the trade between China and Europe. The issue has captured the imagination of Turkish strategists since at least the 1990s. The policy class has long considered the country the quintessential "bridge between east and West" and sought to capitalize on the status, but struggled to create tangible plans. The early AK Party governments began to seriously work on the subject, and when Abdullah Gül became president in 2007, he sought to take the lead on it. Speaking at the ground breaking ceremony of the Baku-Tbilisi-Kars railway in November 2007, he said:[101]

> Today we are not only connecting Baku, Tbilisi, and Kars, we are really connecting China to London. This is a great project. The wagons and locomotives that depart China will cross the Caspian, then they will cross Baku-Tbilisi-Kars, reach Istanbul, and once the Marmaray Project underneath the Bosphorus is finished—and its construction is advancing apace—they will cross

the Bosphorus underneath the water, they will traverse Europe, and there they will cross the channel and reach London.[102]

This was Turkey as the superconnector of globalization, and it would not fail from want of construction prowess. The projects along the path Gül spoke of—including the tunnel underneath the Bosphorus—did indeed advance at speed, but the idea gradually shifted from its liberal emphasis on free trade and globalization to national greatness and connectivity with China.

In 2013, China launched what it first called the One Belt One Road (OBOR) policy, and later rebranded as the Belt and Road Initiative (BRI). This was to be an investment space across Asia, with an emphasis on creating transportation and trade corridors. As Turkey's relations with its Western allies were souring in the 2010s, and China was emerging as the major non-Western power, there was a new political incentive in Ankara to find a framework to engage with Asia. Ankara's diplomats and academics were eager to point out that the world's "economic center of gravity" was shifting Eastward, suggesting that Turkey's Silk Road efforts could be plugged into this process. It wasn't clear, however, how exactly that could take place. A flurry of maps tried to impose structure to this thinking: China and Europe were linked through a "northern corridor" through Russia and a "maritime route" through the Suez Canal, while Turkey was part of the least-developed "middle corridor," which originated in China's industrial heartland, traversed the Turkic Republics of Central Asia via rail, entered Turkey, and eventually connected to Europe, as Gül had described.[103] If this trade route ever became operational, at least parts of the hundreds of billions of dollars' worth of China–Europe trade would flow underneath the Bosphorus straits every year.

In the 2010s, rapid institutional and legal shifts in Ankara created confusion about who was leading Turkey's BRI efforts. The Foreign Ministry was to coordinate Turkey's BRI policy in the mid-2010s, but their effort failed to get high-level attention. BRI coordination fluctuated between the Ministry Transportation and Infrastructure, the Ministry of Trade, and the Ministry of Foreign Affairs (MFA). In 2019, the MFA seemed to be taking the lead as it launched its "Asia Anew" initiative. Echoing the American "Pivot to Asia" under Barack Obama, Asia Anew aimed to highlight Turkey's aspiration to connect with Asian powers on a deeper level. Turkey's ambassador to China argued that BRI was "naturally at the center of this initiative," and it seemed that Turkey sought to signal a greater readiness to work with China on the "middle corridor."[104] In the same year, the first train from China to Europe crossed underneath the Bosporus, an event praised in the media as the realization of a long-held dream.[105] Yet the capacity of the Turkish "middle corridor" remained at most 3–5 percent of that of the northern route through Russia.[106] The Caspian Sea crossing was a major concern, and even though Turkey was eager to streamline bureaucratic hurdles, it proved difficult to work with other countries along the route. Writing in *China Daily*, Jiang Mingxin, an associate researcher at the Chinese Academy of Social Sciences, argued that the northern route had many structural advantages over the relatively underdeveloped central route, but that Turkey's efforts could yield a viable option in the future.[107]

Ankara was learning that in order to make progress in its relations with China, it had to create clearer and more realistic policy framework at home, as well as shape Beijing's perceptions of Turkey. The greatest obstacle to that was the Uyghur issue.

Case Study: The Uyghur Question

The Uyghur question casts a long shadow over Turkey–China relations. Though seldom openly addressed in direct interactions between Chinese and Turkish elites, the issue remains an unarticulated, yet palpable source of tension in the background. Being the larger and more demanding side of the relationship, China uses this issue to keep Turkey on the defensive. Meanwhile, Turkey feels that it must maintain its claims as a protector of Muslim and Turkic people everywhere, while also dispelling Chinese fears of meddling. This nigh-impossible task has been an anchor weighing down relations, and is lodged deep in Central Asian history.

The Uyghur are a Turkic and Muslim people based in East Turkestan, or Xinjiang, in present-day northwestern China. The Qing dynasty conquered the territory in the seventeenth and eighteenth centuries. After the Republic of China was founded in 1912, Turkic-Muslim separatist movements fought China's authority, establishing the "East Turkestan Republic" twice: the first lasting a few months, from November 1933 to April 1934, and the second a few years, from November 1944 to December 1949, before it was annexed back into China.[108] Beijing has been on alert against Uyghur separatism ever since.

Today, China's Xinjiang province is home to about twelve million Uyghurs, as well as some Kazakhs and Kyrgyz, who are also ethnically Turkic, and mostly Muslim.[109] China recognizes the Uyghur as the titular people of Xinjiang province but seeks to snuff out any hint of a separate political identity. Its campaign to assimilate the Uyghur into Han Chinese cultures has included arbitrary mass detentions, forced labor, and involuntary sterilization.[110] The Muslim population of Xinjiang is under intense surveillance, and the area is closed to foreign reporters. Satellite images have documented large complexes where the Chinese government has interned more than one million Uyghurs with the purpose of "re-educating" them.[111] Inmates are indoctrinated in the ideology of the Communist Party of China and are prohibited from practicing Islam in all but its most symbolic aspects. These institutions are meant to peel back the Muslim-Turkic identity of the population to a degree that is acceptable to the central government.[112]

The issue has become a flashpoint in the wider geopolitical struggle between China and the United States. Human rights organizations based in the West have produced incriminating evidence, and the most vocal Uyghur dissidents are based in Western countries. The Biden administration has escalated the issue by accusing Beijing of genocide in its annual human rights report in 2021.[113] China vigorously denies the accusations, arguing that they are a coordinated attempt to weaken its sovereignty and international standing. It claims that it is combating Islamist extremists in Xinjiang province, and that its policies attempt to de-radicalize the Uughur population, rather than to expunge it of its culture. China also argues that its policies have broad support in the province.[114]

Beijing is extremely sensitive to anyone raising criticism on its handling of the Uyghur question, but it is especially vigilant about policing opinions in Turkey. The country, after all, claims to be the protector of Muslims and Turks everywhere. It also became a NATO ally after sending soldiers to the Korean War (1950–3), where the allies fought the Chinese. China seems to fear that the combination of civilizational ties to the Uyghur, as well as an institutional belonging to the West, could make Turkey an asset to a larger Western campaign to encircle it on this issue. Turkey is also a rambunctious—if illiberal—democracy, where political speech is allowed to a far larger degree than in any other Turkic-Muslim polity. Turkish civil society, including Islamist groups, are deeply shaped by Western norms. While right-wing groups are integrated into the state, they also have a tendency to campaign for causes without state approval.

This means that Turkey's new elite once again finds itself in a difficult geopolitical cleavage. On the one hand, they need to publicly address the plight of China's oppressed Muslims. Given the gravity of the accusations and overwhelming amount of evidence, it is fair to assume that the presidential palace understands the depth of China's crimes against the Uyghur, and cannot credibly deny them. On the other hand, China's geopolitical revisionism and massive economic weight means that pursuing good relations with China far outweighs Turkey's concerns for the Uyghur. Accordingly, Turkey could follow the lead of European countries, dealing freely with China while occasionally raising humanitarian concerns about its treatments of the Uyghur. What makes Turkey different, however, is that its concerns are not humanitarian, but civilizational. This presents an opportunity for Ankara. As long as it can divorce its Uyghur advocacy from the Western-dominated humanitarian effort, Beijing won't be alarmed, because Turkey won't be participating in its broader Western encirclement, and Turkish voters can be assured that their state is still carrying the banner of Muslim-Turkic civilization. The task of Turkish diplomacy is therefore once again be "pro-Uyghur" without being "pro-Western."

It took some time for Turkey to feel its way to this position, and nowhere is this more apparent than in Erdoğan's personal actions. The famously outspoken president has long been slamming European countries about their Islamophobia, and what he has called their racist attitudes toward Turkish and Muslim populations. His mantra in Europe has been "no to assimilation, yes to integration," the difference being that the former seeks to strip away the civilizational identity of Muslims and Turks, while the latter maintains it.[115] China's policy was clearly a case of extreme assimilation via extraordinarily coercive measures, and in 2009, then–prime minister Erdoğan called China's Uyghur policy "a kind of genocide."[116] By 2012, however, Erdoğan had softened enough that Chinese authorities received him on a visit to Xinjiang. He was now refraining from any criticism, and, at a dinner with officials in the regional capital of Urumchi, told officials "our ethnic kin are entrusted to you".[117]

The Uyghur issue was largely in the background in the 2000s, but became better known in the 2010s, when international reports of Chinese repression became more prominent. The challenge for the government was to prevent the Uyghur from being perceived as a major Turkic minority, like those in Cyprus and Europe, or oppressed Muslims in places like Palestine and Myanmar. It helps that the "Cause of East Turkistan" (Doğu Türkistan Davası), as it is known, is almost exclusively a matter of the political right, either being Islamist or pan-Turkic nationalist. The left may point at the government's hypocrisy, but seldom claims ownership of the issue enough to protest, publish, or pressure the government on it. Within the right, one's tone on the Uyghur issue depends on which side of Erdoğan one stands. Government supporters who are genuinely concerned with the state of Uyghurs don't usually protest or speak out, since this would put pressure on the government. They trust that President Erdoğan is concerned with the well-being of their fellow Muslims and has their long-term interest at heart. The implication here is that Turkey can only have influence on the issue if it becomes a more powerful country, and that it can only be a more powerful country if it distances itself from the United States and develops better relations with China.

The segment of the political right in the opposition has tried to pressure the government, but hasn't had electoral success with it. The Turkist İYİ Party, a splinter of the AK Party partner MHP, published a document in 2022 entitled "The Human Rights Report on Chinese Uyghur Autonomous Region."[118] It contained a highly detailed treatment of Chinese thinking on the Uyghur issue, carefully researched facts about the internment policy, and harrowing stories from dozens of internment camps survivors. The İYİ Party's chairwoman at the time, Meral Akşener, spoke at the launch event in June 2022, saying that the Erdoğan government was silent because it was after "small calculations." Soon afterward, Akşener attended a China–Turkey volleyball match, where she and her followers displayed an Uyghur flag.[119] The İYİ Party later proposed to establish a parliamentary subcommittee to investigate human rights violations against the Uyghur, but the AK Party rejected it.[120] This may have burnished Akşener's Turkist credentials and appeared to be putting pressure on Erdoğan, but it didn't get the party much attention beyond opposition Turkist circles. The Uyghur question was simply too remote.[121]

Turkish officials walked a fine line in which they made the occasionally strong statement to appease public sentiment. In 2019, for example, a year when the issue was covered especially intensely on the global stage, a spokesperson of the Foreign Ministry said they "call on Chinese authorities to respect the fundamental human rights of the Uyghur Turks and to shut down the concentration camps."[122] Turkey also signed an extradition treaty with China in 2017, but has been stalling its ratification, even as China ratified it in 2020.[123] In their meetings with their Chinese counterparts, Turkish officials sometimes claimed to have brought up the Uyghur issue, and reported that they were assured of the Uyghurs' well being, and that reports to the contrary were the products of a Western disinformation campaigns. In his *Habertürk* interview that same year, Ambassador Önen implied that there were problems on this issue, but that the larger aims that Turkey and China shared would ultimately help them to overcome them. "Our citizens can rest assured that we are defending all the rights of our Uyghur kin to the hilt," he said, "but these sensitive issues need to be contained within the diplomatic channels."[124] And they have been, especially at the highest levels. Erdoğan himself has notably refrained from speaking on the issue in recent years. His government still releases official statements, but these merely signal that they are handling the issue behind the scenes.

As a result, China is cautiously warming up to Turkey. Beijing appears to have had an understanding that, despite the unprecedented centralization of the Erdoğan regime, Turkey was still fairly pluralistic and therefore politically unstable—at least by Asian standards. Turks may have an orientalized image of China, but the Chinese view of Turkey is also distorted. One businessman with experience in the country said to me, "ordinary Chinese people don't know much about Turkey, but the one thing they do sometimes know is our kinship with the Uyghur . . . and that makes us suspect in their eyes."[125] This is why it is very difficult for citizens of Turkey, including businesspeople, to obtain visas to China. Beijing's extreme sensitivity and its surveillance capabilities have created an environment in which Turkish businessmen and diplomats have adopted a strict culture of self-censorship. When I interviewed a Turkish businessman via encypted phone application, for example, I found that he had no problems talking about his long experience in Turkey–China relations.[126] When I asked about the Uyghur issue and whether it ever came up in his dealings with Chinese interlocutors, however, he said it didn't, but his tone suddenly changed, he said that he wouldn't ordinarily have taken an interview request, and cut short what was an otherwise very friendly and forthcoming conversation.

Although the Uyghur issue will probably remain a destabilizing element in Turkey–China relations, the countries are getting better at containing it. "Our soft underbelly is the Uyghur issue, other than that we have no problems," said Ambassador Önen, adding that high-level talks between the two states have reduced distrust significantly.[127] This entailed deflecting negative news as Western disinformation and telling an alternative story with increasing force. Chinese authorities have been more successful at this in more recent years. Speaking in fluent Turkish at an event in May 2019, Chinese consul-general to Istanbul Cui Wei explained that reports of abuse in the Xinjiang region were "hearsay" created by Western outlets. "In Chinese we have a saying: the mouth is in another body," implying that Turks being critical of the issue were really speaking with the mouth of the West.[128] Such attempts on the Chinese side are the strongest indication that policymakers in Beijing are genuinely interested in developing relations further.

The war in Ukraine and the Uyghur question are therefore two policy areas in which Turkey is trying to chart a new path. It refuses to be integrated too deeply into a Western policy framework, and is eager to build relations with Russia and China on its own terms. To hold its own against these powers,

Turkish actors signal their Competitive Occidentalist values in order to reassure their counterparts that they are not part of the Western efforts to contain them. Ultimately, Ankara's ambition is not to fold under these powers, but to become their peers as a major civilization-state. This may seem out of proportion for a country of Turkey's size, but as I will argue in the next chapter, New Turkey is serious about becoming a major geopolitical force of its own.

5

The Vision of Greater Turkey

The important thing isn't what some people are doing. It is whether we can surpass these things, overcome these things, because only that is befitting of a Muslim Turk, and that is what we are doing.[1]

– Recep Tayyip Erdoğan

Introduction

During Erdoğan's campaign ahead of the 2017 constitutional referendum, an ad painted a picture of a new, globally expansive Turkey. It starts with a young Turkish couple at a restaurant in Pakistan, asking for the bill. The waiter talks to his manager, then sends the couple a note. "Erdoğan has paid the bill," it says, and they all smile. The video then takes us to Palestine, Somalia, Iraq, Kazakhstan, and Bosnia, where Turkish infrastructure projects, education, and humanitarian aid are making a difference in people's lives. In France, meanwhile, a man is sitting in the back of a cab, reading the daily *Le Figaro*, which revels in Erdoğan's electoral defeat on June 7, 2015 featuring a derogatory cartoon of the "last Ottoman." His driver sees the paper, and asks his passenger in polite, Turkish-accented French, "you've been writing the same headlines for ten years sir, do you really think you can stop the Turks?" The neckerchief-wearing Frenchman looks up. "A hope," he sighs. The video goes on to Mecca, where people with Turkish flags on their white *ihram* robes are praying, and then to a school in Turkey, where children are enacting the 1915 battle of Gallipoli, in which Turkish forces defended the country against an attack by the British Empire. A child playing Mustafa Kemal Atatürk performs a monologue saying "My soldiers! The world has united against us," and recounting the long history of Selchukid and Ottoman battles, the boy-Atatürk says "do not feel alone. Feel your history. Feel our brethren peoples who pray for you." He implores his boy-soldiers to fight for the motherland and the banner of Islam. Together they raise the flag, and the words "Turkey is greater than Turkey" emblazons the screen in scarlet and white.

Variations of this message have since become staples of the Erdoğan palace's communications. Official state organs now speak of the vision of the "Century of Turkey" or simply "Greater Turkey."[2] The idea is that the recent centuries belonged to Western countries, but that the twenty-first century will be the time when Turkey—and by extension the Islamic world—will rise once again. In this section, I will seek to boil down the vision of Greater Turkey into three areas: territory, population, and military development.

Territory

The ultimate fear of Turkish nationalism is the country's territorial dismemberment. Every child knows of the Treaty of Sèvres (1920), which after the First World War, was to partition the Ottoman Empire among the victorious European powers. It serves as a reminder of how close Turkey once came to complete territorial fragmentation. In the literature on Turkey today, the "Sèvres syndrome" refers to a deeply ingrained fear that this could still happen—that in a moment of national weakness, Western powers could come back and finish the job. They could incite division among Turkey's social "fault lines" and divide the country's riches among themselves. This is why the Turkish public has long been deeply anxious about the possibility of Western-backed Kurdish separatism, Armenian reparation claims, or even a wanton American invasion.[3]

As Turkey has grown into its regime of Competitive Occidentalism, a flip side to the "Sèvres syndrome" has emerged. The country's new elite believes that as Turkey's power grows, its territorial presence should, and inevitably will, expand. Here, "Greater Turkey" is literally a larger country, an echo of the territorial expanse in its imperial history. In Turkey's state-sponsored discourse, the Ottoman Empire is emphatically remembered as a "cihan devleti" (a "world state") that "spread across three continents." This is often expressed in contrast to Western influence. European empires and the lighter footprint postwar global American influence, are referred to as "emperyalizm" in Turkish, while the Ottoman Empire is an "imparatorluk," or simply "Osmanlı." The former is a system of oppression, while the latter is conceived as a just order to which people submitted freely. Its territorial expanse was a sign of its righteousness. Erdoğan knows by heart random factoids like how Sultan Selim "the Grim" expanded

Ottoman lands by "18 million square kilometers" and holds it up as a measure of success.[4] He likes to recite the opening lines of *Dark Tidings* by the romantic poet Abdurrahim Karakoç:[5]

> As flowers bloom in strange lands
> It is snowing in our country
> Who has drawn this border on my soul?
> It is too tight, too tight, my brother.

Here, as in other romantic poetry, there is meaning to be obtained in the expanse of geography. The Turkish nation, in this thinking, has gone through a tightening phase, trapped within the frosty borders drawn by unnamed powers. From that decline, it is emerging once again to what Karakoç has elsewhere called "driliş" or "reawakening." As the national soul now stirs from its slumber, its physical circumstances must accommodate that reality. There are two ways this physical expansion can occur.

First, the expansion can occur within Turkey's current bounds, meaning that the Turkish nation breaks out of the parochial thinking of Kemalist Aspirational Occidentalism and reaches out to the world, building new commercial, cultural, and humanitarian connections. This can fit into the postwar liberal mindset of Western countries, and Turkey therefore advertises its outreach as a sign of its growing power and prestige. Second, the expansion can occur literally, meaning that Turkey uses its military power to expand its control over other territory, with the possibility of it becoming an extension of Turkey's sovereign space in the future.[6] This is an irredentist idea that does not fit into the postwar liberal mindset prevalent in Western countries, and Turkey's new elite is therefore more cryptic and defensive in its communication. I will discuss both ideas next.

Liberal Expansion

Turkey's shift from Aspirational to Competitive Occidentalism has triggered an explosion of activity in the realms of diplomacy, logistics, sports, commerce, and culture. Turkey is eager to be in the room, to imprint its national presence beyond its borders in as forceful a way as possible.

These efforts begin with President Erdoğan as Turkey's evangelist-in-chief, leading the international expansion through incessant travel. He is one of the most itinerant national leaders in the world, having traveled to 120 countries in his almost quarter-century in power. As he said in an interview, "the countries of the world we have not visited are few."[7] In his early years, Erdoğan mostly traveled to Turkey's treaty allies in Europe and North America, while in the 2010s, his focus shifted to the Balkans, Eastern Europe, Africa, the Persian Gulf, and the wider Global South. Erdoğan likes to set up relationships with long-serving right-wing leaders like himself, including Vladimir Putin, Viktor Orbán, and Ilham Aliyev. When home, he spends a lot of time on the phone with other leaders, follows their elections closely, and maintains cordial relations with their representatives in Turkey. Erdoğan's international sociability can come up at odd moments. For example, after speaking at a graduation ceremony at the police academy in Ankara, where international students are also present, Erdoğan chatted with a newly graduated officer from Indonesia, asking her when she would be back home. When the officer responded, Erdoğan remarked that she would be back in time for the upcoming national elections in Indonesia and asked her to pass his regards to President [Joko] Widodo, an especially friendly leader whose humble origins and populist charm mirror that of his own.[8]

Erdoğan is eager to leverage these relationships to project Turkey into areas of global governance where it did not traditionally have a role. The event that set this pattern occurred in 2010. Western countries, led by the Obama administration, were trying to negotiate a deal with Iran to curtail its nuclear production, but a lack of trust on both sides was hampering efforts. To everyone's surprise, Erdoğan and Brazilian leader Luiz Inácio Lula da Silva took initiative to resolve the crisis, proposing a fuel-swap scheme that their countries would oversee.[9] This was strange. The world was used to Western countries grappling with problems far beyond their immediate areas of interest, but countries like Brazil and Turkey were expected to stay in their lanes. That was precisely what the two leaders wanted to change. They sought to show the West that the developing world was ready to take responsibility on the international stage and resolve big geopolitical problems. Turkey also had a rotating seat at the UN Security Council at the time, which boosted its status. In May 2010, Erdoğan, Lula, and Iranian prime minister Mahmoud Ahmadinejad inked the "Tehran Agreement" and sought international approval to put it to work.[10] Western capitals gave the deal a cool reception, eventually sinking it when they proposed and passed UN sanctions on Iran. Iran's parliamentary speaker called this a "humiliation" for Brazil, Iran, and Turkey.[11]

But Erdoğan never stopped trying to mediate international conflicts. He offered himself up as mediator during the 2011 NATO intervention in Libya, and in 2021, in the conflict between Sudan and Ethiopia, and between the two sides of the 2023 Civil War in Sudan.[12] Turkey's most successful mediation was between Ukraine and Russia, where Turkish diplomats negotiated a deal to export grain from the war zones into international markets, as well as prisoner swaps.[13] As covered in the previous chapter, Erdoğan had strong connections to both sides in this conflict. At other times, as in the case of the Gaza war in 2023, Erdoğan offered to mediate between Israel and Hamas, but Israel seemed averse to the idea, and Erdoğan too abandoned it once Israel ramped up its bombing campaign.[14] The United States worked closely with the Gulf countries, especially Qatar, in negotiating hostage releases, while Turkey remained on the sidelines. Analysts close to the Erdoğan palace have come to refer to the president's top-heavy diplomatic efforts as "leadership diplomacy," claiming that it grounds Turkey's international outreach.[15] Implicit in this is a sense that while Western leaders suffocated politics with rules and procedures, Erdoğan is prepared to face the personal dimension of politics, to carry the weight of national sovereignty into the room and use it to drive toward a solution.

In addition to Erdoğan's personal weight, a key factor in Turkey's expanding political footprint is its presence in the humanitarian space. The country presides over a growing ecosystem of Islamist NGOs that provide humanitarian relief. Much of this is concentrated within Turkey's borders, where many refugees from conflict zones, and primarily Syria, live. Depending on the year and measure, Turkey hovers somewhere around the bottom of the world's top twenty economies, but in 2017, the country became the world's most generous provider of humanitarian aid per national income, surpassing the United States.[16] It has built up a sprawling ecosystem of humanitarian aid organizations, many of which are founded on an explicitly Islamist agenda and are spreading across the world. The hardline Islamist Humanitarian Relief Foundation (İnsan Hak ve Hürriyetleri İnsani Yardım Vakfı, IHH), most famous for sending a flotilla to Gaza despite the Israeli blockade in 2010, now operates in 123 countries, including Turkish-controlled territories in northern Syria.

Turkish humanitarian organizations are also active in Africa. A quarter of Turkish official development assistance is devoted to humanitarian aid in the continent, with the country being Somalia's top donor.[17] Faith-based Turkish NGOs have also increased their attention toward Africa since the mid-2000s. They provide food and medical aid, construct schools, roads and mosques, and offer scholarships to students. While Turkey's humanitarian rise occurred within the context of global humanitarianism, it is articulated through a language that combines motifs of anti-colonialism and Muslim solidarity. Like others that fashion themselves as civilization-states, such as China and India, this combination is ingrained in Turkey's brand.[18] Turkey's new elite believes that as a nation, it is historically innocent and pure, while the

West is guilty of the vast majority of suffering in the world. Its humanitarian outreach is therefore uninhibited about propagating Turkish nationalism and exceptionalism.

Turkey's new outreach to the world is also reflected in the amount of physical infrastructure the country maintains abroad. In 2002, the Foreign Ministry had an already impressive 163 missions across the world, but by 2022, it had 257.[19] According to the Lowy Institute's Global Diplomacy index in 2024, Turkey ranks third in the world in terms of its diplomatic missions (if one doesn't count the EU as a whole), coming after China and the United States.[20] Turkish citizens can count on fast and reliable service in consulates, as well as help during emergencies. During the Covid-19 pandemic, Turkey claims to have repatriated more than 100,000 of its citizens from 142 countries and aided thousands of citizens of other countries.[21] At the tip of Turkey's global presence are prestigious construction projects, including a $300 million tower across the street from the UN's headquarters in New York City, a $100 million mosque complex in Virginia, a €35 million mosque in Cologne, and a ¥1.5 billion mosque in Japan.[22] When asked about the 300,000-square-meter presidential palace complex he had built, Erdoğan famously said, "this is a matter of horizons. One does not skimp on reputational matters ['itibardan tasarruf olmaz']. Those who come and go look at these places."[23] The same principle seems to apply to his representation abroad. The majesty of these buildings are to attest to the civilizational weight of the country behind them.

Most Turkish construction sites abroad, however, are more practical. One of the AK Party's biggest election pledges in 2002 was to upgrade the country's roads, and it delivered on this with thousands of kilometers of pavement.[24] Since upgrading the roads in Turkey, those contractors have gone abroad, and aided by presidential phone calls, they've built roads, bridges, and tunnels, especially in the Balkans as well as North and Central Africa.[25] Having one of the biggest truck fleets in Europe, Turkey finds improved road quality in these places to be a significant advantage.[26] In 2023, Erdoğan also signed a deal for a $20 billion project to build a large road and rail corridor from the Turkish–Iraqi border to the port of Basra, marking an aggressive push to extend trade to the Persian Gulf.[27] Turkish air travel too, has also grown relentlessly during the time of the AK Party government, with the flagship carrier Turkish Airlines becoming one of the largest and most valuable airlines in the world.[28] In 2002, it flew to seventy-eight international destinations.[29] As of 2024, it flies to 340 destinations in total, placing it among the top airlines in the world.[30] It helps that Turkish Airlines is based in the newly built, $12 billion Istanbul airport, one of the largest in the world.[31] Like every imperial enterprise, Turkey is therefore a great builder of transport links, a compressor of distances.

The Turkish state also seeks to close the distances between itself and the sizable Turkish diaspora, especially in the West. Erdoğan called assimilation in Europe a "crime against humanity" and called on Turks there to maintain their often conservative Turkish political affinities.[32] Turks abroad were to integrate into the local languages and customs, but never loosen the ties that bonded them to Turkey's civilizational mission. He has thus taken measures to thicken the ties that bind the diaspora to the motherland. The Turkish-Islamic Union of Religious Affairs (Diyanet İşleri Türk-İslam Birliği, or DITIB) was set up in 1984 as an extension of Turkey's Presidency of Religious Affairs, which is the central authority overseeing Hanefi Muslim practice in Turkey. Before the AK Party, DITIB used to appoint a few dozen clerics to Europe to meet the needs of the Turkish diaspora there. Its staff has grown immensely in the last decades, numbering well over 1,500 in 2020.[33] It has built more than 100 mosques abroad, spending tens of millions of dollars.

Turkey is also trying to plant its flag in the realm of international culture, high and low. Until recently, Turkey did not have an equivalent to the likes of the Goethe Institute, Institut Français, the British Council, or the Confucius Institute. Established in 2009, the Yunus Emre Institute, named after the famous thirteenth-century Sufi poet, grew very quickly, having eighty-five branches as of 2023.[34] These offer affordable (or free) Turkish language classes, as well as workshops and instruction in traditional Turkish fine arts and music. Branches have become places where Turkophiles and those interested in Islamic culture can gather for frequent events, and academics in the humanities can hold presentations.

Turkish popular culture is also spreading across the world, and its primary vehicle is TV and streaming. Turkish TV shows have grown rapidly since the early 2000s, and are now second only to those of the English-speaking world.[35] The subjects range across a broad spectrum, including historical conquerors, rags-to-riches love stories, and action heroes, sweeping into markets from Latin America to Asia, but, most of all, in Muslim societies across the world. Exports were set to reach $600 million by the end of 2022, and the Ministry of Culture and Tourism has claimed that the shows have reached more than 750 million people across more than 150 countries.[36] Success here hasn't necessarily been by Ankara's design. During the sector's meteoric rise, the most popular shows have been those from the private sector and had an irreverent bend. *Gümüş* ("Silver," or *"Nour" in Arabic)*, a story rife with sexual affairs and relatively progressive norms, took the Arab and Latin American markets by storm, while *The Magnificent Century*, an occasionally salacious depiction of the court of Sultan Suleiman "the Magnificent," was wildly popular, even among pious audiences. Both ran on private networks in Turkey first, and only later reached international acclaim. The state seems to be pleased to enter new markets, but seeks to control the messaging more tightly, and to this end, launched *Tabii*, its own streaming platform, in 2023. *Tabii* is explicitly geared to counter the "Cultural Hegemony" of Hollywood and create a religiously wholesome, popular culture that can serve as a bond between the population of Turkey and sympathetic, primarily Muslim, audiences abroad.[37]

Put together, these dynamics make up for a country with a wide political footprint, ranging from the highest levels of diplomacy, down to the level of popular culture. They are expressions of Turkey's desire to be a great country, one with economic and cultural influence beyond its demographic and geographic limitations. To realize the idea of "Greater Turkey" in these policy areas, Turkish officials and businesspeople work out of a blueprint developed in Europe, but add their own twist to it, refining the economic, humanitarian and cultural models in ways that make sense for them. Turkey also plays to its natural strengths in transportation and logistics, an unusually entrepreneurial business class, centralized politics, and a vibrant cultural life. These forces may sometimes be conflicting, but the country has managed to integrate them and project them in a way that makes it more influential beyond its borders.

Redrawing the Map

There is also a more literal strand to the idea of "Greater Turkey." In the background of the new regime's thinking lies an older desire of expanding national sovereignty through the acquisition of new territory. The underlying idea is that much of the international arrangements demarcating Turkey's current borders took place at a time when the country was historically weak. Now that it is stronger, some seek to revise these international arrangements. This goes against liberal norms today, and like other forms of irredentism, is therefore expressed more cryptically.

To better understand the vocabulary of these discussions, we need to take a brief look at Turkey's founding moments. In 1919, the First World War was over, Turkey was under occupation, and a rebel movement in Anatolia under the leadership of Mustafa Kemal south to take the country back. But what would that look like? The Ottoman Empire had been losing territory for centuries, and certainly throughout the rebels' lifetimes. Which parts could they realistically save? Which parts did they have to let go? The rebels held two congresses, one in Erzurum and the other in Sivas, in which they discussed the question. They eventually agreed on a territorial demarcation they called the Mîsâk-ı Millî, literally meaning "the National Oath." The Ottoman parliament passed the resolution to the Mîsâk-ı Millî in its last session on January 28, 1920. This was at once a goal the rebels set out for themselves as well as a future negotiating position.

There are, however, some problems in interpreting the Mîsâk-ı Millî. First, it determined the borders verbally, rather than drawing lines on a map. Second, it specified a core territorial mass that was definitely to be within the country, but also a few territories where referenda would be held. The core borders specified are roughly modern Turkey today, with the notable addition of the Mosul area. The areas to be determined via referendum were Western Thrace, the Kars, Ardahan, Batumi area, as well as most of the Arabian peninsula.

The Allies had very different ideas about Turkey's territorial presence. They imposed upon the sultan's government the Treaty of Sèvres, which relegated Turkey into a rump state in Anatolia, with the UK, France, Italy, and Greece dividing up much of the former Ottoman territory. Led by Mustafa Kemal's armies, the rebels fought the allies and defeated them in October 1922. Sèvres was no more, but it was unclear how much of Mîsâk-ı Millî could be obtained. In a series of negotiations, modern Turkey's borders were set. Only Hatay, which had been under French occupation, held a referendum and became part of Turkey. Mustafa Kemal dispatched General İsmet İnönü to Lausanne to sign a new treaty, and Turkey's final borders were set narrower than that of the Mîsâk-ı Millî. Turkey ceded parts of what are today northern Iraq and Syria, as well as a small part of present-day Greece (Western Thrace). Modern Turkey was therefore founded by compromising on the borders set in the "National Oath" of 1920.

For the vast majority of Republican history, this was not considered a problem. Compared to the Treaty of Sèvres, the treaty of Lausanne was a great victory, and the Kemalist nationalist ethos celebrated it as such, to the extent that the compromises of the Mîsâk-ı Millî usually went unmentioned. The official historical narrative did not induce a feeling of having been robbed of parts of Iraq, Syria, Western Thrace, or (to encompass the plebiscite territories) most of the Arabian Peninsula. The collective amnesia was so pronounced that the term Mîsâk-ı Millî changed its meaning accordingly, and up until recently, the phrase

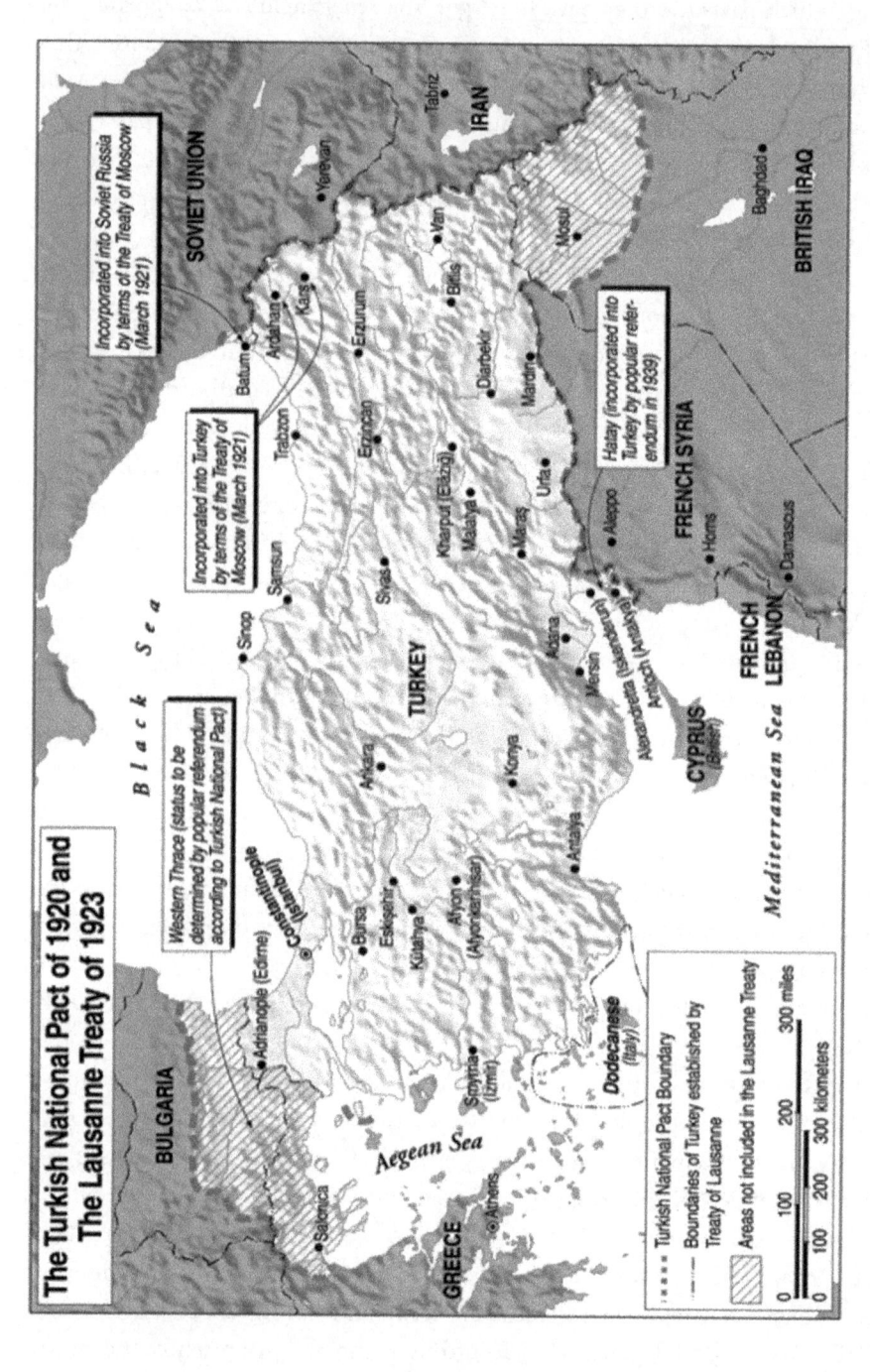

Figure 5 The Turkish National Pact of 1920 and The Lausanne Treaty of 1923. Sean McMeekin, Map 23, *The Ottoman End Game: War, Revolution, and the Making of the Modern Middle East, 1908–1923* (London: Penguin, 2016).

Figure 6 An article on the website of the state news agency Anadolu Agency delineating Mîsâk-ı Millî borders on Turkey's southern border via Google Maps. "Higher Education Numbers," Study in Türkiye, Yükseköğretim Kurulu, https://www.studyinturkey.gov.tr/StudyinTurkey/_PartStatistic.Yasemin Kalyoncuoğlu, "Misakımilli'nin güney sınırları belgelere yansıdı [Mîsâk-ı Millî's southern bounds are reflected in documents]," Anadolu Ajansı, January 27, 2019, https://www.aa.com.tr/tr/turkiye/misakimillinin-guney-sinirlari-belgelere-yansidi/1376163.

was used in daily parlance to refer to the present-day, internationally recognized borders of Turkey.

Starting in the 2010s, there has been a conscious effort among Turkey's new elite to return to the original meaning of Mîsâk-ı Millî as the basis of an irredentist policy.[38] Erdoğan himself weighed in on the discussion in two speeches after the 2016 coup attempt. This was a time when his regime was pushing itself off from the liberalism of the 2000s, and Erdoğan discussed some of his more deeply held ideas for the country's future. He broached the topic in a speech on September 24, 2016:

> Know that July 15 [the coup attempt] is the Turkish nation's second war of independence. What did they [the West] do to us in history? In 1920, they showed us Sèvres, and in 1923 they made us acquiesce to Lausanne. Some tried to make us swallow Lausanne as a victory. Everything is out in the open. You now see the Aegean, don't you? We gave up islands within shouting distance. Is this victory? Those were ours. There are our mosques, our places of worship

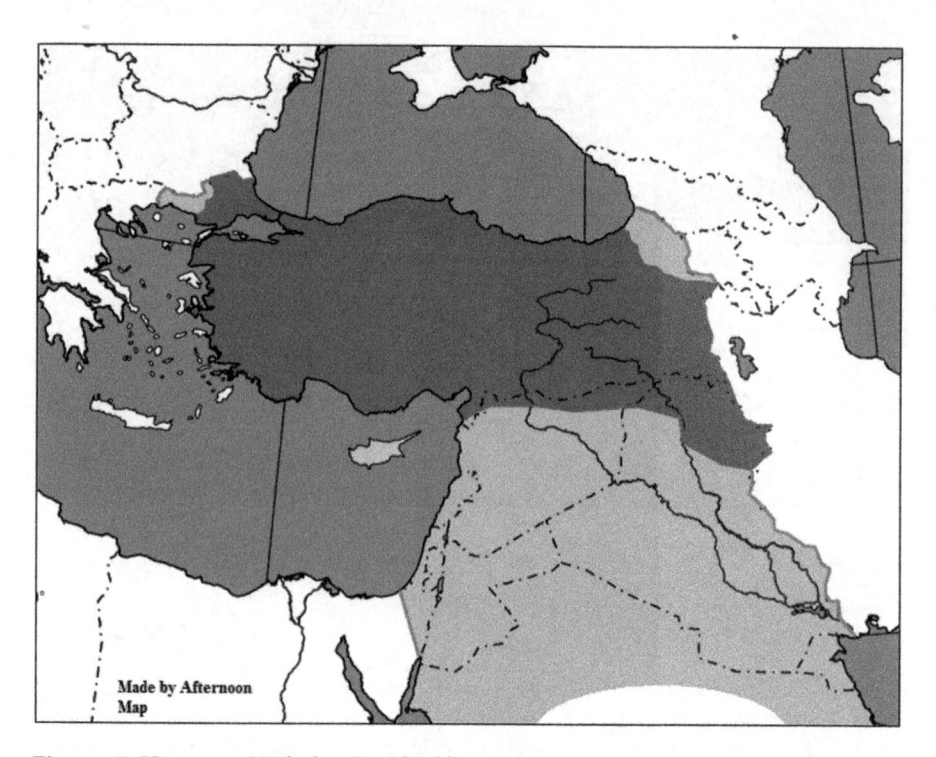

Figure 7 Historian Nicholas Danforth's interpretation of the January 20, 1920, version: "Regions in red were an 'indivisible whole,' while regions in pink would have their status determined by referendum." Nicholas Danforth, "Turkey's National Pact Borders," *The Afternoon Map*, October 21, 2016, http://www.midafternoonmap.com/2016/10/turkeys-national-pact-borders.html.

there. Yet we still talk about what is going to happen in the Aegean, what the continental shelf is going to be, what is going to happen in the air and in the sea, we still struggle on these fronts. Why? Because of those who sat at the table at that treaty [of Lausanne]. Those who sat at the table did not do that treaty justice, and because they didn't, we suffer the consequences.[39]

Erdoğan was squarely attacking the unarticulated founding principle of modern Turkey: that the Republic was founded on victory. Mustafa Kemal Atatürk's foundation of the Republic may have averted the catastrophe of Sèvres, he suggested, but that didn't make it a victory. Turkey had still lost the vast majority of the territories it held in Ottoman times, and did so not because of the country's weakness, but because of the "Westernist" decadence of the Kemalists.

Unfortunately for him, Erdoğan chose to illustrate his point by referring to the Aegean islands, which sparked a debate on the technical limits of the Mîsâk-ı Millî. Had the founders really ceded islands within shouting distance at

Lausanne?⁴⁰ Commentators soon pointed out that the Ottoman Empire lost the twelve islands (the Dodecanese) to Italy in 1911, and Cyprus in the late nineteenth century. At Lausanne, the de-facto situation was merely formalized. Erdoğan's speech was likely influenced by the polemical historian Kadir Mısıroğlu (see Chapter 1) who had also argued that Turkey lost the Dodecanese at Lausanne.

In a speech on October 19, Erdoğan addressed the issue again. He seemed annoyed that the public had gotten lost in the details of his argument. The important thing, he suggested, was that the country would seize on his broader point. In its transition from empire into a modern nation-state, the West had forced Turkey into a physical and mental confines that were unnatural, and caused the country undue suffering:

> Our goal when entering our War of Independence was to protect our Mîsâk-ı Millî borders. Unfortunately, we could not protect our Mîsâk-ı Millî goals on our western and southern borders. There may be those who excuse or try to excuse this situation due to the conditions of the period, but such excuses are only possible up to a point. What is really fatal is to accept the situation that arose from hardship and to imprison ourselves entirely within this shell. We reject this understanding. The aim of those who, since 1923, have imprisoned Turkey in such a vicious cycle, is to make us forget our thousand-year existence in our geography, as well as our Seljuk and Ottoman heritage. Do you know how we came to 780 thousand square kilometers [Turkey's current territory]? If we take a closer look at the past, we came here from 20 million square kilometers.⁴¹

The underlying principles of the argument are the same as in any far-right political movement. Erdoğan was arguing that the nation had been hoodwinked into believing that it was naturally small and subservient, when its true essence was that of a superpower reigning over massive territory. The way to change this mindset was to speak of territory differently. The conceptual basis for Turkey's physical being was not to be the rump state at Sèvres, but the immense expanse of the Ottoman Empire. This mental shift was possible only if the nation began to see the founding of the Republic for the failure it was. Changing the emotional charge of the country's foundation from victory to treasonous defeat would set the political basis for expansion, eventually leading to a revision in the future.

This didn't mean that the Turkish war of independence was a defeat—the opposite was true. It was a righteous and holy war against Western occupiers, but what the Turkish nation won on the battlefield, forces alien to the national spirit had squandered at the negotiating table. Mustafa Kemal's second-in-command, İsmet İnönü, who was at the head of the Turkish delegation in Lausanne, had not only accepted compromises on the Mîsâk-ı Millî but also conceded Turkish territory that was already won. In line with the long-standing Islamist tradition, Erdoğan was attacking İnönü as a proxy for Mustafa Kemal, making him, as Tanıl Bora aptly put it, a "voodoo doll of Kemalism and Mustafa Kemal."[42] This is a way of undermining secular and republican history while avoiding a battle with the cult of Mustafa Kemal. Erdoğan's point was that the Republic had been built on treason against the national struggle, and the celebration of Lausanne sought to cover it up.

While Erdoğan's tropes were tried and tested, his tone was shifting in the post-coup environment. He was almost pleading with his audience to take this seriously, to accomplish the revaluation of the republic with him. This is why he sought to mark the coup attempt as Turkey's "second war of independence." After every war, states sat down to renegotiate borders and entitlements. The coup attempt was therefore to be interpreted as the starting gun for a period of covert confrontation that would result in such renegotiation. Turkey was now stirring with renewed political energy, and was chafing against its diplomatic, economic, military, and territorial confinement. Erdoğan was calling on the nation to get into the mindset of scrapping up old "deals" and negotiating new ones.

The Trumpian overtone is no coincidence here. Donald Trump, who had by mid-2016 won the Republican primaries and was campaigning against Hillary Clinton, suggested that American decline was a choice, and that previous presidents simply fell into this out of a mix of self-interest and complacency. The way he was going to "make America great again" was by renegotiating with the world, this time from a place of patriotic feeling.[43] The negotiations themselves were simple enough—take a maximalist position and be stubborn until you get a good enough deal. Erdoğan was not necessarily inspired by Trump, or by Putin for that matter, but these leaders shared a worldview defined by *ressentiment* and sought to develop an appetite for revision among their constituencies.

As with any attempt to shift norms, the key has been gradualism. It's telling, for example, that Erdoğan started with the islands. Sovereignty over islands might by their nature always feel more fluid than parts of mainland territory. Turkey also had a reasonable claim for the revision of the maritime delineation in the Aegean, and tacking on the islands to those claims gave them a veneer of respectability.[44] Since Erdoğan's speeches, the revisionist narrative has slowly found its way into the country's official history. Government media publishes mini-documentaries that go into detail on how Turkey ceded Batumi to the Soviets, Western Thrace to the Greeks, and Mosul to the British Mandate of Iraq. The official high school textbook gives students a detailed account of the negotiations in 1920–3 and asks them to reflect on why the Mîsâk-ı Millî had to be compromised.[45] The newly emerging official narrative thereby aims to dislodge the idea that the country's borders were a fair, or even desirable, outcome of the many possible outcomes at the time they were negotiated. The political narrative then revalues the facts from the Aspirational Occidentalism of the Kemalist Republic to the Competitive Occidentalism of the Erdoğan palace. Younger generations will grow up with the narrative that Turkey's borders are the product of defeat, that the country is now more powerful, and therefore needs to prepare for a time of new confrontation and negotiation.

When dealing with the outside world, Turkish officials are careful to package irredentist ideas in softer language. Speaking in what is now the Mimar Sinan University in January 2021, where the Mîsâk-ı Millî was signed in 1920, the then-speaker of parliament, Mustafa Şentop, said:

> I believe that it would be beneficial, on the way to a just and lasting peace, to reassess the problems of our country's geography on the basis of the Mîsâk-ı Millî, to solve problems on the principles accepted at the Mîsâk-ı Millî.[46]

Note that Şentop speaks of re-assessment. To him, Mîsâk-ı Millî is no longer something that has served its purpose in the past; it is the basis of solving problems in the future. It isn't to be imposed on the region, but to be presented as a natural solution to the distortion of a Western-imposed order. Erdoğan, for example, is usually eager to say that Turkey has "no eye on a single span of another's soil," sincerely claiming that Turkey respects the sovereignty of its neighbors and intends to act accordingly.[47] What is and is not "another's soil," however, is quickly shifting in the collective imagination of the Turkish right, and perhaps in those of Turkey's neighboring populations as well. Erdoğan's politics is about setting the ideological and material foundations for expansion. It revises Turkey's story in such a way that the country's enemies are alien to the land they inhabit, and its friends are inherently friendly to the expansion of Turkish power. The status of soil, in his understanding, can shift if one makes an emotional investment in it. Celebrating a national holiday in 2021, the president shared what might be considered his personal theory of political belonging:

> Soil does not become a homeland if there hasn't been a spilling of blood. I think of it this way: there are estates [arsa] and there are mere fields [arazi]. To transform a field into an estate, you need to pay a price. Otherwise, the field has no meaning at all. That is how we paid in martyrs to make this soil into a homeland.[48]

If territorial expansion is to be thought of as a transformation of "fields" into "estates" Turkey is in a phase of gathering up estates, meaning that it has to change facts on the ground over a long period of time. Since 2016, Turkey has, for example, been occupying growing parts of Syria and became more active in its operations in Iraq. It began to contest Greek claims in the Aegean with renewed rigor.[49] In 2019, it signed a maritime deal with Libya and became a decisive player in the country's civil war. In 2020, Turkey helped Azerbaijan gain a long-awaited military victory over Armenia and retake Nagorno-Karabakh. It has made claims of naval rights and airspace, but never made territorial claims in any of these involvements. Despite Erdoğan's fondness for Sultan Selim, the government understands that it cannot act in a sixteenth-century fashion, nor even in the way Russia has annexed Crimea. Having no significant hydrocarbon resources and being dependent on international markets as well as on NATO membership, Turkey has to be slow in developing these claims. It has to set itself up for such expansion and wait for a time when "fields" can once again be turned into "estates."

Population

Another core tenet of Turkey's new geopolitical thinking is that it must expand its population. After all, great countries aren't just expansive, they also have large populations. Part of far-right politics is simply about out-existing others, to win a competition of numbers. Erdoğan has never been shy about this point saying at a 2018 wedding:

> What does our Prophet say? The order is very clear. Get married, multiply. It is necessary for Muslims to increase their numbers. I trust the sensitivities of Muslim women on this issue. The terrorist organization [the PKK] is very sensitive on this issue. They have at least 10, 15 children.[50]

Many political leaders are worried about the demographic time bomb. In places like Israel and Turkey, where the state sees hostile populations to its political project, this can have immediate strategic considerations as well. The "enemy" is having more children, so the population supporting state control must rise as well. In this regard, Turkey has ambitions far beyond its midsized frame. For the country to realize the idea of "Greater Turkey," its population must rise far faster than its projected trajectory. This means that it is experimenting with immigration and, therefore, a new model of nationhood.

Who Belongs to the Nation?

Turkey is home to a variety of ethnic and religious groups, but these are not equal in their political representation. The country isn't called "The Republic of Anatolia," it is explicitly the Republic of Turkey, a state of the Turkish nation. Visitors will notice "happy is he who calls himself a Turk," a phrase attributed to Atatürk (literally "father-turk") written in capital letters on the sides of mountains. The iconic motto of *Hürriyet*, formerly the country's biggest newspaper, reads "Turkey belongs to the Turks." Nations usually feel the need to assert themselves repeatedly, but few do it as emphatically.

Turkey's founding fathers did not mean it to be a very diverse place. The Ottoman state had a Hanafi-Turkish core, but ruled over a famously multi-ethnic and multi-denominational empire. By the nineteenth century, diversity had become a dangerous thing. Part of the inter-European rivalry was about reaching into a rival state's population and connecting to their ethnic, linguistic, and religious minorities. As a weak, yet vast multinational imperial state, the Ottoman Empire were deeply vulnerable in this regard. Foreign powers had long-standing relations to its various communities, such as the Greeks and Armenians, and leveraged these connections in their favor. The Turkish response could be brutal. From 1915 to 1917, the Young Turk government rounded up more than a million Anatolian Armenians, and either killed them or marched them into the desert of Syria, where most of them died.[51] As nationalist movements in the Balkans got their independence, they also inflicted immense suffering on the Muslim populations there, driving them out or killing them.

The Kemalist state was also born into this age of demographic engineering. It undertook the 1920s population exchanges, where Turkey and Greece swapped Muslim and Christian populations in order to achieve a semblance of homogeneity. Turkish-speaking and Muslim populations were persecuted minorities in the new Balkan countries, and many migrated to Turkey. The forced homogenization of centuries of layered religious, linguistic, and ethnic diversity was immensely traumatic. In Turkey, leading intellectuals like Ziya Gökalp were influenced by the scientific racism that came out of Europe, conceiving an image of Turkishness in vaguely ethnic terms.[52] In the 1940s, this relaxed considerably, with Turkish civic identity becoming a more cultural and linguistic attribute, but Turkey's numerous ethnic and religious minorities still faring badly.[53] Jewish and Christian groups, including Armenians, Assyrians, and Greeks, were now under threat and emigrated over time. The Alevi, an unorthodox branch of Islam, became the largest religious minority in the country. Most Sunni ethnic minorities, such as the Albanians and Arabs, integrated into the larger umbrella of Sunni Turkishness. Only the Kurds, as the largest ethnic minority, preserved their language, culture, and political distinctiveness. The state has tried to assimilate them, resulting in a great deal of bloodshed, from the 1925 Sheikh Said Rebellion, to the PKK's insurgency from the late 1970s on.

The far right had their own ideas about who should constitute Turkey's population. The Turkist nationalists called for a more ethnically Turkish order, going as far as scientific racism. The popular Turkist writer Nihal Atsız, especially, was known for his criticism of the Kemalist establishment over its perceived liberalism toward minorities.[54] From the Islamist perspective, the Kemalist state was too exclusionary against ethnic groups like the Kurds and Arabs, and not exclusionary enough against non-Muslims and Alevis. In one of his most memorable lines, the Islamist poet Necip Fazıl writes that the spirit of the Anatolian Turk, as represented by the Sakarya river, is "A stranger in your native land, a pariah in your own home!" There was also a concern here that Westernization sought to curb Turkey's population growth. Islamist magazines were dripping with conspiracy theories about Jews and Freemasons spreading cheap contraception in Turkey to sap the country's natural strength.[55] Under these conditions, politics was not merely about seizing power, it was also about biological existence. In 1993—a time when Islamism was on the rise—a mob chanting Islamist slogans surrounded a hotel where Alevi and explicitly atheist writers and cultural figures were staying and burned it down, killing thirty-seven people.[56]

In its early years, the AK Party departed from the Islamist tradition in this area. It renovated churches and synagogues in Turkey and made a point of meeting with Jewish and Christian leaders, especially the Ecumenical Patriarch of Istanbul. This earned the government goodwill in the West and boosted its liberal credentials. Entering the illiberal years of the 2010s and 2020s, Erdoğan continued to invite the leaders of Christian and Jewish communities for important events, such as his presidential swearing-in ceremonies.[57] In 2023, he opened the first church built in the country's Republican history.[58] This policy, however, was about restoring the symbolism of the multi-ethnic empire, rather than promoting actual demographic diversity. Unlike countries like Egypt and Lebanon, Turkey's non-Muslim population was at this point well below 1 percent of the population, and only dwindling further.[59] It was no longer the non-Muslim populations whom the state considered a Western "fifth column" in Turkey, but the opposition, especially leftist and liberal circles. The president's enthusiasm for the non-Muslim religious leaders was about recreating an environment in which he, as the Muslim leader, is powerful, and is willing to be benevolent to those of other faiths. While Western leaders were disrespectful of Muslims in their countries, he thought, he would show that he allowed other faiths to flourish in his domain.

When it comes to demography, Erdoğan's views therefore remain consistent with that of the Islamist tradition. Turkey, to him, must not only be large on the map, it must be populous and young. As a natural sovereign, Erdoğan's language of population sounds more like the notion of "populousness" of seventeenth-century mercantilism than the population as a domain of policy in liberal sense.[60] With his incessant concern with population volume, Erdoğan seems to envisage the country's people as a resource from which to derive greater wealth and power for the state. Adhering to a long-held Turkish rhetorical tradition, Erdoğan often refers to the country by its population size, updating it throughout his tenure, saying, for example, "we are the 70 million" in discussing his electoral platform in 2008, or "the totality of the 80 million deserve praise" during the AK Party congress in 2017, and "all of the 85 million have won" after elections in 2023.[61] He encourages the country to be "yekvücut" meaning a "single body" and frequently summons its vigor with a quote from the Sufi Mystic Haci Bektasi Veli, in saying "let us be one, let us be large, let us be alive!"[62] He also likes to exercise the act of unison at every chance: Erdoğan's rallies in Istanbul can gather well over a million people, as the party-state having made an art of organizing such crowds.[63]

"Population is a country's power," Erdoğan once said during a discussion of geopolitics in Azerbaijan, "it shifts that country's paradigms for the future."[64] Actually getting the nation to continue growing, however, hasn't been as easy for the leader. Like other countries, Turkey's population has been aging as it is becoming more urban. The birth rate has dropped from 6.3 in 1960 to 1.6 in 2022.[65] TürkStat, the country's official statistical institute, has long projected the share of the population above the age of sixty-five is to increase sharply starting in the early 2020s. To boost these numbers, Turkey has implemented policies like providing credit for newlyweds or boosting the availability of childcare options, but these have only had limited success.[66]

Erdoğan has developed a unique way of communicating his concerns about population. Since his earliest years as a politician, the itinerary of the "reis" has included weddings, where he is invariably the chief witness, and is asked to speak. After the initial pleasantries, Erdoğan always says that he is about to impart his classic bit of wisdom. The crowd chuckles, knowing what the great man is about to say. Erdoğan then tells the newlyweds to have "at least three children." The slight nod toward the act of procreation is daringly invasive, but Erdoğan's avuncular air makes it feel genuine, even funny. Listening to the president's remarks at such occasions more closely, however, reveals more somber considerations about history and geopolitics. At a wedding in 2008, for example, then-PM Erdoğan said:

> What do they want to do? They want to eradicate [kökünü kazımak] the Turkish nation. That is what they are doing. If you don't want your population to decline, every family must have three children. The decision is yours [gesturing towards the couple], that is a different matter. I have lived this. I say it because I believe it. Children are a blessing, that we must also know. I have four children. I am happy, I wish I had more. Every one of them has been a blessing. Our population now is young. But if things keep going like this, we will have aged by 2030, which is a danger to us. We do not want to be exposed to this danger. We must balance this out.[67]

These views are a clear expression of the Islamist tradition's concept of population as a source of geopolitical power. The only difference is that given the venue and his status as prime minister, Erdoğan refrains from saying who exactly sought to curb Turkey's population growth, but his audience understands that he is referring to Western powers. One might argue that on a more abstract level, Westernization in Turkey, like anywhere else, makes people more individualistic, marry later in life and have fewer children. It also emancipates women, making them less likely to have as many children. This may be part of the idea, yet Erdoğan is usually describing too conscious and too aggressive an act of demographic sabotage for that to be sufficient.

In the 2010s, the AK Party came to be more selective in its approach to population. Erdoğan's share of the vote had steadily grown from 36 percent of the vote to a slim majority at 52 percent. As discussed in previous chapters, however, this was the extent of his electoral reach. Despite a growing degree of control over the apparatus of state, the government, which during this time evolved into a regime of its own, could not get the support of a comfortable majority within the country. In 2012, Erdoğan held a speech saying that he sought to "raise a pious generation." This, he argued, was a legitimate part of the AK Party's conservative democratic identity.[68] But with every election and referendum, divisions in the country were becoming deeper. Governing circles had always seen the voter base of their opponents as a "fifth column" of the West, but they had assumed that they would eventually come to soften their opposition.[69] They didn't have to vote for Erdoğan's brand of Islamist nationalism, but they did want

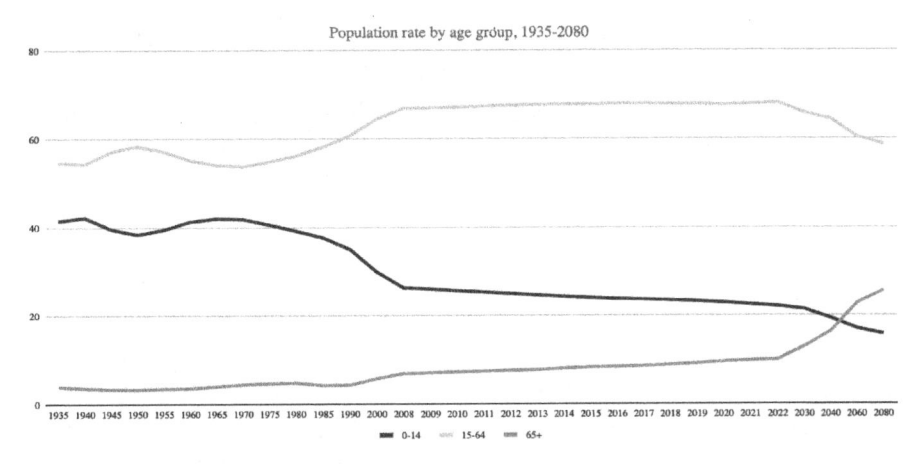

Figure 8 Population rate by age group, 1935–2080. TürkStat.

them to transition to a secular version of Competitive Occidentalism to be part of the new regime.

As with other issues, the 2016 coup attempt gave this problem greater urgency. Thinking of this "second war of independence," Erdoğan's followers couldn't help but think what would have happened if the coup had succeeded. Would there have been a civil war? Many people thought so.[70] But what would have been the lines of division? On the event's first anniversary, Erdoğan said, "on the night of July 15, we gave 250 heroes to the soil," referring to the people who were killed by the putschists, "in order to save the future of a Turkey of 50 million." Turkey's population was roughly eighty million at this point, and Erdoğan never made mistakes about that. It was clear to listeners that this number was the product of the palace's speculation regarding the night of the coup. They seemed to believe that fifty million, meaning slightly more than half of the population, were loyal to Erdoğan's vision, while thirty million would have been willing to overthrow him and cooperate with the enemy.[71] This was the split between Competitive and Aspirational Occidentalism. The political revaluation remained unfinished. A majority of "patriotic" citizens were burdened with presiding over a huge minority of possible traitors. These included liberals, leftists, and roughly half of the Kurdish population. Erdoğan believed that he governed the country better than any leader before him, yet that this unpatriotic, immoral, and irrational group still saw considered him to be illegitimate. He addressed this group in a 2020 speech in the following manner:

> When there is an earthquake, you do your utmost to inflate the numbers of those under the rubble. When there is an attack on our economy, and people

are thinking of their bread and their future, you run after political profit. When there is a coup attempt, and our nation plants itself in front of tanks, flags in hand, a takbir [the phrase "Allahu Akbar"] on their tongue, you applaud the tanks on your balconies, you slurp coffee in front of your televisions. When we stage operations to end harassment on our border, you rise up against us in defense of blood-stained terrorists.[72]

This population of intensely negative and potentially treasonous opposition supporters was to be contained as much as possible. The election campaigns toward the end of the 2010s raised the threat perception to new levels. A touchstone of Erdoğan's pitch to voters was now a well-worn idea of nationalists everywhere: the West aimed to destabilize Turkey's family structure by injecting LGBT culture into the country.[73] In 2021, Turkey left the Istanbul Convention on July 1, 2021, officially known as "The Council of Europe Convention on Preventing and Combating Violence Against Women and Domestic Violence."[74] This European treaty had been hammered out in Istanbul in 2011, at the tail end of the AK Party liberal years. Now regime surrogates deemed it part of an international plot to spread "LGBT deviation" and curb Turkey's population. In many ways, this was a twenty-first-century version of supposed Jewish conspiracies against Muslim populations, and many commentators made the link explicit.[75] There was a large minority within the country that did not conform to Competitive Occidental values of the new regime, and they had to be contained and, over time, diluted.

Muslim Cosmopolitanism and the Secular Turkish Fear of Replacement

If "Greater Turkey" needs more people, and Turkey's population growth isn't enough to supply them, where will the new people come from? For many countries, a demographic deficit is most easily solved by opening the gates to immigration. Especially English-speaking countries like the United States and Britain consider migration to be a key aspect of their economic and political makeup. Postwar Europe has also begrudgingly become a destination for people across the world. As explained earlier, Republican Turkey's approach is rooted in prewar Europe, gearing toward homogeneity. The most difficult question political for Turkey's new regime is whether it can change that. On the one hand, migration could solve many of the Islamists' problems. Injecting a young population would boost the economy and help to ameliorate the "problem of the 30 million." On the other hand, immigration is wildly unpopular and entails a fundamental revision of what it means to be a citizen of Turkey.

Turkey's first new minority arrived in the country at the heels of a political and humanitarian catastrophe. In the early days of the Syrian Civil War in 2011, the Damascus regime bombed cities in northern Syria, and many inhabitants rushed across the Turkish border to escape. Turkey adopted an open-border policy, welcoming millions of refugees from Syria over the years. While the official number is 4.6 million as of 2024, some experts put it far higher.[76] This population first lived in camps along the border regions, but as the war went on, and their numbers increased, many ventured to Turkey's big cities to find work. Over time, many Syrians transplanted their businesses and started new lives across the border.[77] Syrian ghettos formed in major urban areas with their own economic and cultural spheres.[78] Still, many Syrians sought to move on to Europe, but policies there have since turned sharply against accepting refugees. In March 2016, Turkey and the EU came to an understanding in which Turkey agreed to prevent illegal migration to Europe and was paid significant amounts of money to host refugees within its borders.[79] The Syrian refugees shifted Turkey's conception of itself. Throughout its Republican history, Turkey had been a country of emigration to Europe, and in the post–Cold War era was a transition country for migrants from Asia and Africa. Starting in the 2010s, it became a place to settle down, or at least stay for years at a time. The big cities became a crossroads where people from different continents met.

There are roughly four groups of such newcomers. The first are the least fortunate, the people fleeing wars, primarily in Syria, Iraq and Afghanistan, but also economic migrants from across Asia. This group generally found themselves in specific economic sectors: Afghans tend to work in agriculture, Syrians in manufacturing, and Turkmen, Filipino, and Indonesians in the care sector. The second group are tourists and investors, many of whom came from the oil-rich Gulf, Russia, and Europe. Generous new laws offered them citizenship for property purchases for as much as $400,000.[80] Russians and Ukrainians, be they oligarchs or middle class draft-dodgers, have descended on Turkey's long Mediterranean coastline, while wealthy Gulf Arabs bought property on the lush Black Sea coast and around Istanbul shopping districts. In 2023, more than half of all the world's "citizenship purchases," defined as the practice of obtaining citizenship after making large purchases in a country, occurred in Turkey.[81] The third group are students who take up a growing number of state and non-state scholarships to study in Turkey. Many come from non-Western countries and see this as an opportunity to develop long-term ties with Turkey. The fourth group has been a very small cohort of middle-class Muslims from Western countries. Being frustrated with Western progressivism on the one side and Judeo-Christian conservatism on the other, this group seems drawn to the idea of Turkey's status as a stridently non-liberal Muslim-majority country. The community actually committing to a "hijra" to Turkey is still small, but will likely grow in the future.[82]

The idea of cosmopolitanism in recent history has been almost intrinsically Western, but there is now an exciting south–south cosmopolitanism in some of Turkey's major institutions and cities. This is the result of deliberate policy choices. The Erdoğan government seems to believe that a greater circulation of people from the Muslim world, but also generally non-Western countries, will boost the country's chances across business and culture. When secular Turks express unease about this, Turkish officials argue that they are stuck in an old way of thinking about the world. While center–periphery relations defined the unipolar post–Cold War order, they say, we are now entering a time with far greater connectivity between non-Western countries, which is why Turkey has adopted a "360 degree" approach.[83] This has implications to all aspects of life, and in terms of population, it means that Turkey's demography is going to reflect a broader swathe of its neighboring geography. In this sense, the new regime is probing the boundaries of its Occidentalism, experimenting seeking to engage with ideas that are genuinely new.

The problem for Turkey's new elites is that immigration is wildly unpopular. Nearly every opinion survey conducted on refugees, economic migrants, and even wealthier foreigners in Turkey has registered a desire for a return to Turkey's more homogenous past. A poll conducted by Metropoll in August 2021, for example, asked citizens whether "refugees"—often a catch-all term for poor foreigners—should go back to their countries, and found that 81.7

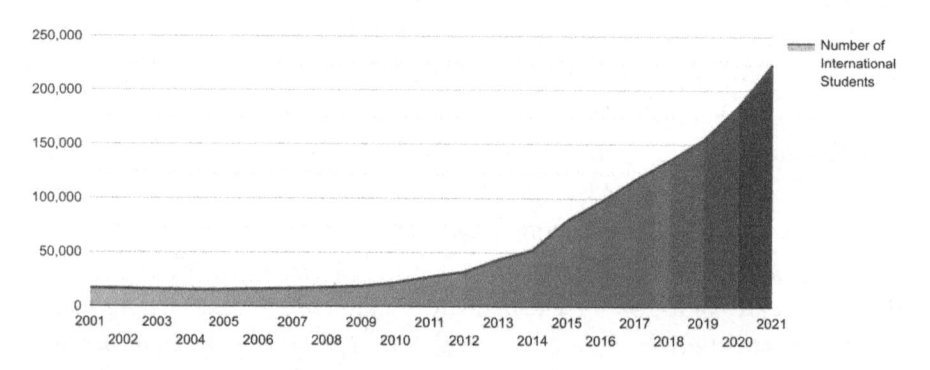

Figure 9 Number of international students 2001–21.

percent responded affirmatively.[84] Opposition voters did so in the high 1980s and 1990s, AK Party supporters were at 84.6 percent, with only the pan-Turkic MHP supporters responding 62.3 percent, perhaps to make up for a perception of racism. Global polls also rank Turkey's residents among the least willing to open their borders for more refugees.[85] This is one of the very few issues that unites young and old, rich and poor, secular and religious.

Opposition parties have strongly aligned against the new immigration policy from a variety of perspectives. The left side of the spectrum has noted that immigration decreases wages and increases housing prices. Politicians among the Kurdish left Peoples' Equality and Democratic Party (DEM), try to speak about immigration in progressive terms, but ultimately know that their base is against it.[86] Many immigrants, especially from Syria and Afghanistan, compete with Kurdish workers in key sectors. Having long been Turkey's largest ethnic minority, the Kurds are also concerned about the country's demographic change, especially as the newcomers seem politically aligned with the state. Parties like the Workers' Party of Turkey (TİP) and the left wing of the main opposition Republican People's Party (CHP) have tried to find a voice that is not xenophobic, humane toward refugees, but also calls for a more stringent border policy. On the right side of the opposition spectrum, there is a more Kemalist resistance to migration, much in the mold of the European right. The CHP's right wing, as well as the pan-Turkic İYİ Party, make up the centrist part of this dyanmic. Founded in 2021, the Victory Party (ZP) is a single-issue, far-right anti-immigrant party, and has pulled the opposition spectrum even further in this direction.[87]

The Erdoğan-led governing coalition was for some time averse to discussing this issue. In the early years of the Syrian Civil War, the AK Party's promise to voters was that Syrians would depart once the conflict was over. "This is not a permanent state, this will not continue for all time. God willing, when conditions in Syria are improved, when the bloody-handed regime in Syria has gone, our brothers and sisters here will return to their cities, their villages, their homes," Erdoğan said in 2014.[88] He repeated the promise throughout the years, sometimes accompanied with plans of extravagant housing projects across the border. Yet with every passing year, the promise becomes less credible.[89] The issue reached boiling point in the 2023 elections, when the opposition's presidential candidate, CHP chairman Kemal Kılıçdaroğlu, underperformed in the first round, signed a secret pact with the hard-right ZP, and campaigned heavily against migrants in the second round. Erdoğan stood his ground during this time, arguing on the basis of an Islamically grounded humanitarianism that refugees could not be forced to return to their countries, and that Turkey had an obligation to take them in. In what appeared to be a carefully scripted question-and-answer session, he also said that refugees who qualified through exams should be free to enter professional tracks in Turkey.[90]

These claims have merit. It isn't too hard to believe that Erdoğan feels kinship, especially to poor Muslims abroad, and feels strongly about giving them a chance at life in Turkey. It is also true, however, that this might obscure other substantial reasons for his pro-immigration stance. The first, as covered earlier, is economic. Migration is clearly convenient to the Islamist elite in a way that isn't for the Erdoğan's working classvoter base, and it is them who have to compete with the newcomers for jobs, housing stock, and educational placement. The second, and more fraught dimension to migration, is about the country's identity. It is not lost on the opposition that migrants are mostly from Muslim countries and tend to support Erdoğan. This has drawn racist attacks on the government's immigration policies. A film entitled *Silent Invasion*, for example, depicts the year 2043, when Arabic has become the national language and Turks are persecuted in their own country.[91] Such imagery invokes the European far right, which has long worried about the "great replacement." It is also common among opposition circles, including among vocal politicians, to claim that the regime has been granting newcomers citizenship with an eye toward winning elections. Successive studies have shown that this is not the case, and that Erdoğan would have won elections regardless of newly naturalized citizens.[92] Projections of Turkey's population growth also suggest that while Syrians are set to become a sizable minority, they are not going to be a large political block anytime soon.[93] Still, population projections in Western countries have often underestimated immigration flows. Once countries open their doors to migrants, a combination of economic interests and family dynamics makes it difficult to stop, leading to an inevitable political transformation. A "white flight" of mostly secular professionals to Western countries is also thinning out institutional capacity in the cities.

Given the political sensitivities around the issue, the Erdoğan regime has tried to avoid it as much as possible, but they won't be able to do so for long. Turkey is on an irreversible course to become a more ethnically and linguistically diverse country, while assuming a more Islamic character. The question then arises: Can Turkey's new regime really be classified as "far right?" After all, it is the opposition that conforms to anti-immigration trends on the Western far right, while the Erdoğan palace's immigration policies are more open than even the most left-wing governments in the West. Erdoğan and his surrogates have made such arguments many times, gleefully out-flanking their Western critics.

The question reflects a broader category error in the classification of political movements. In Western countries, far-right movements favor strict limits on immigration. Left-wing movements label this as a form of racism, seeing in it a belief that people from other countries are immoral or somehow unfit to live in one's society. While this may be true, it misses the civilizational dimension of right-wing politics. France's Marine Le Pen and the Netherlands' Geert Wilders have long campaigned on anti-immigration tickets, and are gaining ground.[94] The Brexit campaign in the UK found out that one of the few issues that moved the needle for voters was the idea that Turkey would eventually be accepted into the EU, and that Turkish migrants would come streaming into Britain.[95] These far-right movements have often pulled the center-right politics in their countries to adopt draconian policies on immigration. Yet the same countries don't generally oppose the free movement of people within Europe. The war in Ukraine has also shown that they are considerably more lenient on refugees from their own continent, than they are toward refugees from the Middle East and Africa, like Syrians, Moroccans, and Kurds.[96] Their detractors claim that far-right nationalists are against any kind of immigration, but that is not quite true. These movements see themselves more as building societies of a homogenous "civilizational" makeup. The problem for the far right, in other words, isn't that immigrants are coming into their countries, it's that immigrants of *foreign civilizations* are coming in.

Hungary's Fidesz and Poland's Law and Justice Party have long boasted that they did not let in any Muslim refugees, often basing these policies explicitly on civilizational thinking.[97] Both countries, however, have been generous recipients of Ukrainian migrants, with Poland hosting about 1.5 million Ukrainian refugees.[98] The far-right governments, including that of Hungary and Italy, have also advocated for policies that would boost birth rates in their countries, framing this as a counter to pro-immigration arguments from liberal quarters.[99] France and Germany, as Europe's leading liberal democracies and longtime recipients of Muslim migrants, on the other hand, have sought to integrate Muslim migrants and refugees, with all the political difficulties this has brought. Yet Erdoğan has very strong relations with Hungary's Viktor Orbán and Poland's Andrej Duda, while he and his surrogates incessantly accuse German and French leaders of Islamophobia.[100] Implicit in these relationships is the idea of maintaining a sort of civilizational hygiene, so that strong national leaders support each other in preventing the mixing of populations. In these circles, the civilizational mixing in liberal democracy has become leverage to be used against these historically powerful countries.

Just like the European far right, Turkey's Islamist tradition therefore takes a civilizational approach on its population. Unlike European countries, however, Turkey has a wider variety of right-wing traditions, which take different positions on Turkey's civilizational place. The Erdoğan palace is a far-right Islamist and, to a lesser extent, Turkist regime, which seeks to fashion the country into the core of wider Muslim-Turkish civilization. This means that the migrants from Islamic countries don't counteract the country's "core identity," but rather help grow the country's imperial body. This has been a theme since the earliest days of Syrian refugees coming in—Turkish politicians, including then—foreign minister Ahmet Davutoğlu, pointed out that Turks and Syrians used to belong to the same empire and were comrades-in-arms against Western invaders.[101] Turkey's Kemalist and Turkist right wings, including the CHP, İYİ, and ZP, on the other hand, consider Turkey to be part of either Western civilization or arguably a Turkic civilization of its own (Turan). To them, the newly arriving migrants are mostly foreign and damaging to the country's identitarian fabric. Erdoğan's ruling coalition therefore faces a different kind of political pressure on migrants. Unlike liberals and leftists, who can safely be labelled as borderline treasonous, the right-wing opposition could be dangerous to Erdoğan. It is easy to imagine that given adverse economic conditions, or weaker leadership in the post-Erdoğan era, the regime's immigration gambit could backfire, resulting in electoral defeats for the AK Party. That is likely why it has treaded carefully and sought to roll out their Islamist cosmopolitanism gradually.

Whether Turkey will choose to take on more migrants or not, the issue will continue to be deeply personal for President Erdoğan. At the eighth annual "Council on the Family," held in the presidential palace complex in October 2023, Erdoğan held a long speech. As usual, he was reading from two teleprompters, alternating between sentences, turning his head from side to side. Having read a few sentences on the average age of marriage rising and divorce becoming more common, the president pulled his gaze away from the two teleprompters and looked straight at the audience for a moment. He was now adding the following statement extemporaneously:

> And the average number of children is declining from day to day. I mean, we aren't saying "at least three children" for nothing. Because this society especially needs it. I can't get into details here. But at this time, it is not enough for our population to be 85 million. We need a much larger population.[102]

With that, Erdoğan fixed his eyes back on the teleprompters. The next line happened to be about how Europe was aging faster than most, which was surely intended to be encouraging. The idea of Greater Turkey was not simply about competing with the West over territory and resources, but in biological existence as well. Success was far from assured, and Turkey needed every advantage it could get.

Military Development and Alliance Structure

The third aspect of Greater Turkey is perhaps the most precarious part of the vision. In order to become a great power in its own right, Turkey's new elite believes that it must acquire the ability to become entirely independent of its treaty allies in the West. This means that it must develop native military technology and defensive alliances. In some ways, this is the last stage of the Competitive Occidentalist transformation. A value system that constantly measures itself up against the West cannot assume that it will remain within its alliance structure indefinitely.

Turkey's Native Arms Industry

Turkey is often said to be the second-largest military force in NATO. This refers to the number of men and women under arms, but says little else.[103] As Turkey's new rulers know all too well, countries also need political will, combat experience, and technology to be a credible military power. Turkey has the first, is acquiring the second, but remains behind on the third. The Islamist tradition has long believed that it was the Islamic world's failure keep pace with Western technology that has been at the root of its decline.[104] And indeed, among the innumerable controversies and contradictory policies, Turkey's new regime is crystal-clear about one thing: it wants to build an entirely self-sufficient defense industry.

This means that Ankara wants to be in a position in which it can produce all of its defense technology without being dependent on any foreign countries, including its treaty allies.[105] It sees any cooperation it maintains with these countries as stepping stones to establishing indigenous capability. In Turkey's new political parlance, this is referred to as the "yerlilik ve millilik oranı," which literally translates as "the degree of localness and nationalness," but is often referred to in English as the "indigenization rate."[106] It isn't clear how the government calculates the figure, but it seems to be based on the monetary value of the parts used in the defense industry.[107] Erdoğan claims that the indigenization rate was at 20 percent when he took office, and periodically reports a rising number.[108] After steady increases for two decades, the Ministry of Defense claimed that the number was above 80 percent in 2023.[109] During the 2023 national elections, the Erdoğan campaign was adamant to point out its achievements in this field, adorning its election posters with natively produced attack helicopters and armored personnel carriers. Weeks before the election, the new flagship of the Turkish navy, the *TCG Anadolu*, docked off the ancient Topkapı Palace in Istanbul, where it received visitors to inspect the indigenously produced, high-tech weapons systems on board. The queue to enter the vessel stretched back 2 kilometers.[110]

As in many other fields, the new regime's eagerness stems from a need to make up for lost time. Turkey began building up an indigenous defense industry in the early years of the Republic, especially in the 1930s and 1940s. This was aided by scientists fleeing Nazi Germany. The General Directorate of Military Factories was formed during this time and presided over a flurry of activity, including in the aviation sector.[111] Turkey, however, sat out nearly all of the Second World War, and its military capabilities remained untested. Within the 1939–57 time window, when Turkey was most pro-American and anti-Soviet (see Chapter 4), the country changed tack. Under the Truman Doctrine, the United States and Turkey signed a deal on July 12, 1947, under which Turkey was to receive American weapons, many of which were holdovers from the recent war in Europe. Turkey quickly became dependent on the US arms industry, the General Directorate of Military Factories was dissolved into another department, and some of the factories that had been built in the initial period were converted for civilian purposes.[112] Infamously, the Turkish Aeronautical Association's plane factory was repurposed as a textiles factory.

Turkey felt the need to reverse this policy decades before the founding of the AK Party. In the 1960s, the Turkish minority in Cyprus was under increasing threat from the Greek majority. Ankara sought to intervene on the island, but in 1964, a letter from US president Lyndon B. Johnson threatened it with an arms embargo if it should do so. This was a bitter rebuke, and Turkey launched a highly public campaign to build up its indigenous capabilities. In 1965, it founded the "Türk Donanma Cemiyeti" (The Turkish Naval Association) and in 1970 the "Türk Hava Kuvvetlerini Güçlendirme Vakfı" (The Foundation for Strengthening the Turkish Air Force).[113] In 1974, Turkey staged the "Cyprus Peace Operation," in which it intervened on the island on behalf of its Turkish-speaking population, and was sanctioned by the United States and other NATO allies. In 1975, ASELSAN, a company aiming to produce communication equipment for the Turkish military, was founded as one of the first technology firms in the defense space.[114] An indigenous defense industry was now on its way, but rather than aiming for complete self-sufficiency, it was simply geared toward reducing Turkey's dependence on its allies.

In 1985, Turkey established the Presidency of Development and Support of the National Defense Industry, launching the modernization of the Turkish Air Force (TAF).[115] The effort was now centralized and advanced with greater urgency. The 1980s had brought a wave of liberalization and economic and industrial growth, and the defense sector grew along with the rest of the economy. Much of this was once again in close cooperation with Turkey's NATO allies. The biggest partnership was the F-16 project, which became the flagship project of the Turkish military aviation industry. Firms like FNSS, ASELSAN, and ROKETSAN grew very quickly, acquiring bigger parts in their joint projects with their American partners. An ecosystem of small and medium-sized enterprises grows around the defense sector.[116]

The first AK Party government of 2002 already began to accelerate the indigenization process. Necmettin Erbakan, the leader of Turkish Islamism and mentor to many of the AK Party's founders, was a German-trained mechanical engineer who was passionate about building up the defense sector independently of Turkey's NATO allies. While it diverged from Erbakan's politics, the young AK Party government followed in his footsteps in the defense sector, and quietly emphasized the growth of indigenous capabilities. In its meeting on May 14, 2004, the Defense Industry Executive Committee (the main decision-making body of the then-SSM) decided that it would abandon the production model of two systems at the time (a battle tank and unmanned drone) and initiate new production plans in which national indigenous companies would be the main contractors.[117] This marked the beginning of a new model in the industry in which indigenous companies were the main contractors, rather than supplementary ones.[118] The economy grew quickly in the 2000s, and once again, the defense industry grew with it. This time, more national companies were experimenting with indigenous designs and concepts. SME clusters developed and attracted skilled engineers from some of Turkey's best universities. The most complex components, such as engines and electronics, were still imported, but much of the design was done in Turkey. Turkish firms were able to develop their own platforms and export to ever-growing markets. One of the stars of this movement, a young MIT-trained engineer and businessman called Selçuk

Bayraktar, married Erdoğan's younger daughter in 2016. Some of the best-known indigenously produced systems of this era were the Bayraktar drone, the Altay tank, and the *MILGEM* warship.

The 2016 coup attempt accelerated indigenization and diversification in the defense industry. Soon after the coup attempt, the SSM (and MİT) were linked directly to the presidency, signaling a new prioritization. Turkey chose to purchase the S-400 Russian air-defense system, which Turkish authorities knew would endanger their place in the program for the F-35, NATO's fifth-generation fighter jet. Turkey had joined the program in 1999, and the air force eagerly anticipated the most important upgrade to its arsenal in decades.[119] Experts made it clear that the F-35 was far more important to Turkey's arsenal than the S-400. Yet in the post-coup environment, Turkey chose to risk the purchase of the S-400, eventually being kicked out of the F-35 program. This was a clear demonstration that the country was taking self-sufficiency seriously. Soon afterwards, Turkey announced plans to build its own fifth-generation fighter jet.[120] As discussed in Chapter 3, this was also a time when Turkey launched cross-border operations into Syria and intensified its efforts on all other fronts. The TSK was now involved in direct combat in Iraq and Syria, and indirectly in conflicts like the Armenia–Azerbaijan war. All this allowed Turkey's defense industry to test its systems under more strenuous conditions and tightened the relationship between developers and end users. Exports of the defense and aerospace industry rose by leaps and bounds in the early 2020s.[121] Between 2002, when the AK Party came to power, and 2022, the number of projects annually increased more than tenfold, from 62 to more than 750.[122] In 2002, the sector's R&D spending was $49 million. By 2020, it had reached $1.24 billion.[123]

Erdoğan's enthusiasm for the "indigenization ratio" became wildly popular, to the extent that the president rarely had to mention himself any more. His son-in-law Selçuk Bayraktar became a national technologist-in-chief, launching "Teknofest," a fair for families with small children, showcasing the latest in Turkish defense technology, including drones, planes, as well as futuristic gadgets with civilian applications. It started to host competitions, often attended by students of elite STEM programs.[124] The media narrative around Teknofest constantly evoked the late 1940s, when Turkey began importing American weapons, abandoned its own defense industry, and was entrapped in an alliance that was foreign to its civilizational core. A documentary series by the state broadcaster TRT, entitled "The Solitary Geniuses of the Defense Industry," for example, portrays figures from this era as patriotic inventors who labored to create defense technology, but were sabotaged by dark forces, presumably being the Kemalist elite and the United States.[125] Among these figures is Nuri Demirağ, a famous industrialist and owner of the shuttered airplane factories, now hailed a "Turkish Elon Musk." More appropriate to fitting to that title, however, is Selçuk Bayraktar himself, a skilled technologist who rejected attractive offers in the United States and returned to build up his father's business in Turkey. Bayraktar likes to argue that Turkey's defense industry was in a "mentality of dependence" which trapped it in a "technological encirclement." Now that it has regained its self-confidence, it has broken through the encirclement and has become a self-confident producer.[126]

Detractors in the opposition often seek to deflate this narrative, pointing out that some of Turkey's highest-profile projects heavily rely on its traditional partners. The engine of the fifth-generation fighter jet "Kaan," for example, which Turkey is developing as a replacement for the F-35, is based on a $125 million deal with BAE Systems based in the UK.[127] Such criticism, however, is missing the point. Surrogates of the Erdoğan palace understand that the country is playing the long game, benefiting from technology transfers until it is able to build and maintain complex weapons platforms on its own.[128] When Kaan made its maiden flight on February 21, 2024, Selçuk Bayraktar released a video, saying, "when future generations look at these years, they will see that this age, which started with the national technology moves of the 2000s, led into the golden age of Turkish aviation." He argued that the nation had accomplished this despite "some political segments" trying to prevent these efforts.[129] When advertising native projects, state media frame them as milestones in a journey toward a fully autonomous weapons industry.

This raises an awkward question. A robust indigenous defense industry is an important part of any country's defense. Yet weapons systems today are too complex for midsized countries to develop on their own. There are certainly no other NATO members preparing for complete, or even near-autarky in their defense sector. Some of the best Turkish experts on the defense industry have also argued autarky is not remotely a practical goal for Turkey.[130] The idea behind Greater Turkey, however, is that it does not behave like a midsized power, but a major power in its own right. What, then, does this mean for the country's membership in the most powerful military alliance in the world?

NATO in the Age of Competitive Occidentalism

There is a taboo against interrogating the compatibility of "Greater Turkey" and the country's NATO membership. There may be several different reasons for this.

For members of Turkey's new elite, especially those communicating its message abroad, the subject is taboo because it would weaken Turkey's standing in the West. From their point of view, it would make sense for Turkey to maximize the benefits of NATO membership until it has acquired self-sustaining defense capabilities, and is less dependent on the alliance.[131] For liberals in Turkey, the taboo is about protecting Turkey's possible future in NATO. They fear that if Turkey's Western allies are made to believe that the country intends to leave the alliance, the process might accelerate and become irreversible.[132] For the liberal political establishment in other NATO countries, the taboo exists for similar reasons: few seek to accelerate Turkey's current geopolitical direction of travel, and given the growing influence of the far right in Europe and the United States, it may also seem inappropriate in these circles to be hard on the alliance's big Muslim-majority member.

Tellingly, there is a group of thinkers who are blissfully free of the taboos regarding Turkey's defense policy. Yusuf Kaplan, one of the foremost contemporary heirs of the Islamist romantics and prominent columnist of the newspaper *Yeni Şafak*, has been writing for some time that Turkey's NATO membership is a great misfortune, a manifestation of the way in which the country has been gaslit to serve its enemies. Now that Turkey has come to realize that the West is not a cradle of freedom, but an evil force bent on suppressing the Islamic world, he believes that that Ankara is gradually preparing to leave. This means that there is an unarticulated civilizational tension between Turkey and its treaty allies:

> By keeping Turkey in NATO, NATO prevents Turkey from shifting towards a different direction, from trying to form its own Islamic orbit. Turkey, meanwhile, by staying in NATO, prevents itself from becoming an open target of NATO. I've said it already, but Turkey knows that NATO stages the coups, that it supports terror, and NATO knows that Turkey knows.[133]

This notion that Turkey and NATO are locked in what we might call a "hostile embrace" is a theme that comes up repeatedly in public discussions. Here is Victory Party leader Ümit Özdağ speaking on the subject:

> If Turkey left NATO today, it would become its target ... our chance of taking back the islands under Greek occupation in the Aegean would disappear ... Turkey would be in the position of an occupier in Cyprus, the Greek part of the island would enter NATO. In summary, remaining within NATO now is a security strategy for Turkey ... without deep-rooted change under objective conditions, saying 'let's leave NATO,' politically, is nothing but drivel.[134]

The idea underpinning much of the right-wing punditry on this issue is that leaving NATO entails counterintuitive measures, and is best not discussed too openly. "Plain logic is suicide of the mind," writes Kaplan, cautioning that "Turkey isn't yet fully independent, and its problems cannot be solved with plain logic."[135]

Plain logic, however, is fairly wide spread among the ruling elite, and sometimes leaks out to the wider public. Ethem Sancak, a businessman, defense contractor, and former AK Party member known for his close ties to Erdoğan (later with the Eurasianist-Kemalist Vatan Party), made similar comments when he was dispatched to Moscow in the early days of Russia's full-scale invasion of Ukraine in 2022. Speaking to a TV channel there, Sancak said that NATO was "a devilish gang," that "NATO membership comes from a shameful part of Turkey's history [geçmişten gelen ayıbıdır]" and that "they will kick us out if we don't leave anyways."[136] The remarks were meant to soften Russian reactions to Turkey's Kyiv-friendly, but Western-skeptic, policy, but they also conveyed the trajectory implicit to Turkey's Competitive Occidentalist geopolitical orientation.

None of this is to say that Turkey is about to leave NATO. The Erdoğan palace has become highly skilled at the "hostile embrace." Officials in the West usually emphasize that despite Turkey's dramatic rhetoric, its participation behind the scenes remains stellar. Occupying a critical geographic area for Western security outfits, Turkey's intelligence and military institutions have been reliable partners to its allies. A frequently used rhetorical device among Turkish officials is to make extremely strong assertions such as "NATO cannot be fathomed without Turkey" or "NATO cannot remain standing without Turkey." These are intended to uphold the taboo against singling out Turkey, as well as to invite Western statesmen to repeat them, and thus uphold the taboo on their side.[137] Turkey thereby seeks to leverage its NATO membership to weaken Western containment of Turkey's indigenous development.

Meanwhile, the idea of an alternative network of cooperation, if not alliance, is brewing in governing circles. This is not a new concept, and its variations go back as far as the dissolution of the Ottoman Empire. Turanists wanted Turkey to lead the Turkic world, while Islamists wanted a pan-Islamic political union, even if it fell short of re-establishing the caliphate. Former prime minister Necmettin Erbakan famously championed the idea of an Islamic superstate with its own currency and defensive alliance. In a video in which Erbakan explains the concept to a room full of eager listeners, we see a young Erdoğan sipping tea.[138] The problem was that at the time, the idea sounded cartoonish. When I asked former Islamists about the reasons they co-founded or supported the

AK Party, which was, after all a draing Islamist splinter movement at the time, several cited one salient memory: the image of Erbakan holding up a coin in front of the press, and saying, "this is an Islamic Dinar," the future currency of the Turkish-led Islamic superstate. It was emblematic of his politics, but to his young protoges, it felt escapist—it may have been an alluring thought, but it was out of tune with the times. The early years of the AK Party sought to correct for that, and link up to the liberalism of the times. More than twenty years after the AK Party's founding, however, the idea of forging bold new alliances no longer sounds as outlandish in Ankara as it once did.[139]

Conclusion

In early 2023, it looked like New Turkey might be approaching its end. People seemed unhappy with the way the country was run. Inflation was at about 60 percent year-on-year, eroding savings and purchasing power. Housing prices were soaring, especially in big cities like Istanbul. Most news reports consisted of reporters going to grocery stores and interviewing people about the price of household goods.

Parliamentary and presidential elections were scheduled for May 14, with a possible presidential runoff to take place on May 28. Hopes were high in opposition circles. Its united presidential candidate, CHP chairman Kemal Kılıçdaroğlu, presented himself as a Kemalist democrat against Erdoğan's Islamist authoritarianism. His campaign song was deeply nostalgic, and the refrain was heard in shops and homes across the major cities: "I promise you spring will come, I promise you hope won't end." Kılıçdaroğlu was going to restore the parliamentary system, free the media, and rebuild bureaucratic competence. Pollsters were highly optimistic about his chances. Most of the debate in the opposition circles was on whether Kılıçdaroğlu would secure a majority in the first round or win in a runoff.[1]

Meanwhile, Erdoğan ran on a heavily nationalistic platform, parading indigenous weapons systems and monumental building projects. His party and state institutions took measures to broaden employment and make sure that neighborhoods loyal to the ruling party were taken care of. Above all, however, they asked their voters for patience. The economic problems were temporary, they said, and voters should keep their eyes on the thing that really mattered: Turkey's national resurgence. Speaking on a government-friendly news channel two weeks before the elections, Mehmet Uçum, the senior presidential advisor and one of the architects of the Erdoğan regime's institutional structure, said that the opposition was assuming that people would vote on pocketbook issues, but that "this election will probably break that orthodoxy [ezber]."[2] The economy was a problem, Uçum said, but Erdoğan's base would ultimately vote on geopolitics. "This is the election where people will ask what Turkey needs to do in order to feel secure. What will be our situation in the Mediterranean, Iraq, and Syria? How will Turkey's role continue in the Russia-Ukraine war? Voters have feelings about this," he said.[3]

The presidential palace took a big risk, and it paid off. In an outcome that stunned all but a few pro-government pollsters, Erdoğan established a nearly 5-point lead over Kılıçdaroğlu in the first round on May 14, almost winning an outright majority. In the second round on May 28, the president was reelected with 52.18 percent. The parliamentary race, too, went overwhelmingly in Erdoğan's favor. His coalition was no longer just the AK Party and the MHP, it now had other flavors of Islamism and Turkism. The "Free Cause Party," (HÜDA-PAR), which had its origins in a Kurdish-Islamist paramilitary group called Hizbullah, (not to be confused with the Lebanese group of the same name) notorious for its violent operations in the South-Eastern provinces in the 1980s and 1990s, received four seats. The New Welfare Party (Yeniden Refah), headed by the son of Erdoğan's mentor Necmettin Erbakan, received five seats. On the opposition side, the CHP had worked with disgruntled right-wingers in a failed attempt to woo Erdoğan voters, so even the opposition ranks now contained Islamists and Turkists. Altogether, this was easily the most far-right parliament in the country's history.

What kind of policy would this yield? One might have thought that it would translate into a more radical form of Competitive Occidentalism, especially in foreign policy. The new government would surely pump more money into the defense sector, adopt a hawkish stand in Syria, Iraq, Libya and the Eastern Mediterranean, be more disruptive in NATO, and cooperate with revisionist and Islamist powers across the region.

That is not what happened. A few days after the election, Erdoğan announced his cabinet, and it was perhaps the most centrist, professional team he had ever put together. The economy was in the hands of Mehmet Şimşek, a strict adherent of neoliberal orthodoxy and darling of London investors. Interior Minister Süleyman Soylu, who was believed by many to have ties to organized crime, and was known for his vicious attacks against the opposition, Kurdish politicians, and "the West," was replaced with Ali Yerlikaya, a quiet bureaucratic type.[4] Foreign Minister Mevlüt Çavuşoğlu, who was thin on substance and merely echoed Erdoğan's scolding remarks against Western leaders, was switched out for the laconic and technocratic Hakan Fidan.[5]

In the following months, Turkey embarked on a major charm offensive in the West. The economics team hired Turkish talent from the United States to fix monetary policy and attract international investment. The interior ministry and intelligence services embarked on a major campaign against organized crime, working with international partners to bust record numbers of drug dealers and money launderers. Foreign Minister Fidan, re-engaged with his European counterparts, reached out to Greece, and tried to untangle relations with the United States.

In such moments, it might seem that Erdoğan's "anti-Western" rhetoric is merely for show, an elaborate act to excite voters while maintaining the country's Western orientation. Turkey, after all, is inextricably bound to Western markets, know-how, and defense infrastructure.

This narrow focus on policy outcomes misses the point of Turkish politics in the last quarter-century. What I have suggested in this book is that Erdoğan's politics of the last twenty years is not a revolution but a revaluation. The Islamist movement does not aim to enforce radical change. The US-dominated liberal order is too broad and powerful to confront head-on, especially for midsized powers like Turkey. For the Erdoğan government, revisionism is a more subtle and long-term project. Its most important goal has been to reverse the value system that Western domination has yielded in Turkey. That is why the monarchist and anti-Kemalist polemicist Kadir Mısıroğlu, whose life and work I have covered in the first chapter, would not have been troubled by this latest rapprochement with the West. To borrow from his analogy, Turkey is going through a change in seasons, from the cold, dark days of Aspirational Occidentalism to the warm summery days of "New Turkey's" Competitive Occidentalism. "When there is a cold day in between, we aren't worried because it is against the essence of the season. Seasons contain contrasts," Mısıroğlu said. And indeed, the revaluation has quietly been continuing. The regime is deepening its control over public and private institutions, as well as overhauling the education system to rewrite the narrative of modern Turkey.[6] The new elite want the next generation of Turkish citizens to grow up with very rigid conceptions of East and West, and be receptive to the message of revisionist nationalism, be it Islamist or Turkist in outlook.

Will they succeed? It's hard to tell. Romantic nationalists may claim that nations have irrepressible essences that remain constant over time, but the rest of us have no reason to share in such beliefs. When looking at his fellow Germans in the late nineteenth century, Nietzsche wrote that they had a past and a future, but they didn't have a present. The question "what is German?" was always fresh to Nietzsche.[7] His countrymen, he thought, were vulgar in comparison to the French, but their virtue lay in their readiness to change, to push the boundaries of what it meant to be German. "Change into the ungermanic has always been the mark of the most able of our people" he wrote.[8] The Turkish people too, are a nation in flux. This is only the most recent in a series of "New Turkeys," and despite what far-right romantics may believe, it isn't any more "essential" to Turkishness than any other. After phases of Aspirational and Competitive Occidentalism, perhaps Turkey will be ready to step out of Occidentalism all together. Perhaps it will leave the politics of catchup and revenge behind, focus more on the welfare of its citizenry, and less on its status among other nations.

Notes

Introduction

1. Interview with author, July 24, 2020.
2. Barack Hussein Obama II, "Inaugural Address," January 20, 2009, https://obamawhitehouse.archives.gov/realitycheck/the_press_office/President_Barack_Obamas_Inaugural_Address.
3. Interview with author, July 24, 2020.
4. *EU-Turkey Relations* (Cham: Palgrave-Macmillan, 2021), 91–2, https://link.springer.com/content/pdf/10.1007/978-3-030-70890-0.pdf.
5. Soner Çağaptay, *Erdoğan's Empire: Turkey and the Politics of the Middle East* (London: I.B. Tauris, 2019), 128–31.
6. Nicholas L. Danforth, "New Turkey versus Old Cliches," *Duvar English*, December 5, 2019, https://www.duvarenglish.com/columns/2019/12/05/new-turkey-versus-old-cliches. Tanıl Bora, "Yeni Türkiye [New Turkey]," *Birikim*, June 7, 2016, https://birikimdergisi.com/haftalik/7718/yeni-turkiye%23.XW-pnpMzaWc.
7. Danforth, "New Turkey versus Old cliches."
8. Ibid.
9. Karaca objected to her song's use, hinting that she did not support the AK Party. The term, however, continued to be used in political discourse. See: "İşte AK Parti'nin seçim şarkısı... [Here is the AK Party's election song...]," May 19, 2007, https://www.haberturk.com/gundem/haber/23725-iste-ak-partinin-secim-sarkisi; Muhittin Ataman, Burhanettin Duran, and Kemal İnat, "Türk Dış Politikası Yıllığı: 2009 [Annual Review of Turkish Foreign Policy: 2009]," *Siyaset, Ekonomi ve Toplum Araştırmaları Vakfı*, March 2011, https://tdpyilligi.setav.org/tdp/turk-dis-politikasi-yilligi-2009.pdf; İbrahim Kalın, "Enine Boyuna Türkiye: Siyaset, Toplum, Kültür [Turkey in Length: Politics, Society, Culture]," *Siyaset, Ekonomi ve Toplum Araştırmaları Vakfı*, June 1, 2009, https://www.setav.org/enine-boyuna-turkiye-siyaset-toplum-kultur/; Ali Ekber Ertürk and Ömer Karahan, "Atam izindeyizi kim makasladı," *Akşam*, May 16, 2007, https://web.archive.org/web/20070519031910/http://www.aksam.com.tr/haber.asp?a=77555,3.
10. Mehmet Ocaktan, "'Felaket senaryoları' boşuna, Türkiye iyi yolda... ['Disaster scenarios' are in vain, Turkey is on the right track...]," *Yeni Şafak*, February 20, 2007, https://www.yenisafak.com/yazarlar/mehmet-ocaktan/felaket-senaryolari-bouna-turkiye-iyi-yolda-3951.

11 For a thorough treatment of the topic, see: Robert A. Schneider, *The Return of Resentment: The Rise and Decline and Rise Again of a Political Emotion* (Chicago, IL: University of Chicago Press, 2023).
12 See Arlie Russell Hochschild, *Strangers in Their Own Land: Anger and Mourning on the American Right* (New York City, NY: The New Press, 2016) and James David Vance, *Hillbilly Elegy: A Memoir of a Family and Culture in Crisis* (New York City, NY: Harper, 2016).
13 İlker Aytürk, "Post-Post-Kemalizm: Yeni Bir Paradigmayı Beklerken [Post-Post-Kemalism: Awaiying a New Paradigm]," in *Post-Post Kemalizm* (Istanbul: İletişim Yayınları, 2022). Nicholas L. Danforth, *The Remaking of Republican Turkey: Memory and Modernity Since the Fall of the Ottoman Empire* (Cambridge: Cambridge University Press, 2021), 6.
14 ibid.
15 "Press Conference by the President, 6-23-09," *The White House, Office of the Press Secretary*, June 23, 2009, https://obamawhitehouse.archives.gov/the-press-office/press-conference-president-6-23-09.
16 "Adalet ve Kalkınma Partisi" literally means "Justice and Development Party." The initials "AK" also spell out the Turkic-rooted word for "white." "Ak" has an Ottoman-era twang (as opposed to "beyaz," which is the contemporary word for white most often used today). "Ak" is used in old proverbs and carries a meaning of a clean slate, or innocence ("Ana sütü gibi *ak*" meaning "*white* as mother's milk"). Both Ak-evler and the AK Party suggest innocence and a fresh beginning.
17 "Akevler Platformu [Akevler Platform]," https://www.akevler.org/Default.aspx; "Ak Evler Nedir? | 1998 | Rıdvan Akar [What are Ak Evler? | 1998 | Rıdvan Akar]," (Gün, 1998), 32, https://www.youtube.com/watch?v=HQLtQ97JQHI.
18 One oft-repeated story was that Captain Jacques Cousteau, a famous French naval officer and explorer, converted to Islam after discovering that salt and sweet waters do not mix in the Strait of Gibraltar, seemingly confirming a Quranic passage.

Chapter 1

1 Robbie Shilliam, *German Thought and International Relations: The Rise and Fall of a Liberal Project* (New York City, NY: Palgrave Macmillan, 2009), 37.
2 Tanıl Bora, *Cereyanlar: Türkiye'de siyasî ideolojiler* [Currents: Political ideologies in Turkey] (Istanbul: İletişim Yayınları, 2017), 442.
3 "Erdoğan eleştirilerinin dozunu artırdı [The dose of Erdoğan criticisms rose]," *CNN Türk*, February 13, 2008, https://www.cnnturk.com/2008/turkiye/02/13/erdogan.elestirilerinin.dozunu.artirdi/428004.0/index.html.

Notes

4 See Yael Tamir, *Why Nationalism* (Princeton, NJ: Princeton University Press, 2019); S. Kapil Komireddi, *Malevolent Republic: A Short History of the New India* (London: Hurst Publishers, 2019); Helge Blakkisrud and Pål Kolstø, *The New Russian Nationalism: Imperialism, Ethnicity and Authoritarianism 2000–2015* (Edinburgh: Edinburgh University Press, 2017); and Maria Hsia Chang, *Return of the Dragon: China's Wounded Nationalism* (Oxford: Routledge, 2018).

5 See: Benedict Anderson, *Imagined Communities: Reflections on the Origin and Spread of Nationalism* (London: Verso, 2016) and Ernest Gellner, *Nations and Nationalism* (Oxford: Blackwell, 1983).

6 See Elie Kedourie, *Nationalism* (Oxford: Blackwell, 1993).

7 See Liah Greenfield, *Nationalism: Five Roads to Modernity* (Cambridge, MA: Harvard University Press, 1992) and Liah Greenfield, "The Formation of the Russian National Identity: The Role of Status Insecurity and Ressentiment," *Comparative Studies in Society and History* 32, no. 3 (July 1990): 549–91.

8 Greenfield, *Nationalism*, 4–5.

9 Liah Greenfield, *Nationalism: A Short History* (Washington, DC: Brookings Institution Press, 2019), 39.

10 Ibid., 46.

11 Ibid., 44–5.

12 Friedrich Wilhelm Nietzsche, Keith Ansell-Pearso, and Carol Diethe, eds., *"On the Genealogy of Morality" and Other Writings* (Cambridge: Cambridge University Press, 2017).

13 Friedrich Wilhelm Nietzsche, *Thus Spoke Zarathustra*, ed. Robert Pippin, trans. Adrian Del Caro (Cambridge: Cambridge University Press, 2006), 111.

14 Max Scheler, *Ressentiment* (New York: The Free Press, 1961), 52; Pankaj Mishra, *Age of Anger: A History of the Present* (New York: Farrar, Strauss, and Giroux, 2017), 333.

15 Ibid., 50; Greenfeld, *Nationalism*, 75.

16 Mishra, *Age of Anger*, 174; John H. Zammito, Karl Menges, and Ernest A. Menze, "Johann Gottfried Herder Revisited: The Revolution in Scholarship in the Last Quarter Century," *Journal of the History of Ideas* 71, no. 4 (2010): 669–70.

17 Richard Samuel, "III. Goethe—Napoleon—Heinrich Von Kleist: Ein Beitrag Zu Dem Thema: Napoleon Und Das Deutsche Geistesleben," *Publications of the English Goethe Society* 14, no. 1 (January 1939): 50.

18 Friedrich Nietzsche and Daniel Breazeale, eds., *Nietzsche: Untimely Meditations* (Lexington: University of Kentucky Press, 1997), 6.

19 German History in Documents and Images: Volume 5, Wilhelmine Germany and the First World War, 1890-1918; Bernhard von Bülow on Germany's "Place in the Sun" (1897), https://germanhistorydocs.ghi-dc.org/pdf/eng/607_Buelow_Place%20in%20the%20Sun_111.pdf.

20 Peter Padfield, *The Great Naval Race: The Anglo-German Naval Rivalry, 1900-1914* (New York City, NY: D. McKay Company, 1974), 44–5.
21 Robert E. Kelly, "Comparing China and the Kaiser's Germany (part 1): Similarities," *Lowy Institute*, March 12, 2014, https://www.lowyinstitute.org/the-interpreter/comparing-china-kaiser-s-germany-part-1-similarities; Walter Russell Mead, "In the Footsteps of the Kaiser: China Boosts US Power in Asia," *The American Interest*, September 26, 2010, https://www.the-american-interest.com/2010/09/26/in-the-footsteps-of-the-kaiser-china-boosts-us-power-in-asia; Robert Kirchubel and Sorin Adam Matei, "How Xi Jinping's China Is Wilhelmine Germany Come Again," *The National Interest*, April 20, 2021, https://nationalinterest.org/blog/buzz/how-xi-jinping%E2%80%99s-china-wilhelmine-germany-come-again-183190.
22 H. Ozan Özavcı, "The Ottoman Imperial Gaze: The Greek Revolution of 1821–1832 and a New History of the Eastern Question," *Journal of Modern European History* 21, no. 2 (2023): 223.
23 M. Şükrü Hanioğlu, *A Brief History of the Late Ottoman Empire* (Princeton, NJ: Princeton University Press, 2008), Chapter II: Initial Ottoman Responses to the Challenge of Modernity.
24 Miroslav Hroch, Michal Kopeček, and Balázs Trencsényi, *National Romanticism: The Formation of National Movements* (Budapest: Central European University Press, 2007), 94–7.
25 Bora, *Cereyanlar*, 25.
26 Hasan Aksakal, *Türk Politik Kültüründe Romantizm* [Romanticism in Turkish Political Culture] (Istanbul: İletişim Yayınları, 2015), 15.
27 For an in-depth discussion of the term, see Ian Burma and Avishai Margalit, *Occidentalism: The West in the Eyes of its Enemies* (New York: Penguin Gorup, 2004).
28 Greenfeld and Chirot argue that some strands of nationalism contain more ressentiment than others, which makes them more likely to engage in moralistic and, ultimately, violent behavior. Russia, she argues, is one such country. A similar argument could be made about Turkey, requiring an in-depth analysis of Ottoman and republican Occidentalist views and class relations. See Daniel Chirot and Liah Greenfeld, "Nationalism and Aggression," *Theory and Society* 23, no. 1 (February 1994): 79–130.
29 See "Chapter III: The Scientism of the Young Turks," in M. Şükrü Hanioğlu, *Atatürk: An Intellectual Biography* (Princeton, NJ: Princeton University Press, 2011).
30 Hanioğlu, *A Brief History of the Late Ottoman Empire*, 125, 142.
31 Ryan Gingeras, *Eternal Dawn: Turkey in the Age of Atatürk* (New York: Oxford University Press, 2019), 72–4.
32 Amit Bein, *Kemalist Turkey and the Middle East International Relations in the Interwar Period* (Cambridge: Cambridge University Press, 2020), 19–20; Nicholas

L. Danforth, *The Remaking of Republican Turkey: Memory and Modernity Since the Ottoman Empire* (Cambridge: Cambridge University Press, 2021), 164.

33 Hasan Rıza Soyak, *Atatürk'ten Hatıralar* [Memories from Atatürk] (Istanbul: Yapı Kredi Yayınları, 2004).

34 Soyak quotes him as saying "şaşarım aklı perişanına," an exclamation peculiar to Atatürk.

35 Ibid.

36 Ziya Önis, "Globalization, Democratization and the Far Right: Turkey's Nationalist Action Party in Critical Perspective," *Democratization* 10, no. 1 (2003): 27–52.

37 İlker Aytürk and Tanıl Bora, "Yetmişli Yıllarda Sağ ve Sol Kutuplaşması [Polarization of Right and Left in the Seventies]," in *Türkiye'nin 1970'li Yılları* [Turkey's Seventies], ed. Mete Kaynar (İstanbul: Iletişim Yayınları, 2020), 318–20.

38 Corey Robin has a similar definition. See Corey Robin, *The Reactionary Mind: Conservatism from Edmund Burke to Sarah Palin* (Oxford: Oxford University Press, 2011).

39 Aytürk and Bora, "Yetmişli Yıllarda Sağ ve Sol Kutuplaşması," 322–3.

40 Aytürk's classification can be applied to the contemporary politics of other nations. An analogous moment in American politics was Donald Trump's inauguration speech, also known as the "American Carnage" speech. Here, Trump argued that the center of government had been hijacked by "globalists," and that his presidency marked the restoration. "January 20th 2017, will be remembered as the day the people became the rulers of this nation again," he said.

41 James Ryan, "Ideology on Trial: The Prosecution of Leftists and Pan-Turkists at the Dawn of the Cold War in Turkey, 1944-1947," *PRISMS*, 2022, 32–4.

42 Bora writes that the Anatolianists "drew a strong line between Islamism and nationalism," see: Bora, *Cereyanlar*, 371.

"Mukaddesatçı" literally translated into "those in favor of the sacred." For a full English-language treatment of the term, see Talha Köseoğlu, "*Mukaddesatçılık*: A Cold War Ideology of Muslim Turkish Ressentiment," *International Journal of Middle East Studies* 55, no. 1 (February 2023): 84–105.

43 The Turkists had (and continue to have) the Ülkü Ocakları" or "Idealist Hearths" and the Islamists had the National Turkish Student Union (Milli Türk Talebe Birliği, or MTTB).

44 Tanıl Bora and Kemal Can, *Devlet Ocak Dergâh: 12 Eylül'den 1990'lara Ülkücü Hareket* [State, Hearth, Convent: the Nationalist Movement from September 12 to the 1990s] (Istanbul: İletişim Yayınları, 1991), 74–9.

45 Turkist ideology features quasi-mystical symbols like the she-wolf who led the ancestral Turks out of a great crisis. Literalist Muslims consider this heresy.

46 Samuel J. Hirst and Onur İşçi, "Smokestacks and Pipelines: Russian-Turkish Relations and the Persistence of Economic Development," *Diplomatic History* 44, no. 5 (November 1, 2020): 834–59.

47 For an early interpretation of the Turkish far right as a movement of Nietzschean *ressentiment*, see the reprinting of the 1996 article by Fethi Açıkel in *Kutsal Mazlumluktan Makyavelist Despotizme: AKP Otoriterliğinin psikopatolojisi* [From Sacred Oppression to Machiavellian Despotism: The Psychopathology of AKP Authoritarianism] (Istanbul: İletişim Yayıcılık A.Ş., 2023).
48 Sadi Irmak, "Atatürk'ü anarken [Remembering Atatürk]," *Atatürk Araştırma Merkezi Dergisi* 1, no. 1 (1984): 164–6.
49 Necip Fazıl Kısakürek, *Bâbıâli* (Istanbul: Büyük Doğu Yayınları, 2007).
50 Köseoğlu, *"Mukaddesatçılık,"* 86–7.
51 Ibid., 10.
52 Necip Fazıl Kısakürek, *O ve ben* (Cağaloğlu, İstanbul: Büyük Doğu Yayınları, 1965).
53 "Üstad Kadir Mısıroğlu - Tasavvuf, Hatıralar - Cumartesi Sohbetleri [CS84 - Ustad Kadir Mısıroğlu - Sufism, Memories - Saturday Talks]," *Üstad Kadir Mısıroğlu Resmî*, December 21, 2013, https://www.youtube.com/watch?v=UKzr-Eiym1g&t =4434sl (accessed May 16, 2021).
54 Hasan Aksakal, *Türk Muhafazakârlığı: Terennüm, Tereddüt, Tahakküm* [Turkish Conservatism: Singing, Hesitation, Domination] (Istanbul: Alfa Basım Yayınları, 2017), 142–4.
55 Ibid., 143.
56 Ibid., 159.
57 TRT, the Turkish state broadcaster, produces a series commemorating the thinkers behind Turkey's "reawakening." Episode 9 is devoted to Atilhan: https://www.youtube.com/watch?v=BahVqAwKg3M.
58 Köseoğlu, *"Mukaddesatçılık,"* 86–7.
59 See my translation of Sakarya Türküsü: Koru, "Sakarya Türküsü," *Kültürkampf*, https://kulturkampftr.substack.com/p/sakarya-turkusu (accessed August 31, 2023); Necip Fâzıl Kısakürek, *Doğru yolun sapık kolları: arınma çağında İslâm*. 14. basım. Cağaloğlu (İstanbul: Büyük Doğu, 2005); Bora, *Cereyanlar*, 442.
60 Yalman survived. He came from an elite family and held a PhD from Columbia university. He was no friend of the Kemalist state either, opposing its crimes against the Kurdish and Alevi populations, and going to jail for it. Selma Çetinkaya, "Ahmet Emin Yalman Suikastı Ve Etkileri," *Balkan ve Yakın Doğu Sosyal Bilimler Dergisi* 2, no. 1 (2016): 42–57.
61 Bora, *Cereyanlar*, 444.
62 Necip Fâzıl Kısakürek, "Başyücelik Emirleri – Kadın Kılığı," in *İdeolocya Örgüsü* (Istanbul: Fatih Matbaası, 1968), 183–4.
63 In his book on ideologies, he invariably mentions Fascism and Nazism side by side: Necip Fâzıl Kısakürek, *İdeolocya Örgüsü*. 22. Basım (Kadıköy, İstanbul: Büyük Doğu Yayınları, 2016).

64 "Necip Fazıl'ın Ayasofya hitabesi (sansürsüz) [Necip Fazıl's Hagia Sophia sermon]," *Millî Gazete*, July 25, 2020, https://www.milligazete.com.tr/haber/5048361/necip-fazilin-ayasofya-hitabesi-sansursuz.

65 Recep Tayyip Erdoğan, "Millete sesleniş konuşması [Public address speech]," *T.C. Cumhurbaşkanlığı*, https://www.tccb.gov.tr/konusmalar/353/120589/millete-seslenis-konusmasi; Selim Koru, "Turkey's Islamist Dream Finally Becomes a Reality," *The New York Times*, July 14, 2020, https://www.nytimes.com/2020/07/14/opinion/hagia-sophia-turkey-mosque.html.

66 "Cumhurbaşkanı Erdoğan: Necip Fazıl, Türkiye merkezli bir dünya tasavvurunun vücut bulmuş haliydi [President Erdoğan: Necip Fazıl was the Embodiment of a Turkey-centered Vision of the World]," *T.C. Cumhurbaşkanlığı İletişim Başkanlığı*, June 11, 2023, https://www.iletisim.gov.tr/turkce/haberler/detay/cumhurbaskani-erdogan-necip-fazil-turkiye-merkezli-bir-dunya-tasavvurunun-vucut-bulmus-haliydi.

67 "Cumhurbaşkanı Erdoğan: Ayasofya, Üstad Necip Fazıl'ın dediği gibi açıldı [President Erdoğan: The Hagia Sophia was Opened Like Master Necip Fazıl said it would be]," *TRT Haber*, May 13, 2022, https://www.trthaber.com/haber/gundem/cumhurbaskani-erdogan-ayasofya-ustad-necip-fazilin-dedigi-gibi-acildi-680035.html.

68 Necip Fazıl's 1968 play *Abdülhamit Han* is the basis of the sultan's contemporary status among the far right. It serves as the basis for the Payitaht Abdülhamit TV series running on state broadcaster TRT from 2017 to 2021.

69 Muharrem ÇOLAK, "İslamcılık, Said Nursi, Mehmet Akif, Abdülhamit, Sebilürreşad. Kadir Mısıroğlu Anlatıyor [Islamism, Said Nursi, Mehmet Akif, Abdulhamit, Sebilürreşad. Kadir Mısıroğlu explains]," *YouTube*, October 30, 2010, https://www.youtube.com/watch?v=l4cXigQBtK4.

70 Kadir Mısıroğlu, *Lozan Zafer Mi Hezimet Mi?* (Istanbul: Sebil Yayınevi, 1965), 5.

71 Mısıroğlu discusses the territorial losses in detail in the second volume of his book. See: Kadir Mısıroğlu, *Lozan Zafer Mi Hezimet Mi?* (Istanbul: Sebil Yayınevi, 1973).

72 Kaidr Mısıroğlu, *Lozan Zafer Mi Hezimet Mi?*, 16.

73 Üstad Kadir Mısıroğlu Resmî Sayfasıdır !, "Rıza Nur'un Ruhsal Sorunları Var Mıydı, Yoksa İftira Mı Ediliyor? [Did Rıza Nur Have Mental Problems or Is He Being Slandered?]," *YouTube*, July 4, 2015, https://www.youtube.com/watch?v=4ViBldI4Yxk.

74 He did not shy away from criticizing others in his ranks. He said if he ever spoke of Necip Fazıl's deeds, "you would think sewer waters had exploded." Mehmet Akif Ersoy was "nothing more than a bum." See "CS84 - Üstad Kadir Mısıroğlu - Tasavvuf, Hatıralar - Cumartesi Sohbetleri [CS84 - Ustad Kadir Mısıroğlu - Sufism, Memories - Saturday Talks]," *Üstad Kadir Mısıroğlu Resmî*, December 21, 2013, https://www.youtube.com/watch?v=UKzr-Eiym1g&t=4434sl (accessed May 16,

2021); "Kadir Mısıroğlu Mehmet Akif Ersoy'a Pezevenk Diyor! [Kadir Mısıroğlu Calls Mehmet Akif Ersoy a Pimp!]," *Türkiye Gerçekleri*, November 19, 2012, https://www.youtube.com/watch?v=rXDoao-wd1k; https://www.youtube.com/watch?v=UKzr-Eiym1g&t=4434s (accessed May 16, 2021).

75 Musa Alcan, "Tarihin gerçekliği yoluna adanmış bir ömür [A Life Dedicated to the Path of the Truth of History]," *Anadolu Ajansı*, May 6, 2019, https://www.aa.com.tr/tr/portre/tarihin-gercekligi-yoluna-adanmis-bir-omur/1471312.

76 "Sebil Yayınevi [Sevil Publishing House]," http://sebilyayinevi.com/.

77 Here he was reciting the Quran's Surah Al-Isra, verse 81, in a strong Turkish accent.

78 Üstad Kadir Mısıroğlu Resmi Sayfasıdır !, "Rıza Nur'un Ruhsal Sorunları Var Mıydı, Yoksa İftira Mı Ediliyor?."

79 "Turgut Özal Hakkında [About Turgut Özal]," *Üstad Kadir Mısıroğlu Resmi*, July 7, 2015, https://www.youtube.com/watch?v=ZQaTFrzMWbE (accessed February 16, 2022).

80 Necmettin Erbakan was the head of Turkey's Islamist movement from the 1970s until the AK Party's rise in the 2000s. He was also a mentor to Recep Tayyip Erdoğan.

81 Üstad Kadir Mısıroğlu Resmî Youtube Sayfasıdır !, "Üstad Kadir Mısıroğlu - Ben 'Ahrâr'dan Adamım! Kınsız Kılıç Gibi..! [Master Kadir Mısıroğlu - I am a man from 'Ahrâr'! Like a Sword Without a Sheath..!," *YouTube*, April 17, 2021, https://www.youtube.com/watch?v=c_7bDPhaeRA.

82 "Kadir Mısıroğlu'nun cenaze vasiyeti ne olacak? [What will be Kadir Mısıroğlu's funeral will?]," *Sözcü*, May 6, 2019, https://www.sozcu.com.tr/kadir-misiroglunun-cenaze-vasiyeti-wp4685779.

83 "Ülkemizi muasır medeniyet seviyesinin üzerine çıkarma mücadelesini, Millî Mücadele ruhuyla sürdürüyoruz [In the Spirit of the National Struggle, we continue the struggle to raise our country above the level of contemporary civilization]," *Presidency of the Republic of Turkey*, February 12, 2019, https://www.tccb.gov.tr/haberler/410/150141/-ulkemizi-muasir-medeniyet-seviyesinin-uzerine-cikarma-mucadelesini-mill-mucadele-ruhuyla-surduruyoruz- .

Chapter 2

1 *Türkiye Cumhuriyeti Devlet Teşkilat Rehberi: Özet Kitap* [The Republic of Turkey State Institution Guide: Summary Book] (Ankara: Türkiye ve Orta Doğu Amme İdaresi Enstitüsü, 2014).

2 *The United States Government Manual*, https://www.usgovernmentmanual.gov/(X(1)S(i1nosltypvb04jjzy52p1uhc))/Home.aspx?AspxAutoDetectCookieSupport=1 (accessed December 22, 2020).

3 Özcan Yıldırım, "Ülke yönteiminde yeni dönem [A New Era in the Country's Administration]," *Anadolu Ajansı*, July 10, 2018, https://www.aa.com.tr/tr/turkiye/ulke-yonetiminde-yeni-donem/1199998.
4 Elektronik Kamu Bilgi Yönetim Sistemi (KAYSİS) [The Electronic Public Information Management System], https://www.kaysis.gov.tr/.
5 Carl Schmitt, *The Concept of the Political* (Chicago, IL: University of Chicago Press, 2007), 25–7.
6 Ibid.
7 "Turkey's Only Presidential Candidate Withdraws from Election," *The New York Times*, May 6, 2007, https://www.nytimes.com/2007/05/06/world/europe/06iht-turkey.1.5583899.html.
8 Nick Birch, "Gul Abandons Presidential Bid in Face of Second Boycott," *The Guardian*, May 7, 2007. https://www.theguardian.com/world/2007/may/07/turkey.international.
9 "Dev Cumhuriyet Mitingi [Giant Republic Rally]," *BBC Türkçe*, May 14, 2007, https://www.bbc.co.uk/turkish/news/story/2007/05/070514_turkeyrallyupdate.shtml.
10 Sabrina Tavernise, "Ruling Party in Turkey Wins Broad Victory," *The New York Times*, July 22, 2007, https://www.nytimes.com/2007/07/22/world/europe/22cnd-turkey.html. "Genel Seçim 2007 [General Election 2007]," *Habertürk*, July 22, 2007, https://www.haberturk.com/secim2007.
11 Mehmet Ali Birand, "22 Temmuz seçimleri, dengeleri değiştirdi [The July 22 Elections Changed the Balance]," *Hürriyet*, December 26, 2007, https://www.hurriyet.com.tr/22-temmuz-secimleri-dengeleri-degistirdi-7921144.
12 "Abdullah Gül 367 şartı ve 27 Nisan engelini aşa aşa Çankaya Köşkü'ne çıktı [Abdullah Gül Went to Çankaya Mansion, Overcoming the 367 Condition and the April 27 Obstacle]," *Habertürk*, August 7, 2014, https://www.haberturk.com/gundem/haber/977543-abdullah-gul-367-sarti-ve-27-nisan-engelini-asa-asa-cankaya-koskune-cikti.
13 Abdullah Gül, "insan gerçekten hayret ediyor [One Really Wonders Sometimes.]," *Twitter*, April 7, 2011, https://x.com/cbabdullahgul/status/56016866145079296.
14 Gül, "Erdoğan'ın sakinleştirmeye çalıştı [Gül worked to calm Erdoğan]," *Hürriyet*, May 10, 2014, https://www.hurriyet.com.tr/gundem/gul-erdoganin-sakinlestirmeye-calisti-26391430.
15 "Kurtulmuş, AKP'nin 'hedefini' açıkladı: Güçlendirilmiş başkanlık [Kurtulmuş announced the AKP's target: Reinforced Presidency]," *Diken*, November 14, 2016, http://www.diken.com.tr/kurtulmus-akpnin-hedefini-acikladi-guclendirilmis-baskanlik-gundemimiz/.

16 Salih Bayram, *Türkiye'de Başkanlık Sistemi Tartışmaları* [*Discussions of the Presidential System in Turkey*] (Istanbul: SETA Yayınları, 2016), http://file.setav.org/Files/Pdf/20160105130350_bt_web.pdf (accessed November 15, 2020).
17 "Erdoğan'ı üzecek anket, [The Poll that will Upset Erdoğan]," *Milliyet*, December 15, 2011, https://www.milliyet.com.tr/siyaset/Erdoğani-uzecek-anket-1475863; and "Bu Anket Başbakanı Gerçekten Ağlatacak [This Poll is Really Going to Make the Prime Minister Cry]," *Sözcü*, August 23, 2013, https://www.sozcu.com.tr/2013/yazarlar/ugur-dundar/bu-anket-basbakani-gercekten-aglatacak-362019/.
18 "Erdoğan: Taraflı Cumhurbaşkanı Olacağım! [Erdoğan: I will be a President who Chooses a Side!]," *Kanal 7*, July 8, 2014, https://www.haber7.com/partiler/haber/1177823-Erdoğan-tarafli-cumhurbaskani-olacagim.
19 "Erdoğan 12. Cumhurbaşkanı oldu [Erdoğan Became the 12th President]," *Anadolu Ajansı*, August 10, 2014, https://www.aa.com.tr/tr/politika/erdogan-12-cumhurbaskani-oldu/132741.
20 "AKP'nin tercihi Davutoğlu [AKP's Preference, Davutoğlu]," *BBC News*, August 21, 2014, https://www.bbc.com/turkce/haberler/2014/08/140821_yeni_basbakan.
21 "Erdoğan tarafsızlık yemini çiğnedi [Erdoğan Violated the Oath of Neutrality]," *Sözcü*, January 31, 2015, https://www.sozcu.com.tr/2015/gundem/erdogan-tarafsizlik-yemini-cignedi-728944/; Fahrettin Altun, "Muhalefetin mızıkçılığı, Erdoğan'ın tarafsızlığı [The Opposition's Whining, Erdoğan's Impartiality]," *Sabah*, May 14, 2015, https://www.sabah.com.tr/yazarlar/fahrettinaltun/2015/05/14/muhalefetin-mizikciligi-erdoganin-tarafsizligi.
22 "İşte son kamuoyu araştırmaları… Türkiye başkanlık istiyor mu? [Here are the Latest Polls… Does Turkey Want a Presidency?]," *Hürriyet*, May 5, 2015, https://www.hurriyet.com.tr/gundem/iste-son-kamuoyu-arastirmalari-turkiye-baskanlik-istiyor-mu-40010465.
23 "Bakanlık sisteminin öğrenilmesini istemiyorlar [They Do Not Want the Presidential System to be Learned About]," *TRT Haber*, January 29, 2015, https://www.trthaber.com/haber/gundem/baskanlik-sisteminin-ogrenilmesini-istemiyorlar-164997.html.
24 "Çift-başlı kampanya 'meydanları zayıflatır' dendi, Erdoğan paralel miting programından vazgeçti [Double-headed Campaign 'Weakens the Squares', said, Erdoğan Abandons Parallel Rally Program]," *Bir Gün*, April 10, 2015, https://www.birgun.net/haber/cift-basli-kampanya-meydanlari-zayifilatir-dendi-erdogan-paralel-miting-programindan-vazgecti-77438; "Erdoğan kasanın anahtarını değiştirdi [Erdoğan Changed the Key of the Safe]," *Sözcu*, September 24, 2015, https://www.sozcu.com.tr/2015/gundem/erdogan-kasanin-anahtarini-degistirdi-943254/; Mehmet Gökhan Genel, "Türkiye Basınında Başkanlık Sistemi Tartışmaları: Köşe Yazarları Özelinde Bir Araştırma [Presidential System Debates

in the Turkish Press: A Study Specific to Columnists]," *AJIT--e: Online Academic Journal of Information Technology* 6, no. 19 (Spring 2015), https://dergipark.org.tr/en/download/article-file/1114206.

25 Fundanur Öztürk, "Oyu Batı'da artan, Doğu'da azalan HDP 'Türkiyelileşti' mi? [Has the HDP, Whose Votes Increased in the West and Decreased in the East, 'Become of Turkey'?]," June 26, 2018, https://www.bbc.com/turkce/haberler-turkiye-44613327.

26 "Demirtaş'tan Davutoğlu'na çok sert yanıt [Very harsh response from Demirtaş to Davutoğlu]," *Cumhuriyet*, October 10, 2015, https://www.cumhuriyet.com.tr/haber/demirtastan-davutogluna-cok-sert-yanit-385453.

27 Akin to the difference between the French "tu" and "vous." or the Spanish "tú" and "usted."

28 "Demirtaş, tarihin en kısa grup toplantısını yaptı! [Demirtaş has held the Shortest [Parliamentary] Group Meeting in History!]," *T24*, March 17, 2015, https://t24.com.tr/haber/Demirtaş-hdp-grup-partisini-tek-cumleyle-bitirdi,290709.

29 After 2016, Erdoğan's team would cave to the polling and call the new system "the local and national presidency" and retain the official title of "Cumhurbaşkanı." Informally, however, Erdoğan never gave up trying to be a "başkan." On his inauguration day as the nation's first elected president, the first question he received from a journalist was, "what should we call you?" Erdoğan replied, "you may call me 'my president,'" using the American term without the cumhur- prefix ("başkanım diyebilirsiniz"). Everything about the day was minutely planned, meaning that the question was likely planted. It seemed Erdoğan couldn't help himself. He wanted to be called a "başkan," even if it couldn't be his official title. Today, usage of the term is one of the many rhetorical cleavages between Erdoğan supporters and the opposition. Erdoğan's loyalists insist on referring to him as "Başkan Erdoğan," while those in the opposition or outer circles use the official "Cumhurbaşkanı." See: "'Sistemin adı başkanlık değil, Cumhurbaşkanlığı olacak," *TRT Haber*, June 12, 2016, https://www.trthaber.com/haber/gundem/sistemin-adi-baskanlik-degil-cumhurbaskanligi-olacak-286380.html.

30 Erdoğan would never forgive Demirtaş. Once he attained his emergency powers after the 2016 coup attempt, Demirtaş became the first and only party leader to be imprisoned, and remains so to this day. Demirtaş was imprisoned in Edirne, which is the farthest point in the country from Diyarbakir, where his family resides. His wife, Basak Demirtaş, and his two daughters have to regularly travel to Edirne to see him. The personalized nature of the punishment inflicted on Demirtaş highlights the force of his speech, as well as the importance of the executive presidency.

31. "Osman Baydemir anlatıyor: Çözüm süreci nasıl bitti? [Osman Baydemir Explains: How did the Peace Process Come to an End?]," *Kısa Dalga*, December 7, 2020, https://www.kisadalga.net/osman-baydemir-anlatiyor-cozum-sureci-nasil-bitti/.
32. "A Sisyphean Task? Resuming Turkey-PKK Peace Talks," *International Crisis Group*, Crisis Group Europe Briefing no. 77 (December 2015): 7.
33. "5 ayda 5 milyon oy: Kasım 2015 genel seçimleri [5 Million Votes in 5 months: November 2015 General Elections]," *Yeni Şafak*, https://www.yenisafak.com/secim-2015-kasim.
34. Abdülkadir Selvi, "Zirvede çatlak söz konusu mu [Is there a Crack in the Summit]," *Hürriyet*, April 6, 2016, https://www.hurriyet.com.tr/yazarlar/abdulkadir-selvi/zirvede-catlak-soz-konusu-mu-40082208.
35. Turkish diplomats have long sought to gain visa-free travel in the Schengen zone for Turkish passport-holders. In the deal that Davutoğlu struck with EU leaders, Turkey was to attain this right contingent on reforms in its policies relating to migrants and changes in its anti-terror laws. After Davutoğlu stepped down, the Erdoğan government failed to enact the reforms, and the EU did not grant visa-free travel.
36. Reporting later revealed that the post had been written from the offices of "Bosphorus Global," directed by Hial Kaplan, a powerful opinion maker, and allegedly funded at the time by Erdoğan's son-in law Berat Albayrak. Daniel Bellut and Hülya Schenk, "Turkey's Pelican Group: A State within a State," *Deutsche Welle*, March 16, 2020, https://www.dw.com/en/turkeys-pelican-group-a-state-within-a-state/a-52798624; "Eski 'Pelikan'cıdan şok itiraflar: Hilal Kaplan ve kocası…[Shocking Confessions from the ex-Pelican: Hilal Kaplan and her husband…]," *Cumhuriyet*, April 24, 2014, https://www.cumhuriyet.com.tr/haber/eski-pelikancidan-sok-itiraflar-hilal-kaplan-ve-kocasi-727401. "Pelikan Dosyası [Pelikan Dossier]," https://pelikandosyasi.wordpress.com/.
37. The incident is remembered for the "Pelikan File," a blog post authored by the Bosphorus Group, a PR firm loyal to the Erdoğan government and close to son-in-law Berat Albayrak.
38. Christiaan Triebert, "'We've Just Shot Four People. Everything's Fine' The Turkish Coup Through the Eyes of its Plotters," *Bellingcat*, July 24, 2016. https://www.bellingcat.com/news/mena/2016/07/24/the-turkey-coup-through-the-eyes-of-its-plotters/
39. Karim El Bar, "3 Helicopters Sent to 'Kill or Capture' Erdoğan at Hotel During Coup, Leaks Say," *Middle East Eye*, July 18, 2016, https://www.middleeasteye.net/news/3-helicopters-sent-kill-or-capture-Erdoğan-hotel-during-coup-leaks-say.
40. "Meral Akşener'den olağanüstü kurultay çağrısı [Call for Extraordinary Congress from Meral Akşener]," *TRT Haber*, November 30, 2015, https://www.trthaber.com/haber/turkiye/meral-aksenerden-olaganustu-kurultay-cagrisi-219325.html.

41 "Beştepe'de Erdoğan-Bahçeli görüşmesi [Erdoğan-Bahçeli meeting in Beştepe]," *NTV*, November 2, 2016, https://www.ntv.com.tr/turkiye/bestepede-Erdoğan-bahceli-gorusmesi,Hk4PJ24NjECyrGAPm_FP2w; "Leadership Battle in Turkey's Nationalist Opposition Hangs in Legal Llimbo," *Reuters*, May 13, 2016, https://www.reuters.com/article/turkey-politics-nationalists-idINKCN0Y41TZ.

42 "Milliyetçi Hareket Partisi Genel Başkanı Sayın Devlet Bahçeli'nin TBMM Grup Toplantısında Yaptıkları Konuşma 11 Ekim 2016 [The Speech Nationalist Movement Party Chairman, the Honorary Devlet Bahçeli held at the Grand National Assembly of Turkey on October 11 2016]," *Nationalist Movement Party*, http://www.mhp.org.tr/htmldocs/genel_baskan/konusma/4136/index.html.

43 Selim Koru, "Turkey's Last Coup: What I Saw in Ankara," *War on the Rocks*, July 16, 2016, https://warontherocks.com/2016/07/turkeys-last-coup-what-i-saw-in-ankara/.

44 The new office was again to be called *Cumhurbaşkanlığı* rather than the foreign-sounding *Başkanlık*. See: Türey Köse, "'Türk Tipi Başkanlık' TBMM Genel Kurulu'nda [The 'Turkish Type Presidency' is at the GNA General Assembly]," *BBC Türkçe*, January 8, 2017, https://www.bbc.com/turkce/haberler-turkiye-38529200.

45 Jon Henley, "Turkey Threatens to Pull out of Migrant Deal as Dutch Row Intensifies," *The Guardian*, March 13, 2017, https://www.theguardian.com/world/2017/mar/13/turkey-summons-dutch-envoy-over-riot-police-tactics-in-rotterdam.

46 Author interview with anonymous AK Party member, November 2020.

47 "Turkish Referendum on Erdoğan Powers Passed by 51.4 Percent: Final Figures," *Reuters*, April 27, 2017, https://www.reuters.com/article/us-turkey-politics-referendum-idUSKBN17T2SL.

48 "Türkiye Cumhuriyeti Cumhurbaşkanlığı: Görev ve Yetkiler [Republic of Turkey Presidency: Task and Authorities]," , *Türkiye Cumhuriyeti Cumhurbaşkanlığı*, https://www.tccb.gov.tr/cumhurbaskanligi/gorev_yetki/#:~:text=Cumhurba%C5%9Fkan%C4%B1n%C4%B1n%20g%C3%B6rev%20s%C3%BCresi%20be%C5%9F%20y%C4%B1ld%C4%B1r,y%C3%BCz%20bin%20se%C3%A7men%20aday%20g%C3%B6sterebilir.

49 Ibid.

50 "2019 Cumhurbaşkanlığı Seçimi [2018 Presidential Election]," *Habertürk*, June 24, 2018, https://www.haberturk.com/secim/secim2018/cumhurbaskanligi-secimi.

51 "Türkiye Cumhuriyeti Anayasası [Constitution of the Republic of Turkey]," November 9, 1982, https://www.icisleri.gov.tr/kurumlar/icisleri.gov.tr/IcSite/illeridaresi/Mevzuat/Kanunlar/Anayasa.pdf.

52 Interview with author, July 2020.

53 Ahmet Eşref Fakıbaba resigned in October 2022. "Kulisler hareketli... AKP'den ve milletvekilliğinden istifa eden Fakıbaba'nın adresi belli oldu [The Lobbies

are Abuzz… The Address of Fakıbaba, who Resigned from the AKP and as Parliamentarian, has Become Evident]," *Cumhuriyet*, October 20, 2022, https://www.cumhuriyet.com.tr/siyaset/kulisler-hareketli-akpden-ve-milletvekilliginden-istifa-eden-fakibabanin-adresi-belli-oldu-1994260.

54 "Milletin iradesinin üzerinde irade tanımayarak demokrasimizi ileriye taşıdık [We have Carried our Democracy Forward by Not Recognizing Any will Above the will of Our People]," *Presidency of the Republic of Turkey*, February 12, 2019, https://www.tccb.gov.tr/haberler/410/101951/-milletin-iradesinin-uzerinde-irade-tanimayarak-demokrasimizi-ileriye-tasidik-.

55 Kemal Gözler, "Cumhurbaşkanlığı Hükümet Sisteminin Uygulamadaki Değeri: Bir Buçuk Yıllık Bir Bilanço [An Evaluation of the Presidential System of Government in its Implementation: The Balance Sheet of One and a Half Years]," *Turkish Constitutional Law*, December 27, 2019, https://www.anayasa.gen.tr/cbhs-bilanco.htm.

56 "An Overwhelming Majority of Nurses Intend to Vote Labour," *Nursing Notes*, August 25, 2021, https://nursingnotes.co.uk/news/politics/overwhelming-number-healthcare-workers-plan-vote-labour/; Julie Flint, Murray Jones, and Sascha Levin, "Military Matters: 91% of Veterans from the Main Political Parties are Conservatives," *Byline Times*, October 22, 2021, https://bylinetimes.com/2021/10/22/military-matters-91-of-mps-with-armed-forces-background-are-conservatives/.

57 David A. Hollinger, "Rich, Powerful, and Smart: Jewish Overrepresentation Should Be Explained Instead of Avoided or Mystified"" *Jewish Quarterly Review* 94, no. 4 (2004): 595–602; "Onward Christian Soldiers," *The Economist*, May 25, 2019, https://www.economist.com/erasmus/2019/05/25/onward-christian-soldiers.

58 The Turkist "Idealists" (Ülkücü) are mostly represented by the Nationalist Action Party (MHP), which is in Erdoğan's governing coalition, as well as the Good Party (İYİ), which is in the opposition. While they are traditionally strong in what is called the "armed bureaucracy," namely, the police, military, and intelligence forces, they have boosted their presence across other parts of the public sector in recent years.

59 İlyas Söğütlü, "Cumhuriyet Türkiyesi'nde Modernleşme ve Bürokratik Vesayet [Modernization and Bureaucratic Tutelage in Republican Turkey]," *Kocaeli University Journal of Social Sciences* no. 49 (June 1, 2010), https://dergipark.org.tr/en/pub/kosbed/issue/25701/271204.

60 "Erdoğan: Bürokratik oligarşi bizi parmağında oynatıyor [Erdoğan: Bureaucratic oligarchy play with us in their hand]," *Hürriyet*, June 8, 2003, https://www.hurriyet.com.tr/ekonomi/erdogan-burokratik-oligarsi-bizi-parmaginda-oynatiyor-38471519.

61 "Kuvvetler Ayrılığı Engel [The Seperation of Powers is an Obstruction]," *Radikal*, December 18, 2012, http://www.radikal.com.tr/turkiye/kuvvetler-ayriligi-engel-1112491/.
62 For example: "Erdoğan Atatürk'ün Evinde [Erdoğan is in Atatürk's Home]," *Hürriyet*, June 21, 2003, https://www.hurriyet.com.tr/gundem/Erdoğan-ataturkun-evinde-154712.
63 "Gül'e 'bekle' mesajı [A 'Wait' Message to Gül]," *Cumhuriyet*, August 12, 2014, https://www.cumhuriyet.com.tr/haber/gule-bekle-mesaji-105157; "Başbakanlık Misafir Konutunda Basın Toplantısı | Pakistan | 16 Haziran 2003 [Press Conference at the Prime Ministry Guest House | Pakistan | 16 June 2003]," from Recep Tayyip Erdoğan, *Yeni Türkiye Vizyonu: Efendi Değil Hizmetkar Olmak-1* [The New Vision of Türkiye: Being a Servant, Not a Master-1] (Ankara: Cumhurbaşkanlığı Yayınları, 2019), 162.
64 "2002 Genel Seçimleri: Seçim Beyannamesi [2002 General Elections: Party Program]," *AK Parti*, https://www.akparti.org.tr/media/318780/3-kasim-2002-genel-secimleri-secim-beyannamesi-sayfalar.pdf.
65 With universities being deeply left-leaning or secular in Turkey, the government has had difficulty in hollowing them out and has only met some success after the 2016 coup attempt. In recent years, however, even the oldest and most prestigious universities have been breached by government appointment. Institutions like the Middle East Technical University and Boğaziçi University used to maintain a precarious balance between the government and their critical faculties. That balance has now tipped in the government's favor. See: Bethan McKernan, "Istanbul University Students Clash with Police over Rector Appointment," *The Guardian*, January 6, 2021, https://www.theguardian.com/world/2021/jan/06/istanbul-university-students-clash-with-police-over-rector-appointment. Institutions like Ankara University, which has a historically leftist makeup that is close to the Kurdish movement, has been under relentless pressure, and its most critical faculty has effectively been purged. See: Suzy Hansen, "'The Era of People Like You Is Over': How Turkey Purged Its Intellectuals," *New York Times*, July 29, 2019, https://www.nytimes.com/2019/07/24/magazine/the-era-of-people-like-you-is-over-how-turkey-purged-its-intellectuals.html.
66 While many of the AK Party's founding leaders were sympathetic to the *cemaat* of İskenderpaşa, this was a very loose association that largely did not reflect on their institutional choices.
67 Vinny Vella, "The Cleric Next Door: Pocono Neighbors Weigh in on Fethullah Gülen, the Man Turkey Wants Back," *Philadelphia Inquirer*, January 16, 2016, https://www.inquirer.com/news/pennsylvania/fethullah-gulen-movement-turkey-Erdoğan-saylorsburg-pennsylvania-camp-20190116.html.

68 The recording can be found here: Medyascope, "Gülen'in 1999'da yayınlanan olay videosu: 'Sivrilirsek sonumuz Cezayir gibi olur' [Gülen's Incident Video published in 1999: 'If we Excel, we will End up Like Algeria']," *YouTube*, August 18, 2016, https://www.youtube.com/watch?v=7Y_cLmsmOuY&ab_channel=Medyascope. The group's central narrative explicitly aims at what one would recognize as state capture through the work of the "golden generation," the network that would eventually seize the levers of power.

69 Natalie Martin, "Allies and Enemies: The Gülen Movement and the AKP," *Cambridge Review of International Affairs* 35, no. 1 (2022): 113–16; Gareth H. Jenkins, "Between Fact and Fantasy: Turkey's Ergenekon Investigation," *Central Asia - Caucasus Institute Silk Road Studies Center*, August 2009, https://www.silkroadstudies.org/resources/pdf/SilkRoadPapers/2009_08_SRP_Jenkins_Turkey-Ergenekon.pdf.

70 Sedat Ergin, "Aleviler Neden Rencide Oldu? [Why are were the Alevi Offended?]," *Hürriyet*, September 17, 2010, https://www.hurriyet.com.tr/aleviler-neden-rencide-oldu-15801716.

71 "Hayır ve Ötesi raporu: 'Mezardakiler kalkıp oy kullansa' sözü gerçek oldu [No and Beyond report: 'If Only Those in the Graves Stood up and Voted' Would Come True]," *Diken*, April 25, 2017, https://www.diken.com.tr/hayir-ve-otesi-raporu-mezardakiler-kalkip-oy-kullansa-sozu-gercek-oldu/; "Fethullah Gülen'in referandum yorumu [Fethullah Gülen's referendum comment]," *Habertürk*, August 1, 2010, https://www.haberturk.com/polemik/haber/537886-fethullah-gulenin-referandum-yorumu.

72 "Turkey's Electoral Board Makes Public Official Results of Referendum," *Anadolu Ajansı*, September 23, 2010, https://www.aa.com.tr/en/archive/turkeys-electoral-board-makes-public-official-results-of-referendum/421328.

73 Laurel Leaves, "Referandum 2010 - Recep Tayyip Erdogan'in Tesekkürleri, Okyanus Ötesine Mesaji [Referendum 2010 - Recep Tayyip Erdogan's Thanks, Message to Across the Ocean]," *YouTube*, September 10, 2010, https://www.youtube.com/watch?v=9YIcZDnjDs4.

74 Interview with author, June 2020.

75 The Gülenists were so dominant that they caused a subtle change in the Turkish language. Turkish does not have definite or indefinite articles, but one may think of any public utterance of the term *cemaat* in those years as having a silent definite article. People were not talking about *a cemaat*, they were talking about *the cemaat*. Nobody had to specify that they were talking about the *Gülenists cemaat*; the term automatically implied them. Once the state declared the Gülenists to be terrorists, it became inappropriate to refer to them as *cemaat*, and the word snapped back to its original usage. A person speaking of a *cemaat* without any definitive adjectives today may once again be asked which *cemaat* he is referring to.

76 Interview with author, July 2020.
77 Ahmet Şık, *İmam'ın Ordusu: 15 Temmuz Darbe Girişimi İncelemesiyle Birlikte* [The Imam's Army: With an Examination of the July 15 Coup Attempt] (Istanbul: Kırmızı Kedi, 2017).
78 Yeni Şafak Temsilcisi, "Erdoğan, 2011'de 'Fethullah Hoca, bu kirli yapının tam göbeğinde' demişti [*Yeni Şafak* Representative: Erdoğan said in 2011 that 'Fetullah Gülen is at the center of this dirty construct']," *T24*, December 28, 2015, https://t24.com.tr/haber/yeni-safak-temsilcisi-Erdoğan-2011de-fethullah-hoca-bu-kirli-yapinin-tam-gobeginde-demisti,322075.
79 Martin, "Allies and Enemies," 117.
80 Ibid.
81 Cem Gurbetoğlu, "'FETÖ'den suçlananlara ilişkin rapor: 35 intihar yaşandı [Report on those accused of FETÖ: 35 suicides]," *Evrensel*, April 29, 2017, https://www.evrensel.net/haber/317685/fetoden-suclananlara-iliskin-rapor-35-intihar-yasandi; "İntihar eden yarbay FETÖ'cüleri olay günü saymış [FETÖ Members Count the Day of the Event of the Suicide of the Lieutenant Colonel]," *Anadolu Ajansı*, February 2, 2017, https://www.aa.com.tr/tr/turkiye/intihar-eden-yarbay-fetoculeri-olay-gunu-saymis/954666; "İntihar eden Nazlıgül Üsteğmen komutanı FETÖ'cü çıktı [First Lieutenant Commander Nazlıgül who Committed Suicide Turns out to be a FETÖ Member]," *Memurlar*, March 27, 2018, https://www.memurlar.net/haber/599774/intihar-eden-nazligul-ustegmen-komutani-feto-cu-cikti.html.
82 Interview with author, April 2020.
83 Yıldıray Oğur and Ceren Kenar, "Who was Behind the 15th July Coup in Turkey?," *Medium*, March 21, 2017, https://medium.com/@15thJulyCoup/who-was-behind-the-15th-july-coup-in-turkey-19f75a5771c5.
84 The opposition usually blames the government for collaborating with the Gülenists in its early years and allowing them to grow in power. Erdoğan, in turn, accuses the opposition of approaching them in the time between the events of December 17-25, 2013 (widely referred to as the "events of 17-25"), when they leaked the corruption tapes, and the July 15, 2016, coup attempt.
85 "AKP ve MHP 'Susurlukçu' Drej Ali'nin düğününde buluştu [The AKP and MHP met at 'Susrluk's' Drej Ali]," *Cumhuriyet*, September 9, 2019, https://www.cumhuriyet.com.tr/haber/akp-ve-mhp-susurlukcu-drej-alinin-dugununde-bulustu-1570540.
86 Bahadır Özgür, "Çeteler parlıyor: Devletteki yeni cerahat [The Gangs are Shining: The New pus of the State]," *Gazete Duvar*, September 17, 2019, https://www.gazeteduvar.com.tr/yazarlar/2019/09/17/ceteler-parliyor-devletteki-yeni-cerahat.
87 Salim Çevik, "Erdoğan's Comprehensive Religious Policy: Management of the Religious Realm in Turkey," SWP Comment: No. 12, March 2019, 6–7, https://www.swp-berlin.org/publications/products/comments/2019C12_cvk.pdf; "TÜGVA

belgeleri tartışması [TÜGVA documents debate]," *Deutsche Welle*, October 13, 2021, https://www.dw.com/tr/t%C3%BCgva-belgeleri-tart%C4%B1%C5%9Fmas%C4%B1/a-59496193; "CHP'li Emre TÜGVA ve TÜRGEV'e aktarılan kamu kaynaklarının araştırılması için önerge verdi [CHP's Emre Submitted a Proposal to Investigate Public Resources Transferred to TÜGVA and TÜRGEV]," *Evrensel*, November 1, 2021, https://www.evrensel.net/haber/446613/chpli-emre-tugva-ve-turgeve-aktarilan-kamu-kaynaklarinin-arastirilmasi-icin-onerge-verdi.

88 "FETÖ'den boşalan yerler yeni tarikatlarla dolduruldu [The Places Vacated by FETO were Filled with New sects]," *Bir Gün*, August 11, 2017, https://www.birgun.net/haber/feto-den-bosalan-yerler-yeni-tarikatlarla-dolduruldu-174268; Dilan Ayırkan, "Menzil cemaati liderinin cenazesi sonrası, akademisyenler Türkiye'deki tarikatları değerlendirdi: Laikliğe savaş açıldı [After the Funeral of the Leader of the Menzil Community, Academics Evaluated the sects in Turkey: War on Secularism]," *Cumhuriyet*, July 14, 2023, https://www.cumhuriyet.com.tr/siyaset/menzil-cemaati-liderinin-cenazesi-sonrasi-akademisyenler-turkiyedeki-tarikatlari-degerlendirdi-laiklige-savas-acildi-2099071; "Yargıtay üyesi: Yargı iki tarikatın kontrolünde, Cumhurbaşkanlığı ve Adalet Bakanlığı da biliyor [Supreme Court Member: Judiciary is under the Control of Two sects, Presidency and Ministry of Justice also know]," *Artı Gerçek*, October 19, 2021, https://artigercek.com/guncel/yargitay-uyesi-yargida-her-tarikatin-whatsapp-grubu-var-haremlik-selamlik-182759h; Erdi Tütmez, "Dr. Deniz Parlak: Tarikatların rolleri ve tehditleri sanılanın oldukça ilerisinde [Dr. Deniz Parlak: The Roles and Threats of the sects are Far Beyond what is Believed]," *Evrensel*, July 19, 2023, https://www.evrensel.net/haber/494980/dr-deniz-parlak-tarikatlarin-rolleri-ve-tehditleri-sanilanin-oldukca-ilerisinde.

89 Menzil is the name of the village in Adıyaman Province, where the order is based. There are regular buses to the village from city centers, such as Istanbul and Ankara, as well as to the group's secondary base in Eskişehir province. Journalist Saygı Öztürk estimated in 2019 that 35-40 such buses arrive in Menzil daily and that a helicopter landing ground often brings VIP guests. He quotes the head of the order at the time (since deceased and succeeded by his sons) having said that as many as 10 ministers have visited him at the same time. According to Öztürk, Menzil's influence over the Ministry of Health has somewhat waned since the term of former minister Recep Akdağ, who was a longtime member of the *cemaat*. Fahrettin Koca, who assumed office in 2018, is of the Iskenderpasa *cemaat*, which is also powerful in the health industry. See: Saygı Öztürk, *Menzil: Bir Tarikatın İki Yüzü* [Menzil: Two Faces of an Order] (Istanbul: Doğan Kitap, 2019).

90 In 2019, the average judge in Turkey had two and a half years of experience, according to the head of the Turkish Bars Association. Carlotta Gall, "Erdogan's Purges Leave Turkey's Justice System Reeling," *The New York Times*, June 21, 2019,

https://www.nytimes.com/2019/06/21/world/asia/erdogan-turkey-courts-judiciary-justice.html.

91 The statement made national news, often as a "scandalous admittance" of a widely talked about, but unacknowledged, trend. The governor later said that his statement was truncated and that it was intended as a joke. He is neither an *Imam Hatip* graduate, nor from Trabzon, which suggests that his statement expressed personal frustration more than anything else. "AKP'li belediye başkanı: Makam sahibi olmak için bir imam hatipli bir de Trabzonlu olacaksın [AKP Mayor: to hold Office, You have to be an Imam Hatip Graduate and be from Trabzon]," *Cumhuriyet*, December 19, 2019, https://www.cumhuriyet.com.tr/video/akpli-belediye-baskani-makam-sahibi-olmak-icin-bir-imam-hatipli-bir-de-trabzonlu-olacaksin-1709735.

92 The health ministry employed 1.62 million people health personnel in 2020.

93 The MFA has small offices in Istanbul and Izmir. The properties it manages abroad are subject to the laws of host states. It has about 2,500 career diplomats and a total of about 6,000 staff. In comparison, according to information published in March 2019 by CCN Holding, Ankara's "City Hospital" alone has 2,700 academics, doctors, and surgeons, as well as 6,300 health professionals and 4,000 managerial staff. CCN Holding built the Ankara City Hospital.

94 Gülenists were not replaced at the working level, more than one banker claimed, because they did not significantly contribute to the day-to-day tasks of the bank. "I remember how they'd make fun of us saying, 'I could write an inflation report in two days,'" one said, adding, "They thought writing reports was the work of a peon [amele]. They didn't come as workers, they came as managers [yönetici]." This kind of sentiment is prevalent, especially in small and systemically important institutions (interview with author, December 2020).

95 Interview with author, July 2020.

96 Caitlin Ostroff, "Foreign Investors Flee Turkey's Bond Market," *Wall Street Journal*, July 24, 2020, https://www.wsj.com/articles/foreign-investors-flee-turkeys-bond-market-11595583002.

97 Lütfi Elvan, who came up as a bureaucrat in Turkey's prestigious State Planning Agency (DPT), was apparently preparing for retirement when Erdoğan called upon him to replace Albayrak.

98 Hatice Şenses Kurukız, Kaan Bozdoğan, Hanife Sevinç, Semra Orkan, Kaan Bozdoğan, and Hikmet Faruk Başer, "Cumhurbaşkanı Erdoğan: Macron senin zaten süren az kaldı. Gidicisin [President Erdoğan: Macron, Your Time has Nearly Run out Anyways. You are a Goner]," *Anadolu Agency*, September 12, 2020, https://www.aa.com.tr/tr/turkiye/cumhurbaskani-erdogan-macron-senin-zaten-suren-az-kaldi-gidicisin/1971570.

99 "Bahçeli'den Bülent Arınç'a sert tepki [Strong reaction by Bahçeli towards Bülent Arınç]," *Dünya*, November 24, 2020, https://www.dunya.com/gundem/bahceliden-bulent-arinca-sert-tepki-haberi-601258.

100 Levent Köker, "Başkancı rejim: Popülist yarışmacı otoriterlik mi, diktatörlük mü? [The Presidential System: Populist Competitive Authoritarianism or Dictatorship?]," *Birikim*, September 2020, https://birikimdergisi.com/dergiler/birikim/1/sayi-377-eylul-2020/10048/baskanci-rejim-populist-yarismaci-otoriterlik-mi-diktatorluk-mu/11902.

101 Ayşe Sayın, "İYİ Parti ve Gelecek Partisi 'parlamenter sistem' üzerine çalışacak [The IYI Party and the Future Party to Work on the Parliamentary System]," *BCC Türkçe*, November 16, 2020, https://www.bbc.com/turkce/haberler-dunya-54960757.

102 Mehmet Uçum, "Güçlendirilmiş parlamenter sistem ne anlama geliyor? [What Does the Reinforced Parliamentary System Mean?]," *Sabah*, December 5, 2020, https://www.sabah.com.tr/yazarlar/perspektif/mehmet-ucum/2020/12/05/guclendirilmis-parlamenter-sistem-ne-anlama-geliyor.

103 "Narendra Modi threatens to Turn India into a One-party State," *The Economist*, November 28, 2020, https://www.economist.com/briefing/2020/11/28/narendra-modi-threatens-to-turn-india-into-a-one-party-state.

104 Gidi Weitz, "Netanyahu: 'Deep State' Controls Israel, There's No Democracy Here," *Haaretz*, April 5, 2020, https://www.haaretz.com/israel-news/2020-04-05/ty-article/netanyahu-deep-state-israel-no-democracy-here-lieberman/0000017f-e06e-d804-ad7f-f1fecd800000.

105 Max Fisher, "Stephen K. Bannon's CPAC Comments, Annotated and Explained," *The New York Times*, February 24, 2017, https://www.nytimes.com/2017/02/24/us/politics/stephen-bannon-cpac-speech.html.

106 Tamsin Shaw, "William Barr: The Carl Schmitt of Our Time," *The New York Review*, January 15, 2020, https://www.nybooks.com/daily/2020/01/15/william-barr-the-carl-schmitt-of-our-time/; also see Adrian Vermeule and Eric Posner, *The Executive Unbound: After the Madisonian Republic* (New York City, NY: Oxford University Press, 2011).

107 Birsen Altaylı and Hümeyra Pamuk, "Pollsters see Support for Erdogan's AKP Largely Unscathed Despite Quake," *Reuters*, March 3, 2023, https://www.reuters.com/world/middle-east/pollsters-see-support-erdogans-akp-largely-unscathed-despite-quake-2023-03-03/.

108 Uçum, Mehmet, "Güçlendirilmiş Parlamenter sistem ne anlama geliyor?" ["What does the Reinforced Parliamentary System Mean?"], *Sabah*, December 5, 2020, https://www.sabah.com.tr/yazarlar/perspektif/mehmet-ucum/2020/12/05/guclendirilmis-parlamenter-sistem-ne-anlama-geliyor.

109 "Cumhurbaşkanı Erdoğan: 50+1 şartının değişmesi isabetli olur [President Erdoğan: It would be Appropriate to Change the 50+1 Condition]," *TRT Haber*,

November 18, 2023, https://www.trthaber.com/haber/gundem/cumhurbaskani-erdogan-501-sartinin-degismesi-isabetli-olur-813836.html.

Chapter 3

1 Bülent Aras and Rabia Karakaya Polat, "From Conflict to Cooperation: Desecuritization of Turkey's Relations with Syria and Iran," *Security Dialogue* 39, no. 5 (October 2008): 495–515; Hatem Ete and Taha Özhan, "Kürt Meselesi: Problemler ve Çözüm Önerileri," *SETA Analiz*, January 1, 2008, https://www.academia.edu/36454363/K%C3%BCrt_Meselesi_Problemler_ve_%C3%87%C3%B6z%C3%BCm_%C3%96nerileri.

2 This took the form of the "Greater Middle East Initiative" in 2004. The matter was discussed at a G8 summit in Georgia in June of 2004. Then-PM Erdoğan was invited as a guest to discuss the matter. In following years, the initiative ("Büyük Ortadoğu Projesi," or BOP in Turkish) came to be thought of as a formal arrangement for Turkey to become an outpost to manage the Middle East on behalf of the United States. Opposition figures still accuse Erdoğan of being a part of BOP. See: Tamara Coffman Wittes, "The New U.S. Proposal for a Greater Middle East Initiative: An Evaluation," *Brookings Institution*, May 10, 2004, https://www.brookings.edu/research/the-new-u-s-proposal-for-a-greater-middle-east-initiative-an-evaluation/; Aslı Aydıntaşbaş, "Erdoğan'ın BOP pazarlığı [Erdoğan's BOP bargain]," June 8, 2004, http://arsiv.sabah.com.tr/2004/06/08/gnd102.html.

3 One early framework for such responsibility was Turkey's role in the formation of the Baghdad Pact in the 1950s. The pact was to be what NATO was to Europe: an American-led alliance to contain the Soviet Union. The Menderes administration at the time was eager to build it up, but the United States wasn't able to gather regional support, especially that of Egypt, which it believed to have been critical for success.

4 The Milli Güvenlik Kurulu (National Security Council, or MGK), in "Old Turkey," used to be a summit between senior politicians and the military leadership, mostly with the latter telling the former what to do.

5 The Turkish word is "kalemşör," a play on the word "silahşör," which means "gunslinger" (or "swordsman", anyone carrying and wielding a weapon).

6 In the 1997 film *Wag the Dog*, by Barry Levinson, an American president hires a spin doctor and a movie producer (Robert de Niro and Dustin Hoffman) to distract the public from his sex scandal. The duo then produce a phony war against Albania. Turkish viewers watched this movie intently, and op-ed writers still frequently reference it. There are different ways of watching the movie. On one level, it is a satire about the relationship between entertainment and politics. A more literal way to watch it is to see it as an expose of the American willingness to manipulate

the lives of foreigners for nothing more than the convenience (and immorality) of their own political class. Competitive Occidentalists tend to watch it in the latter way (and their columnists still refer to it in their writing), while at the same time imitating the methods of political manipulation it portrays in their own practices. The hallmark of Competitive Occidentalism is to contain that contradiction seamlessly.

7 Ahmet Köroğlu, "Türkiye'de 1990'lı Yıllarda Ortaya Çıkan Siyasi Liberalizm Pratikleril," *İnsan ve Toplum* 2, no. 2 (2012): 119–38.
8 The CHP's 1973 election slogan under the charismatic leadership of Bülent Ecevit was "to white days" "ak günlere," so the AK Party was not the first to evoke this imagery. See Mustafa Çolak, *Bülent Ecevit* (İstanbul: İletişim Yayınları, 2016).
9 Author interview, March 8, 2023.
10 As with many liberal institutions at the time, both parties developed links (or depending on one's perspective, were infiltrated by) the Gülenist network. They were critical of the government in the early 2010s and were shut down after the 2016 coup attempt.
11 Hakan Akpınar, "5 gün 5 ülke yordu [He walked 5 countries in 5 days]," *Hürriyet*, November 21, 2002, https://www.hurriyet.com.tr/gundem/5-gun-5-ulke-yordu-110890; "Erdoğan Bush'la Görüşüyor - 2002-12-10 [Erdoğan meets with Bush - 2002-12-10]," *Amerika'nın Sesi*, December 10, 2002, https://www.amerikaninsesi.com/a/a-17-a-2002-12-10-8-1-87862857/796938.html.
12 A popular pro-government account on Twitter called "Mastermind Games" (@UstAkilOyunlari), most likely run by people who work in the presidential palace, actually uses a photo of Brzezinski as its profile picture. In its profile description, it reads "Üst Aklın, Nam-ı diğer; Gizli Ecnebi Örgüt'ün, tarih boyunca yaptığı, ve insanlığın geleceği üzerine planladığı oyunlar...!" ["The games the Mastermind, also known as the Secret Foreign Organization, which have aimed to chart the future of humanity throughout history...!"]
13 This remains the legal name of the foundation. Later, new departments were founded, including Foreign Policy, and Human Rights and Law.
14 Interview, September 17, 2023.
15 Ibid.
16 Ahmet Davutoğlu, "Yay-ok ya da Asya-Avrupa etkileşimi içinde Türkiye'nin strateji arayışı [Bow-arrow or Turkey's Search for Strategy within Asia-Europe Interaction]," *Yeni Şafak*, August, 17, 1996, https://www.yenisafak.com/yazarlar/ahmet-davutoglu/yay-ok-ya-da-asya-avrupa-etkileimi-icinde-turkiyenin-strateji-arayii-2026992.
17 Behlül Özkan, "SETA: From the AKP's Organic Intellectuals to AK-paratchicsk," in *Turkey's New State in the Making: Transformations in Legality, Economy and Coercion*, ed. Pınar Bedirhanğlu (London: Zed Books, 2020), 226–42.

18 Cengiz Çandar, "Turkey's 'Soft Power' Strategy: A New Vision for a Multi-Polar World," *SETA Policy Brief*, December 2009.
19 Interview, September 17, 2023.
20 Ibid.
21 Interview, July 24, 2020.
22 *Today's Zaman* was the English-language version of the Gülenist flagship newspaper *Zaman*. The state shut it down in 2016. A version of the column is available on the SETA website: İbrahim Kalın, "Erdoğan, Peres and the Unclothed Emperor," *Siyaset, Ekonomi ve Toplum Araştırmaları Vakfı*, February 5, 2009, https://www.setav.org/en/erdogan-peres-and-the-unclothed-emperor/.
23 Paul White, *The PKK: Coming Down from the Mountains* (London: Zed Books, 2015).
24 Hatem Ete and Taha Özhan, "Kürt Meselesi Problemler ve Çözüm Önerileri," *SETA Vakfı Analiz*, November 2008.
25 Ibid., 12.
26 Ibid., 16.
27 Hüseyin Yayman, "Şark Meselesinden Demokratik Açılıma Türkiye'nin Kürt Sorunu Hafızası [Turkey's Memory of the Kurdish Question, from the Eastern Question to the Democratic Initiative]," *Siyaset, Ekonomi ve Toplum Araştırmaları Vakfı*, February 2011.
28 For a full discussion of the peace process, see Gülay Türkmen, *Under the Banner of Islam: Turks, Kurds, and the Limits of Religious Unity* (Oxford: Oxford University Press, 2021).
29 "Akil insanların tam listesi [Complete List of Wise People]," *TRT Haber*, April 3, 2013, https://www.trthaber.com/haber/gundem/akil-insanlarin-tam-listesi-80941.html.
30 Lisel Hintz, *Identity Politics Inside Out: National Identity Contestation and Foreign Policy in Turkey* (New York, NY: Oxford University Press, 2018), 107.
31 See Gönül Tol, *Erdoğan's War: A Strongman's Struggle at Home and in Syria* (New York City, NY: Oxford University Press, 2021).
32 "Erdoğan: Esad'a halkı da inanmıyor, biz de [Erdoğan: The People Don't Believe in Assad, Nor Do We]," *BBC News Türkçe*, September 14, 2011, https://www.bbc.com/turkce/haberler/2011/09/110914_Erdoğan_syria.
33 Mensur Akgün, Perçinoğlu Gökçe, Sabiha Senyücel Gündoğar, and Levack Jonathan, "The Perception of Turkey in the Middle East 2010," *TESEV Foreign Policy Programme*, February 2, 2011, https://www.tesev.org.tr/wp-content/uploads/report_The_Perception_Of_Turkey_In_The_Middle_East_2010.pdf; Gönül Tol, "The "Turkish Model" in the Middle East," *Middle East Institute*, https://www.mei.edu/publications/turkish-model-middle-east-0.
34 Ufuk Ulutaş, "Nasıl 'Ortadoğu uzmanı' olunur? [How to become a 'Middle East expert'?]," *Star*, September 16, 2012, https://www.star.com.tr/acik-gorus/nasil-ortadogu-uzmani-olunur-haber-689234/.

35 Egemen Bezci, *Turkish Intelligence and the Cold War: The Turkish Secret Service, the US and the UK* (London: I.B. Tauris, 2021), 15.

36 Ibid.

37 Hakan Fidan, "Intelligence and Foreign Policy: A Comparison of British, American and Turkish Intelligence Systems," *The Institute of Economics and Social Sciences, Bilkent University*, May 1999, https://repository.bilkent.edu.tr/server/api/core/bitstreams/175b39d3-23a8-4668-829f-9ba6acfe15fb/content.

38 "Milli İstihbarat'tan Dışişleri'ne: Erdoğan'ın 'sır kutusu' Hakan Fidan kimdir? [From National Intelligence to the Ministry of Foreign Affairs: Erdoğan's 'Box of Secrets' Who is Hakan Fidan?]," *Euronews*, June 6, 2023, https://tr.euronews.com/2023/06/06/milli-istihbarattan-disislerine-erdoganin-sir-kutusu-hakan-fidan-kimdir.

39 Fehim Taştekin, "AKP Seeks to 'Legalize' PKK Peace Talks," *Al-Monitor*, June 27, 2014. https://www.al-monitor.com/originals/2014/06/tastekin-legal-turkey-peace-process-kurds-pkk-akp-erdogan.html

40 İsmail Sağıroğlu, "Fidan'ın Hatay çıkarması [Fidan's Hatay landing]," *Radikal*, February 17, 2012, http://www.radikal.com.tr/turkiye/fidanin-hatay-cikarmasi-1079006/.

41 The MİT officer who led the action, Önder Sığırcıklıoğlu, later fled prison and made statements to the media outlet OdaTV, claiming that his motivations were political, and that there was no reward involved. He said that Ankara was supporting radical Islamist groups in Syria and that he sought to work against that policy. MİT pressed charges against journalist Ömer Ödemiş, who broke the story, and OdaTV, which was ordered to take part of the story offline. "Hapisten kaçan MİT'çi konuştu: Binlerce cihatçı Suriye'ye sokuldu [MİT Member who Escaped from Prison Spoke: Thousands of jihadists were Smuggled into Syria]," *Sol TV*, January 13, 2015, https://haber.sol.org.tr/turkiye/hapisten-kacan-mitci-konustu-binlerce-cihatci-suriyeye-sokuldu-105146; "Odatv'ye MİT soruşturması [MİT investigation into Oda TV]," June 2, 2015, https://www.odatv.com/medya/odatvye-mit-sorusturmasi-76678; "Katiller AFAD'ın arabalarıyla taşındı [The murderers were transported with AFAD's cars]," *Oda TV*, January 14, 2015, https://www.odatv.com/guncel/katiller-afadin-arabalariyla-tasindi-70112.

42 "ÖSO Komuta Merkezi Türkiye'den Taşındı [FSA Command Center Moved from Turkey']," *Bianet*, September 24, 2012, https://bianet.org/haber/oso-komuta-merkezi-turkiye-den-tasindi-141027.

43 Aaron Stein, *The US War Against ISIS: How America and Its Allies Defeated the Caliphate* (London: I.B. Tauris, 2022), 74–5.

44 Saliha Çolak, "MİT Kanunu'nda değişiklik teklifi komisyondan geçti [The Proposal to Amend the MİT Law Passed the Commission]," *HaberTürk*, February 14, 2012, https://www.haberturk.com/gundem/haber/715659-mit-kanununda-degisiklik-teklifi-komisyondan-gecti.

45 Ibid..
46 In 2014, footage was leaked (most likely by Gülenist sources in government) confirming that MİT was transporting military supplies to fighters in Syria. The government decided to punish both leakers and publishers (Cumhuriyet newspaper) for the leak.
47 Erdoğan confirmed that these leaks were authentic. See "Erdoğan, Suriye'ye dair ses kaydını doğruladı [Erdoğan confirmed the audio recording regarding Syria]," *Evrensel*, March 27, 2014, https://www.evrensel.net/haber/81071/erdogan-suriyeye-dair-ses-kaydini-dogruladi.
48 Aaron Stein has made the same point: Aaron Stein, "Turkey's Syria Policy: Why Seymour Hersh Got It Wrong," *Arms Control Wonk*, April 8, 2014, https://www.armscontrolwonk.com/archive/604329/turkeys-syria-policy-why-seymour-hersh-got-it-wrong/.
49 Kazım Civelekoğlu, "Ahmet Davutoğlu-Hakan Fidan Gerekirse Kendi Ülkemize Füze Atarız ! [Ahmet Davutoğlu-Hakan Fidan If Necessary, We Will Fire Missiles at Our Own Country !]," YouTube, February 9, 2015, https://www.youtube.com/watch?v=X-4VWADux4Y.
50 Ibid..
51 Stein, *The US War Against ISIS*, 69–83.
52 Later reporting based on sources from the State Department confirm Davutoğlu's status as a "channel for many U.S. officials to convey their thoughts and concerns." See John Hudson, "America Loses Its Man in Ankara," *Foreign Policy (blog)*, May 5, 2016, https://foreignpolicy.com/2016/05/05/america-loses-its-man-in-ankara/.
53 "BM Daimi Temsilciliğine Feridun Hadi Sinirlioğlu atandı [Feridun Hadi Sinirlioğlu was Appointed as Permanent Representative to the UN]," *Haberturk*, August 16, 2016, https://www.haberturk.com/gundem/haber/1282498-bm-daimi-temsilciligine-feridun-hadi-sinirlioglu-atandi.
54 Barçın Yinanç, "Why the Turkish–US train-equip Program Failed in Syria," *Hurriyet Daily News*, August 10, 2015, https://www.hurriyetdailynews.com/opinion/barcin-yinanc/why-the-turkishus-train-equip-program-failed-in-syria-86749; Michael D. Shear, Helene Cooper and Eric Schmitt, "Obama Administration Ends Effort to Train Syrians to Combat ISIS," *The New York Times*, October 9, 2015, https://www.nytimes.com/2015/10/10/world/middleeast/pentagon-program-islamic-state-syria.html.
55 Kurds refer to the territories of Kurdistan by cardinal directions in Kurdish. Turkey's Kurdish region is "Bakur" (north), Iran's is "Rojhilat" (east), Iraq's is "Başûr" (south), and Syria's is "Rojava" (west). These names are considered irredentist in the four countries concerned.
56 Amberin Zaman, "Salih Muslim: Syria's Kurdish Problems will be Solved by Syrians, not Turkey," *Al-Monitor*, February 26, 2018, https://www.al-monitor.com/originals/2018/02/salih-muslim-syria-kurds-turkey-arrest.html#ixzz8Q2C0fE6L.

57 Newsha Tavakolian, "Meet the Women Taking the Battle to ISIS," *Time*, April 2, 2015. https://time.com/3767133/meet-the-women-taking-the-battle-to-isis/

58 Joost Jongerden, "Colonialism, Self-Determination and Independence: The New PKK Paradigm," in *Kurdish Issues: Essays in Honor of Robert W. Olson*, ed. Michael Gunter (Costa Mesa, CA: Mazda Publishers, 2016), 106–21.

59 "Cumhurbaşkanı Erdoğan: Türkiye'nin sosyal güvenlik ve sağlık hizmetleri reformu, tüm dünyaya örnek olmuştur [President Erdoğan: Turkey's Social Security and Health Services Reform has Set an Example for the Whole World]," *Türkiye Cumhuriyeti Cumhurbaşkanlığı İletişim Başkanlığı*, https://www.iletisim.gov.tr/turkce/pozitif_iletisim_kampanyalari/detaylar/cumhurbaskani-erdogan-turkiyenin-sosyal-guvenlik-ve-saglik-hizmetleri-reformu-tum-dunyaya-ornek-olmustur.

60 Interview, September 17, 2023.

61 Burhanettin Duran, "Kürt milliyetçi söyleminin savrulması [The drift of Kurdish nationalist discourse]," *Sabah*, November 4, 2014, https://www.sabah.com.tr/yazarlar/duran/2014/11/04/kurt-milliyetci-soyleminin-savrulmasi.

62 "Kurds Celebrate Gains Amid Blow to Turkey's Ak Party," *Al Jazeera*, June 8, 2015, https://www.aljazeera.com/news/2015/6/8/kurds-celebrate-gains-amid-blow-to-turkeys-ak-party.

63 Burcu Karakas, "Suruç Katliamı: Yedi yıldır süren adalet arayışı [Suruç Massacre: The Seven-year Search for Justice]," *DW*, July 20, 2022, https://www.dw.com/tr/suru%C3%A7-katliam%C4%B1-yedi-y%C4%B1ld%C4%B1r-s%C3%BCren-adalet-aray%C4%B1%C5%9F%C4%B1/a-62531252.

64 "Şanlıurfa'da 2 polis şehit oldu, saldırıyı terör örgütü PKK üstlendi [2 policemen killed in Şanlıurfa, terrorist organization PKK claimed responsibility for the attack]," *Habertürk*, July 22, 2015, https://www.haberturk.com/gundem/haber/1106043-sanliurfada-2-polis-sehit-oldu; Mahmut Hamsici, "Kandil: Çözüm süreci yeniden başlatılabilir, zor değil [Kandil: The Peace Process can Begin Again, it's Not Hard]," *BBC Türkçe*, July 29, 2015, https://www.bbc.com/turkce/haberler/2015/07/150728_kandil_roportaj.

65 This is, of course, relative and reflects how the government saw the state at the time (and into the present day). One could take a more expansive view of the Turkish state and claim that it was actually benefiting more from the peace process because it was resolving the long-standing issue that obstructed democratic progress in the country.

66 "Turkey's PKK Conflict: A Visual Explainer," *International Crisis Group*, https://www.crisisgroup.org/content/turkeys-pkk-conflict-visual-explainer.

67 Ibid.

68 Özkan Öztaş, "Kurdun dişi Kürdün düşü [Wolf's Tooth Kurd's Dream]," *Haber Sol*, November 29, 2015. https://haber.sol.org.tr/yazarlar/ozkan-oztas/kurdun-disi-kurdun-dusu-137755

69 "Bu Kafa Yapısı Çözüm Değil, Sorun Üretir! Kaynak: Bu Kafa Yapısı Çözüm Değil, Sorun Üretir! [This Mindset Produces Problems, Not Solutions! Source: This Mindset Produces Problems, Not Solutions!]," *Haksöz Haber*, November 15, 2015, https://www.haksozhaber.net/bu-kafa-yapisi-cozum-degil-sorun-uretir-67864h.htm.

70 "Mete Yarar Kimdir? Kendi Hayat Hikayesini Anlatıyor. Eski Bordo Bereli Mete Yarar Kim? [Who is Mete Yarar? He Tells His Own Life Story. Who is Old Maroon Beret Mete Yarar?]," https://www.youtube.com/watch?v=3oc7WaCTdes.

71 "Keskin Nişancıların Operasyon Hazırlıkları | Şahit Olun [Operation Preparations of Snipers | Witness]," *TRT Belgesel*, https://www.youtube.com/watch?v=khIJ62ZY8ZU.

72 Hülya Karabağlı, "Darbe girişimi sırasında MİT Müsteşarı Hakan Fidan ne yaptı? [What did MİT Undersecretary Hakan Fidan Do during the Coup Attempt?]," *T24*, December 22, 2016, https://t24.com.tr/haber/darbe-girisimi-sirasinda-mit-mustesari-hakan-fidan-ne-yapti,378443.

73 Mahmut Hamsici and Osman Kaytazoğlu, "15 Temmuz: Kritik noktalarda neler yaşandı? [July 15: What Happened at Critical Points?]," *BBC Türkçe*, July 13, 2018, https://www.bbc.com/turkce/resources/idt-sh/temmuz_darbe_girisimi#:~:text=15%20Temmuz%20%C3%87at%C4%B1%20Davas%C4%B1%27n%C4%B1n,faaliyeti%20saat%2020.30%20s%C4%B1ralar%C4%B1nda%20ba%C5%9Flad%C4%B1.

74 Medyascope, "Darbe gecesi Erdoğan'ın CNN Türk'ten önce yaptığı ama yayınlanmayan ilk konuşması [Erdoğan's First Speech on the Night of the Coup, Made before CNN Türk but Not Broadcast]," *YouTube*, November 19, 2016, https://www.youtube.com/watch?v=MA1h_B-ElU0.

75 Mahmut Hamsici and Osman Kaytazoğlu, "15 Temmuz: Kritik noktalarda neler yaşandı? [July 15: What Happened at Critical Points?]," *BBC Türkçe*, July 13, 2018, https://www.bbc.com/turkce/resources/idt-sh/temmuz_darbe_girisimi#:~:text=15%20Temmuz%20%C3%87at%C4%B1%20Davas%C4%B1%27n%C4%B1n,faaliyeti%20saat%2020.30%20s%C4%B1ralar%C4%B1nda%20ba%C5%9Flad%C4%B1.

76 "Zekai Aksakallı ilk kez konuştu... Hulusi Akar'a ikinci salvo... 15 Temmuz öncesi defterler yeniden açıldı [Zekai Aksakallı Spoke for the First Time... Second salvo against Hulusi Akar... The Books were Reopened before July 15]," *OdaTV*, July 13, 2023, https://www.odatv.com/guncel/zekai-aksakalli-roportaj-67834325; Cüneyt Özdemir, "Ömer Halisdemir Darbe Gecesi Semih Terzi'yi Öldürmeseydi Neler Olacaktı? [What Would have Happened if Ömer Halisdemir had Not Killed Semih Terzi on the Night of the Coup?]," *YouTube*, July 13, 2017, https://www.youtube.com/watch?v=8kJji_0zBLk.

77 These are versions of the Fiat 131 that were indigenously produced in the 1980s and 1990s. There is a lively market for maintaining and modifying them.

78 Tanju Özkaya, "FETÖ'nün darbe girişiminin üzerinden 7 yıl geçti [7 Years have Passed since FETO's Coup Attempt]," *Anadolu Ajansı*, July 13, 2023, https://www.aa.com.tr/tr/15-temmuz-darbe-girisimi/fetonun-darbe-girisiminin-uzerinden-7-yil-gecti/2944540; "TSK İlk Açıklama: Ölü ve Yaralılar Var [TSK First Statement: There Are Dead and Injured]," *Bianet*, July 16, 2016, https://bianet.org/haber/tsk-ilk-aciklama-olu-ve-yaralilar-var-176787.

79 Turkish politics is an information-poor environment, and there is no conclusive evidence linking the event to an order of Gülen himself. On the morning of the coup, several known Gülenists who had no formal affiliation with the military were found and arrested on military grounds. The most senior was Adil Öksüz, who is believed to have orchestrated the coup attemopt. He was detained at the coup's headquarters on the morning after the coup but was able to flee and eventually travel abroad. His wherabouts are currently unknown. Zia Weise, "Where in the World is Adil Öksüz?," *POLITICO*, December 20, 2017, https://www.politico.eu/article/where-in-the-world-is-adil-oksuz-turkey-coup/.

80 Egemen Gök, "Umut Vakfı: "Bireysel silahlanma bir yıl içinde yüzde 27 arttı" [Umut Foundation: 'Individual Armament Increased by 27 percent in One Year']," *Medyascope*, September 28, 2017. https://medyascope.tv/2017/09/28/umut-vakfi-bireysel-silahlanma-1-yil-icinde-yuzde-27-artti/; "Umut Vakfı– Türkiye Silahlı Şiddet Haritası 2017 [Umut Foundation – Türkiye Armed Violence Map 2017]," https://www.umut.org.tr/umut-vakfi-turkiye-silahli-siddet-haritasi-20172/#:~:text=%C4%B0lk%20%C3%A7al%C4%B1%C5%9Fmam%C4%B1z%C4%B1%202015%20y%C4%B1l%C4%B1nda%20yapm%C4%B1%C5%9F,25%20art%C4%B1%C5%9Fla%202721%20olay%20yans%C4%B1m%C4%B1%C5%9Ft%C4%B1 (accessed November 19, 2023).

81 Perhaps the most popular one is Süleyman Kocabıyık, whose firm claims to have ten locations in Turkey, and provides training to civilians as well as official bodies, in Turkey and abroad: http://www.suleymankocabiyik.com.

82 Rachel Monroe, "I Am Not a Soldier, but I Have Been Trained to Kill," *Wired*, January 15, 2021, https://www.wired.com/story/america-civilian-tactical-training-industry/; Myke Cole, "The Sparta Fetish Is a Cultural Cancer," *The New Republic*, August 1, 2019, https://newrepublic.com/article/154563/sparta-myth-rise-fascism-trumpism.

83 "Sevda Noyan: 'Bu ülkede kim darbe yapıyorsa karşısındayım, elime ne geçiyorsa hakkımı savunurum' [Sevda Noyan: 'I am Against Whoever is Making a Coup in this Country, I will Defend my Rights with Whatever I can']," *BBC News Türkçe*, May 9, 2020, https://www.bbc.com/turkce/haberler-turkiye-52599442; Selim Koru, "Erdoğan's Turkey and the Problem of the 30 Million," *War on the Rocks*, June 4, 2020, https://warontherocks.com/2020/06/erdogans-turkey-and-the-problem-of-the-30-million/.

84. The most acute skills shortage was in fighter pilots. Nearly all of Turkey's F-16 pilots were believed to be Gülenists. It took years to train up new groups of pilots. See "F-16 pilotlarının neredeyse tümü FETÖ'cü çıktı [Almost all F-16 Pilots Turned Out to be FETÖ Members]," *Anadolu Ajansı*, March 23, 2017, https://www.aa.com.tr/tr/15-temmuz-darbe-girisimi/f-16-pilotlarinin-neredeyse-tumu-fetocu-cikti/777801; "Yolcu uçağı pilotluğundan F-16'ya geçmek kaç yıl sürer, pilotların hangi eğitimlerden geçmesi gerekiyor? [How Many Years does it Take to Transition from a Passenger Plane Pilot to an F-16, and what Training Do Pilots Need to Undergo?]," *T24*, August 22, 2016, https://t24.com.tr/haber/yolcu-ucagi-pilotlugundan-f-16ya-gecmek-kac-yil-surer-pilotlarin-hangi-egitimlerden-gecmesi-gerekiyor,356246.

85. "Cumhurbaşkanı Erdoğan: Türkiye'nin güvenliği Halep'te başlar [President Erdoğan: Turkey's Security Begins at Aleppo]," *Anadolu Ajansı*, January 5, 2017, https://www.aa.com.tr/tr/gunun-basliklari/cumhurbaskani-erdogan-turkiyenin-guvenligi-halepte-baslar/720916.

86. Sarp Özer, "Yedek astsubaylığa yoğun ilgi," August, 4, 2019, https://www.aa.com.tr/tr/turkiye/yedek-astsubayliga-yogun-ilgi/1548986; Selim Koru, "The Fart Of A Soldier," May 19, 2022, https://kulturkampftr.substack.com/p/the-fart-of-a-soldier.

87. Sarp Özer, "Bakan Akar yeni askerlik sisteminin tüm detaylarını açıkladı [Minister Akar Announced All the Details of the New Military Service System]," May 22, 2019, https://www.aa.com.tr/tr/turkiye/bakan-akar-yeni-askerlik-sisteminin-tum-detaylarini-acikladi/1484069; Murat Aslan, "Yeni Asker Alma Sistemi [New Registration System]," March, 2019, https://setav.org/assets/uploads/2019/03/232.-Yeni-Askerlik-Sistemi.pdf.

88. Kıymet Sezer, "Savunmada büyük dönüşüm: TSK tam profesyonel [Big Transformation in Defense: TAF is Fully Professional]," May 4, 2022, https://www.yenisafak.com/gundem/savunmada-buyuk-donusum-tsk-tam-profesyonel-3818176.

89. Haber Merkezi, "TSK'da Din İşleri Subaylığı yeniden hayata geçiyor [Religious Affairs Officer in TAF is Being Brought Back to Life]," December 3, 2020, https://www.yenisafak.com/gundem/tskda-din-isleri-subayligi-yeniden-hayata-geciyor-3587857.

90. "Türkiye'nin yeni savunma karargahı: Ay Yıldız [Turkey's New Defense Headquarters: Crescent and Star]," *TRT Haber*, September 1, 2021, https://www.trthaber.com/haber/gundem/turkiyenin-yeni-savunma-karargahi-ay-yildiz-605652.html.

91. Nate Schenkkan, "Turkey just Snatched Six of its Citizens from Another Country," *The Washington Post*, April 1, 2018, https://www.washingtonpost.com/news/democracy-post/wp/2018/04/01/turkey-just-snatched-six-of-its-citizens-from-another-country/.

92 "Milli İstihbarat Teşkilatı Yeni Hizmet Binası'nın Açılış Töreni'nde Yaptığı Konuşma [His Speech at the Opening Ceremony of the New Service Building of the National Intelligence Organization]," *Türkiye Cumhuriyeti Cumhurbaşkanlığı*, January 6, 2020, https://www.tccb.gov.tr/konusmalar/353/115196/milli-istihbarat-teskilati-yeni-hizmet-binasi-nin-acilis-toreni-nde-yaptigi-konusma.

93 Utku Şimşek, "Milli İstihbarat Akademisinin ilk raporu yayımlandı [The First Report of the National Intelligence Academy was Published]," *Anadolu Ajansı*, January 11, 2024, https://www.aa.com.tr/tr/gundem/milli-istihbarat-akademisinin-ilk-raporu-yayimlandi/3105766.

94 Berrin Sönmez, "SETA'da kim kimi tasfiye etti? [Who Liquidated whom in SETA?]," *Gazete Duvar*, June 25, 2021, https://www.gazeteduvar.com.tr/setada-kim-kimi-tasfiye-etti-haber-1526518.

95 Richard Falk, "Davutoglu's Brilliant Statecraft," *Al Jazeera*, November 11, 2011, https://www.aljazeera.com/opinions/2011/11/11/davutoglus-brilliant-statecraft; James Traub, "Turkey's Rules," *The New York Times*, January 21, 2011, https://www.nytimes.com/2011/01/23/magazine/23davutoglu-t.html.

96 Daniel Bessner, *Democracy in Exile: Hans Speier and the Rise of the Defense Intellectual* (Ithaca, NY: Cornell University Press, 2018); Mircea Alexandru Platon, "'Protracted Conflict': The Foreign Policy Research Institute "Defense Intellectuals" and Their Cold War Struggle with Race and Human Rights," *Du Bois Review: Social Science Research on Race* 12, no. 2 (2015): 407–39.

Chapter 4

1 Islamists read Huntington and were inspired by his civilizational view of the world, but also offended by his characterization of Islam as being angry and having "bloody borders."

2 İbrahim Karagül, "Türkiye'nin yeni serüveni [Turkey's New Adventure]," *Yeni Şafak*, March 8, 2000, https://www.yenisafak.com/yazarlar/ibrahim-karagul/turkiyenin-yeni-seruveni-47813.

3 İbrahim Karagül, "Soykırımı onaylamak… [To Endorse the Genocide…]," *Yeni Şafak*, April 15, 2000, https://www.yenisafak.com/yazarlar/ibrahim-karagul/soykirimi-onaylamak-48956.

4 İbrahim Karagül, "Bloklar savaşı ve Türkiye'nin yeri [The War of Blocks and Turkey's Place]," *Yeni Şafak*, June 16, 2001, https://www.yenisafak.com/yazarlar/ibrahim-karagul/-bloklar-savai-ve-turkiyenin-yeri-52210.

5 Islamists often portray this as a purge, but by the standards of the Erdoğan government in the 2010s (as well as state repression of the PKK tradition), it was mild. Many who were removed from public jobs, for example, appealed decisions

in court and were reinstated. Islamist politicians were not persecuted anywhere near the level of the repression of the Kurdish and leftist politicians were repressed in the 2010s and continue to be in the 2020s.

6 İbrahim Karagül, "Amerika ile kavga, Avrupa ile barış [Fight with America, Peace with Europe]," *Yeni Şafak*, March 29, 2000, https://www.yenisafak.com/arsiv/2000/mart/29/ikaragul.html.

7 *The Economist* was alarmed by the former spymaster's background, but thought that he should be given the benefit of the doubt. Richard Haass from the Brookings institute thought Putin's Russia "an odd mixture of weakness and strength. It is filled with resentment over its diminished status in the world" and that it would not be a partner for the United States in the post–Cold War world. "Putin the Great Unknown," *The Economist*, January 16, 2000, https://www.economist.com/leaders/2000/01/06/putin-the-great-unknown; Richard N. Haass, "Putin's Rule May Leave U.S. Cold," *Brookings Institution*, January 3, 2000, https://www.brookings.edu/opinions/putins-rule-may-leave-u-s-cold/.

8 İbrahim Karagül, "Ankara'daki Rus lobisi kazandı, Türkiye kaybetti… [The Russian Lobby in Ankara Won, Turkey Lost…]," *Yeni Şafak*, May 24, 2000, https://www.yenisafak.com/yazarlar/ibrahim-karagul/ankaradaki-rus-lobisi-kazandi-turkiye-kaybetti-51909.

9 İbrahim Karagül, "Sonu gelmeyecek savaşlar [Wars That Won't Come to an End]," *Yeni Şafak*, September 25, 1999, https://www.yenisafak.com/yazarlar/ibrahim-karagul/sonu-gelmeyecek-savalar-43978.

10 İbrahim Karagül, "Globalleşme bizi yok edecek [Globalization will Destroy us]," *Yeni Şafak*, June 28, 2000, https://www.yenisafak.com/yazarlar/ibrahim-karagul/globalleme-bizi-yok-edecek-53366. For an example of Western coverage, see Thomas Fuller, "Malaysia Leader Urges Modernization to Foil Muslims' Oppressors: Mahathir Tells Islam To Embrace Technology," *The New Tork Times*, June 28, 2000, https://www.nytimes.com/2000/06/28/news/malaysia-leader-urges-modernization-to-foil-muslims-oppressors-mahathir.html.

11 İbrahim Karagül, "21. yüzyıla ilişkin öngörüler [Predictions Relating to the Twenty-first Century]," *Yeni Şafak*, January 5, 2000, https://www.yenisafak.com/yazarlar/ibrahim-karagul/21-yuzyila-ilikin-ongoruler-45544.

12 İbrahim Karagül, "Freedom House ve 17 Aralık ortaklığı [Freedom House and the December 17 Partnership]," *Yeni Şafak*, May 12, 2014, https://www.yenisafak.com/yazarlar/ibrahim-karagul/21-yuzyila-ilikin-ongoruler-45544; İbrahim Karagül, "'6'lı Masa'nın Anayasa planına baktım [I Looked at the Constitutional Plan of the Table of Six]," *Twitter*, November 28, 2022, https://twitter.com/ibrahimkaragul/status/1597169649187028992.

13 İbrahim Karagül, "Şanghay ve BRICS'e tam ortaklık: Bütün tehditler neden Batı'dan? Türkiye bir ülke değil, coğrafyadır [Full Partnership with Shanghai

and BRICS: Why Are All Threats from the West? Turkey is Not a Country, It Is Geography]," *Yeni Şafak*, July 30, 2018, https://www.yenisafak.com/yazarlar/ibrahim-karagul/sanghay-ve-bricse-tam-ortaklik-butun-tehditler-neden-batidan-turkiye-bir-ulke-degil-cografyadir-2046660.

14. See İbrahim Karagül, "*Türkistan da bizim Filistin de.* Enver de bizim Şeyh Yasin de.* Kimler, kimlerin düdüğünü çalıyor, biz bunu iyi biliriz. [Türkistan is our Palestine. Enver is our Sheikh Yasin. Who]," *Yeni Şafak*, January 12, 2019, https://www.yenisafak.com/yazarlar/ibrahim-karagul/-turkistan-da-bizim-filistin-de-enver-de-bizim-seyh-yasin-de-kimler-kimlerin-dudugunu-caliyor-biz-bunu-iyi-biliriz-2048872. "Ukrayna krizi büyütülür. Batı, Karadeniz'e çöker. Türkiye-Rusya savaşı Batı'nın ana hedefidir. - Erdoğan ve Putin bunu durdurmalı! [The Ukraine Crisis Grows. The West Will Claim the Black Sea. A Turkey-Russia War Is the West's Greatest Goal. - Erdoğan and Putin Should Stop This!]," *Yeni Şafak*, February 8, 2022, https://www.yenisafak.com/yazarlar/ibrahim-karagul/-ukrayna-krizi-buyutulur-bati-karadenize-coker-urkiye-rusya-savasi-batinin-ana-hedefidir-Erdoğan-ve-putin-bunu-durdurmali-2061927.

15. This is a popular idea in New Turkey, and is often expressed as "Turkey is greater than Turkey" (Türkiye Türkiye'den büyüktür.) In the United States, similar discussions are held about countries like Iran or the United States itself: Erka Medya, "Türkiye Türkiyeden Büyüktür. Erdoğan Hesabı Ödedi. Turkey Big Boss Recep Tayyip Erdoğan [Turkey Is Greater Than Turkey. Erdoğan has Paid the Bill. Turkey Big Boss Recep Tayyip Erdoğan.]," *YouTube*, March 27, 2017, https://www.youtube.com/watch?v=bwFv6JpBmwc; James Mackenzie Fallows, "America as an Idea," *United States Studies Centre*, November 8, 2009, https://www.ussc.edu.au/analysis/america-as-an-idea; Doyle McManus, "Iran's Dilemma: A Country or a Cause," *The Los Angeles Times*, January 24, 2016, https://www.latimes.com/opinion/op-ed/la-oe-0124-mcmanus-iran-symbolism-20160124-column.html.

16. "Joe Biden: Former Vice President of the United States," *The New York Times*, January 17, 2020, https://www.nytimes.com/interactive/2020/01/17/opinion/joe-biden-nytimes-interview.html.

17. Galip Dalay and E. Fuat Keyman, "Has Turkey's Quest for 'Strategic Autonomy' Run its Course?," *German Marshall Fund*, July 26, 2021, https://www.gmfus.org/news/has-turkeys-quest-strategic-autonomy-run-its-course.

18. Stuart Williams, "The Uneasy Alliance Between Putin and Erdoğan," *New Lines Magazine*, March 11, 2021, https://newlinesmag.com/essays/the-uneasy-alliance-between-putin-and-Erdoğan/.

19. Galip Dalay, "Turkey and Russia are Bitter Frenemies," *Foreign Policy*, May 28, 2019, https://foreignpolicy.com/2019/05/28/turkey-and-russia-are-bitter-frenemies/; Galip Dalay, "Turkey's Recurring Quest for Security, Status, and

Geopolitical Identity," *German Marshall Fund*, April 1, 2022, https://www.gmfus.org/news/turkeys-recurring-quest-security-status-and-geopolitical-identity.

20 Liana Fix and Michael Kimmage, "What If Russia Wins? A Kremlin-Controlled Ukraine Would Transform Europe," *Foreign Affairs*, February 18, 2022, https://www.foreignaffairs.com/articles/ukraine/2022-02-18/what-if-russia-wins; "Virtual Event | Turkey's Role in the Ukraine Crisis," *Hudson Institute*, February 11, 2022, https://s3.amazonaws.com/media.hudson.org/Transcript-Turkey's%20Role%20in%20the%20Ukraine%20Crisis.pdf.

21 Selim Koru, "NATO's Prodigal Son Is Not Returning," *War on the Rocks*, July 31, 2023, https://warontherocks.com/2023/07/natos-prodigal-son-is-not-returning/.

22 Samuel J. Hirst and Onur İşçi, "Smokestacks and Pipelines: Russian-Turkish Relations and the Persistence of Economic Development," *Diplomatic History* 44, no. 5 (2020): 834–59.

23 Ibid., 838–9.

24 Ibid., 841.

25 Ibid., 844–5.

26 Ibid., 848–50.

27 For liberal reforms in the Russian economy in the early 2000s, see Chris Miller, *Putinomics: Power and Money in Resurgent Russia* (Chapel Hill, NC: University of North Carolina Press, 2018), chapter 3.

28 Daniel Fried and Kurt Volker, "The Speech in Which Putin Told Us Who He Was," *POLITICO*, February 18, 2022, https://www.politico.com/news/magazine/2022/02/18/putin-speech-wake-up-call-post-cold-war-order-liberal-2007-00009918.

29 Lisel Hintz, *Identity Politics Inside Out: National Identity Contestation and Foreign Policy in Turkey* (New York, NY: Oxford University Press, 2018), 107.

30 Keith Richburg, "Giscard Declares Turkey Too 'Different' to Join EU," *The Washington Post*, November 9, 2022, https://www.washingtonpost.com/archive/politics/2002/11/09/giscard-declares-turkey-too-different-to-join-eu/826842dd-b769-4ef8-bc37-c8fa2fe80928/.

31 Burns, Nicholas and Alexander Vershbow, "Opinion | Istanbul Summit: Building a Partnership with Russia," *The New York Times*, June 26, 2004, https://www.nytimes.com/2004/06/26/opinion/IHT-istanbul-summit-building-a-partnership-with-russia.html.

32 Liah Greenfeld, "The Formation of the Russian National Identity: The Role of Status Insecurity and Resentment," *Comparative Studies in Society and History* 32, no. 3 (July 1990): 549–91.

33 "Mermiler Uçağa Yetişmiyor [Bullets Cannot Reach the Plane]," *Yeni Şafak*, November 22, 2015, https://www.yenisafak.com/gundem/mermiler-ucaga-yetismiyor-2344546; "Humus Katliamı [Homs Massacre]," *Yeni Şafak*, October 16, 2015, https://www.yenisafak.com/dunya/humus-katliami-2324729.

34 Rengin Arslan, "Rusya'nın Suriye sahasına girişi Türkiye için ne anlam ifade ediyor? [What does Russia's Entrance into Syria Mean for Turkey?]," *BBC Türkçe*, October 3, 2015, https://www.bbc.com/turkce/haberler/2015/10/151003_rengin _rusya_turkiye_analiz.

35 Aaron Stein, "How Russia beat Turkey in Syria," *Atlantic Council*, March 27, 2017, https://www.atlanticcouncil.org/blogs/syriasource/how-russia-beat-turkey-in -syria/.

36 Thomas Gibbons-Neff, "The Last Time a Russian Jet was Shut Down by a Nato Jet was in 1952," *The Washington Post*, November 24, 2015, https://www .washingtonpost.com/news/checkpoint/wp/2015/11/24/the-last-time-a-russian-jet -was-shot-down-by-a-nato-jet-was-in-1952/

37 Seda Başıhoş, Can İtez, and Ayşegül Taşöz, "Rusya ile Yaşanan Krizin Ekonomiye Olası Etkilerine Nasıl Bakılabilir [How to Approach the Potential Economic Effects of the Crisis with Russia]," *TEPAV Değerlendirme Notu, N201538*, December 2015, https://www.tepav.org.tr/upload/files/1451058729-9.Rusya_ile_Yasanan_Krizin _Ekonomiye_Olasi_Etkilerine_Nasil_Bakilabilir.pdf.

38 Julian Borger, "NATO and UN Seek Calm over Turkish Downing of Russian Jet," *The Guardian*, November 24, 2015, https://www.theguardian.com/world/2015/nov /24/nato-and-un-seek-calm-over-turkish-downing-of-russian-jet.

39 Jeffrey Mankoff, "Why Russia and Turkey Fight," *Foreign Affairs*, February 24, 2016, https://www.foreignaffairs.com/articles/turkey/2016-02-24/why-russia-and -turkey-fight.

40 "Erdoğan NATO'nun yüzünden Karadeniz Rus Gölüne Döndü [Erdoğan NATO'nun yüzünden Karadeniz Rus Gölüne Döndü [Erdoğan: The Black Sea Turned into a Russian Lake Because of NATO]," *Haber Sol*, May 11, 2016, https:// haber.sol.org.tr/toplum/erdogan-natonun-yuzunden-karadeniz-rus-golu-oldu -155577.

41 "Adım Adım Türkiye ve Rusya'nın Normalleşme Süreci [The Normalization Process of Turkey and Russia, Step by Step]," *TRT Haber*, December 3, 2016, https://www.trthaber.com/haber/gundem/adim-adim-turkiye-ve-rusyanin -normallesme-sureci-285992.html.

42 Nazlı Yüzbaşıoğlu, "Darbe Girişiminşn Karşısında Türkiye'nin Yanında Durdular [They Stood Against the Coup Attempt by Turkey]," *Anadolu Ajansı*, July 14, 2019, https://www.aa.com.tr/tr/15-temmuz-darbe-girisimi/darbe-girisiminin-karsisinda -turkiyenin-yaninda-durdular/1531276.

43 Simon A. Waldman, "Erdogan's Big Lie: Why Turkey's President Rewrote the History of the 2016 Coup," *Haaretz*, July 14, 2021, https://www.haaretz.com/ middle-east-news/2021-07-14/ty-article-opinion/.premium/erdogans-big-lie-why -turkeys-president-rewrote-the-history-of-the-2016-coup/0000017f-dbf6-d856 -a37f-fff6210c0000; "15 Temmuz darbe girişimi: Türkiye neden ABD'yi suçluyor,

Amerikan yönetimi ne diyor? [July 15 Coup Attempt: Why does Turkey Blame the USA, what does the American Administration Say?]," *BBC Türkçe*, February 5, 2021, https://www.bbc.com/turkce/haberler-dunya-55952909.

44 Ibid.

45 "FETÖ ve Arkasındaki Güçlerin Türkiye-Rusya İlişkilerine de Kastettiği Anlaşılıyor [It is Understood that FETÖ and the Forces Behind it also Mean Turkey-Russia Relations]," *Türkiye Cumhuriyeti Cumhurbaşkanlığı*, August 9, 2016, https://www.tccb.gov.tr/haberler/410/49946/feto-ve-arkasindaki-guclerin-turkiye-rusya-iliskilerine-de-kastettigi-anlasiliyor.

46 Hakan Ceyhan Aydoğan and Ali Cura, "Rusya FETÖ'nün hüsrana uğradığı ilk ülkelerden biriydi [Russia was One of the First Countries that FETO was Disappointed by]," *Anadolu Ajansı*, August 15, 2016, https://www.aa.com.tr/tr/turkiye/rusya-feto-nun-husrana-ugradigi-ilk-ulkelerden-biriydi/628841; "FETÖ Rusya'da etkin olmayı başaramadı [FETO Failed to be Effective in Russia]," *TRT Haber*, October 8, 2016, https://www.trthaber.com/haber/dunya/feto-rusyada-etkin-olmayi-basaramadi-265388.html.

47 Nerdun Hacıoğlu, "O gece Ruslar da uyumadı [That Night the Russians did Not Sleep Either]," *Hürriyet*, October 24, 2019, https://www.hurriyet.com.tr/yasasin-demokrasi/o-gece-ruslar-da-uyumadi-40163428

48 "Rus uçağı FETÖ'nün talimatı ile düşürüldü [Russian Plane was Shot Down on the Instructions of FETÖ]," *Star*, July 24, 2016, https://www.star.com.tr/guncel/rus-ucagi-fetonun-talimati-ile-dusuruldu-haber-1128175/; "Ahmet Zeki Üçok: Rusya uçağını düşürenler FETÖ'cü [Ahmet Zeki Üçok: Those who Shot Down the Russian Plane are FETO Members]," *CNN Türk*, August 10, 2016, https://www.cnnturk.com/video/turkiye/ahmet-zeki-ucok-rusya-ucagini-dusurenler-fetocu; Ufuk Ulutaş, "5 Soru: Rus Büyükelçi Karlov'a Düzenlenen Suikast [5 Questions: Assassination of Russian Ambassador Karlov]," *SETAV*, December 21, 2016, https://www.setav.org/5-soru-rus-buyukelci-karlova-duzenlenen-suikast/

49 "Erdoğan ile Putin St. Petersburg'da bir araya geldi [Erdoğan and Putin in St. Met in St. Petersburg]," *BBC Türkçe*, August 9, 2016, https://www.bbc.com/turkce/haberler-dunya-37020971.

50 "Dugin AKP grup toplantısında [Dugin at the AKP group meeting]," *Sözcü*, November 8, 2016, https://www.sozcu.com.tr/2016/gundem/dugin-akp-grup-toplantisinda-1496219/; Meltem Öztürk, "Rus stratejist Dugin: Putin Türkiye'ye dostluk elini uzatıyor [Russian strategist Dugin: Putin extends the hand of friendship to Turkey]," *Anadolu Ajansı*, November 8, 2016. https://www.aa.com.tr/tr/turkiye/rus-stratejist-dugin-putin-turkiyeye-dostluk-elini-uzatiyor/681122

51 Edebali Murat Akca, Abdullah Keşvelioğlu, Alpaslan Oğuz, and Muhammed Lütfi Türkcan, "Turkey's Procurement of the S-400 System: An Explainer," *TRT World*

Research Centre, August 2019, https://researchcentre.trtworld.com/wp-content/uploads/2020/11/S400.pdf.

52. Aaron Stein, "The Crete Mirage: Why Rapprochement with Turkey May be a Long Way Off," *Foreign Policy Research Institute*, February 10, 2021, https://www.fpri.org/article/2021/02/the-crete-mirage-why-rapprochement-with-turkey-may-be-a-long-way-off/.

53. Serhat Güvenç and Lerna K. Yanık, "Turkey's Involvement in the F-35 Program: One Step Forward, Two Steps Backward?," *International Journal* 68, no. 1 (2012): 111–29; Srdjan Vucetic and Kim Richard Nossal, "The International Politics of the F-35 Joint Strike Fighter," *International Journal* 68, no. 1 (2012): 3–12.

54. Aaron Stein, "A Pilrouette, Not a Pivot," *War On The Rocks*, May 24, 2023. https://warontherocks.com/2023/05/a-pirouette-not-a-pivot/; Patrick Tucker, "Why the S-400 and the F-35 Can't Get Along," *Defense One*, July 17, 2019. Patrick Turner, "Why the S-400 and the F-35 Can't Get Along," *Defense One*, July 17, 2019, https://www.defenseone.com/technology/2019/07/why-s-400-and-f-35-cant-get-along/158504/.

55. "First Shipment of Russian S-400 Systems Delivered to Turkey," *AlJazeera*, July 12, 2019, https://www.aljazeera.com/news/2019/7/12/first-shipment-of-russian-s-400-systems-delivered-to-turkey.

56. Joe Gould and Aaron Mehta, "Lawmakers say Trump is Locked into Turkey Sanctions," *Defense News*, July 16, 2019, https://www.defensenews.com/congress/2019/07/16/trump-cuts-off-f-35-for-turkey-and-lawmakers-say-sanctions-are-coming/; "Turkey: U.S. Sanctions Under the Countering America's Adversaries Through Sanctions Act (CAATSA)," *Congressional Research Service*, December 16, 2020, https://sgp.fas.org/crs/mideast/IN11557.pdf.

57. Gazete Duvar, "Erdoğan: S-400 tarihimizin en önemli anlaşması [Erdoğan: S-400 is the Most Important Deal in Our History]," July 14, 2019, https://www.gazeteduvar.com.tr/gundem/2019/07/14/Erdoğan-s-400-tarihimizin-en-onemli-anlasmasi.

58. Ibid.

59. This argument is also prevalent among Turkist nationalists like Ümit Özdağ, who argued against leaving NATO because "if Turkey left NATO today, it would become its target." See: Cansu Çamlıbel, "Zafer Partisi Genel Başkanı Ümit Özdağ: Kılıçdaroğlu kazansa üç bakanlık ve MİT Başkanlığını alacaktık, yazılı mutabakat var [Victory Party Chairman Ümit Özdağ: If Kılıçdaroğlu Won, We Would Get Three Ministries and the MİT Presidency, There Is a Written Agreement]," *T24*, July 17, 2023, https://t24.com.tr/yazarlar/cansu-camlibel/zafer-partisi-genel-baskani-umit-ozdag-kilicdaroglu-kazansa-uc-bakanlik-ve-mit-baskanligini-alacaktik-yazili-mutabakat-var,40818.

60 Fazlı Şahan, "Oyunun kuralları değişiyor [The Rules of the Game Change]," *Yeni Şafak*, April 4, 2018, https://www.yenisafak.com/gundem/oyunun-kurallari-degisiyor-3192649.

61 "İdlib'de 34 asker şehit oldu, tüm rejim unsurları nokta atışlarıyla vuruluyor [34 Soldiers Were Martyred in Idlib, All Regime Elements Are Being Hit with Precise Shots]," *TRT Haber*, February 29, 2020, https://www.trthaber.com/haber/gundem/idlibde-34-asker-sehit-oldu-tum-rejim-unsurlari-nokta-atislariyla-vuruluyor-463839.html.

62 Alex Gatopoulos, "Largest Drone War in the World: How Airpower Saved Tripoli," *Al Jazeera*, May 28, 2020, https://www.aljazeera.com/news/2020/5/28/largest-drone-war-in-the-world-how-airpower-saved-tripoli.

63 On Ukraine's Revolution of Dignity, see Joung Ho Park and Yuriy Shveda, "Ukraine's Revolution of Dignity: The Dynamics of Euromaidan," *Journal of Eurosian Studies* 7, no. 1 (2016): 85–91.

64 UkrHaber, https://www.ukrhaber.com/; Ukrayna Hayat, https://ukraynahayat.com/.

65 Fabrice Deprez, "Ukraine: Zaporizhia Bridge Emerges as Measure of Zelensky's Progress," *Eurasianet*, October 27, 2020, https://eurasianet.org/ukraine-zaporizhia-bridge-emerges-as-measure-of-zelenskys-progress.

66 Kadir Çurku, "Kiev'de, Hreşçatik Caddesi onarımı için 740 milyon harcanacak: İhaleyi Onur İnşaat kazandı [In Kyiv, Onur Construction Won the Tender for 740 Million gryvnia Repairs to Khreschatyk Street]," *UKR Haber*, November 29, 2021, https://www.ukrhaber.com/blog/kievde-hrescatik-caddesi-onarimi-icin-740-milyon-harcanacak-ihaleyi-onur-insaat-kazandi/#.Yo81tpPMJhE and Kadir Çurku, "Onur Taahhüt'ün Kiev-Borispol Havaalanı yolu onarımı havadan görünümü (video) [The View of Onur Taahhüt's Repair of the Kyiv-Boryspol Airport Road (video)]," *UKR Haber*, June 30, 2021, https://www.ukrhaber.com/blog/onur-taahhutun-kiev-borispol-havaalani-yolu-onarimi-havadan-gorunumu-video/#.Yo89TZPMJhE.

67 Matthew Luxmoore and Jared Malsin, "Turkey, Ukraine Sign Free-Trade, Drone Deals as Erdoğan Visits Kyiv," *The Wall Street Journal*, February 3, 2022, https://www.wsj.com/articles/turkey-ukraine-sign-free-trade-drone-deals-as-Erdoğan-visits-kyiv-11643911532.

68 "Türkiye – Ukrayna Ticari ve Ekonomik İlişkileri [Turkey-Ukraine Trade and Economic Relations]," October 2018, https://www.deik.org.tr/uploads/ukrayna-bilgi-notu-ekim-2018.pdf.

69 There appear to be only a handful of countries for which the DEİK report mentions corruption, and none surveyed for this research bring it up as prominently as the one on Ukraine.

70 "Maintaining the Momentum of Decentralisation in Ukraine," *Organisation for Economic Cooperation and Development*, June 15, 2018, https://www.oecd.org/

countries/ukraine/maintaining-the-momentum-of-decentralisation-in-ukraine-9789264301436-en.htm.

71 Alexander Clarkson, "Post-Soviet Saviours? Ukraine, Russia and the Dark Side of the War against Corruption," *Political Insight*, April 2018; "Annual Municipal Survey of Ukraine Reveals Satisfaction with Local Governments," *International Republican Institute*, September 15, 2021, https://www.iri.org/resources/annual-municipal-survey-of-ukraine-reveals-satisfaction-with-local-governments/. Ukrainian mayors are often leaders of regional business networks. Some have been accused of corruption and organized crime, but have been elected multiple times: Ben Farmer, Tanya Kozyreva, and Simon Townsley, "'We'll Fight to the End': Odesa's Pistol-packing Mayor Gets City Fired up for Russian Attack," *The Telegraph*, March 6, 2022, https://www.telegraph.co.uk/world-news/2022/03/06/gennadiy-leonidovich-trukhanov-odesa-ukraine-invasion-russia/.

72 Ben Hall, "Military Briefing: Ukraine's Battlefield Agility Pays Off," *Financial Times*, May 26, 2022, https://www.ft.com/content/9618df65-3551-4d52-ad79-494db908d53b.

73 Terms that convey regional governance are often used with regard to the Kurdish issue in Turkey, and right wing circles view them with deep suspicion, even hostility. Examples include: federalism, regional governance [yerel yönetim], decentralization [adem-i merkeziyetçilik] are or smaller settings, terms like two-headedness [çift başlılık]. Under the Erdoğan regime, the separation of powers has joined the list of undesirable (and foreign-imposed) divisions of sovereign power.

74 İbrahim Karagül, "TÜSİAD'da bir 'kurucu adam,' bir büyük dava [A 'Founding Man' at TÜSİAD, a Big Case]," *Yeni Şafak*, September 18, 2014, https://www.yenisafak.com/yazarlar/ibrahim-karagul/tusiadda-bir-kurucu-adam-bir-buyuk-dava-55949.

75 Hilal Kaplan, "Ateş altındaki #Ukrayna halkına destek olmak başka," *Twitter*, February 27, 2022, https://twitter.com/hilal_kaplan/status/1497918359349993481.

76 "Murat Çiçek ile 'Yüz Yüze' / Cumhurbaşkanı Sözcüsü İbrahim Kalın - 11 10 2022 ['Face to Face' with Murat Çiçek / Presidential Spokesperson İbrahim Kalın - 11 10 2022]," *24 TV*, October 11, 2022, https://www.youtube.com/watch?v=n8OFcbwEB_4.

77 Steven A. Cook, "There's Always a Next Time to Betray the Kurds," *Foreign Policy*, October 11, 2019, https://foreignpolicy.com/2019/10/11/kurds-betrayal-syria-erdogan-turkey-trump/.

78 Hatice Şenses Kurukız, Sefa Mutlu, and Hanife Sevinç, "Cumhurbaşkanı Erdoğan: NATO daha kararlı bir adım atmalıydı [President Erdoğan: NATO Should Have Taken a More Decisive Step]," *Anadolu Ajansı*, February 25, 2022, https://www.aa.com.tr/tr/gundem/cumhurbaskani-Erdoğan-nato-daha-kararli-bir-adim-atmaliydi/2514498.

79 "'Savaşın bir an önce sona erdirilmesine yönelik olarak Rusya ve Ukrayna ile yoğun temas hâlindeyiz' ['We are in Intensive Contact with Russia and Ukraine to End the War as Soon as Possible']," *Türkiye Cumhuriyeti Cumhurbaşkanlığı*, March 24, 2022, https://tccb.gov.tr/haberler/410/136243/-savasin-bir-an-once-sona-erdirilmesine-yonelik-olarak-rusya-ve-ukrayna-ile-yogun-temas-h-lindeyiz-.

80 "Estimated Value of Weapon Deliveries to Ukraine from January to November 2022, by Country," *Statista Research Department*, May 22, 2024, https://www.statista.com/statistics/1364467/ukraine-weapon-deliveries-value-by-country/.

81 Burak Ege Bekdil, "Turkey's Baykar to Spend $100 Million on Ukraine Drone Production," *C4ISRNET*, October 10, 2023, https://www.c4isrnet.com/global/europe/2023/10/10/turkeys-baykar-to-spend-100-million-on-ukraine-production-plant/.

82 Anthony Capaccio, Natalia Drozdiak, and Selcan Hacaoğlu, "US Turns to Turkey for Explosives as War in Ukraine Saps Supply," *Bloomberg*, March 27, 2024, https://www.bloomberg.com/news/articles/2024-03-27/us-taps-turkey-to-replenish-ukraine-s-ammunition-supply-amid-russia-s-war.

83 "Murat Çiçek ile 'Yüz Yüze' / Cumhurbaşkanı Sözcüsü İbrahim Kalın - 11 10 2022 ['Face to Face' with Murat Çiçek / Presidential Spokesperson İbrahim Kalın - 11 10 2022]," *T24*, October 11, 2022, https://www.youtube.com/watch?v=n8OFcbwEB_4.

84 "İbrahim Kalın: 'AB, Türkiye'nin güvenlik endişelerini dikkate almıyor' [İbrahim Kalın: 'The E.U. does Not Take Attention to Turkey's Security Concerns']," *CNN Türk*, March 1, 2022, https://www.youtube.com/watch?v=fvOGxlwzN58.

85 "Συνέντευξη Ζελένσκι στην ΕΡΤ: Η Τουρκία, η Ελλάδα και οι αντιδράσεις για την εμφάνιση στην Βουλή και τους Αζόφ [Zelensky Interview on ERT: Turkey, Greece and the Reactions to the Appearance in the Parliament and the Azov]."

86 "Zelenskiy'den Türkiye'ye 'çifte standart' eleştirisi ['Double Standards' Criticism from Zelenskiy to Turkey]," *EuroNews*, May 2, 2022, https://tr.euronews.com/2022/05/02/ukrayna-devlet-baskan-zelensky-den-turkiye-ye-cifte-standart-elestirisi.

87 Recep Tayyip Erdoğan, "Turkey, China Share a Vision for Future," *Global Times*, July 1, 2019, https://www.globaltimes.cn/content/1156357.shtml.

88 Bringing large abstract policy notions down to a single, easily visualized thought is a typical example of Erdoğan's thought process. Murat Birsel, "Çin Başbakanı Erdoğan'a şiir dersi verdi [The Prime Minister of China Gave Erdoğan a Poetry Lesson]," *Gazete Vatan*, January 14, 2003, https://www.gazetevatan.com/yazarlar/murat-birsel/cin-basbakani-Erdoğana-siir-dersi-verdi-3397.

89 Sumru Öz, "Küresel Rekabette Yükselen Bir Güç: Çin [A Rising Power in Global Competition: China]," 2006, https://tusiad.org/tr/yayinlar/raporlar/item/download/7827_f29cdf2368beafb3797118b4e7c011f5; Fuat Kabakcı, "MÜSİAD, Türkiye-Çin iş birliğini perçinleyecek [MÜSİAD Clinches Turkey-China Cooperation]," October 20, 2018, https://www.aa.com.tr/tr/dunya/musiad-turkiye-cin-is-birligini

-percinleyecek/1287648; "TÜSİAD 'Çin'i Anlamak & Çin ile İş Yapmak' konulu bir konferans düzenledi [TÜSİAD Organized a Conference with the Topic of Understanding China and Making Cooperation with China]," https://tusiad.org/tr/tum/item/9560-tusiad-cin-i-anlamak-cin-ile-is-yapmak-konulu-bir-konferans-duzenledi.

90. Bahri Yılmaz, "Trade Relations between China and Turkey: A Comparison with the European Union," *Stiftung Wissenschaft und Politik, German Institute for International and Security Affairs* no. 1 (May 2022), https://www.swp-berlin.org/publications/products/arbeitspapiere/WP01_22_FG7_Yilmaz_China_Turkey.pdf; Yalkun Uyuyol, "Partnership with Limits: China Turkey Relations in the Late AKP Era," *Heinrich Böll Stiftung*, March 20, 2024, https://tr.boell.org/en/2024/03/20/partnership-limits-china-turkey-relations-late-akp-era.

91. "Arçelik, 8 milyon dolara satın aldığı Çin'deki üretim tesisini 16,5 milyon dolara sattı [Arçelik Sold Its Production Facility in China, Which It Bought for 8 million dollars, for 16.5 million dollars]," *Independent Türkçe*, October 1, 2020, https://www.indyturk.com/node/252156/ekonomi%CC%87/ar%C3%A7elik-8-milyon-dolara-sat%C4%B1n-ald%C4%B1%C4%9F%C4%B1-%C3%A7in%E2%80%99deki-%C3%BCretim-tesisini-165-milyon-dolara.

92. Author's interview, May 25, 2022.

93. In mid-2022, the website of the ministry of trade listed six staff across four cities. As of December 2023, the number of staff was eight. Even assuming that Turkey has more staff devoted to working on trade between the countries, the numbers are low. https://ticaret.gov.tr/dis-iliskiler/yurt-disi-teskilatimiz.

94. Government media and think tanks generally focus their international coverage on Europe and the United States, often with a subheading on the Islamophobia in those regions. China is usually tucked into an "Asia Pacific" section. Anadolu Ajansı, the government's main news agency, has a Beijing office, but its only broadcast center in East Asia is in Jakarta, Indonesia. See https://www.aa.com.tr/uploads/userFilesShared/pazarlama%2FGLOBALYAPI_2021_TR_B.jpg.

95. "Türkiye'nin Pekin Büyükelçisi: Artık Çin'den bir şey alma zamanı değil buraya bir şey satma zamanı [Turkey's Beijing Ambassador: it's Already Not Time to Take Something from China, It's Time to Sell Something]," *Habertürk*, July 1, 2019, https://www.haberturk.com/turkiyenin-pekin-buyukelcisi-artik-cin-den-bir-sey-alma-zamani-degil-buraya-bir-sey-satma-zamani-2500080.

96. Ibid.

97. Ibid.

98. "Koronavirüsle Mücadele Eşgüdüm Toplantısı Öncesi Yaptıkları Konuşma [Speech Before the Coordination Meeting Against the Coronavirus]," *T.C. Cumhurbaşkanlığı*, March 18, 2020, https://www.tccb.gov.tr/konusmalar/353/117032/koronavirusle-mucadele-esgudum-toplantisi-oncesi-yaptiklari-konusma.

99 "'Tüm öncü göstergeler, ülkemizin çok ciddi bir sıçramanın eşiğinde olduğuna işaret ediyor' ['All Leading Indicators Point to Our Country Being on the Verge of a Very Serious Leap']," *Türkiye Cumhuriyeti Cumhurbaşkanlığı*, June 27, 2020, https://www.tccb.gov.tr/haberler/410/120497/-tum-oncu-gostergeler-ulkemizin-cok-ciddi-bir-sicramanin-esiginde-olduguna-isaret-ediyor-.

100 Hacer Boyacıoğlu, "Türkiye 11 sektörde çok iddialı [Turkey is Very Assertive in 11 Sectors]," *Hürriyet*, May 31, 2020, https://www.hurriyet.com.tr/ekonomi/turkiye-11-sektorde-cok-iddiali-41529372.

101 "BTK demiryolu projesinin temeli atıldı [BTK Railway Project Foundation Laid]," *CNN Türk*, November 21, 2007, https://www.cnnturk.com/2007/ekonomi/genel/11/21/btk.demiryolu.projesinin.temeli.atildi/406247.0/index.html.

102 Abdullah Gül, "Bakü-Tiflis-Kars Demiryolu Temel Atma Töreni'nde Yaptıkları Konuşma [Speech at the Groundbreaking Ceremony of the Baku-Tbilisi-Kars Railway]," November 21, 2007, http://www.abdullahgul.gen.tr/konusmalar/371/56507/bakutifliskars-demiryolu-temel-atma-toreninde-yaptiklari-konusma.html.

103 "Türkiye's Multilateral Transportation Policy," *Republic of Türkiye Ministry of Foreign Affairs*, https://www.mfa.gov.tr/turkey_s-multilateral-transportation-policy.en.mfa.

104 Emre Aytekin, "Pekin Büyükelçisi Musa: Çin, Türkiye'nin Yeniden Asya Girişimi'nin merkezinde yer alıyor [Beijing Ambassador Musa: China is at the Center of Turkey's Asia Again Initiative]," *Anadolu Ajansı*, October 25, 2023, https://www.aa.com.tr/tr/dunya/pekin-buyukelcisi-musa-cin-turkiyenin-yeniden-asya-girisiminin-merkezinde-yer-aliyor/3032484.

105 "Çin'den Avrupa'ya giden ilk yük treni Kapıkule'de [First Train from China to Europe at Kapikule]," *TRT Haber*, November 7, 2019, https://www.trthaber.com/haber/turkiye/cinden-avrupaya-giden-ilk-yuk-treni-kapikulede-439925.

106 "Middle Corridor Unable to Absorb Northern Volumes, Opportunities Still There," *RailFreight.com*, March 18, 2022, https://www.railfreight.com/specials/2022/03/18/middle-corridor-unable-to-absorb-northern-volumes-opportunities-still-there/.

107 Jiang Mingxin, "Opportunities Rising from and for Middle Corridor," *China Daily*, December 29, 2021, http://www.chinadaily.com.cn/a/202112/29/WS61cbbde9a310cdd39bc7e0b1.html.

108 Nabijan Tursun, "1933 ve 1944 Yıllarında Kurulan Doğu Türkistan Cumhuriyetleri Hakkındaki Kaynaklar ve Bu Kaynakların Değeri [Sources About the East Turkestan Republics Established in 1933 and 1944 and the Value of These Sources]," *Uluslararası Uygur Araştırmaları Dergisi* no. 16 (2020): 234–35.

109 James A. Millward, *Eurasian Crossroads: A History of Xinjiang*, rev. and upd. ed. (New York City, NY: Columbia University Press, 2022), 301.

110 John Sudworth and the BBC News Visual Journalism Team, "Xinjiang Police Files: Inside a Chinese Internment Camp," *BBC News*, May 24, 2022, https://

www.bbc.co.uk/news/resources/idt-8df450b3-5d6d-4ed8-bdcc-bd99137eadc3; "OHCHR Assessment of Human Rights Concerns in the Xinjiang Uyghur Autonomous Region, People's Republic of China," *Office of the United Nations High Commissioner for Human Rights*, August 31, 2022, https://www.ohchr.org/sites/default/files/documents/countries/2022-08-31/22-08-31-final-assesment.pdf.

111 Allison Killing and Megha Rajagopalan, "The Factories in the Camps," *Buzzfeed News*, December 28, 2020, https://www.buzzfeednews.com/article/alison_killing/xinjiang-camps-china-factories-forced-labor.

112 "Break Their Lineage, Break Their Roots: China's Crimes Against Humanity Targeting Uyghurs and Other Turkic Muslims," *Human Rights Watch*, April 19, 2021, https://www.hrw.org/report/2021/04/19/break-their-lineage-break-their-roots/chinas-crimes-against-humanity-targeting.

113 John Hudson, "As Tensions with China Grow, Biden Administration Formalizes Genocide Declaration Against China," *The Washington Post*, March 30, 2021, https://www.washingtonpost.com/national-security/china-genocide-human-rights-report/2021/03/30/b2fa8312-9193-11eb-9af7-fd0822ae4398_story.html.

114 "Fact Check: Lies on Xinjiang-related Issues Versus the Truth," *Xinhuanet*, February 5, 2021, http://www.xinhuanet.com/english/2021-02/05/c_139723816.htm.

115 "Asimilasyona hayir, entegrasyona evet [No to Assimilation, Yes to Integration]," *AK Parti*, June 19, 2014, https://www.akparti.org.tr/haberler/asimilasyona-hayir-entegrasyona-evet/.

116 "Turkey Attacks China Genocide," *BCC News*, July 10, 200, http://news.bbc.co.uk/1/hi/8145451.stm

117 Yayha Bostan, "Urumçi'de sevgi seli [Flood of Love in Urumqi]," *Sabah*, April 9, 2014, https://www.sabah.com.tr/gundem/2012/04/09/uygur-halki-basbakan-erdogani-bagrina-basti.

118 "Çin Uygur Özerk Bölgesi İnsan Hakları Raporu [Chinese Uyghur Autonomous Region Human Rights Report]," August 17, 2022, https://www.uyghurreport.org/wp-content/uploads/The_Human_Rights_Report_on_Uyghur-Turkish.pdf.

119 "Akşener, Türkiye-Çin maçını Doğu Türkistan bayrağı altında izledi [Akşener Watched the Turkey-China Match under the East Turkistan Flag]," *Diken*, June 3, 2022, https://www.diken.com.tr/aksener-turkiye-cin-macini-dogu-turkistan-bayragi-altinda-izledi/.

120 Levent Kenez, "Turkish Parliament Rejects Establishment of Special Committee to Investigate Human Rights Violations against Uyghurs," *Nordic Monitor*, July 25, 2023, https://nordicmonitor.com/2023/07/turkish-parliament-rejects-a-special-commission-on-human-rights-violations-against-uyghurs/.

121 The only time Erdoğan has successfully been outflanked from the right on a comparable issue was in the regional elections of 2024, when the Islamist New

Welfare Party campaigned against Erdoğan's relatively weak response to Israel's bombing of Gaza. See Selcan Hacaoğlu and Fırat Kozok, "Islamist Gains Are Fresh Headache for Erdogan After Vote Defeat," *Bloomberg*, April 2, 2024, https://www.bloomberg.com/news/articles/2024-04-02/turkey-s-erdogan-faces-new-headache-from-islamist-party-after-istanbul-election.

122 Tevfik Durul, "Uygur Türklerinin durumu 2019'da dünya gündemine oturdu [The Situation of Uyghur Turks was on the World Agenda in 2019]," *Anadolu Ajansı*, December 26, 2019. https://www.aa.com.tr/tr/dunya/uygur-turklerinin-durumu-2019da-dunya-gundemine-oturdu/1684242.

123 "Turkey and China Keep Relations on Track Despite Uighur Dispute," *Middle East Eye*, February 5, 2022, https://www.middleeasteye.net/news/turkey-china-uighur-relations-track-despite-dispute; Daren Butler, "Looming China Extradition Deal Worries Uighurs in Turkey," *Reuters*, March 8, 2021, https://www.reuters.com/article/idUSKBN2B01E1/.

124 "Türkiye'nin Pekin Büyükelçisi: Artık Çin'den bir şey alma zamanı değil buraya bir şey satma zamanı [Turkey's Ambassador to Beijing: Now is Not the Time to Buy Something from China, it is Time to Sell Something]."

125 Author's interview, May 25, 2022.

126 Author's interview, 2020.

127 "Türkiye'nin Pekin Büyükelçisi: Artık Çin'den bir şey alma zamanı değil buraya bir şey satma zamanı [Turkey's Ambassador to Beijing: Now is Not the Time to Buy Something from China, it is Time to Sell Something].".

128 "Çin İstanbul Başkonsolosu: Cami yıkmıyoruz, 100'e yakın tarihi cami de restore ediliyor [Chinese Consul General in Istanbul: We are Not Demolishing Mosques, Nearly 100 Historical Mosques are Being Restored]," *Demiroren Haber Ajansi*, May 14, 2019, https://www.youtube.com/watch?v=-5cPMnn0W5U.

Chapter 5

1 Ali Kemal Akan, Yıldız Nevin Gündoğmuş, Merve Yıldızalp, and Ferdi Türkten, "Cumhurbaşkanı Erdoğan: Sene sonuna kadar 100 milyon yardımcı kaynağı öğrencilerimize ulaştıracağız [President Erdoğan: We will Deliver 100 million Aid Resources to Our Students by the End of the Year]," *Anadolu Ajansı*, June 2, 2022. https://www.aa.com.tr/tr/gundem/cumhurbaskani-erdogan-sene-sonuna-kadar-100-milyon-yardimci-kaynagi-ogrencilerimize-ulastiracagiz/2603913.

2 The phrase the regime uses is "Büyük Türkiye" which literally means "Great Turkey," but the comparative form is implied there. That is also why official sources and pro-government media translate the phrase as "Greater Turkey." The phrase is also not to be confused with the pan-Turkic vision of a wider Turkic world

(Turan). See: "Turkey's First President Elected by Popular Vote," *President of the Republic of Türkiye*, August 28, 2014, https://www.tccb.gov.tr/en/news/542/3205/turkeys-first-president-elected-by-popular-vote; "Erdoğan Underlines AK Party's Values in his Letter to Former District Chairs," *Daily Sabah*, February 11, 2020. https://www.dailysabah.com/politics/2020/02/11/erdogan-underlines-ak-partys-values-in-his-letter-to-former-district-chairs.

3 On Armenia fear: Okan Müdderisoğlu, "3T Planı ve ABD-Türkiye ilişkileri… [The 3T Plan and U.S.-Turkey Relations…]," *Sabah*, April 29, 2021. https://www.sabah.com.tr/yazarlar/muderrisoglu/2021/04/29/3t-plani-ve-turk-abd-iliskileri; on fears of American invasion: Soli Özel, "The Gathering Storm," *Foreign Policy*, July 1, 2005. https://web.archive.org/web/20100212033933/http://www.foreignpolicy.com/articles/2005/07/01/the_gathering_storm; on Sèvres syndrome: Nicholas Danforth, "Forget Sykes-Picot. It's the Treaty of Sèvres That Explains the Modern Middle East," *Foreign Policy*, August 10, 2015, https://foreignpolicy.com/2015/08/10/sykes-picot-treaty-of-sevres-modern-turkey-middle-east-borders-turkey/.

4 "Cumhurbaşkanı Erdoğan'dan sürpriz ziyaret [A Surprise Visit from President Erdoğan]," *Yeni Şafak*, March 28, 2017. https://www.yenisafak.com/gundem/cumhurbaskani-erdogandan-surpriz-ziyaret-2635080.

5 "Erdoğan çok anlamlı Abdurrahim Karakoç şiiri [Erdoğan and Abdurrahim Karakoç's Very Meaningful Poem]," *Haber7*, November 4, 2015. https://www.haber7.com/siyaset/haber/1638073-erdogan-cok-anlamli-abdurrahim-karakoc-siiri.

6 MHP leader Devlet Bahçeli, for example, recited the lines when threatening Bashar Assad that Turkey would reconquer Syrian territory if the Damascus continued to work with "terror groups." "Bahçeli: Suriye yönetimi teröristle iş yaparsa, 100 yıl önceki topraklarımızın bir kısmını elimizde tutmanın yolu açılacaktır [Bahçeli: If the Syrian Administration does Business with Terrorists, it will Open the Way for us to Keep Some of our Lands from 100 Years Ago]," *PolitikYol*, March 6, 2018. https://www.politikyol.com/bahceli-suriye-yonetimi-teroristle-is-yaparsa-100-yil-onceki-topraklarimizin-bir-kismini-elimizde-tutmanin-yolu-acilacaktir/.

7 [this is for the quote, need citation for the countries as well] Hilal Kaplan, "Son dakika haberi! Başkan Erdoğan'dan Soçi dönüşü flaş açıklamalar! 'Suriye konusunda Putin ile mutabık kaldık' [Breaking News! Flash Statements from President Erdoğan on the Return of Sochi! 'We agreed with Putin on Syria']," *Sabah*, August 6, 2022. https://www.sabah.com.tr/gundem/2022/08/06/son-dakika-haberi-baskan-erdogandan-soci-donusu-flas-aciklamalar-suriye-konusunda-putin-ile-mutabik-kaldik.

8 "Erdoğan'dan Endonezya'ya selam [A Greeting from Erdoğan to Indonesia]," *Yeni Şafak*, July 27, 2023. https://www.yenisafak.com/video-galeri/gundem/erdogandan-endonezyaya-selam-4548481.

9 "İran, Türkiye ve Brezilya ile nükleer anlaşmayı imzaladı [Iran Signed a Nuclear Agreement with Turkey and Brazil]," *BBC News Türkçe*, May 17, 2010. https://www.bbc.com/turkce/haberler/2010/05/100517_turkey_iran.
10 "17.05.2010 Joint Declaration of the Ministers of Foreign Affairs of Turkey, Iran and Brazil," *Republic of Türkiye Ministry of Foreign Affairs*, May 17, 2010, https://www.mfa.gov.tr/17_05_2010-joint-declaration-of-the-ministers-of-foreign-affairs-of-turkey_-iran-and-brazil_.en.mfa.
11 Julian Borger, "Cool Response to Iran's Nuclear Fuel Swap with Turkey," *The Guardian*, May 18, 2010. https://www.theguardian.com/world/2010/may/17/iran-nuclear-fuel-swap-turkey; "İran, Türkiye ve Brezilya aşağılandı [Iran, Turkey, and Brazil were Humiliated]," *Hürriyet*, July 20, 2010, https://www.hurriyet.com.tr/dunya/iran-turkiye-ve-brezilya-asagilandi-15365742.
12 "Türkiye'den Libya'da arabuluculuk teklifi [Turkey Offers Mediation in Libya]," *BBC News Türkçe*, March 28, 2011, https://www.bbc.com/turkce/haberler/2011/03/110327_guardian_erdogan; "Erdoğan, Sudan ve Etiyopya arasında arabuluculuk teklif etti [Erdoğan Offered Mediation between Sudan and Ethiopia]," August 19, 2021, https://tr.euronews.com/2021/08/19/erdogan-sudan-ve-etiyopya-aras-nda-arabuluculuk-teklif-etti; Murat Paksoy, "Cumhurbaşkanı Erdoğan, Sudan Egemenlik Konseyi yetkilileriyle telefonda görüştü [President Erdoğan Spoke on the Phone with Officials of the Sudanese Sovereignty Council]," *Anadolu Ajansı*, April 20, 2023, https://www.aa.com.tr/tr/politika/cumhurbaskani-erdogan-sudan-egemenlik-konseyi-yetkilileriyle-telefonda-gorustu/2877465.
13 Drew Hinshaw, James Marson, Joe Parkinson, and Aruna Viswanatha, "A Secluded Runway, a Turkish Spymaster and No Guns: the New World of Hostage Exchanges," *The Wall Street Journal*, December 19, 2023, https://www.wsj.com/world/american-hostages-exchange-turkey-russia-f173d8b4.
14 "Erdogan Renews Offer for Turkish Mediation in Israeli-Hamas Conflict," *Reuters*, October 10, 2023, https://www.reuters.com/world/middle-east/turkeys-erdogan-discusses-israeli-palestinian-conflict-with-uns-guterres-turkish-2023-10-10/.
15 Şuay Nilhan Açıkalın, "15 Temmuz Darbe Girişimi Sonrası Türk Dış Politikasında Otonomi ve Lider Diplomasisi [Autonomy and Leader Diplomacy in Turkish Foreign Policy After the July 15 Coup Attempt]," *Kriter*, July 1, 2023, https://kriterdergi.com/dosya-7-yilinda-15-temmuz/15-temmuz-darbe-girisimi-sonrasi-turk-dis-politikasinda-otonomi-ve-lider-diplomasisi.
16 Turkey remained as the largest humanitarian donor per national income in 2018 and 2019 as well. Gökhan Ergöçün, "Turkey Continues to be Ranked Among Top Donor Countries," *Anadolu Ajansı*, July 10, 2021, https://www.aa.com.tr/en/world/turkey-continues-to-be-ranked-among-top-donor-countries/2300237.

17 Hurcan Asli Aksoy, Salim Çevik, and Nebahat Tanrıverdi Yaşar, "Visualising Turkey's Activism in Africa," *Centre for Applied Turkey Studies*, June 3, 2022, https://www.cats-network.eu/topics/visualizing-turkeys-activism-in-africa.
18 See Dennis Dijkzeul and Zeynep Sezgin eds., *The New Humanitarians in International Practice: Emerging Actors and Contested Principles* (New York, NY: Routledge, 2021).
19 "Türkiye Cumhuriyeti Dışişleri Bakanlığı Tarihçesi [History of the Ministry of Foreign Affairs of the Republic of Türkiye]," *Türkiye Cumhuriyeti Dış İşleri Bakanlığı*, https://www.mfa.gov.tr/turkiye-cumhuriyeti-disisleri-bakanligi-tarihcesi.tr.mfa#:~:text=Coğrafi%20dağılım%20bakımından%20257%20dış,diplomatik%20kariyer%20memuru%20görev%20yapmaktadır (accessed December 25, 2023); Betül Usta, "Turkey Set to Increase Number of Global Diplomatic Missions to 255," *Daily Sabah*, May 5, 2022, https://www.dailysabah.com/politics/diplomacy/turkey-set-to-increase-number-of-global-diplomatic-missions-to-255.
20 "Lowy Institute Global Diplomacy Index: Country Ranking," Lowy Institute, https://globaldiplomacyindex.lowyinstitute.org/country_ranking.
21 "Kültürel Diplomasi 2020-2021 [Cultural Diplomacy 2020-2021]," *Türkiye Cumhuriyeti Dışişleri Bakanlığı*, 2021, https://www.mfa.gov.tr/site_media/html/TKGM-Prestij-Kitabi-2020-2021.pdf.
22 Ken Moriyasu and Sinan Tavsan, "Erdogan Opens Turkish Skyscraper with Ottoman Influence in Heart of N.Y.," *Nikkei Asia*, September 21, 2021, https://asia.nikkei.com/Politics/Erdogan-opens-Turkish-skyscraper-with-Ottoman-influence-in-heart-of-N.Y; Samanth Subramanian, "How $100m Muslim Centre is Building Bridges in the US Amid Islamophobic Climate," *The National*, April 1, 2016, https://www.thenationalnews.com/world/how-100m-muslim-centre-is-building-bridges-in-the-us-amid-islamophobic-climate-1.137544; Jonas Panning, "Erdogan-Besuch in Köln: Die lange Geschichte der Ditib-Moschee [Erdogan Visit to Cologne: The Long History of the Ditib Mosque]," *Deutschlandfunk*, September 28, 2018, https://www.deutschlandfunk.de/erdogan-besuch-in-koeln-die-lange-geschichte-der-ditib-100.html.
23 "'1150 odası var, itibardan tasarruf olmaz' ['It has 1,150 Rooms, there is No Saving on Reputation']," *Evrensel*, December 6, 2014, https://www.evrensel.net/haber/99108/1150-odasi-var-itibardan-tasarruf-olmaz.
24 There is debate on how many thousands of kilometers were actually constructed. "AK Parti Döneminde Yapılan Yollar Ne Kadar? [How Many Roads Were Built During the AK Party Period?]," *Doğruluk Payı*, October 18, 2016, https://www.dogrulukpayi.com/iddia-kontrolu/binali-yildirim/14-yilda-6-bin-100-kilometrenin-uzerine-18-bin-500; "AK Parti ile birlikte 26 bin 764 km bölünmüş yol [26 Thousand 764 km of Divided Roads with the AK Party]," *Memurlar.net*,

August 15, 2019, https://www.memurlar.net/haber/849162/ak-parti-ile-birlikte-26-bin-764-km-bolunmus-yol.html#google_vignette.
25. "Turkish Contractors Turning to Balkan Countries," *Hürriyet Daily News*, May 9, 2023, https://www.hurriyetdailynews.com/turkish-contractors-turning-to-balkan-countries-182982.
26. Akın Arslan, "Turkey Possesses Europe's Largest Truck Fleet, 90% of Domestic Freight by Volume is Handled by Trucking and Road Transport. Some 850,000 Trucks Made up Fleets Across the Country," *Medium*, July 13, 2020, https://akin-10877.medium.com/turkey-possesses-europes-largest-truck-fleet-90-of-domestic-freight-by-volume-is-handled-by-50379ea8ad60.
27. Sabena Siddiqui, "Can $20B Iraq Development Road Project Rival India-Middle East Corridor?" *Al-Monitor*, April 27, 2024, https://www.al-monitor.com/originals/2024/04/can-20b-iraq-development-road-project-rival-india-middle-east-corridor.
28. "Turkish Airlines Remains at Top with Largest Network," *Hürriyet Daily News*, December 31, 2021, https://www.hurriyetdailynews.com/turkish-airlines-remains-at-top-with-largest-network-170454.
29. Koray Kaplıca, "THY'nin Uçuş Noktaları Ne Kadar Arttı? [How Much Have Turkish Airlines' Flight Destinations Increased?]," *Doğruluk Payı*, October 9, 2017, https://www.dogrulukpayi.com/iddia-kontrolu/recep-tayyip-erdogan/yurtdisi-ucus-noktalari-sayisini-60-tan-296-ya-cikardik-dunyada-destinasyon-sayisi-acisindan-birinci-thy-dir; "Turkish Airlines Annual Report 2002," *Türk Hava Yolları*, https://investor.turkishairlines.com/documents/ThyInvestorRelations/download/yillik_raporlar/faaliyetRaporu2002_en.pdf.
30. "Our Story," *Turkish Cargo*, https://www.turkishcargo.com/en/about-us/about-turkish-cargo/our-story.
31. "Istanbul Airport ranks 2nd Among World's Top Airports: Survey," *Daily Sabah*, September 9, 2021, https://www.dailysabah.com/business/transportation/istanbul-airport-ranks-2nd-among-worlds-top-airports-survey; Tuba Şahin, "Turkish Airlines' Net Income Rises to $959M in 2021," *Anadolu Ajansı*, March 1, 2022, https://www.aa.com.tr/en/economy/turkish-airlines-net-income-rises-to-959m-in-2021/2520051; Graham Dunn, "Turkish Airlines Lifts Q3 Profits by One Quarter," *FlightGlobal*, November 2, 2023, https://www.flightglobal.com/airlines/turkish-airlines-lifts-q3-profits-by-one-quarter/155639.article#:~:text=It%20continues%20the%20strong%20run,nine%20months%20of%20the%20year.
32. "Erdoğan'dan Köln'de Adeta Seçim Öncesi Propagandası [Pre-Election Propaganda from Erdoğan in Cologne]," *Bianet*, February 11, 2018, https://bianet.org/haber/erdogan-dan-koln-de-adeta-secim-oncesi-propagandasi-104793.
33. Mustafa Mert Bildircin, "Diyanet yurtdışına 'taştı' [Diyanet 'overflowed' abroad]," *Bir Gün*, March 27, 2020, https://www.birgun.net/haber/diyanet-yurtdisina-tasti-293427.

34 "Yunus Emre Enstitüsü [Yunus Emre Institute]," *Yunus Emre Enstitüsü*, https://www.yee.org.tr/tr/kurumsal/yunus-emre-enstitusu.

35 Fatima Bhutto, "How Turkish TV is Taking over the World," *The Guardian*, September 13, 2019, https://www.theguardian.com/tv-and-radio/2019/sep/13/turkish-tv-magnificent-century-dizi-taking-over-world.

36 "'Türkiye's Series Exports to Exceed $600 mln this Year,'" *Hürriyet Daily News*, October 19, 2022, https://www.hurriyetdailynews.com/turkiyes-series-exports-to-exceed-600-mln-this-year-177782.

37 Hilal Kaplan, "Kültürel hegemonyaya TABİİ direniş [TABİİ Resistance to Cultural Hegemony]," *Sabah*, May 5, 2023, https://www.sabah.com.tr/yazarlar/hilalkaplan/2023/05/05/kulturel-hegemonyaya-tabii-direnis.

38 Nicholas Danforth, "Turkey's New Maps Are Reclaiming the Ottoman Empire," *Foreign Policy*, October 23, 2016, https://foreignpolicy.com/2016/10/23/turkeys-religious-nationalists-want-ottoman-borders-iraq-erdogan/.

39 "Cumhurbaşkanı Erdoğan: Birileri Lozan'ı zafer diye yutturmaya çalıştı [President Erdoğan: Someone Tried to Make Lausanne a Victory]," *Anadolu Ajansı*, September 29, 2016, https://www.aa.com.tr/tr/gunun-basliklari/cumhurbaskani-erdogan-birileri-lozani-zafer-diye-yutturmaya-calisti/654904.

40 Çınar Livane Özer, "Haritanın Lozan'da kaybedilen adaları gösterdiği iddiası [The Claim that the Map Shows the Islands Lost in Lausanne]," *Teyit*, October 2, 2016, https://teyit.org/analiz/gokcek-feribot-sefer-haritasini-lozanda-verilen-adalar-saniyor; "'Adalar, Lozan Antlaşması'ndan 10 yıl önce kaybedildi' ['The Islands were Lost 10 Years before the Lausanne Treaty']," *Sözcü*, October 3, 2016, https://www.sozcu.com.tr/adalar-lozan-antlasmasindan-10-yil-once-kaybedildi-wp1424721.

41 "28. Muhtarlar Toplantısında Yaptıkları Konuşma [Their Speech at the 28th Mukhtars' Meeting]," *Türkiye Cumhuriyeti Cumhurbaşkanlığı*, October 19, 2016, https://www.tccb.gov.tr/konusmalar/353/55704/28-muhtarlar-toplantisinda-yaptiklari-konusma.

42 Tanıl Bora, "Kaçıncı İnönü? [Which İnönü?]," *Birikim*, February 9, 2022, https://birikimdergisi.com/haftalik/10906/kacinci-inonu.

43 Binyamin Appelbaum, Alexander Burn, and Nick Corasaniti, "Donald Trump Vows to Rip Up Trade Deals and Confront China," *The New York Times*, June 28, 2016, https://www.nytimes.com/2016/06/29/us/politics/donald-trump-trade-speech.html.

44 "Turkey and Greece: Time to Settle the Aegean Dispute," *International Crisis Group, Europe Briefing* no. 64 (July 19, 2011), https://www.crisisgroup.org/sites/default/files/b64-turkey-and-greece-time-to-settle-the-aegean-dispute.pdf.

45 Akif Çevik, Gül Koç, and Koray Şerbetçi, *Türkiye Cumhuriyeti İnkılap Tarihi ve Atatürkçülük* [History of the Revolution of the Turkish Republic and Atatürkism]

(Ankara: Devlet Kitapları, 2018), 89, http://aok.meb.gov.tr/kitap/aol-kitap/INKILAP-Tarihi/inkilap_tarihi_1_2.pdf.

46 "'Misak-ı Milli, milletimizin tüm dünyaya ilan ettiği bir istiklal bildirisidir' ['The Mîsâk-ı Millî is the Independence Declaration Our Nation Declares to the Entire World']," *TRT Haber*, January 29, 2021, https://www.trthaber.com/haber/gundem/misak-i-milli-milletimizin-tum-dunyaya-ilan-ettigi-bir-istiklal-bildirisidir-551889.html.

47 Aynur Ekiz, Barış Kılıç, and Ferdi Türkten, "Cumhurbaşkanı Erdoğan: Kimsenin tek karış toprağında gözümüz yok [President Erdoğan: We are not eyeing anyone else's land]," *Anadolu Ajansı*, August 30, 2019, https://www.aa.com.tr/tr/turkiye/cumhurbaskani-erdogan-kimsenin-tek-karis-topraginda-gozumuz-yok/1569361.

48 "Cumhurbaşkanı Erdoğan: Toprak kan dökülmemişse vatan olmaz, ben bunu hep şuna benzetiyorum; araziyi, arsaya dönüştürmek için belli bedel ödemek gerekiyor [President Erdoğan: The Land will Not Become a Homeland if Blood has Not Been Shed, I Always Liken it to this; It is Necessary to Pay a Certain Price to Convert the Field into Estates]," *T24*, April 23, 2021, https://t24.com.tr/video/cumhurbaskani-erdogan-toprak-kan-dokulmemisse-vatan-olmaz-ben-bunu-hep-suna-benzetiyorum-araziyi-arsaya-donusturmek-icin-belli-bedel-odemek-gerekiyor,38265.

49 Turkey has been contesting Greek claims for decades. Part of this is because the Greeks have a very unique position of claiming air space greater than the size of their islands would usually merit. Turkish contestation here isn't necessarily about expansionist ideas, but about insisting on international norms.

50 "Nikah masasında Erdoğan'dan izin alarak 'Evet' dedi [She said 'Yes' at the Wedding table with Permission from Erdoğan]," *Cumhuriyet*, May 7, 2018, https://www.cumhuriyet.com.tr/haber/nikah-masasinda-erdogandan-izin-alarak-evet-dedi-970237.

51 Feroz Ahmad, "The Young Turk Revolution," *The Journal of Contemporary History* 3, no. 3 (1968): 19–36. For the Armenian genocide, see Uğur Ümit Üngör, *The Making of Modern Turkey: Nation and State in Eastern Anatolia, 1913–1950* (Oxford: Oxford University Press, 2011).

52 Fikret Adanır, "Kemalist Authoritarianism and Fascist Trends in Turkey during the Inter-War Period," in *Fascism outside Europe: The European Impulse against Domestic Conditions in the Diffusion of Global Fascism*, ed. Stein Ugelvik Larsen (Boulder, CO: Social Science Monogrpahs, 2001), 313–61; Ayça Alemdaroğlu, "Politics of the Body and Eugenic Discourse in Early Republican Turkey," *Body & Society* 11, no. 3 (2005): 61–76.

53 İlker Aytürk, "The Racist Critics of Atatürk and Kemalism, from the 1930s to the 1960s," *Journal of Contemporary History* 46, no. 2 (2011), 308–33.

54 Ibid., 308.

55 This was a trope among a variety of Islamist magazines and writers. Kadir Mısıroğlu specifically claimed throughout his life that Jewish conspirators like the Rockefeller Foundation were employing secret methods to decrease the fertility of Turkey's population, such as putting chemicals into vaccines that were used in Turkey. He maintained that this was the reason behind Turkey's demographic decline. Meanwhile, the same forces were encouraging Israel's population to grow. *Sebil*, Issue 230, June 5, 1980, https://katalog.idp.org.tr/pdf/6534/11678.

56 Sertaç Aktan, "Sivas Katliamı'nın 30. yılı: Madımak Oteli'nde neler yaşandı? [30th Anniversary of the Sivas Massacre: What Happened at Madımak Hotel?]," *Euronews*, July 2, 2023, https://tr.euronews.com/2023/07/02/sivas-katliaminin-26-yili-madimak-insanlik-tarihinde-kara-bir-leke; Nil Mutluer, "The Looming Shadow of Violence and Loss: Alevi Responses to Persecution and Discrimination," *Journal of Balkan and Near Eastern Studies* 8, no. 2 (February 22, 2016): Identity, race, and nationalism in Turkey.

57 Mümin Altaş, Ferdi Türkten, and Zafer Fatih Beyaz, "Cumhurbaşkanı Erdoğan'dan "Göreve Başlama Töreni"ne katılanlara özel teşekkür [Special thanks from President Erdoğan to those who attended the "Inauguration Ceremony]," *Anadolu Ajansı*, June 3, 2023. https://www.aa.com.tr/tr/politika/cumhurbaskani-erdogandan-goreve-baslama-torenine-katilanlara-ozel-tesekkur/2913642.

58 "Cumhuriyet tarihinin ilk kilisesi açıldı [The First Church was Opened in the History of the Republic]," *TRT Haber*, October 8, 2023, https://www.trthaber.com/haber/kultur-sanat/cumhuriyet-tarihinin-ilk-kilisesi-acildi-801680.html.

59 "Türkiye farklı inançlara sağlanan ibadet yeri sayısında Batı'nın 5 kat önünde [Turkey is 5 Times Ahead of the West in the Number of Places of Worship Provided for Different Faiths]," *Anadolu Ajansi*, July 11, 2020. https://www.aa.com.tr/tr/ayasofya-camii/turkiye-farkli-inanclara-saglanan-ibadet-yeri-sayisinda-batinin-5-kat-onunde/1907134#:~:text=verdi%C4%9Fi%20%C3%B6nemi%20g%C3%B6steriyor.-,T%C3%BCrkiye%27de%20180%20bin%20854%20Hristiyan%20ve%20yakla%C5%9F%C4%B1k%2020%20bin,da%20oldu%C4%9Fu%20435%20ibadethane%20bulunuyor.

60 Bruce Curtis, "Foucault on Governmentality and Population," *Canadian Journal of Sociology* 27, no. 4 (2002): 508.

61 "Erdoğan: Atatürk resimlerini paradan CHP çıkarttı [Erdoğan: CHP Removed Atatürk Pictures from Money]," *Sabah*, April 13, 2008, https://arsiv.sabah.com.tr/2008/04/13/haber,2D1CDFD6C5674A9F89AB1F972D6601C4.html; "Cumhurbaşkanı Erdoğan'ın 3. Olağanüstü Büyük Kongresinde yaptığı konuşma [President Erdoğan's speech at the 3rd Extraordinary Grand Congress]," May 21, 2017, https://www.akparti.org.tr/haberler/cumhurbaskani-erdogan-in-3-olaganustu-buyuk-kongremizde-yaptigi-konusma/; "Cumhurbaşkanı Erdoğan: 85 milyon kazandı, Türkiye Yüzyılı'nın kapısını açtık [President Erdoğan: 85 million

Won, we Opened the Door of the Turkey Century," *TRT Haber*, May 28, 2023, https://www.trthaber.com/haber/gundem/cumhurbaskani-erdogan-85-milyon-kazandi-turkiye-yuzyilinin-kapisini-actik-770617.html.

62 "Cumhurbaşkanı Erdoğan, TRT özel yayınına katıldı [President Erdoğan Joined in the TRT Special Broadcast]," *Türkiye Cumhuriyeti Cumhurbaşkanlığı*, December 9. 2019, https://tccb.gov.tr/haberler/410/113863/cumhurbaskani-erdogan-trt-ozel-yayinina-katildi.

63 "AK Parti'nin Büyük İstanbul Mitingi'ne 1 milyon 300 bin kişi katıldı [1 million 300 Thousand People Attended the AK Party's Great Istanbul Rally]," *Anadolu Ajansı*, June 17, 2018, https://www.aa.com.tr/tr/turkiye/ak-partinin-buyuk-istanbul-mitingine-1-milyon-300-bin-kisi-katildi/1177304; Mikail Bıyıklı and Serkan Köymen, "AK Parti'nin 'Büyük İstanbul Mitingi'ne rekor katılım: 1 milyon 700 bin kişi [Record Participation in AK Party's 'Great Istanbul Rally': 1 million 700 Thousand People]," *Hürriyet*, May 7, 2023, https://www.hurriyet.com.tr/gundem/ak-partinin-buyuk-istanbul-mitingi-bugun-erdogan-halka-seslenecek-42263303.

64 "Cumhurbaşkanı Erdoğan, Azerbaycan Cumhurbaşkanı Aliyev ile ortak basın toplantısında konuştu [President Erdoğan Spoke at a Joint Press Conference with Azerbaijani President Aliyev]," *Türkiye Cumhuriyeti Cumhurbaşkanlığı İletişim Başkanlığı*, June 13, 2006, https://www.iletisim.gov.tr/turkce/haberler/detay/cumhurbaskani-erdogan-azerbaycan-cumhurbaskani-aliyev-ile-ortak-basin-toplantisinda-konustu.

65 Berat Yücel, "Demografik geçiş ekseninde gelecekte bizi neler bekliyor? [What Awaits us in the Future in Terms of Demographic Transition?]," *Türkiye Ekonomi Politikaları Araştırma Vakfı*, August 2023, 3–6, https://www.tepav.org.tr/upload/mce/2023/notlar/demografik_gecis_ekseninde_gelecekte_bizi_neler_bekliyor.pdf; "Doğum İstatikleri, 2022 [Birth Statistics, 2022]," *Türkiye İstatistik Kurumu*, May 15, 2023, https://data.tuik.gov.tr/Bulten/Index?p=Dogum-Istatistikleri-2022-49673.

66 Uğur Duyan, "30 yaşından önce 2 çocuk teşviki [Incentive for 2 Children before the Age of 30]," *Yeni Şafak*, June 1, 2024, https://www.yenisafak.com/dunya/30-yasindan-once-2-cocuk-tesviki-4624996; "Hükümetten 'evlilik' teşviki ['Marriage' Promotion from the Government]," *Cumhuriyet*, July 30, 2013, https://www.sozcu.com.tr/hukumetten-evlilik-tesviki-wp344834; *Yüzyılın Sosyal Politikaları* [Social Policies of the Century], Türkiye Cumhuriyeti Cumhurbaşkanlığı İletişim Başkanlığı and Türkiye Cumhuriyeti Cumhurbaşkanlığı Sosyal Politikalar Kurulu (Ankara: Cumhurbaşkanlığı İletişim Başkanlığı Yayınları, 2023), 53–8, https://www.iletisim.gov.tr/images/uploads/dosyalar/yuzyilin-sosyal-politikalari.pdf.

67 "Erdoğan: En az 3 çocuk yapın [Erdoğan: At Least have Three Children]," *Yeni Şafak*, July 3, 2008, https://www.yenisafak.com/gundem/erdogan-en-az-3-cocuk-yapin-104290.

68 "Dindar gençlik yetiştireceğiz [We will Raise Religious Youth]," *Hürriyet*, February 2, 2012, https://www.hurriyet.com.tr/gundem/dindar-genclik-yetistirecegiz-19825231.

69 "Başkan Erdoğan'ın bahsettiği 5. kol faaliyeti nedir? Beşinci kol faaliyetleri neleri kapsıyor? [What is the 5th Column Activity that President Erdoğan Mentioned? What Do Fifth Column Activities Include?]," *A Haber*, January 27, 2021, https://www.ahaber.com.tr/video/gundem-videolari/baskan-erdoganin-bahsettigi-5-kol-faaliyeti-nedir-besinci-kol-faaliyetleri-neleri-kapsiyor.

70 "Darbe Başarılı Olsaydı İç Savaş Çıkacaktı [If the Coup Had Been Successful, a Civil War Would Have Broke Out]," *Türkiye Cumhuriyeti Adalet Başkanlığı, Basın ve Halkla İlişkiler Müşavirliği*, September 1, 2016, https://basin.adalet.gov.tr/darbe-basarili-olsaydi-ic-savas-cikacakti; Hikmet Faruk Başer and Adem Demir, "'Hainler başarsaydı iç savaş olacaktı' ['If the Traitors had been Successful, there would have been a Civil War]," *Anadolu Ajansı*, August 1, 2016, https://www.aa.com.tr/tr/15-temmuz-darbe-girisimi/hainler-basarsaydi-ic-savas-olacakti/619428; Ahmet Çakar, "Sadece bir darbe değil onbinlerce insanın öleceği bir iç savaş planlamışlar [They Planned Not Just a Coup, but a Civil War in which Tens of Thousands of People would Die]," *Sabah*, July 21, 2016, https://www.sabah.com.tr/yazarlar/spor/cakar/2016/07/21/sadece-bir-darbe-degil-onbinlerce-insanin-olecegi-bir-ic-savas-planlamislar; "İçişleri Bakanı Ala: Orgeneral Galip Mendi'nin zaten son senesiydi bir daha dönmeyecek [Minister of Internal Affairs Ala: It was the Last Year of General Galip Mendi and he will Not Return Again]," *A Haber*, July 22, 2016, https://www.ahaber.com.tr/gundem/2016/07/22/icisleri-bakani-ala-orgeneral-galip-mendinin-zaten-son-senesiydi-bir-daha-donmeyecek.

71 For a detailed discussion, see Selim Koru, "Erdoğan's Turkey and the Problem of the 30 Million," *War on the Rocks*, June 4, 2020, https://warontherocks.com/2020/06/erdogans-turkey-and-the-problem-of-the-30-million/.

72 "Cumhurbaşkanı Erdoğan: 'Normal hayata dönüşü kademe kademe başlatacağız' [President Erdoğan: 'We will Start the Return to Normal Life Gradually']," *Türkiye Cumhuriyeti İletişim Başkanlığı*, May 4, 2020, https://www.iletisim.gov.tr/turkce/haberler/detay/cumhurbaskani-erdogan-normal-hayata-donusu-kademe-kademe-baslatacagiz.

73 "Erdoğan yine LGBTİ+'ları hedef aldı: LGBT gibi sapkın bir yapıyla mücadele edeceğiz [Erdoğan Targeted LGBTI+ People Again: We will Fight Against a Perverted Structure Like LGBT]," *Artı Gerçek*, April 19, 2023, https://artigercek.com/politika/erdogan-lgbt-gibi-sapkin-bir-yapiyla-mucadele-edecegiz-246832h.

74 "Türkiye İstanbul Sözleşmesi'nden 1 yıl önce çekildi: Kadınlar sözleşmeden vazgeçmiyor [Turkey Withdrew from the Istanbul Convention 1 Year Ago: Women Do Not Give up on the Contract]," *Evrensel*, March 19, 2022, https://www.evrensel

.net/haber/457416/turkiye-istanbul-sozlesmesinden-1-yil-once-cekildi-kadinlar-sozlesmeden-vazgecmiyor.

75 "LGBT'nin arkasındaki gizli oluşum ortaya çıktı [The Secret Organization behind LGBT has been revealed]," *Yeni Akit*, May 18, 2020, https://www.yeniakit.com.tr/haber/lgbtnin-arkasindaki-gizli-olusum-ortaya-cikti-1243995.html; Sinan Okuş, "Batı Zehirlenmesinin Yeni Adı; Erdoğan Korkusu [The New Name of Western Poisoning; The Fear of Erdoğan]," *Yörünge*, August 1, 2018, https://www.yorungedergi.com/2018/08/yazar-alev-alatlidan-yorungeye-aciklamalar-bati-zehirlenmesinin-yeni-adi-erdogan-korkusu/.

76 "Mülteci karşıtlığı durdurulamıyor: Türkiye'de kaç mülteci yaşıyor? [Anti-refugee Sentiment Cannot be Stopped: How Many Refugees Live in Turkey?]," *Medyascope*, September 25, 2023, https://medyascope.tv/2023/09/25/multeci-karsitligi-durdurulamiyor-turkiyede-kac-multeci-yasiyor/#:~:text=G%C3%B6%C3%A7%20%C4%B0daresi%20Ba%C5%9Fkanl%C4%B1%C4%9F%C4%B1%2C%20T%C3%BCrkiye%27deki,638%20bin%20461%20m%C3%BClteci%20ya%C5%9F%C4%B1yor.

77 Sibel Güven, Omar Kadkoy, Murat Kenanoğlu, and Taylan Kurt, "Syrian Entrepreneurship and Refugee Start-ups in Turkey: Leveraging the Turkish Experience," 2018, 16, https://www.tepav.org.tr/upload/files/1566830992-6.TEPAV_and_EBRD___Syrian_Entrepreneurship_and_Refugee_Start_ups_in_Turkey_Lever....pdf.

78 Omar Kadkoy and Asmin Kavas, "Syrians and Post-War Ghetto in Turkey," June 2018, https://www.tepav.org.tr/upload/files/1528374080-0.Syrians_and_Post_War_Ghetto_in_Turkey.pdf.

79 "EU Facility for Refugees in Turkey: €6 billion to Support Refugees and Local Communities in Need Fully Mobilised," *European Commission*, December 10, 2019, https://ec.europa.eu/commission/presscorner/detail/es/ip_19_6694.

80 Murat Ağırel, "400 bin dolara kaç vatandaşlık alınır?n [How Many Citizenships can be Obtained for 400 Thousand Dollars?]," *Cumhuriyet*, January 20, 2023, https://www.cumhuriyet.com.tr/yazarlar/murat-agirel/400-bin-dolara-kac-vatandaslik-alinir-2023197.

81 Marco d'Eramo, "Selling Citizenship," *The New Left Review*, December 15, 2023, https://newleftreview.org/sidecar/posts/selling-citizenship; Kristin Surak, *The Golden Passport Global Mobility for Millionaires* (Cambridge, MA: Harvard University Press, 2023), 18.

82 This is still less than 1 percent of Turkey's population of university students. The rapid increase, however, is being felt in big cities. Ezgi Toprak, "Büyüteç: Üniversitelerdeki yabancı öğrenci verileri ne söylüyor? [Magnet: What do foreign student data at universities say?]," *Teyit*, May 26, 2022, https://teyit.org/dosya/buyutec-universitelerdeki-yabanci-ogrenci-verileri-ne-soyluyor.

83 "Türkiye Finds its Own Axis in the World: Presidential Spokesperson," *Daily Sabah*, April 26, 2023, https://www.dailysabah.com/politics/diplomacy/turkiye-finds-its-own-axis-in-the-world-presidential-spokesperson.

84 "Metropoll: Halkın yüzde 82'si, AKP seçmeninin yüzde 85'i Suriyelilerin geri dönmesini istiyor [Metropoll: 82 Percent of the Public and 85 Percent of AKP Voters Want Syrians to Return]," *T24*, March 17, 2022, https://t24.com.tr/haber/metropoll-halkin-yuzde-82-si-akp-secmeninin-yuzde-85-i-suriyelilerin-geri-donmesini-istiyor,1021483.

85 "World Refugee Day: Global Attidues towards Refugees," *IPSOS*, June 2019, https://www.ipsos.com/sites/default/files/ct/news/documents/2019-06/World-Refugee-Day-2019-Ipsos.pdf.

86 "Kürt Z Kuşağı'nın Sığınmacı ve Göçmenlere Yönelik Algı ve Tutumları [Perceptions and Attitudes of Kurdish Generation Z Towards Asylum Seekers and Refugees]," *Spectrum House Düşünce ve Araştırmalar Merkezi*, http://spectrumhouse.com.tr/kurt-z-kusaginin-siginmaci-ve-gocmenlere-yonelik-algi-ve-tutumlari/.

87 Evren Balta, Ezgi Elçi, Deniz Sert, "Göçmen Karşıtı Tutumların Siyasi Parti Temsili Türkiye Örneği," *Heinrich Böll Shiftung and Özyeğin University*, December 2022.

88 "Erdoğan: Suriyeli kardeşlerimiz geri dönecek [Erdoğan: Our Syrian brothers will return]," *Haber7*, August 7, 2014, https://www.haber7.com/partiler/haber/1188694-erdogan-suriyeli-kardeslerimiz-geri-donecek.

89 "Erdoğan'dan Güvenli Bölge'de ev önerisi: 'Suriyelilere bahçeli evler yapsak, orada ekip biçseler' [Erdoğan's House Proposal in the Safe Zone: 'Let's Build Houses with Gardens for Syrians, so they can Cultivate and Harvest there']," *EuroNews*, September 5, 2019, https://tr.euronews.com/2019/09/05/erdogandan-guvenli-bolge-de-ev-onerisi-suriyelilere-bahceli-evler-yapsak-orada-ekip-bicse; "Suriyelilerin eve dönüşü için briket ev yapımı devam ediyor [Briquette House Construction Continues for Syrians to Return Home]," *TRT Haber*, May 20, 2023, https://www.trthaber.com/haber/dunya/suriyelilerin-eve-donusu-icin-briket-ev-yapimi-devam-ediyor-768778.html; "Cumhurbaşkanı Erdoğan: Hedefimiz Suriyelilerin tamamının evlerine dönmesi [President Erdoğan: Our Goal is for All Syrians to Return to their Homes]," *NTV*, June 21, 2018, https://www.ntv.com.tr/turkiye/hedefimiz-suriyelilerin-tamaminin-evlerine-donmesi,zmSC_mCSMkGZtGx_cII4EQ.

90 Recep Tayyip Erdoğan, "Gençlerimizin Aklına Takılan Soruları Samimiyetle Cevaplandırdığım Buluşmamız [Our Meeting Where I Sincerely Answered the Questions Our Young People Had in Their Minds]," *YouTube*, https://www.youtube.com/watch?v=i6HQhJvhUrw.

91 Hande Karacasu, "SESSİZ İSTİLA [SILENT INVASION]," *YouTube*, May 3, 2022, https://www.youtube.com/watch?v=EpPo5vjC2bE.

92 Dilge Temiz, "2023 seçimlerinin kaderini yabancı seçmen mi belirledi? [Did Foreign Voters Decide the Fate of the 2023 Elections?]," *Teyit*, June 15, 2023, https://teyit.org/demec-kontrolu/2023-secimlerinin-kaderini-yabanci-secmen-mi-belirledi.

93 "'2050 yılı için en uç projeksiyonda bile Suriyeli nüfus Türkiye nüfusunun yüzde 8'i olabiliyor' ['Even in the Most Extreme Projection for 2050, the Syrian Population can be 8 Percent of the Turkish population']," *Serbestiyet*, August 30, 2023, https://serbestiyet.com/featured/2050-yili-icin-en-uc-projeksiyonda-bile-suriyeli-nufus-turkiye-nufusunun-yuzde-8i-olabiliyor-140951/#.

94 Koen Verhelst, "Surrounded by Colonial History, Wilders Campaigns Against Migration before EU Vote," *POLITICO*, June 5, 2024, https://www.politico.eu/article/surrounded-by-colonial-history-wilders-campaigns-against-migration-before-eu-vote/; Becky Branford and Marysia Novak, "France Elections: What Makes Marine Le Pen far right?" *BBC News*, February 10, 2017, https://www.bbc.com/news/world-europe-38321401.

95 See James Ker-Lindsay, "Turkey's EU Accession as a Factor in the 2016 Brexit Referendum," *Turkish Studies* 19, no. 1 (2018): 1–22.

96 Shweta Desai, "French Far-right Politicians Change their Tune on Immigration," *Anadolu Ajansı*, March 11, 2022, https://www.aa.com.tr/en/europe/french-far-right-politicians-change-their-tune-on-immigration/2531428.

97 Emily Schultheis, "Viktor Orbán: Hungary doesn't want 'Muslim invaders,'" *POLITICO*, January 8, 2018. https://www.politico.eu/article/viktor-orban-hungary-doesnt-want-muslim-invaders/; "As Election Nears, Polish PM Warns of 'Islamic Fighters' among Migrants," *Reuters*, October 12, 2023, https://www.reuters.com/world/europe/election-nears-polish-pm-warns-islamic-fighters-among-migrants-2023-10-12/#:~:text=The%20nationalist%20Law%20and%20Justice,Morawiecki%20told%20a%20press%20conference.

98 Marie Jamet, "War in Ukraine: Which European Countries Host the Most Refugees?" *Euronews*, September 20, 2023, https://www.euronews.com/2023/09/20/war-in-ukraine-which-european-countries-host-the-most-refugees#:~:text=In%20absolute%20numbers%2C%20Poland%20(1.5,Ukraine%20according%20to%20UNHCR%20figures.

99 "Europe's Conservative Populists Pit Migrants against Babies," *The Economist*, September 20, 2023, https://www.economist.com/europe/2023/09/20/europes-conservative-populists-pit-migrants-against-babies

100 "Cumhurbaşkanı Erdoğan: Dünyanın pek çok yerinde İslam düşmanlığı hastalığı tıpkı kanser hücresi gibi hızla yayılıyor [President Erdoğan: The Disease of Islamophobia is Spreading Rapidly in Many Parts of the World, Just Like a Cancer Cell]," *Anadolu Ajansı*, May 25, 2021. https://www.aa.com.tr/tr/turkiye/cumhurbaskani-erdogan-dunyanin-pek-cok-yerinde-islam-dusmanligi-hastaligi

-tipki-kanser-hucresi-gibi-hizla-yayiliyor/2253418; Özcan Hıdır, "Macron'un İslam'a yönelik hezeyanları [Macron's Delusions about Islam]," *Anadolu Ajansı*, October 8, 2020, https://www.aa.com.tr/tr/analiz/macron-un-islam-a-yonelik-hezeyanlari/1999725.

101 "Başbakan Davutğlu, TBMM grup toplantısında konuştu [Prime Minister Davutoğlu Spoke at the Turkish Grand National Assembly Group Meeting]," *Adalet ve Kalkınma Partisi*, April 26, 2016, https://www.akparti.org.tr/haberler/basbakan-davutoglu-tbmm-grup-toplantisinda-konustu-1-2/

102 "Cumhurbaşkanı Erdoğan, 'Türkiye Yüzyılı'nda Ailemiz, İstikbalimiz' temasıyla düzenlenen 8. Aile Şurası'na katıldı [President Erdoğan attended the 8th Family Council held with the theme 'Our Family, Our Future in the Turkey Century']," *Türkiye Cumhuriyeti İletişim Başkanlığı*, October 27, 2023, https://www.iletisim.gov.tr/turkce/yerel_basin/detay/cumhurbaskani-erdogan-turkiye-yuzyilinda-ailemiz-istikbalimiz-temasiyla-duzenlenen-8-aile-surasina-katildi.

103 Are we to assume for example, that Turkey is a superior military power to France and Britain, both of which have nuclear capabilities, as well as the ability and experience to stage military operations in faraway theaters of war?

104 Growing up in the Islamist tradition, there is a phrase one encounters persistently is: "do not take on the morals of the West, take on their *ilim*." The Arabic-rooted word refers to higher learning in general, but in this context refers to science and technology.

105 "'Hedefimiz yüzde 100 yerlilik' ['Our Goal is One Percent Indigeneity']," *Bloomberg HT*, May 13, 2018, https://www.bloomberght.com/haberler/haber/2120235-hedefimiz-yuzde-100-yerlilik.

106 Another country that makes frequent use of this term is India, which is also made "New" again under the Hindu nationalist Bharatia Janata Party (BJP); see Dhruva Jaishankar, "The Indigenization of India's Defence Industry," *Brookings India*, August 2019, https://www.brookings.edu/wp-content/uploads/2019/08/The-Indigenisation-of-India-Defence-Industy-without-cutmar-for-web.pdf.

107 "Türk savunma sanayiinin 2021 yılı performansı [The performance of the Turkish defense industry in 2021]," *Türkiye Cumhuriyeti Cumhurbaşkanlığı, Savunma Sanayii Başkanlığı (SSB)*, https://www.ssb.gov.tr/WebSite/contentlist.aspx?PageID=48&LangID=1.

108 "Cumhurbaşkanı Erdoğan: "Savunma sanayinde son 17 yılda yaptığımız hamlelerle yerlilik ve millilik oranı yüzde 20'lerden yüzde 70'lere çıkmış durumda [President Erdoğan: With the Moves we have Made in the Last 17 Years in the Defense Industry, the Rate of Localization and Nationality has Increased from 20 Percent to 70 Percent]," *Türkiye Cumhuriyeti İletişim Başkanlığı*, February 5, 2020, https://www.iletisim.gov.tr/turkce/haberler/detay/cumhurbaskani-erdogan-savunma-sanayinde-son-17-yilda-yaptigimiz

-hamlelerle-yerlilik-ve-millilik-orani-yuzde-20lerden-yuzde-70lere-cikmis-durumda.
109 "Millî Savunma Bakanlığında Haftalık Basın Bilgilendirme Toplantısı Düzenlendi [Weekly Press Information Meeting Held at the Ministry of National Defense]," *Milli Savunma Bakanlığı*, December 7, 2023, https://www.msb.gov.tr/SlaytHaber/28e06ddedea943568eb8ada6e6876a16
110 Sinan Tavsan, "Erdogan's Defense-heavy Campaign Shows Off New 'Drone Carrier,'" *Nikkei Asia*, April 22, 2023. https://asia.nikkei.com/Politics/Erdogan-s-defense-heavy-campaign-shows-off-new-drone-carrier
111 Arda Mevlütoğlu, "Türk Savunma Sanayiinin Dönüşümü [The Return of the Turkish Defense Industry]," *Perspektif*, April 17, 2020, https://www.perspektif.online/turk-savunma-sanayiinin-donusumu/.
112 Ibid.
113 Ibid.
114 Ibid.
115 This is the precursor to the Undersecretariat of National Security Industry (Savunma Sanayii Müsteşarlığı, SSM), which under the presidential system is now again a presidency (Defense Industry Agency, Savunma Sanayii Başkanlığı (SSB)).
116 Arda Mevlütoğlu, "Türk Savunma Sanayiinin Dönüşümü…"; Sıtkı Egeli, Serhat Güvenç, Çağlar Kurç, and Arda Mevlütoğlu, " From Client to Competitor: The Rise of Türkiye's Defence Industry," *Center for Foreign Policy and Peace Research and the International Institute for Strategic Studies*, May 2024.
117 "Tank ve helikopter ihaleleri iptal edildi [Tank and Helicopter Tenders were Cancelled]," *Hürriyet*, May 14, 2004, https://www.hurriyet.com.tr/ekonomi/tank-ve-helikopter-ihaleleri-iptal-edildi-225670.
118 Arda Mevlütoğlu, "Türk Savunma Sanayiinin Dönüşümü…"
119 Serhat Güvenç and Lerna K. Yanık, "Turkey's Involvement in the F-35 Program: One Step Forward, Two Steps Backward?" *International Journal* 68, no. 1 (2012): 111.
120 Valerie Insinna, "Turkish Aerospace Industries Reveals Indigenous TF-X Fighter as S-400 Dispute Looms," *Defense News*, June 17, 2019, https://www.defensenews.com/digital-show-dailies/paris-air-show/2019/06/17/turkish-aerospace-industries-reveals-indigenous-tf-x-fighter-as-s-400-dispute-looms/.
121 Cem Devrim Yaylali, "Turkey's Defense, Aerospace Exports Rose by 25% Last Year," *Defense News*, January 8, 2024, https://www.defensenews.com/industry/2024/01/08/turkeys-defense-aerospace-exports-rose-by-25-last-year/.
122 Bahadır Özgür, "Koç'tan Sancak'a: Türkiye'nin 'savaş makinası' [From Koç to Sancak: Turkey's 'War Machine']," *Gazete Duvar*, February 23, 2021, https://www.gazeteduvar.com.tr/koctan-sancaka-turkiyenin-savas-makinasi-makale-1514116; "Bakan Akar: Türkiye'nin ve Kıbrıs'taki kardeşlerimizin hakkını korumakta

kararlıyız [Minister Akar: We are Determined to Protect the Rights of Turkey and Our Brothers in Cyprus]," *TRT Haber*, August 11, 2022, https://www.trthaber.com/haber/gundem/bakan-akar-turkiyenin-ve-kibristaki-kardeslerimizin-hakkini-korumakta-kararliyiz-700857.html.

123 "Rakamlarla yerli savunma sanayii... Proje sayısı 10 kat arttı [Local Defense Industry in Numbers... the Number of Projects Increased Ten-fold]," *CNN Türk*, February 5, 2022, https://www.cnnturk.com/video/turkiye/rakamlarla-yerli-savunma-sanayii-proje-sayisi-10-kat-artti.

124 "Turkey Invests in Youth with Biggest Tech Fest: Minister," *Daily Sabah*, September 8, 2021, https://www.dailysabah.com/business/tech/turkey-invests-in-youth-with-biggest-tech-fest-minister.

125 "Savunma Sanayiinin Yalnız Dehaları [The Solitary Geniuses of the Defense Industry]," *TRT Belgesel*, https://www.trtbelgesel.com.tr/tarih/savunma-sanayiinin-yalniz-dehalari-trt-belgeselde/savunma-sanayiinin-yalniz-dehalari-10900725.

126 Efsun Erbalaban Yılmaz and Halil Fidan, "TEKNOFEST Yönetim Kurulu Başkanı Bayraktar: TEKNOFEST dünyanın daha önce şahit olmadığı zihinsel bir devrime imza atıyor [TEKNOFEST Chairman of the Board of Directors Bayraktar: TEKNOFEST is Signing a Mental Revolution that the World has Never Witnessed Before]," *Anadolu Ajansı*, September 29, 2023, https://www.aa.com.tr/tr/teknofest/teknofest-yonetim-kurulu-baskani-bayraktar-teknofest-dunyanin-daha-once-sahit-olmadigi-zihinsel-bir-devrime-imza-atiyor/3002158.

127 "Türkiye's Indigenous Fighter Jet Completes 2nd Flight," *Daily Sabah*, May 6, 2024, https://www.dailysabah.com/business/defense/turkiyes-indigenous-fighter-jet-completes-2nd-flight.

128 Okan Müderrisoğlu, "İstanbul... kim, kimin rakibi? [Istanbul... Who, whose Rival?]," *Sabah*, January 13, 2024, https://www.sabah.com.tr/yazarlar/muderrisoglu/2024/01/13/istanbul-kim-kimin-rakibi.

129 Selçuk Bayraktar, "Tarihe Not: 21.2.2024 TÜRK HAVACILIĞININ ALTIN ÇAĞI [Note to History: 21.2.2024 THE GOLDEN AGE OF TURKISH AVIATION]," February 21, 2024, https://twitter.com/Selcuk/status/1760392156957585567.

130 Sıtkı Egeli, Serhat Güvenç, Çağlar Kurç, and Arda Mevlütoğlu, "From Client to Competitor: The Rise of Türkiye's Defence Industry," *Center for Foreign Policy and Peace Research and the International Institute for Strategic Studies*, May 2024, 25–6.

131 If the taboo is to be maintained, this group of people believe that the United States staged the failed military coup in Turkey (as is axiomatic in these circles), but they also want to remain a member of NATO and depend on it for Turkey's defense. So if we argue that the New Turkey elite fully see Turkey's future in NATO, they have somehow made peace with the notion that their allies are willing to violently topple their regime.

132 Most leftists in Turkey don't believe that the Erdoğan regime intends to leave NATO. It's too often the case that one conceives of one's enemies as being in league. The Turkish left dislike NATO and Erdoğan, and therefore tend to see the ways in which they act together. The formative ideas here come from the Cold War, in which the NATO establishment and Turkey's anti-Communist right-wing (including the far-right) acted together against the Turkish left (including the far left).

133 Yusuf Kaplan, "Biz NATO'ya yok olmamak için girdik, yok olmamak için çıkacağız yeri ve zamanı geldiğinde… [We Entered NATO Not to Perish, we will Leave Not to Perish, when the Place and Time Comes…]," *Yeni Şafak*, July 4, 2022, https://www.yenisafak.com/yazarlar/yusuf-kaplan/biz-natoya-yok-olmamak-icin-girdik-yok-olmamak-icin-cikacagiz-yeri-ve-zamani-geldiginde-2063370.

134 Cansu Çamlıbel, "Zafer Partisi Genel Başkanı Ümit Özdağ: Kılıçdaroğlu kazansa üç bakanlık ve MİT Başkanlığını alacaktık, yazılı mutabakat var [Victory Party Chairman Ümit Özdağ: If Kılıçdaroğlu won, we would Get Three Ministries and the MİT Presidency, there is a Written Agreement]," *T24*, July 17, 2023. https://t24.com.tr/yazarlar/cansu-camlibel/zafer-partisi-genel-baskani-umit-ozdag-kilicdaroglu-kazansa-uc-bakanlik-ve-mit-baskanligini-alacaktik-yazili-mutabakat-var,40818

135 Yusuf Kaplan, "Biz NATO'ya yok olmamak için girdik…," *Yeni Şafak*, July 4, 2022.

136 "Ethem Sancak Rus medyasına konuştu: NATO Erdoğan'ı seçimle devirmek istiyor [Ethem Sancak Spoke to the Russian Media: NATO Wants to Overthrow Erdoğan with elections]," *Artı Gerçek*, March 4, 2022, https://artigercek.com/haberler/ethem-sancak-rus-televizyonuna-konustu-bayraktar-lari-satarken-boyle-kullanilacagini-bilmiyorduk.

137 "Bakan Akar: Türkiyesiz NATO hayal bile edilemez [Minister Akar: NATO Without Turkey Cannot be Imagined]," *Hürriyet*, January 17, 2023, https://www.hurriyet.com.tr/gundem/bakan-akar-turkiyesiz-nato-hayal-bile-edilemez-42205242; "NATO Türkiye'siz ayakta kalamaz [NATO Cannot Survive Without Turkey]," *Yeni Şafak*, November 30, 2022, https://www.yenisafak.com/dunya/nato-turkiyesiz-ayakta-kalamaz-3893059.

138 "İslam Birliğinden Maksadımız Nedir Erbakan Hocamız Açıklıyorlar [Our Hodja Erbakan Explains What is Our Purpose from the Islamic Union?]," https://www.youtube.com/watch?v=nQQuT4NFHFg.

139 Nicholas Danforth, "Make New Friends, but Keep the Old? Turkey's Precarious Balancing Act," *War on the Rocks*, July 30, 2018, https://warontherocks.com/2018/07/make-new-friends-but-keep-the-old-turkeys-precarious-balancing-act; Soner Cağaptay, *Erdogan's Empire: Turkey and the Politics of the Middle East* (London: Bloomsbury Publishing, 2020), 232–3.

Conclusion

1 Ateş İlyas Başsoy, "14 Mayıs'ta bir mucize gerçekleşecek mi? [Will a Miracle Happen on May 14?]," *Bir Gün*, May 8, 2023, https://www.birgun.net/makale/14-mayista-bir-mucize-gerceklesecek-mi-435317.
2 Interview with Mehmet Akif Ersoy, Habertürk, May 1, 2023.
3 Ibid.
4 Bahadır Özgür, "Suç örgütlerine operasyon 'Soylu'nun tasfiyesi' ile sınırlı değil: Geçmişin değil, bugünün kavgası [The Operation Against Criminal Organizations is Not Limited to the 'Liquidation of Soylu': It is a Fight of Today, Not of the Past]," *Bir Gün*, September 28, 2023, https://www.birgun.net/makale/suc-orgutlerine-operasyon-soylunun-tasfiyesi-ile-sinirli-degil-gecmisin-degil-bugunun-kavgasi-471865; Ruşen Çakır, "Ruşen Çakır'ın konuğu Bahadır Özgür: Tüm yönleriyle Türkiye'nin suç ekonomisi [Ruşen Çakır's guest Bahadır Özgür: Turkey's Criminal Economy in all its Aspects]," *Medyascope*, December 4, 2023, https://medyascope.tv/2023/12/04/rusen-cakirin-konugu-bahadir-ozgur-tum-yonleriyle-turkiyenin-suc-ekonomisi/..
5 Serkan Kaya and Mehmet Tosun, "Cumhurbaşkanı Erdoğan kabine üyelerini açıkladı [President Erdoğan Announced the Cabinet Members]," *Anadolu Ajansı*, June 3, 2023, https://www.aa.com.tr/tr/politika/cumhurbaskani-erdogan-kabine-uyelerini-acikladi/2913641.
6 Merve Kara-Kaşka, "'Türkiye Yüzyılı Maarif Modeli': Yeni müfredat Milli Eğitim Bakanlığı'nca onaylandı ['Turkey Century Education Model': The New Curriculum was Approved by the Ministry of National Education]," *BBC Türkçe*, May 16, 2024, https://www.bbc.com/turkce/articles/cjk442g5zvdo; "Eğitim Askıda: Eğitim Reformu Girişimi'nin Millî Eğitim Bakanlığı Taslak Öğretim Programları İnceleme ve Değerlendirmesi [Education on Suspension: Review and Evaluation of the Education Reform Initiative's Draft Curriculum of the Ministry of National Education]," *Eğitim Reformu Girişimi*, May 2024, https://www.egitimreformugirisimi.org/wp-content/uploads/2024/05/EGITIM-ASKIDA_ERGnin-MEB-Taslak-Ogretim-Programlari-Inceleme-ve-Degerlendirmesi.pdf.
7 Raymond Geuss, "Nietzsche's Germans," in *The New Cambridge Companion to Nietzsche*, ed. Tom Stern (Cambridge: Cambridge University Press, 2019), 415.
8 Friedrich Nietzsche and R. J. Hollingdale, eds., *Human, All Too Human: A Book for Free Spirits* (Cambridge: Cambridge University Press, 1996), 287.

Index

Note: Page numbers followed by "n" refer to notes

AANES, see Autonomous Administration of North and East Syria (AANES, "Rojava")
Abdülhamid II 23, 24, 32, 33, 35, 100
acquis communautaire 111
"Adil Düzen" (Just Order) 7
Ağa, İ. 65
Ağbal, N. 67
AK, see Justice and Development (Adalet ve Kalkýnma (AK)) Party
Akar, H. 85
Akdağ, R. 198 n.89
Aksakal, H. 22
Akşener, M. 138
Albayrak, B. 67
Albayrak, E. 65
Aliyev, I. 144
Altun, F. 101
ANAR 74
Anderson, B. 16
Ankara University 73
Arab Spring 81, 94
Aras, B. 76
Arçelik 131
Arınç, B. 46
armed bureaucracy 64, 93
Armenia 72
Armenian Secret Army for the Liberation of Armenia (ASALA) 82
Article 105 56, 57
Arvâsî, A. 29
ASALA, see Armenian Secret Army for the Liberation of Armenia (ASALA)
ASELSAN 171
Aspirational Occidentalism 10, 22–5, 31, 35, 38, 43, 143, 155, 161, 162, 179
al-Assad, B. 81, 87, 112
Atalay, B. 1, 2, 47, 74

Atatürk, M. K. 3, 4, 6–8, 23, 38–9, 110, 141, 148, 152, 157
  leadership in war of independence 26, 33
  mausoleum 39
  tenth-year speech 38
  on Westernization 24
Atilhan, C. R. 29, 30
Atlantic, The 86
Atsız, N. 26, 158
Autonomous Administration of North and East Syria (AANES, "Rojava") 88
Aytürk, İ. 25
Azerbaijan 72
Aznar, J. M. 75

Babacan, A. 47
BAE Systems 173
Bahçeli, D. 54–5, 68, 224 n.6
Banking Regulation and Supervision Agency (BDDK) 66
al-Banna, H. 26–7
"Başyüce" 32
"Başyücelik Emirleri" (the orders of the Başyücelik) 32
Baydemir, O. 52
Bayraktar, S. 173
BBC 57
BDDK, see Banking Regulation and Supervision Agency (BDDK)
Belt and Road Initiative (BRI) 134–5
Biden, J. 108, 136
BİSAV, see Science and Art Foundation (Bilim ve Sanat Vakfı, BİSAV)
Blair, T. 73
Boğaziçi University 76, 87, 195 n.65
Bookchin, M. 89
Book of Honor 38
BOP, see "Greater Middle East Initiative" ("Büyük Ortadoğu Projesi," BOP)

Bora, T.   3, 25
Bozdağ, B.   50
BRI, *see* Belt and Road Initiative (BRI)
BRICS   107
Britain
    National Health Service (NHS)   57
British Council   147
Brzezinski, Z.   75
BTK, *see* Information and Communication Technology Authority (BTK)
"bureaucratic-institutional tutelage" (*Bürokratik-kurumsal vesayet*)   69
"bureaucratic oligarchy" (*bürokratik oligarşi*)   59, 62, 64
Bush, G. W.   75
Bush administration   2
Büyük Doğu (Great East)   28, 29
Büyük Doğu Cemiyeti (Great Asia Society)   29

CAATSA, *see* Countering America's Adversaries Through Sanctions Act (CAATSA)
Çalýk Holding   120
Çandar, C.   73
capitalism   19, 30
    global   79–80
    Western   29
"Cause of East Turkistan" (Doğu Türkistan Davası)   137
Çavuşoğlu, M.   178
CCN Holding   199 n.93
Cem, İ.   104
cemaat   11, 45, 60, 65, 66, 68, 195 n.66, 196 n.75, 198 n.89
Center for Economics and Foreign Policy Studies (EDAM)   80
Center for Middle Eastern Studies (ORSAM)   80
Central Bank   66, 67
Chamber of Mechanical Engineers (TMMOB)   58
Chechnya   103
China
    Belt and Road Initiative (BRI, One Belt One Road (OBOR))   13, 134–5
    Communist Party of China   129, 136
    Great Leap Forward   133
    and Turkey, relationship between   12–13, 129–35
China Daily   135
Chirot, D.   184 n.28
CHP, *see* Republican People's Party (CHP)
City Hospitals   59
civilizational destiny   10
civil resistance movement   48
Clinton, B.   73
Cold War   5, 6, 9, 12, 38, 71–3, 75, 78, 103, 108–10, 112, 116, 119, 124, 163, 164, 238 n.132
    Atlanticist framework of   87
    Islamism   105
    Turkish Far Right during   25–8
colonialism   6
Committee of Union and Progress (CUP)   23
Competitive Occidentalism   10, 23, 24, 28, 36–8, 43, 72, 97, 102, 112, 119, 126, 142, 143, 155, 161, 173–6, 178–80, 201 n.6
"confidential service" (*mahrem hizmet*)   63
Confucius Institute   147
conservatism   26, 164
Copenhagen School of International Relations   71
Council of Europe   119
"Council of Europe Convention on Preventing and Combating Violence Against Women and Domestic Violence, The", *see* Istanbul Convention
Council of Higher Education (YÖK)   60
"Council on the Family"   168–9
Countering America's Adversaries Through Sanctions Act (CAATSA)   115
coup attempt   94–101
Cousteau, J.   182 n.18
Covid-19 pandemic   67, 70, 132, 146
Crimean War   108
cultural progressivism   4
Cumhurbaşkanı   51–2, 191 n.29
CUP, *see* Committee of Union and Progress (CUP)
Customs Union   120
Cyprus   87, 110, 111, 153

and Turkey, relationship between 2
   Turkish minority in 170
"Cyprus Peace Operation" 170
Czech Republic 111

Danforth, N. 152
Dark Tidings 143
Davutoğlu, A. 47, 49, 53, 75–6, 102, 113, 168, 192 n.35
   "bow and arrow" theory 76
   as foreign minister 78, 83–6, 88
DCFTA, *see* Deep and Comprehensive Free Trade Area (DCFTA)
Death of the Grey Wolves, The 27
Deep and Comprehensive Free Trade Area (DCFTA) 120
Defense Industry Executive Committee 171
DEİK, *see* Foreign Economic Relations Board of Turkey (DEİK)
DEM, *see* Peoples' Equality and Democratic Party (DEM)
Demirağ, N. 173
Demirel, S. 26, 47
Demirtaş, S. 50, 52, 191 n.30
Democratic-leaning Brookings Institution 73
Democratic Union Party (PYD) 88
diriliş 26
DITIB, *see* Turkish-Islamic Union of Religious Affairs (Diyanet İşleri Türk-İslam Birliği, DITIB)
Dodecanese 153
DPT, *see* State Planning Organization (Devlet Planlama Teşkiları, DPT)
Duda, A. 167
Dugin, A. 114
Duran, B. 91

Eastern Communism 29
Easternness 23
Eastern Question 21
East Turkistan (Xinjiang) 103
Ecevit, B. 86–7, 103, 104
Economic Policy Research Foundation of Turkey (TEPAV) 80
economic relations 12, 119, 121, 130, 131
e-coup 47

EDAM, *see* Center for Economics and Foreign Policy Studies (EDAM)
Egypt
   popular protests 81
Ekrem, S.
   Turkey, Old and New 3
El Roman, R.
   "Macera Dolu Amerika" ("America, full of Adventure") 9
Energy Market Regulatory Authority (EPDK) 66
Enka 120
Ensaroğlu, Y. 80
EPDK, *see* Energy Market Regulatory Authority (EPDK)
equality 2, 18
Erbakan, N. 48, 104, 171, 176, 178
Erdoğan, B. 38, 65
Erdoğan, R. T. 1–3, 6, 21, 28, 33, 38, 45, 46, 77–8, 141, 177–9
   abandoning peace process with the PKK 12
   "bureaucratic-institutional tutelage" (*Bürokratik-kurumsal vesayet*) 69
   and China–Turkey relationship 13, 129–33, 137
   and City Hospitals project 59
   and coup attempt 94–100
   international sociability 144
   on Kısakürek 31–2
   leadership diplomacy 145
   and liberal expansion 143–7
   and military development and alliance structure 169, 170, 172, 173, 175, 176
   on political impartiality 49
   on population 156, 158–62, 164–9
   presidency 49–53, 56, 63, 66–8
   and presidential system 11
   relationship with Gül 47, 48
   and Russia–Turkey relationship 12, 108, 110–18
   and Syrian Civil War 81, 83, 84, 86–8, 91, 92
   trip to Moscow 114
   and Ukraine–Turkey relationship 118–21, 123, 125–9
   visit to Atatürk's mausoleum 39
   visit to Beijing 132

Erdoğan–Gülen civil war 66, 84
Erenköy 65
Ersoy, M. Â. 27, 32
Ete, H. 76
    "Kurdish Issue: Problems and Recommendations for Its Resolution, The" 78–89
EU, see European Union (EU)
"Euphrates Shield" 98
Eurasian Economic Union 119
Eurasianist-Kemalist nationalism 65
Eurasianist-Kemalist Vatan Party 175
Euromaidan protests of 2013-14 121, 122
Europe 80
    Christian Democrats 2
    resentment 17–21
    revaluation 17–21
    romanticism 17–21
European Council 113
European Court of Human rights 119
European modernity 22
European Parliament 3
European Union (EU) 2, 42, 72, 119, 126, 162, 166
    Council 111
European Union–Ukraine Association Agreement 119
executive presidency 45–57

fascism 24, 69, 106
February 28 Process 104
FETÖ, see Fetullahist Terrorist Organization (FETÖ)
Fetullahist Terrorist Organization (FETÖ) 64, 114
Feyzioğlu, M. 48
Fidan, H. 63, 82–4, 88, 94, 102, 178, 179
    "Intelligence and Foreign Policy: A Comparison of British, American and Turkish Intelligence System" 83
"fifty plus one" rule 70
First World War 6, 23, 33, 124, 142, 148
FNSS 171
Foreign Economic Relations Board of Turkey (DEİK) 121
Foreign Ministry 66, 80, 87, 138, 146

Foundation for Political, Economic and Social Research (Siyaset, Ekonomi ve Toplum Araştırmaları Vakfı, SETA) 4, 76–9, 90, 91, 101
FP, see Virtue Party (FP)
France 17, 19, 21, 80, 108, 141, 149, 167, 236 n.103
"Free Cause Party" (HÜDA-PAR) 178
free markets 73
Free Syrian Army (FSA) 84, 88
FSA, see Free Syrian Army (FSA)

Gellner, E. 16
General Directorate of Military Factories 170
genocide 6, 136, 137
geopolitical proportions, career of 103–7
Germany 10, 13, 19–21, 25, 26, 34, 57, 80, 104, 131, 167, 170
Gezi Park protests of 2013 3, 4, 48, 50
global capitalism 79–80
globalization 2, 9, 105, 134
GNP, see Grand National Assembly (GNP)
Goethe Institute 147
Gökalp, Z. 24, 157
Gökçek, M. 77
Goldberg, J. 86
Gözler, K. 57
Grand National Assembly (GNP) 54
    General Assembly 54
"Greater Middle East Initiative" ("Büyük Ortadoğu Projesi," BOP) 201 n.2
Great Leap Forward 133
Greenfeld, L. 16, 17, 184 n.28
Gül, A.
    presidency 46–9, 133–4
    as prime minister 75
    relationship with Erdoğan 47, 48
Gülen, F. 60, 61, 96–8, 207–8 n.79
Gülenist movement 37–8
Gülenists 53, 61, 63–5, 84, 90, 99, 100, 114, 196 n.75, 199 n.94, 208 n.79
Gülen network 53, 62, 116
Güler, Y. 84–6
Güven Hospital 96

Haber, A 122
Habertürk 132, 138
Hagia Sophia 31–3

Harmoush, H. 83
HDP, *see* Peoples' Democratic Party (HDP)
Herder, J. G. 19
High Council for Privatization 41
Hirst, S. J. 109
"How Does One Become a Middle East Expert?" (Ulutaş) 82
"Human Rights Report on Chinese Uyghur Autonomous Region, The" (İYİ Party) 138
humiliation 16–19, 54, 144
Hungary
  Fidesz 167
Hürriyet 22, 157

"Idealist Hearths" ("Grey Wolves," *Ülkü Ocakları*) 5, 58
IHH, *see* Islamist Humanitarian Relief Foundation (İnsan Hak ve Hürriyetleri İnsani Yardım Vakfı, IHH)
Imam Hatip School 7, 65–6
IMF, *see* International Monetary Fund (IMF)
imperialist globalists 69
İnce, M. 56
India 3
individualism 10
inequality 2, 25
Information and Communication Technology Authority (BTK) 42
"Innovationists" (yenilikçi) 74–5
İnönü, İ. 8, 33, 49, 153
Institut Français 147
institutional transformation 11, 45
"Intelligence and Foreign Policy: A Comparison of British, American and Turkish Intelligence System" (Fidan) 83
International Monetary Fund (IMF) 74
Iraq 72
İşçi, I. 110
ISIS, *see* Islamic State of Iraq and the Levant (ISIS)
İskenderpaşa 65
Islamic State of Iraq and the Levant (ISIS) 88, 89, 92
Islamic University of Malaysia 76

Islamism 15, 74, 79, 158, 179
  Cold War 105
  pan-Islamism 176
  political 29
Islamist Humanitarian Relief Foundation (İnsan Hak ve Hürriyetleri İnsani Yardım Vakfı, IHH) 145
Islamist "Milli Görüş" (National Vision) 74
Islamist National Salvation Party 34
Islamist "Nurcu" movement 27
Islamist politics 5
  authoritarian 30
Islamophobia 137, 167, 220 n.65
Israeli Supreme Court 69
Israel–Palestine issue 78
Israel–Turkey relationship 2
Istanbul Convention 162
Istanbul Technical University (İTÜ) 26
Italy 167
İTÜ, *see* Istanbul Technical University (İTÜ)
İYİ Party 165, 194 n.58
  "Human Rights Report on Chinese Uyghur Autonomous Region, The" 138

JÖH (Gendarmerie Special Operations) 93
Johnson, L. B. 170
Judeo-Christian conservatism 164
Justice and Development (Adalet ve Kalkýnma (AK)) Party 1–6, 9, 10, 33, 34, 46, 47, 50–3, 56, 59, 61, 64, 66, 67, 70, 71, 74, 75, 77, 101, 103, 105, 171, 172, 176, 178, 182 n.16
  2002 election 146
  2015 election 52
  2017 election 55–6
  and China–Turkey relationship 130–3, 138
  and coup attempt 96
  electoral tactics 37
  intellectual defense complex 11
  on population 158, 161, 162, 165
  and Russia–Turkey relationship 114
  and Syrian Civil War 81–5, 90–2
  Turkish Type Presidential System 55

Kalın, İ.   76–8, 100, 102, 124–5, 128
Kaplan, H.   123, 192 n.36
Karaca, I.   4
Karagül, İ.   103, 105–7, 123
  "Globalization Is Going to Destroy Us"   105
Karagülle, S.   7
Karakoç, A.   143
Karlov, A.   116
Kavcıoğlu, Ş.   67
Kedourie, E.   16
Kemal, N.   22
Kemalism   24, 32, 34, 35, 38, 73, 75, 78, 154
Kemalist establishment   5, 158
Kemalist order   29–31, 38, 47, 60
Kemalist Republic   6, 11, 25, 33, 34, 155
Kemalist secularism   78
Kılıçdaroğlu, K.   165, 177, 178
King, M. L.   6
Kısakürek, N. F.   11, 17, 28–33, 91, 158
  Abdülhamit Han   187 n.68
  and *Büyük Doğu Cemiyeti* (Great Asia Society)   29
  Him and I (O ve Ben)   29
  Kaldırımlar (Sidewalks)   28
  and Kemalist order   29–31
  opposition against Kemalist state   32
  "This Is Me" (ben buyum)   30–1
Kissinger, H.   75
Kocabıyık, S.   208 n.81
Konya Chamber of Commerce   59
Konyans   58
Korean War   110, 113, 136
"Kurdish Issue: Problems and Recommendations for Its Resolution, The" (Özhan and Ete)   78–9
Kurdistan Workers' Party (Partiya Karkerên Kurdistanê, PKK)   50, 52, 63, 78, 79, 83, 88, 90, 93, 94, 117, 156, 158
  anarchism   89
  confederalism   89
  and coup attempt   98–9
  feminism   89
  peace talks with Damascus   89
Kurds   81–94
Kutan, R.   74

Lausanne Treaty of 1923   150
Le Figaro   141
Le Pen, M.   167
Levinson, B.   201 n.6
Lewis, B.   75, 101
liberal democracy   4, 168
liberalism   3, 11, 24, 73, 75, 151, 158, 176
  neoliberalism   15
  third way   11
  Western   10, 74
liberalization   72–80, 111
Libya   72
  Libyan National Army (LNA)   117
Limak   120
Lowy Institute
  Global Diplomacy index   146
Lula da Silva, L. I.   144

Magnificent Century, The   148
Marshall Plan   110
Maududi, A. A.   27
Menderes, A.   8, 96, 110
Menzil   65
Meriç, C.   27
Merkel, A.   80, 111
Metropoll   50, 164
MFA, *see* Ministry of Foreign Affairs (MFA)
MHP, *see* Nationalist Action Party/Nationalist Movement Party (MHP)
Middle East Public Governance Institute   41, 42
Middle East Technical University   195 n.65
Midnight Express (1978)   123
military development and alliance structure
  native arms industry   169–74
Millî Türk Talebe Birliği (National Turkish Student Union, MTTB)   31
Mingxin, J.   135
Ministry of Culture and Tourism   147
Ministry of Defense   170
Ministry of Finance   66
Ministry of Foreign Affairs (MFA)   199 n.93

"Asia Anew" initiative   134
Ministry of Health   65
Ministry of Interior   66, 96
Ministry of Trade   134
Ministry Transportation and Infrastructure   134
Mîsâk-ı Millî ("the National Oath")   149, 151–5
Mısıroğlu, K.   11, 17, 33–8, 153, 179, 229 n.55
  Black Muslim Movement in America, The   35
  on Gülenist movement   37–8
  Lausanne, Victory or Defeat?   33, 35
  Pages from the CHP's Gallery of Sins   35
  on Rıza Nur   34
  Sebil Yayınevi   34–5
  Three Persons of the Caliphate   35
  on transition from Old to New Turkey   35–7
  on Turkish delegation in Lausanne   33–4
MİT, *see* National Intelligence Organization (Milli İstihbarat Teşkilatı, MİT)
modernity   8, 10, 19, 39
  European   22
  Western   2, 9, 15, 22, 23, 31
Montreaux Convention of 1936   127
morality   10
Morris, C.
  New Turkey: The Quiet Revolution on the Edge of Europe, The   3
MTTB, *see* Millî Türk Talebe Birliği (National Turkish Student Union, MTTB)
Mubarak, H.   81, 82
Muhammed, M.   105
Muhbir   22
Mülkiye   73
Munich Security Conference of 2007   111
MÜSİAD   131
Muslim, S.   88
Muslim civilization   2
Muslim cosmopolitanism   162–9

Nakşibendi order   65
National Intelligence Organization (Milli İstihbarat Teşkilatı, MİT)   63, 82–5, 99, 100, 172
  Intelligence Academy   100–1
nationalism   20, 38, 65, 66, 96, 142, 146, 160, 179, 184 n.28
  civic   24
  ethnic   24
  far-right   5, 25
  Kurdish   92
  pan-Turkic   15
  reactionary   3, 31
  romantic   19, 27
  theory of   16
Nationalist Action Party/Nationalist Movement Party (MHP)   5, 47, 52, 54, 56, 68, 92, 178, 194 n.58
native arms industry   169–74
NATO   13, 27, 37, 81, 86, 94, 99, 108–16, 119, 122, 126–8, 144, 169, 171, 173, 178, 179
  in the age of Competitive Occidentalism   173–6
NATO-Russia Council   111
Nazi Germany
  revanchism   25
Nazi-Soviet pact of 1939   110
neoliberalism   15
new normal   100–2
New Turkey   3–6, 10–12, 16, 20, 76–7, 129, 139
  executive presidency   45–57
  institutional structure of   41–70
  oligarchic networks   57–68
  solar system of institutions   41–5
New Welfare Party (Yeniden Refah)   178
New York Times, The   108
Nietzsche, F.   179
  David Strauss: The Confessor and the Writer   19–20
  Genealogy of Morals   17
  Thus Soke Zarathustra   18
Nour   147–8
Nur, R.   34
Nursi, S.   27
Nye, J.   76

Obama, B.   2, 3, 6, 86, 114, 134, 144
OBOR, *see* One Belt One Road (OBOR)
Öcalan, A.   78, 89, 91
OdaTV   204 n.41
OIC, *see* Organization of Islamic Cooperation (OIC)
Old Turkey   3, 4, 11, 12, 16, 17, 20, 39, 43, 52, 61, 65, 68, 101, 201 n.4
   presidency   46
   oligarchic networks   57–68
One Belt One Road (OBOR), *see* Belt and Road Initiative (BRI)
Önen, E.   132
Önhon, Ö.   88–9
oppression   8, 103, 106, 136, 137, 142
Orbán, V.   69, 144, 167
Organization of Islamic Cooperation (OIC)   105
ORSAM, *see* Center for Middle Eastern Studies (ORSAM)
Ottoman Empire   6, 8, 16, 17, 23, 26, 32, 33, 42, 142, 148, 153, 157, 175
Özal, T.   26, 47
Özdağ, Ü.   174
Özhan, T.   76
   "Kurdish Issue: Problems and Recommendations for Its Resolution, The"   78–9
Öztürk, S.   198 n.89

pan-Islamism   176
Patriotic Revolutionary Youth Movement (Yurtsever Devrimci Gençlik Hareketi, YDG-H)   92
People's Alliance, The   68
Peoples' Democratic Party (HDP)   50–1, 53, 68, 91, 92
Peoples' Equality and Democratic Party (DEM)   165
Peres, S.   77
PKK, *see* Kurdistan Workers' Party (Partiya Karkerên Kurdistanê, PKK)
PÖH (Police Special Operations)   93
Poland   111
   Law and Justice Party   167
political Islamism   29
Political Parties Law   56
population   156–69
Presidency Digital Transformation Office   42
Presidency of Development and Support of the National Defense Industry   171
Presidential Executive System   43, 44
"presidential system" (*Başkanlık Sistemi*)   49
"problem of merit" (*liyakat sorunu*)   70
"problem of survival" ("beka sorunu") campaign   71
prodigal son fallacy   109, 110
Putin, V.   12, 104, 108, 111, 113, 114, 144
PYD, *see* Democratic Union Party (PYD)

Quran   8, 26, 35, 36

reactionary nationalism   3, 31
reawakening   26, 31, 59, 143
Republican People's Party (CHP)   46, 59, 68, 165, 178
Republic of Turkey State Institution Guide, The   41, 42
resentment   17–21
   resentment paradigm   5
ressentiment   28–38, 75, 104, 112
resurrection   26
revaluation   17–21
revanchism   25
Revival of the Grey Wolves, The   27
right-wing movements   5, 25, 27
right-wing politics   5, 25, 96, 167
ROKETSAN   171
romanticism
   in Europe   17–21
   Turkish   21–5
Russian Empire   108, 125
Russia–Turkey relationship   12, 107–18

Safa, P.   28
Şafak, Y.   103
Sakarya Türküsü   33
Sancak, E.   175
Sarkozy, N.   80, 111
Scheler, M.   18
Schmitt, C.   43, 45
Science and Art Foundation (Bilim ve Sanat Vakfı, BİSAV)   75, 76
scientific racism   29, 31, 157, 158

SDF   88, 89
Sebil Yayınevi   34–5
Second World War   6, 26, 29, 101, 110, 170
secularism   10
    Kemalist   78
    leftist   79
secular Turkish fear of replacement   162–9
securitization   71, 79, 101
"securitized policies" (güvenlikçi politikalar)   71
Şehir University   91
self-censorship   139
Şentop, M.   155
SETA, *see* Foundation for Political, Economic and Social Research (Siyaset, Ekonomi ve Toplum Araştırmaları Vakfı, SETA)
SET Foundation   76
Sèvres syndrome   142
Sezer, A. N.
    presidency   46
Shanghai Cooperation Council   107
Sheikh Said Rebellion (1925)   158
Şık, A.
    Imam's Army, The   62
Silent Invasion   166
Şimşek, M.   67, 178
Sinirlioğlu, F.   84, 87, 88
slavery   6
socialism   24
social justice   2
solar system of institutions   41–5
sovereignty   12, 26, 43, 69, 80, 95, 97, 106, 114, 119, 123, 127, 136, 145, 148, 154, 155
Sovereign Wealth Fund   57
Soviet Communism   10
Soyak, H. R.   24
Speier, H.   102
state formation   19
State Planning Organization (Devlet Planlama Teşkilatı, DPT)   74
status anxiety   5, 16, 17
Stone, O.   123–4
Stratfor   73
Strausz-Hupé, R.   102
Sudan
    2023 Civil War   144

Sunnah   26
Supreme Board of Judges and Prosecutors   62
Supreme Court   62
Syria   72
    Turkish-American strategy on   88
Syrian Civil War   2, 81–94, 100, 108, 112, 117, 163

Tabii   148
TAF, *see* Turkish Air Force (TAF)
technological encirclement   173
Tehran Agreement   144
Teknofest   172–3
TEPAV, *see* Economic Policy Research Foundation of Turkey (TEPAV)
territory   142–56
    liberal expansion   143–8
    map, redrawing   148–56
Terzi, S.   95
third way liberalism   11
TİKA, *see* Turkish Development and Cooperation Agency (TİKA)
TİP, *see* Workers' Party of Turkey (TİP)
TMMOB, *see* Chamber of Mechanical Engineers (TMMOB)
Today's Zaman   78, 202 n.22
Topçu, N.   27
"Traditionalists" (gelenekçi)   74
"Train and Equip" program   88
Treaty of Sèvres (1920)   33, 142
"trench operations" (hendek operasyonları)   92, 97
TRT   172
Truman Doctrine   170
Trump, D.   5, 69, 154
    "American Carnage" speech   185 n.40
TSK   99, 172
TTB, *see* Turkish Medical Association (TTB)
TÜGVA (The Service for Youth and Education Foundation of Turkey)   65
Tunisia
    popular protests   81
Turanism   15
TÜRGEV (Turkish Foundation to Serve the Youth and Education)   65

"Türk Donanma Cemiyeti" (The Turkish
  Naval Association) 170
"Turkey's Memory of the Kurdish
  Question" (Yalman) 79
"Türk Hava Kuvvetlerini Güçlendirme
  Vakfı?" (The Foundation for
  Strengthening the Turkish Air
  Force) 170
Turkish Aeronautical Association 170
Turkish Air Force (TAF) 170
Turkish Airlines 146
Turkish Development and Cooperation
  Agency (TİKA) 83
Turkish Great Leap Forward 133
Turkish-Islamic Union of Religious Affairs
  (Diyanet İşleri Türk-İslam Birliği,
  DITIB) 147
Turkish Medical Association (TTB) 58
Turkish National Pact of 1920 and 150
Turkish Occidentalism 22, 23
Turkism 15, 178
Türkiyeli 50
Türköne, M. 73
TÜSİAD 131

Uçum, M. 69, 70, 177
Ufuk Group 82
UK, *see* United Kingdom (UK)
Ukraine 112
  decentralization 125, 127
  lost to freedom 122–9
  national sovereignty 124
  "Revolution of Dignity" 119
  and Turkey, relationship between
    (during the war) 118–29
Ukraine on Fire (2016) 123–4
Ulu Hakan (The Great Khan) 33
Ulutaş, U.
  "How Does One Become a Middle East
    Expert?" 82
United Kingdom (UK) 99
  Brexit campaign 167
  third way liberalism 11
United States (US) 3, 13, 53, 57–8, 75,
  80, 84, 99, 136, 173, 178
  arms industry 170
  civil rights movement 2, 6
  Congress 43, 110

Evangelical Christians 57
hegemony in Europe 104
National Security Council 72, 73
Pivot to Asia 134
State Department 73
third way liberalism 11
"Train and Equip" program 88
United States Government
  Manual 41
White House 43
UN Security Council 144
US, *see* United States (U.S.)
"Üst Akıl" ("the Mastermind") 75, 95
Uyghur Muslims 104, 106–7
Uyghur question over Turkey–China
  relations 135–40

Vahdettin Pavilion 115
Veli, H. B. 159
Victory Party (ZP) 165, 166
Virtue Party (FP) 74
Volksgeist 19, 22, 26
von Bülow, B. 20
von Kleist, H.
  Die Herrrmannsschlacht 19
Vulgärmaterialismus 23

Wag the Dog (1997) 201 n.6
war of independence 8, 24, 26, 29, 33,
  34, 151, 153, 154, 161
war on terror 2, 75
Wei, C. 139
Western capitalism 29
Western hegemony 75
Westernization 24, 34, 38, 49, 79, 122,
  123, 125, 126, 129, 158, 160
  Kemalist 27, 28
  policy 118
  reforms 39
Western liberalism 10, 74
Western modernity 2, 9, 15, 22, 23, 31
Westernness 23, 80
Widodo, J. 144
Wilders, G. 167
"Witness" (Şahit Olun) 93
Workers' Party of Turkey (TİP) 165
World Bank 74

Yalman, A. E. 30
Yanukovych, V. 119
Yayman, H.
 "Turkey's Memory of the Kurdish Question" 79
YDG-H, *see* Patriotic Revolutionary Youth Movement (Yurtsever Devrimci Gençlik Hareketi, YDG-H)
Yeneroğlu, M. 56
Yeni Şafak 105, 122
Yerlikaya, A. 178
Yıldırım, B. 53

YÖK, *see* Council of Higher Education (YÖK)
Young Turk movement 34
Young Turks 23, 100, 157
 "Special Organization" (Teşkilat-ı Mahsusa) 100
Yunus Emre Institute 147

Zaporizhzhia Bridge 120
Zelenskyy, V. 125, 127, 129
ZP, *see* Victory Party (ZP)